Prelude to Pearl Harbor

Prelude to Pearl Harbor

Ideology and Culture in US-Japan Relations, 1919–1941

John Gripentrog

ROWMAN & LITTLEFIELD
Lanham • Boulder • New York • London

Published by Rowman & Littlefield
An imprint of The Rowman & Littlefield Publishing Group, Inc.
4501 Forbes Boulevard, Suite 200, Lanham, Maryland 20706
www.rowman.com

6 Tinworth Street, London SE11 5AL, United Kingdom

Copyright © 2021 by The Rowman & Littlefield Publishing Group, Inc.

All rights reserved. No part of this book may be reproduced in any form or by any electronic or mechanical means, including information storage and retrieval systems, without written permission from the publisher, except by a reviewer who may quote passages in a review.

British Library Cataloguing in Publication Information Available

Library of Congress Cataloging-in-Publication Data

Names: Gripentrog, John, 1961– author.
Title: Prelude to Pearl Harbor : ideology and culture in US-Japan relations, 1919–1941 / John Gripentrog.
Other titles: Ideology and culture in US-Japan relations, 1919–1941
Description: Lanham : Rowman & Littlefield, [2021] | Includes bibliographical references and index.
Identifiers: LCCN 2020052299 (print) | LCCN 2020052300 (ebook) | ISBN 9781538149430 (cloth) | ISBN 9781538149447 (epub) | ISBN 9781538166505 (pbk.)
Subjects: LCSH: United States—Foreign relations—Japan. | Japan—Foreign relations—United States. | United States—Foreign relations—20th century. | Japan—Foreign relations—1912–1945. | Internationalism. | Regionalism—East Asia—History—20th century. | World War, 1939–1945—Causes.
Classification: LCC E183.8.J3 G75 2021 (print) | LCC E183.8.J3 (ebook) | DDC 327.7305209/04—dc23
LC record available at https://lccn.loc.gov/2020052299
LC ebook record available at https://lccn.loc.gov/2020052300

∞ ™ The paper used in this publication meets the minimum requirements of American National Standard for Information Sciences Permanence of Paper for Printed Library Materials, ANSI/NISO Z39.48-1992.

For A.E.Y.G.

*I many times thought Peace had come
When Peace was far away....*

*How many the fictitious Shores—
Before the Harbor be—*

—Emily Dickinson, *Poems*

Contents

Acknowledgments		xi
Notes on Usage		xiii
Introduction		1
1	"Too Proud to Fight": The Dream World of Orderly Processes (1919–1930)	11
2	Toward Two Worlds: The Manchurian Crisis (1931–1933)	37
3	Japan's Charm Offensive (1933–1934)	65
4	The High Tide of Cultural Diplomacy (1935–1936)	95
5	A New Order in East Asia (1937–1938)	125
6	"This Mad World of Ours" (1939–1940)	153
7	"So Many Unexplainable Things Are Happening" (1940–1941)	181
Epilogue		209
Notes		217
Bibliography		243
Index		259
About the Author		269

Acknowledgments

In many ways the genesis of this book—and its many debts—traces back to my travels throughout China in 1986 and more than two years of residence in Japan. The friendships and formative experiences there spurred a lifetime of interest in the history and culture of East Asia. I am especially grateful to Haruno Tokitaro for his generosity and care—and uncommon introduction to Japan. I am also thankful to the history faculty at Cal State Los Angeles for encouraging me to pursue a Ph.D., and a return to my undergraduate alma mater, the University of Wisconsin–Madison.

At UW-Madison I had the fortune of learning from and working with superb faculty in a variety of specialized fields. This study profited, in particular, from the continued scholarly support and feedback of John M. Cooper Jr. and Louise Young. John's timely and careful readings of my manuscript chapters provided rare insights that invariably steered me in more fruitful directions. Louise's inspiration and guidance, during graduate school and many years since, leaves an indelible mark. I could not have asked for more supportive "bookends" in researching and writing a manuscript on US-Japan relations in the 1930s than eminent historians of early twentieth-century United States and interwar Japan, respectively. I am also grateful to Jim Lenburg and the anonymous peer reviewers for their constructive edits and suggestions. The manuscript has been greatly improved as a result of their efforts.

For the yearlong sabbatical that granted me the requisite time to complete this project, I extend deep bows of gratitude to Mars Hill University and the Appalachian College Association. The Faculty Enrichment and Renewal Committee at MHU also provided key travel funding. I am similarly grateful to Wendy Mullis at UNC-Asheville for providing me with a study room in the womblike quietude of the library basement. Of course, the writing of this book would have been impossible without the expert assistance of numerous librarians and archivists. I am particularly indebted to the archivists at the Franklin D. Roosevelt Presidential Library; the National Archives and Records Administration in College Park, Maryland; Kurita Junko at the Japan Foundation in Tokyo; and Sarah Patton at the Hoover Institution Library and Archives. Special acknowledgment is extended to Bev Robertson's superb staff at the Mars Hill University Library, especially Rachel Mitchell and Linda Ray, for their efficient handling of many interlibrary loan requests. At Rowman & Littlefield, I wish to thank Senior Executive Editor Susan McEachern and Assistant Editor Katelyn Turner for their enthusiastic support and guidance.

Also helping this book come to fruition were a host of colleagues and friends, including Jorje Chica, Cletus Hasslinger, and Patrick Michelson, who lent a critical eye to earlier drafts. The diligent work of student research assistants in the history program at Mars Hill University—Roman Blevins, Ben Phillips, Jacob Ashley, and Daniel Nelson—was indispensable. This project also benefited from the excellent research assistance of Fukamatsu Ryota as well as from Naito Yuka and Ruiz Asri. Stephen Gripentrog helped greatly with images, and Peggy Fender and Kristie Hollifield offered critical administrative assistance. Moral support and collegiality, meanwhile, came regularly from colleagues at MHU, especially Lucia Carter, Karen Paar, Matthew Baldwin, Hal McDonald, Brett Johnson, Jennifer Brown, Dan Koster, Marc Mullinax, David Gilbert, Jonathan McCoy, Felice Lopez-Bell, Craig Goforth, Joanna and Jason Pierce, Phyllis Smith, Kathy Newfont, Kathy Meacham, and George Peery. Many other colleagues and friends across historical disciplines offered helpful advice and encouragement along the way, including Edward Frantz, Chris Wells, Alexander Shashko, Anthony Gaughan, Greg Bond, Will Barnett, Tom McGrath, and the late Rob Neufeld.

Above and beyond the mechanics of scholarship, I extend deep gratitude to a core group of longtime friends who have enriched my life and sustained me in the course of completing this manuscript: David Brittain, Jeffrey Schmidt, Todd and Jan Graveline, Markus Giolas and Tammi Franke, Steven Ihrke, Ted Houston, Richard Brittain, and the late Jon Krill.

Finally, I owe a tremendous debt to my family—to my late mother and father, who granted me the freedom to roam early on in life; to seven supportive siblings; and inimitable in-laws. Special acknowledgment goes to Ann Bernier for her critical analytical support in diverse matters. Most of all, I want to thank my wife, Alison, whose unswerving encouragement was both humbling and inspiring.

Parts of a couple chapters of this book are drawn from previously published articles in *Diplomatic History* and the *Pacific Historical Review*. I would like to thank the editors for allowing me to reprint.

Notes on Usage

Japanese names appear in customary style, with family name preceding given name. Exceptions are made for sources published in English in which author names are given according to Western usage. Macrons are used to identify long vowels. Romanization of Chinese names and places goes by the modern pinyin system, but first mention often includes, in parentheses, transliterations based on the outdated Wade–Giles system. Examples: Beijing (Peking); Nanjing (Nanking). Rare exceptions include names and places that remain historically relevant by the older systems, such as Chiang Kai-shek (Jiang Jieshi), the Kuomintang (Guomindang), and Manchukuo (Manzhouguo).

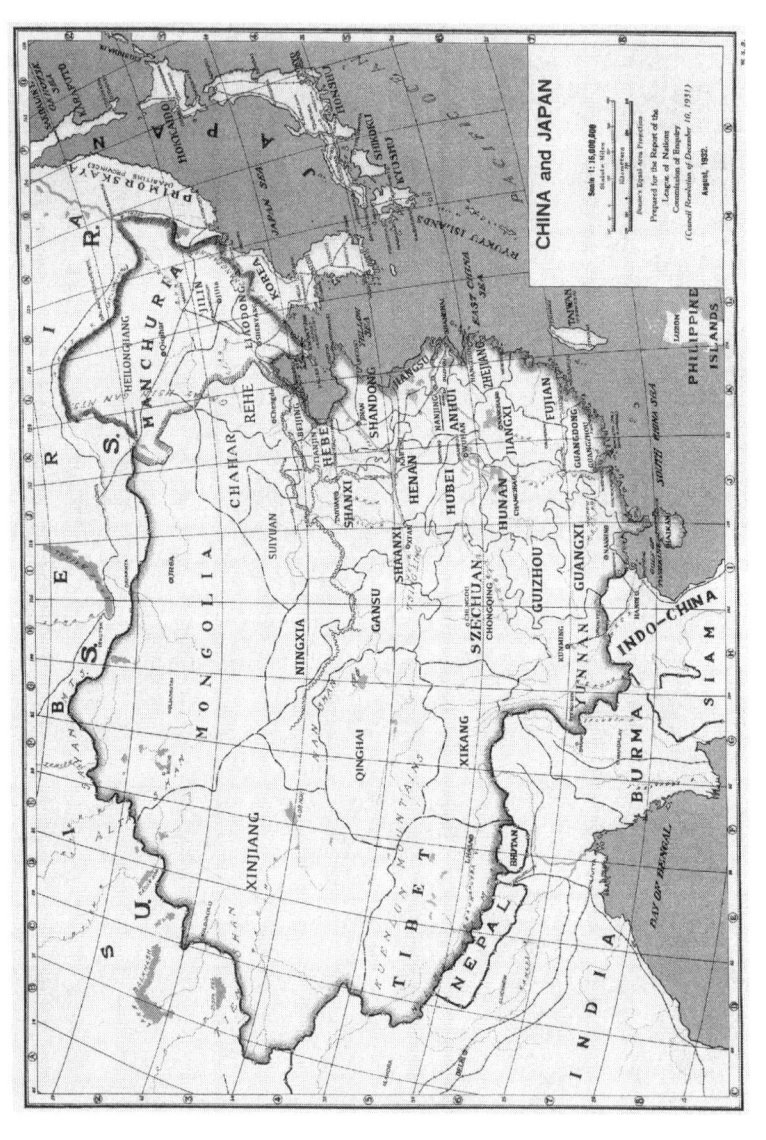

Map of China and Japan, 1930s. (League of Nations, ed., *Appeal by the Chinese Government*, Report of the Commission of Enquiry [Geneva: League of Nations, 1932]; appendix, map 1. Courtesy of the US Air Force Academy, McDermott Library. With select pinyin modification.)

Introduction

On August 15, 1945, a recorded broadcast by Emperor Hirohito announced the surrender of Imperial Japan to Allied forces. World War II in Asia and the Pacific was over. Peering backward through the tunnel of time, as if watching a film in reverse, the signposts of the war's appalling suffering and devastation come into sharp focus: Six days before the emperor's broadcast, the atomic bombing of Nagasaki. Just three days before that, the hellfire of Hiroshima. In the preceding months, the firebombing of sixty-plus Japanese cities. The horrific battle for Okinawa, the final destination of a slow-moving slaughter across the Pacific. Iwo Jima. Peleliu. Saipan, where Japanese civilians jumped from cliffs into the rocky ocean below. Eniwetok. Kwajalein. Tarawa. A series of amphibious landings by American troops—miniature D-Days played out on pockmarked Pacific islands and obscure atolls. Marines coming off beachheads bearing the "thousand-yard stare," having faced withering fire from Japanese soldiers ordered to die honorably by never surrendering. Guadalcanal. The Bataan death march. The surprise attack at Pearl Harbor. Before unspooling, the "film" also provides fleeting images of Japan's initial aggression in China, including indiscriminate aerial bombings of numerous cities, the "Rape of Nanjing," and the sexual enslavement of thousands of imported Korean "comfort woman."

The human cost of the Asia-Pacific War was profound. Between July 1937 and August 1945, military deaths numbered approximately 2.5 million Japanese and 2 million Chinese soldiers. The war also claimed the lives of an estimated 8 to 10 million Chinese civilians and 672,000 Japanese civilians. In the Pacific theater, nearly 100,000 American troops died.[1] Such daunting figures necessarily raise the question: what led to this human calamity and, specifically, the tragic collision between Japan and the United States?

The standard "road to war" narratives explain that Japan's invasion of Manchuria in 1931 strained relations with the United States, a situation severely aggravated by the empire's invasion of China proper in 1937, and then brought to a breaking point in 1941 by Japan's advance into southern Indochina. In response, the administration of President Franklin D. Roosevelt froze Japan's assets in the United States and placed a full embargo on oil. Japan's leaders, unable to find common ground with the United States, launched a surprise attack on Pearl Harbor. But if Japanese expansion into southern Indochina and the subsequent oil ban provided the initial "spark" of the Pacific War, then what was the "gunpowder" that lay behind the belligerency? What explains the underlying growing hostility between Japan and America in the 1930s? The answer is crucial to understanding why the United States ultimately concluded it had no option but to resort to freezing assets and embargoing oil, and why Japan chose to abandon diplomacy and resort to war.

A prominent postwar thesis stresses Japan's "search for economic security" in Asia and the construction of an autarkic "yen bloc." This "realist" perspective argues that Japan's expansionism in the 1930s stemmed primarily from rational calculations aimed at enhancing national security—in particular, the demand to secure external markets and access to natural resources in an increasingly protectionist world. Indeed, there was much talk in Japan at the time about the nation's alleged "have-not" status and unquestionable right to vital "lifelines."[2] Explaining the Asia-Pacific War as a result of Japan's drive for autarky—and America's efforts to contain it—is an important part of the story. But it also tends to construct an image of a Japanese regime single-mindedly focused on cold calculations of economic security. Underappreciated is how these strategic pursuits were undergirded by an ideology profoundly at odds with America's core convictions about world order.

The ideological aspects of the clash between Imperial Japan and the United States guide the premise of this synthetic narrative history, which has two main ambitions. Foremost, *Prelude to Pearl Harbor* underscores the importance of two competing ideologies of world order—"liberal internationalism" and "Pan-Asianist regionalism"—at the heart of the conflict between the United States and Japan during the 1930s. Across a troubled decade, from the Manchurian crisis of 1931 up through fruitless negotiations in the fall of 1941, discord consistently turned on basic principles about world governance, tied to rising geopolitical stakes. *Prelude to Pearl Harbor* also explores American reception of the Japanese government's efforts to shape American public opinion in the 1930s through a vigorous program of cultural diplomacy. By tapping the empire's cultural riches or "soft power," Japan's leaders hoped to combat negative perceptions in the United States and legitimize their regionalist aspirations on the continent.

Ideology is an elusive and expansive term. One scholar asserts that "nobody has yet come up with a single adequate definition of ideology." Historian Michael Howard has pointed to two semantic divergences. On one hand, Howard notes, the word is often used to "describe a particularly rigorous, comprehensive and dogmatic set of integrated values, based on a systematic philosophy, which claims to provide coherent and unchallengeable answers to all the problems of mankind." Thomist Christianity, Marxism-Leninism, and Nazism, he suggests, all fall under this cloistered meaning of ideology. In contrast to this specificity is John Plammentz's definition of ideology as "a set of closely related beliefs or ideas, or even attitudes, characteristic of a group or community." *Prelude to Pearl Harbor* hews to this more broadly conceived meaning of ideology, which comes closer to expressing a worldview or *mentalité*.[3] In particular, this study is concerned with core political beliefs and values related to a crucial normative question: how should the international system be structured and managed? In the 1930s, following a decade of general agreement, Japanese and American leaders held distinctly antagonistic positions on this question of world order. Simply stated, the United States promoted a universalistic framework based on an ideology of liberal internationalism, while Japan pursued an exclusive regionalist arrangement with an emphasis on being the "stabilizing force" in Asia.

Liberal internationalist thinking gained traction after the prolonged agony of World War I, in which unprecedented mechanized killing had shaken to the core all previous assumptions about world order. The balance-of-power system, or concert of power, so esteemed since the Congress of Vienna (1814–1815), lay momentarily discredited on more than nine million graves. "Civilization" itself—an increasingly interdependent global society—now seemed vulnerable to the rages of modern warfare. President Woodrow Wilson, the preeminent advocate for a liberal order, articulated a momentous agenda for the Paris peacemakers in 1919—to ensure perpetual peace. Toward this end, liberal internationalists placed a premium on what they called "orderly processes" in world affairs, or a rules-based system of multilateral cooperation, involving respect for the sanctity of treaties. Nations were asked to buy into a series of liberal principles such as democracy, self-determination, disarmament, and collective security. Underwriting the entire system was reliance on a largely novel and untested phenomenon—the moral sanction of world opinion, a consequence of the technological revolution in mass communication. Liberal internationalism thus combined moralism and legalism, or high-minded principles bound by a signature on a treaty.

As is well known, irony hit fast and hard. Wilson's ideals got diluted in Paris and pummeled in Washington. The result in the United States was a kind of "halfway internationalism," epitomized by the Senate's rejection of the League of Nations. And yet, as Michael Hunt has noted, "far from espousing isolationism," Republican administrations in the 1920s "agreed in broad terms with Wilson that the United States had achieved an eminence in world affairs and with it a duty to promote a better ordered, more just, freer world system."[4] Consequently, Americans worked with the Japanese and British on naval disarmament, and with eight other nations to guarantee China's "territorial and administrative integrity." The ideology of liberal internationalism reached high tide in 1928 with the signing of the Kellogg–Briand Peace Pact, a treaty of mutual self-denial that "outlawed war" as an instrument of national policy.

An important takeaway from all this postwar activity is that Americans and Japanese built internationalist structures together in the 1920s. If Japan's embrace of Wilsonian internationalism was somewhat cautious, it nonetheless was more evident on paper than it was for the United States. Japan not only joined the League of Nations but held a permanent seat on the prestigious Council. Japan accepted naval disarmament and signed the 1928 Peace Pact.[5] Critically, however, at the same time, a strong undercurrent of Japanese intellectuals, politicians, diplomats, and military officials chafed against the new international status quo, which they deemed a ruse for Anglo-American supremacy. While Japan's governments adhered to the internationalist canon, disconsolate voices pointed to apparent contradictions, including Britain's vast colonial enterprise, the United States' prejudicial immigration policies and de facto hegemony in the Americas, and the two powers' disproportionate control over the world's natural resources. The Manchurian crisis (1931–1933) galvanized this discontent and punctured the internationalist spirit. Historians commonly regard the Manchurian crisis as a turning point in interwar history and an important impetus to World War II. *Prelude to Pearl Harbor* accepts that premise but stresses the importance of an emerging ideological divide between liberal internationalism and Japanese regionalism.

In explaining Japan's aggression in Manchuria, Louise Young has written that "many [historical] currents flowed together to produce the sea-change of the early 1930s."[6] Two of the most conspicuous currents were global capitalism's collapse and the rise of Chinese nationalism. The latter threatened Japanese interests attained during the heyday of imperialism in the late nineteenth and early twentieth centuries. Another strong current was the evolving ideological rationale that undergirded Japan's military actions in Manchuria. Historians have long identified the importance of legalistic rights and realpolitik interests in Japan's continental perspective, but only in the past two decades has a moralistic rationale—Japan's Pan-Asian-inspired "special responsibility" in the region—begun to receive its due.[7] *Prelude to Pearl Harbor* benefits from this scholarship and contextualizes the impact of "Asian regionalism" on US-Japan relations.

The ideology of Pan-Asianism first appeared in the late nineteenth century as a response to the West's geopolitical and cultural hegemony and attendant ethnocentrism. From India to Japan, intellectuals extolled the spiritual and cultural solidarity among an idealized Asian family of nations. Japanese philosopher Okakura Tenshin (Kakuzō), for example, criticized Westerners' unwillingness to learn from nonwhite cultures. In his *Book of Tea* (1906), Okakura asked, "When will the West understand or try to understand the East?" In a mild admonishment, he called on Westerners to move beyond patronizing stereotypes of Asian civilization—quaintness, childishness, exoticism—and appreciate its philosophical undercurrents. "Why not amuse yourselves at our expense?" he queried.[8] Okakura imagined a genuinely holistic Pan-Asian community, with Japan as a vital but nondominating asset, as well as an enriching fusion between Western and Asian cultures.

By the time of the Manchurian Incident, however, a more chauvinistic brand of Asianism permeated Japan's ruling class, one that combined resentment against the West with condescension toward the East. Leading Japanese intellectuals, officials, and opinion leaders self-consciously cultivated the "self-evident truth" that Japan's emperor-based polity was unparalleled, that Japan was an exceptional nation, destined to lead and oversee Asia. In some ways, this paternalistic strain of Pan-Asianism revived the underlying rationale of imperialism's "civilizing mission," in which an "enlightened" power had a moral duty to elevate allegedly benighted peoples. Ideologically loaded stock phrases subsequently carried the decade—in particular, that Japan was "the stabilizing force" or "influence" in Asia. As historian Eri Hotta has made clear, this ethnocentric strand of Asianism was not a mere "'assertion,' 'opinion,' or even 'belief,'" but rather a "potent" and "pervasive" force among Japan's leaders in the 1930s. Moreover, as Christopher Szpilman and Sven Saaler argue, by the 1930s, the fundamental premises of radical Pan-Asianism had come to be accepted by the mainstream of Japanese society.[9]

As competing ideologies of world order in the 1930s, the differences between liberal internationalism and Japan's more radical iteration of Asianism were critical, and ultimately, irreconcilable. Although some scholarship has pointed to areas of convergence between the two worldviews—for instance, shared ideals of self-determination and autonomy—such congruency is compelling mainly in comparisons between liberalism and the nondominating strand of Asianism. The latter, however, was most prominent among Japanese political elites around the turn of the century, not the 1930s.[10] What stands out are the fundamental differences. Again, central to the premises of liberal internationalism was a reliance on so-called orderly processes, with states pledging to abide by self-denying strictures, the most hallowed of which was the repudiation of force in the pursuit of national interest. In the event of conflict, nations were to settle their differences within a cooperative framework, through frank discussion and arbitration, either through the League of Nations or with signatories to multilateral treaties. Although the world remained a messy place, strewn with ironies, inequities, and hypocrisies, the idea was to collectively put out small fires and prevent a spiral into another global conflagration. Conversely, Japan's Asianism in the 1930s, while stressing the threat of Western imperialism and a mission to rescue Asia, tended toward a unilateral framework of arbitrary processes, associated with the imperatives of power politics. The goal was a Japanese-led regionalism, and ultimately the promotion of a world order divided by exclusive spheres, carved out by force, if necessary.

In the early 1930s, following the Manchurian crisis, the Roosevelt administration avoided provoking Japan, but it nonetheless reiterated its adherence to liberal treaties and refused to recognize Japan's regionalist claims. *Prelude to Pearl Harbor* illustrates how Japan's leaders, in response, sought to mollify American disapproval of Japanese ambitions on the Asian continent through a vigorous cultural diplomacy—a foreign policy strategy that scholar Joseph S. Nye Jr. has famously described as "soft power." According to Nye, the goal of a nation employing soft power is to get "other countries *to want* what it wants . . . in contrast with the hard or command power of *ordering* others to do what it wants." The underlying logic is clear: "If a state," Nye argues, "can make its power seem legitimate in the eyes of others, it will encounter less resistance to its wishes."[11] Indeed, it was toward this end, in 1934, that the Japanese government created the Society for International Cultural Relations (Kokusai Bunka Shinkōkai, or KBS) to promote the image of a highly civilized nation. To reach American audiences, the KBS published English-language books on a variety of Japanese art forms, sponsored art exhibitions in the United States, and invited American elites on cultural tours of Japan.[12]

On one level, the KBS's depiction of Japan as a highly sophisticated civilization contrasted with the image of marauding militarists, suggesting that, at heart, Japan remained a respectable member of the international community. On another level, this depiction reinforced Japan's Pan-Asian metanarrative that the greatness of Japanese civilization gave the empire a special responsibility to oversee Asia, and that Japan's regional aspirations were legitimate. KBS projects and materials, as artifacts of self-representation, therefore, were not innocent "cultural exchange" but rather a unidirectional campaign of cultural propaganda that sought to provide "correct information" about Japan. Put another way, KBS programs soft-pedaled the empire's rationale for regional primacy. Thus, *Prelude to Pearl Harbor*, as part of the "cultural turn" in international history, delineates a compelling linkage between power and culture (by culture, I mean in a more granular, specific way "the arts," rather than in broadly anthropological terms).[13]

To be sure, the empire's foreign policy goals ultimately were not realized. While Japan's carefully conceived displays of its national culture won the admiration of many urbane Americans, this did not mean that individuals like Ambassador Joseph C. Grew and others were more likely to accept Japan's claims in Asia. Tokyo's soft power campaign thus also demonstrates the limits of cultural tools, especially as the intended message becomes too alien from realities on the ground. The significant point, in terms of causality, however, is that Japan's political leadership consciously sought to use culture because it provided a *possibility for a desired outcome*. As historian Frank A. Ninkovich has noted, "[Culture] is not a cause in the commonly understood scientific sense. Rather, it is the field of possibility for what can and cannot be done."[14]

Instead what happened, also historically significant, is that Japan's soft power initiatives tended to bolster prevailing American assumptions of an exaggerated civilian/military split among Japan's leaders—with the consequent American hope that civilian moderates would regain power and return Japan to the principles of the liberal world order. Paradoxically, the Japanese individuals that Americans designated as "moderates" invariably supported the empire's expansionism on the continent. The result was another layer of confusion in already confused transpacific relations, but one that gave American leaders and commentators pause during the mid-1930s. Moreover, the dualistic stereotypes of Japan's polity survived the war years to influence America's postwar occupation policy. *Prelude to Pearl Harbor* thus illuminates not only the connection between culture and power but also the wages of misperception and unintended consequences in bilateral relations.

Japan's invasion of China in the summer of 1937, and its formal Asianist declaration of a "New Order in East Asia" in 1938, shattered the ambivalence in US-Japan relations. The outbreak of war in Europe further reinforced Tokyo's and Washington's deeply antithetical worldviews. President Roosevelt increasingly emphasized ideological convergence between Imperial Japan, Nazi Germany, and Fascist Italy—and the conviction that radical regimes posed an existential threat. In this way, ideology became increasingly interwoven with rising geopolitical stakes, a dynamic explored by David Reynolds.[15] Negotiations between Tokyo and Washington in 1941 and the introduction of an unofficial peace proposal (the so-called Draft Understanding) laid bare the ideological chasm. Often depicted as a last great chance for a rapprochement, the Draft Understanding, *Prelude to Pearl Harbor* demonstrates, instead of bridging the ideological divide merely confirmed it.

***

What follows is a study of ideology, cultural interactions, and conventional diplomacy in US-Japan relations in the 1930s, within a global context—mainly through a study of American perceptions of and reactions to Japanese policies and cultural programs. Tokyo spent much of the 1930s, in particular, trying to win over American officials and opinion makers to its view of world order; thus, rather than illuminating the inner governmental and intellectual formulation of Pan-Asianism, as Japan scholars have done, sources are used to show how the Japanese publicly articulated their regionalist ideology to American audiences and the rest of the world. The preponderance of primary sources, therefore, are those directly in English (which was the language of diplomacy and record for international treaties) or Japanese-language sources translated into English by Japanese officials and distributed through the mass-circulation press. Exceptions include Japanese-language sources related to Japanese officials' analysis of their cultural programs aimed at Americans.

Chapter 1 examines the transformation in international relations following the Great War. However well plowed in scholarship, I believe US-Japan hostilities in the 1930s can be properly understood only by grappling with the postwar trauma and repeated attempts to revolutionize diplomacy between 1919 and 1930, like the Nine-Power Treaty and no-war pact. The ensuing ideological declarations in the 1930s by Tokyo and Washington and comments on both sides make little sense without this fundamental understanding. As such, I stress the new diplomacy's reliance on rules-based "orderly processes" and how Japan and the United States played important roles in outlining the terms of liberal internationalism in four postwar conferences between 1919 and 1930.

Chapter 2 explores the transformation of the Manchurian Incident into an ideological crisis and a turning point in world affairs and US-Japan relations. As the first real test case for liberal internationalism, the Manchurian crisis became the focal point of a tempestuous ideological drama, in which Japan, the United States, and the League of Nations debated the meaning and merits of the new diplomacy. Toward this end, I discuss the Japanese government's guiding rationale for its seizure of Manchuria, which includes the evolving premises of a more radical Pan-Asianism.

Chapter 3 examines Japan's initial endeavor to avoid isolation in the aftermath of the Manchurian crisis and win recognition of a new regionalist framework justified by historical rights, strategic interests, and, increasingly, an ideology of Pan-Asianism. Strategies by Japan's Ministry of Foreign Affairs included both official demarches as well as seemingly "unofficial" diplomacy, including goodwill trips by eminent Japanese and an emergent soft power campaign involving cultural propaganda. Despite a somewhat scattershot approach, evidence suggests the Japanese government's "charm offensive" further propagated a "dualism" in American perceptions of Japan among the press and Ambassador Grew—one that created an unrealistic turnaround in Japan's foreign policies.

Chapter 4 analyzes how Japan's regionalist policy in the mid-1930s was hardening even as the empire's efforts to finesse American opinion through the Kokusai Bunka Shinkōkai intensified. These efforts included a number of expansive cultural initiatives, such as art exhibitions at the Metropolitan

Museum of Art in New York and the Museum of Fine Art in Boston and an exclusive garden tour in Japan. This chapter also explores a complementary dynamic between the KBS-directed message of Japanese cultural refinement and American acknowledgments of Japanese modernity.

Chapter 5 examines Japan's invasion of China and the sudden deepening of bilateral estrangement between Japan and the United States. After hostilities erupted in North China in July 1937, Japan's leaders issued strongly worded Pan-Asianist statements and set out to realize an autarkic order on the continent. The Kokusai Bunka Shinkōkai, meanwhile, persisted in extolling the empire through cultural activities—including the establishment of a cultural institute in New York. In Washington, President Roosevelt, facing an isolationist Congress committed to neutrality, sought to awaken Americans to the perceived threat of global war.

Chapter 6 explores the impact of the war in Europe on US-Japan relations. By 1939, Japan's leadership focused on consolidating power on mainland China while contemplating a closer relationship with Germany. In the United States, President Roosevelt became vigilant in what became a kind of personal mission to alert Americans to the perceived ideological convergence among revisionist powers and the grave strategic threat they posed to the liberal democracies. Confident of public backing, the administration notified Japan in July 1939 that it intended to terminate the US-Japan commercial treaty of 1911.

Finally, chapter 7 scrutinizes the slippery slope to transpacific war. As would be the case through the attack on Pearl Harbor, Germany's stunning victories emboldened Japanese expansionism, which, in turn, stiffened American resistance. In September 1940, Japanese leaders signed the Tripartite Pact, which foresaw "new orders" in Europe and Asia. The pact's stated intention of carving the world into hegemonic blocs only confirmed the Roosevelt administration's global assumptions about the existential threat resulting from the interconnectedness between ideology and geopolitical ambitions among the Axis powers. In 1941, protracted negotiations between Japan and the United States revealed a yawning ideological gulf. Although a number of Japanese leaders began to harbor doubts about going to war against the United States, it was not because these men had abandoned their dreams of a Japanese-guided regional order; rather, they believed that war would undermine such aspirations. Regrettably, eleventh-hour negotiations could do little to erase the fundamental ideological divide that separated the two nations on the eve of Japan's surprise attack, or alter the historical context of the previous ten years.

Chapter One

"Too Proud to Fight"

The Dream World of Orderly Processes (1919–1930)

Around 10:20 p.m. on September 18, 1931, Japanese troops based in southern Manchuria dynamited a small section of a Japanese-owned railway outside of Shenyang (Mukden) and blamed it on Chinese saboteurs. The railway was part of the 1,400-square-mile Kwantung Leased Territory, which Japan administered through the semigovernmental South Manchurian Railway Company—and which the Japanese troops, known as the Kwantung Army, were there to protect. Although a southbound train passed over the area without incident moments later, the alarm went out according to plan. The Kwantung Army subsequently used the manufactured incident as a pretext to launch attacks against Chinese troops with the intent to extend Japanese influence in Manchuria.

Telegrams from the Japanese consulate in Shenyang to Foreign Minister Shidehara Kijūrō in Tokyo made clear that local Chinese troops were not resisting and that the Kwantung Army likely planned the bombing. On September 19, the Japanese government agreed to contain the conflict, and yet several days later it retroactively sanctioned sending field units across the Yalu River into Manchuria from Japan's neighboring colony in Korea. Emperor Hirohito also endorsed the reinforcements, invoking a passive Japanese expression, "It cannot be helped."[1]

By September 22, the hostilities got the attention of US Secretary of State Henry L. Stimson, who expressed concern to Japanese Ambassador Debuchi Katsuji, saying he hoped each side would refrain from further action. When fighting continued, Stimson confessed, "We really have no idea what is going on in Manchuria." On October 8, the secretary's confusion turned to shock after Japanese planes bombed the city of Jinzhou, 129 miles southwest of Shenyang. Stimson said he asked Foreign Minister Shidehara "pretty direct questions" about whether Tokyo had authorized the operation. Upon receiving an ambiguous reply, one that downplayed the importance of events, it was almost as if Stimson's heart may have skipped a beat as he sensed the initial tremors of an emergent ideological fault line between Japan and the United States.[2]

There is little doubt as to basis of Stimson's distress. The aerial bombing of a Chinese city far from Japan's leased territory suggested a military campaign not a leaseholder's grievance. It was starting to look like naked aggression. And the world had come together several times since the Great War to establish rules-based processes to prevent this very thing. But what if aggressors ignored the process? The postwar treaties were underwritten mainly by self-restraint and the moral sanction of public opinion. These were limited and mostly untested deterrents. As the prospect of collective impotence dawned on Stimson, he noted in his diary, "The whole world looks on to see whether the treaties are good for anything or not, and if we lie down and treat them like scraps of paper nothing will happen, and in the future the peace movement will receive a blow that it will not recover from for a long time." Then, in November 1931, after Japan began massing troops on the outskirts of Jinzhou, Stimson remarked to Debuchi that an assault on the city would upset "the whole apple cart" of multilateral treaties.[3]

Stimson's warning proved prophetic. Japan's aggression in Manchuria marked the beginning of the empire's retreat from the newly established international norms and rising ideological tension with the United States. It is no small irony that the bomb Japanese troops exploded on the railway in Manchuria caused minimal damage to the track but irrevocable damage to the post–World War I peace structure. To understand better the Manchurian crisis as a turning point in Japan and America's ideological estrangement, and an important tributary to the cataclysm of World War II, we need to backtrack to the First World War. We need to appreciate how the war's trauma stimulated a new temperament, a new way of thinking about international relations—about war and peace—that later became known as "liberal internationalism." Although old diplomatic norms did not go by the wayside en masse, methods and behaviors and underlying assumptions were thrown wide open to the critical eye. The United States and Japan played major roles in negotiating and defining the terms of liberal internationalism in four postwar conferences: the Paris Peace Conference (1919), the Washington Conference (1921–1922), the Kellogg–Briand Paris conference (1928), and the London Naval Conference (1930).

***

By 1914, Europe had enjoyed a century of peace. To be sure, it was an imperfect peace. No one who fought in the Crimean or Franco-Prussian or Second Boer or Russo-Japanese Wars would label the peace as lasting a century. Still, the absence of large-scale, protracted conflict since the Napoleonic Wars was no small achievement. Indeed, it would have been reasonable to wonder at the time whether those patrician diplomats at the Congress of Vienna had bequeathed an enduring miracle. The long peace provided incubation for technological innovation and the accelerated expansion of the "second" industrial revolution. In Europe's major cities, world fairs periodically touted new inventions. Imposing, steel-framed railroad stations stood as cathedrals of modernity. In the arts, brilliantly original movements—Impressionism, Post-Impressionism, Fauvism, Expressionism, and Cubism—burst forth in dizzying succession. Despite intermittent socioeconomic turmoil, Europe came to be viewed as the advance guard of civilization. Not surprisingly, Europe's great powers commonly justified their far-flung colonies with claims of bringing "civilization and enlightenment" to allegedly primitive peoples.

By the end of 1914, Europeans and their allies were killing and maiming each other with unprecedented ferocity. Looking back, it is as if the ominously dissonant chords in Igor Stravinsky's *Rite of Spring*, which premiered in 1913, foreshadowed what writers would come to describe as the "cataclysm," "maelstrom," and eventually the Great War. The extraordinary bloodletting persisted for more than four years. Soldiers withdrew to the zigzag maze of trenches, suffered artillery bombardment, occasionally launched offensive charges against insurmountable odds, and died. Death often came suddenly and savagely, and from a distance, thanks to advanced and more pernicious weapons of the "age of progress."

Japan and the United States took very different paths in the world war. Japan intervened in August 1914 on the side of the Entente, eyeing easy war spoils in Germany's possessions in Asia. In the United States, President Woodrow Wilson endeavored to maintain American neutrality, with the eventual goal of mediating a "peace without victory" among the belligerents.[4] In the spring of 1917, however, two months after Germany resumed unrestricted submarine warfare, Wilson asked Congress for a declaration of war. Contrary to casual assumptions, Wilson did not base his decision for war solely to uphold neutral principles or eliminate German militarism. The president's guiding motives were more idealistic. Wilson had come to believe the United States needed to enter the war to hasten its end and guarantee a permanent peace. Concluding his message to Congress, Wilson evoked Martin Luther's principled stand at Worms, declaring, "God helping her [America], she can do no other." The president's morally charged words planted the seeds of a more assertive American role in world affairs as a self-described "indispensable" nation.[5]

The guns finally fell silent on November 11, 1918. "The fires of hell have been put out," reported a correspondent from the front.[6] The war took the lives of more than nine million people. Despite the obvious relief of the war's end, a momentous new reality hovered like a vulture over the human wreckage: modern war had become a genuine threat to the increasingly interdependent global society built on mutual interests and social and economic processes—including finance, trade, shipping, technology transfer, communication, migration, and global markets. Historian Frank Ninkovich has noted that American cosmopolitans since the end of the nineteenth century had come to view the stability and "good health" of global society as a vital interest. This concern now intensified in the wake of the world war. It was not just Americans, however, who grew apprehensive about the perceived vulnerability of global society. British Prime Minister David Lloyd George warned, "If this is not the last war there are men here today who will see the last of civilization." In fact, such fears were present even in the early stages of the war. As the mayor of Tokyo, Sakatani Yoshirō, opined in 1914, a major war in the heart of Europe would threaten Japan and beyond because the world was "intimately entwined."[7] All of which raised a fundamental question about the international system: *how* to achieve lasting peace in a rapidly changing world that offered both promise and peril? This near compulsion, arising out the ashes of the Great War, is one of the reasons the conflict became a watershed event.

There is little historical disagreement that President Wilson led the charge to "remake the world" following the First World War. In speeches and statements before, during, and immediately after America's participation in the conflict, the president repeatedly asserted the world could no longer afford to conduct international relations the "old way." The world must have a plan, said Wilson, which "does not contain the germs of another war." Wilson's allusion to the "old way" meant the peace resulting from the Congress of Vienna. The basis of that peace had been reliance on a "balance of power." En route to the Paris Peace Conference, Wilson again excoriated the "balance of power" system, saying it produced only "aggression and selfishness and war."[8] Wilson seldom alluded to the stampede of imperialism in the late nineteenth century, but that global rivalry was another element in the war's lethal combustion. The great powers had engaged in one of the most expansive orgies of territorial aggrandizement in world history, carving up most of Africa, South and Southeast Asia, and Oceania and obtaining leaseholds in China. Japan had taken Taiwan (Formosa) and Korea and acquired leased territories in Manchuria and Fujian provinces, while the United States seized the Philippines, Guam, Puerto Rico, and Hawaiʻi.

Blaming the old diplomacy for the world's recent trauma, of course, only made the elephant in the room loom larger than ever: what was to be done? By the time he arrived at the peace conference, Wilson had been dwelling on the problem for well over a year. To be sure, the president was hardly alone in calling for a new international framework. At home and abroad the issue stimulated a robust debate, including a more radical model advanced by communist revolutionaries V. I. Lenin and Leon Trotsky. Wilson, however, became the undisputed visionary of a liberal peace. The rhetoric was often lofty and lifting, the nuts and bolts somewhat ambiguous. Wilson had issued his most detailed outline, the Fourteen Points, in January 1918. Though many of the proposals drew from nineteenth-century British liberalism,[9] Wilson gave the ideas new relevancy and cogency. Moreover, his commitment to a just peace as an "associated power"—Wilson refused to enter the war as an official ally of the Entente powers—added an aura of credibility to the Fourteen Points. Indeed, the Fourteen Points soon became regarded by peoples around the world as the rightful blueprint for a new world order, and the basis for discussions among the thousands of delegates who arrived in Paris just two months after the end of the bloodiest war in human history.

PARIS PEACE CONFERENCE, 1919

The Paris Peace Conference convened on January 18, 1919. Twenty-nine countries were represented, although the "Big Five" on the winning side of the war—Great Britain, France, Italy, the United States, and Japan—dominated the proceedings. After March, however, the heavy lifting took place among the sequestered Council of Four, made up of three prime ministers and a president: France's Georges Clemenceau, Britain's Lloyd George, Italy's Vittorio Orlando—and Wilson. The official explanation for Japan's exclusion was that its delegation was not led by a head of state. The more likely reason was the impression that Japan's contribution to the war had been limited to minor conflict in Asia (a view that conveniently overlooked Japan's naval assistance convoying troops and materials for the Allied cause). The conference's agenda, meanwhile, ran along two main tracks: a settlement with Germany and a new framework for world peace. Although the treaty with Germany often converged at various switching points with the second objective, for the purposes of this book's subject matter, the primary focus will be on the establishment of a new international peace structure.

In putting forth his Fourteen Points, Wilson was asking his fellow peacemakers to buy into and internalize a broad range of liberal ideas, what later became known as the ideology of "liberal internationalism." Some of these concepts included diplomatic transparency, freedom of seas, disarmament, free trade, popular government, and "self-determination," or the right of peoples to shape their own national destiny. As the conference proceeded, however, many of these ideas became prescribed as ideals to which the world should aspire rather than new norms. The immediate result of self-determination, for example, was the creation of a few new states in Europe, while the vast collection of colonies around the world continued to exist. If morally convoluted, the approach was emblematic of Wilsonian internationalism: plant an idea, inculcate a sense of "shared beliefs," establish precedents, and then build on them through an evolutionary, orderly process. As Erez Manela has shown, this "Wilsonian moment" offered marginalized groups "unprecedented opportunities to advance claims in the name of . . . emerging national identities and thus bolster and expand their legitimacy both at home and abroad." Put simply, white domination over people of color could no longer be taken for granted.[10]

If some ideas at Paris became diluted or redirected, the heart and soul of the liberal peace program—a League of Nations—found widespread support. The league's guiding premise was that the use of force in the pursuit of national interests was no longer acceptable. With its reliance on collective security—what Wilson called a "community of power"—the league represented a radical experiment in keeping peace among nations. In Article X of the League Covenant, members pledged to guarantee the "territorial integrity" of all member nations. In other words, member states promised to safeguard each other's territorial boundaries as if they were their own borders. Such a reliance on universal selflessness was uncharted territory indeed.

In the case of aggression, league members possessed several "weapons" that could be used to uphold "territorial integrity." First and foremost was moral condemnation through the "organized opinion of mankind." In light of the expansion of the telecommunications revolution, and anticipating the spread of mass participation politics, Wilson placed enormous faith in the power of world opinion to deter or alter the behavior of aggressors. As Wilson explained it,

> The most dangerous thing for a bad cause is to expose it to the opinion of the world. The most certain way that you can prove that a man is mistaken is by letting all his neighbors know what he thinks, by letting all his neighbors discuss what he thinks, and if he is in the wrong you will notice that he will stay at home, he will not walk on the street. He will be afraid of the eyes of his neighbors. He will be afraid of their judgment of his character.[11]

The expectation, of course, was that an ironclad consensus of views, representing the conscience of the world, could shame an aggressor into peaceful retreat.

A second "weapon" in collective security's reserve against an aggressor involved what Wilson called "the most complete boycott ever conceived in a public document," including economic sanctions and a ban on mail, telephone, telegraph, and travel privileges. "Their frontiers," declared Wilson, "would be hermetically sealed." A third and final measure involved the use of military force as a last resort. As Wilson affirmed, "Armed force is in the background in this program, but it is in the background, and if the moral force of the world will not suffice, the physical force shall." This force element is often overlooked because critics tend to caricature Wilson as a man of excessive idealism. In doing so, they gloss over what historian Arthur S. Link refers to as the "higher realism" of the president's program. As we shall see, there were serious problems with the league's collective security approach, but it was not because, as Henry Kissinger has argued, power was "ignored or left in disarray."[12]

On April 28, 1919, the Covenant of the League of Nations was approved in a plenary session of the Paris Peace Conference and announced to the world. The fury of modern war and its perceived threat to "civilization" had compelled the world powers to discard the balance-of-power system for a liberal program. Amid the recent fever of imperialism, secret treaties, jingoistic nationalism, and rearmament, the powers had agreed in principle to seek peaceful resolutions to conflict, to scrap the idea that "might is right" and instead embrace the liberal mantra that "right is right." Many people around the world experienced the same hope and excitement as that of Hugh Byas, the Scottish-born editor of the English-language *Japan Advertiser*, who wrote from Tokyo that "the world's great age begins anew."[13]

But if the world was beginning anew, it also carried with it seeds of discontent and instability. All the major peacemakers contributed to this instability. For example, despite Wilson's opposition, Premier Clemenceau insisted on a vindictive peace. Germany ultimately was forced to pay indemnities, cede territory in the Saar for at least fifteen years, demilitarize the Rhineland, and renounce its colonies. Particularly misguided was the victors' demand that Germany take all the blame for starting the war (Article 231). As one historian recently concluded, "There is no smoking gun in this story; or, rather, there is one in the hands of every major character."[14] Precisely how punitive the final settlement with Germany was remains a source of great debate. What is more certain is that both psychologically and materially the treaty was at odds with Wilson's vision. But having lost crucial leverage after the armistice, and fearing an erosion of support for a League of Nations, Wilson relented.

Wilson also yielded to Japan in what he considered his single greatest concession at the conference. The Japanese delegation had arrived in Paris walking an ideological tightrope—sensitive to "world trends" and the momentum of Wilsonian internationalism, but cautious about abandoning the old diplomacy. Back home, Tokyo University professor Yoshino Sakuzō, a Wilsonian enthusiast, declared that Japan must come to terms with the "rule of morality," which was triumphing over the "rule of naked power." Foreign Minister Uchida Kōsai was less convinced. He instructed his chief plenipotentiaries to maintain harmony with the other peacemakers but "to avoid binding restrictions as much as possible" and to delay a decision on the

League Covenant until the great powers' views on issues important to Japan became clearer.[15] Above all, Japan's delegation was intent on consolidating war spoils.

Japan's most coveted prize was Germany's leased territory in the province of Shandong, China, which Japanese troops captured early in the war. Germany had acquired the concession in 1898 during the imperialist carve-up of China. At the turn of the century, a crumbling Qing dynasty had agreed to lease vast swaths of its coastal territory, typically for ninety-nine years,[16] to Great Britain, France, Germany, Russia, and Japan. The imperialist powers developed railways and mining interests and built naval bases in their leaseholds; they also held exclusive control over customhouses and the court system. In 1904 Japan went to war against Russia and seized the tsar's leasehold in the Liaodong peninsula in Manchuria (which Russia previously had prevented Japan from taking). The Qing dynasty fell in 1912, but China remained in a highly distressed state—politically fragmented, subject to the whims of warlords, and subordinate to imperial powers. During the world war, Japan exploited this instability. In 1915, a year after seizing Shandong from Germany, Japan coerced the nominal Chinese government in Beijing to transfer the kaiser's concession rights to the empire. The transfer occurred as one part of a sweeping ultimatum known as the Twenty-One Demands. Japan's delegation at Paris subsequently insisted that the conferees officially recognize the Shandong transfer.

Such recognition, however, would have violated one of the peace program's most hallowed principles to respect "territorial integrity." This point was made abundantly clear by China's Western-educated plenipotentiaries, V. K. Wellington Koo (Columbia University) and Wang Zhengting (Yale University). Despite their distinctive regional attachments—Koo to the government in Beijing; Wang to Nationalists in Guangdong province—the two delegates eloquently laid out the legal and moral justifications for the return of Shandong. Japan, they argued, had seized the territory under duress; what's more, in 1917 China itself had entered the war against Germany, Shandong's original occupier. In response, Japan's delegates brandished China's signatures on the Twenty-One Demands. They also laid bare promises that France and Great Britain made to Japan in 1917 in support of Tokyo's wartime ambitions in China, as well as secret agreements the Beijing government made with Japan regarding Shandong in 1918.[17]

Wilson sympathized with China but felt caught between fidelity to his principles and a fear that Japan would spurn the League of Nations. In fact, Japanese delegates had intimated that very thing if the conference deprived Japan of Shandong; the historical record suggests they were not bluffing. Tokyo also used as leverage an earlier Japanese proposal to insert into the final treaty a "racial equality" clause. The proposal, which stemmed from the repeated slights Japanese nationals suffered overseas, would have compelled league members to accord "equal and just treatment" to all peoples regardless of race or nationality. The antidiscrimination initiative had not been contrived as leverage. As one scholar has argued, it was a sincere effort to overturn a "Western-centric definition of a great power." Indeed, despite Japan's own discriminatory treatment of Koreans—Korea's concurrent March First Movement against Japanese colonialism was inspired by the promise of Wilsonianism—the amendment was a forward-thinking, liberal statement.[18] It won wide support at the conference except from the Australian, British, and American delegations, who faced domestic political backlash from a mixture of anti-immigration agitators, xenophobes, and racists. Wilson therefore suppressed the clause, an unjustifiable action the Japanese then used to pressure the president further on Shandong. Wilson surrendered, with the stipulation that Japan promise to retrocede the leased territory to China at a future date.

If the Shandong transfer represented an unavoidable political trade-off, it also portended liberal internationalism's limits as well as future ideological discord between Japan and the United States. When the decision was made public, students in Beijing exploded in protest, unleashing the May Fourth Movement. China refused to sign the Treaty of Versailles, the only nation at Paris to do so (it joined the league in 1920). Wilson later told the American people he loathed all of the Chinese leaseholds but that the League of Nations eventually would find a just solution. If and when that happened, however, the United States would not play a role. As is well known, the Republican-led and politically fractured US Senate refused to consent to the League Covenant. The United States never joined the League of Nations—a strikingly unilateralist message to a world about to embark on a novel experiment in multilateral cooperation. The Senate's rejection resulted principally from conflicting views over national sovereignty. Theoretically, collective security demanded that nations surrender a significant degree of foreign policy making to an international institution. There was the impression—*not necessarily the reality*—that each member of the league was expected to send troops into zones of conflict, no matter how large or small, or distant.[19]

It takes but a moment to grasp the tragic irony of the Senate's decision for Wilson. The president had argued for intervention in the Great War in large part to help create a new world order. He had spent nearly *five months* in Paris making certain that would happen. American scholar-diplomat George Kennan later vilified Wilson's "colossal conceit" in thinking he could remake international life in his image.[20] Kennan's appraisal was neither fair nor accurate. Wilson, of course, had drawn extensively from nineteenth-century liberalism. Most important, the president and his fellow peacemakers faced unique circumstances in a world that had undergone unprecedented change since the Napoleonic Age, including the rise of new nation-states like Germany and Italy. The unconcealed fact was that the balance-of-power

Figure 1.1. "The Gap in the Bridge," which draws attention to the irony and weight of America's absence in the League of Nations. Note also the curious inclusion of Belgium and omission of Japan. (Leonard Raven-Hill, *Punch*, December 10, 1919. From Internet Archive.)

system had broken down and filled cemeteries with more than nine million human beings. That Wilson approached the shattered world with an innovative plan is understandable. That the peace program ultimately failed reminds us more about the intractable problem of human conflict and world governance.

Notwithstanding its early setbacks, the ideology of liberal internationalism emerged from the peace conference already having planted roots. Delegates from all over the world had spent six months together discussing the problem of world order. They had answered the normative question about how an international system ought to be structured and managed in entirely novel ways. The new norms proceeded from the principle that naked aggression no longer was acceptable behavior in international relations. And when disputes arose, they were to be dealt with multilaterally through rules-based "orderly processes." By the end of the 1920s—even without the United States (or the Soviet Union) in the league—these "new world trends" had evolved into something approximating a universal ideology, however tenuous. As Ishii Kikujirō, a Japanese representative at the League of Nations, explained at the time,

> World currents of peace, stirred by the lessons of the Great War, have drifted toward Geneva and given to that place the peculiar air known as the Geneva atmosphere.... This atmosphere is a specific remedy for lowering the fever of military aggression.... It is universally accepted that the best way to bring about the peaceful settlement of international disputes is to recognize as binding the duty of submitting such disputes to arbitration.[21]

Toward this end, in the mid-1920s, the league facilitated a series of security and territorial agreements collectively known as the Locarno Treaties, after which Germany became a member.

In substantive ways both Japan and the United States extended the roots of the liberal order during the 1920s. In Japan, despite a cynical undergrowth of nationalist critics who claimed that Wilsonianism was simply a fig leaf for Anglo-American domination, mainstream diplomacy followed in the spirit of an imperial rescript proclaimed in the name of Emperor Taishō. Declaring that world affairs had "completely changed," the rescript instructed Japanese officials to help build an internationalist order. Japan's Foreign Ministry, under the leadership of Shidehara Kijurō, gravitated toward an Anglo-American bias, convinced that cooperation with the world's leading powers was the most effective way to advance Japan's foreign policy goals. Japan's rising global status (one of only four permanent members on the League of Nations Council) gave added incentive for the empire to conform to the new diplomacy. To be sure, this did not mean the unqualified subordination of regional interests to internationalist imperatives; still, Japan's "cooperative diplomacy" during the 1920s was remarkable for its consistency.[22]

As for the United States, although it had spurned the league, it nonetheless remained mostly committed to an internationalist approach. On one hand, the succession of Republican administrations in the 1920s tended to stress capital investment and trade to facilitate world peace. On the other hand (and more ironically, given the League of Nations fight), they also took the lead on a number of initiatives to augment the liberal order. The irony is less striking, however, if one appreciates how the ideology of Wilsonianism evoked aspects of conservativism, in that it sought to avoid upheaval by privileging "orderly processes." As Frank Costigliola has noted, Republicans wanted to "strike a balance between order and change."[23] This was a dominant trait of Progressive-era reforms, which many moderate Republicans had supported. It was a characteristic that consequently guided Republican administrations in a series of multilateral conferences.

WASHINGTON CONFERENCE, 1921–1922

In a campaign speech during the 1920 presidential election, Republican nominee Warren G. Harding called for a return to simpler times and less international engagement. In strained prose, he declared, "America's present need is not . . . submergence in internationality, but sustainment in triumphant nationality." During his first year in office, however, Harding told the US Senate, "We crave peace [in the Pacific] as we do on the continent, and we should be remiss in performing a national duty if we did not covenant the relations which tend to guarantee it."[24] The use of the phrase "national duty" in connection with preserving peace far from the contiguous United States is not what one would have expected from the leader of a party that had jilted the League of Nations. In addition to exposing the cliché of American isolationism in the 1920s, the speech sheds important light on the era's internationalist thrust—especially the fear of another great war and the vigilance required to prevent its outbreak.

The American president and his secretary of state, Charles Evans Hughes, agreed that the area of the Pacific and East Asia was particularly vulnerable to violent disorder. Not only did interests of the world's three largest naval powers—Great Britain, the United States, and Japan—converge there, but the region contained the seeming tinderbox of China. Harding and Hughes were not alone in their geopolitical anxiety. The concern had been palpable at the Paris Peace Conference as well. President Wilson, for example, remarked that "the greatest dangers for the world can arise in the Pacific." The State Department's China specialist, Paul S. Reinsch, similarly stated there was "no single problem in Europe" that challenged the "future peace of the world" more than that of East Asia. The region's tensions, Reinsch asserted, made "a huge armed conflict absolutely inevitable within one generation." And Chinese diplomat Wellington Koo predicted a war in East Asia by 1930 if nothing were done to resolve issues regarding Chinese sovereignty.[25]

The lingering anxieties in Asian-Pacific affairs—as well as political pressures at home—eventually prompted Harding and Hughes to organize an international conference in Washington, DC, in the fall and winter of 1921–1922.[26] The goal was twofold: to prevent a naval arms race and to promote stability in China, where 400 million people continued to live among a patchwork of autonomous political units and foreign-controlled leaseholds. Although the Washington Conference focused on very specific issues among a very specific group of actors, the summit nonetheless embodied the Wilsonian emphasis on "orderly processes" and the sanctity of treaties. Hughes further channeled Wilsonianism by directly tackling disarmament and territorial integrity. Wilson had addressed both issues in his Fourteen Points.

Participants at the conference included the world's largest naval powers as well as nations with vested interests in China. The secretary, however, had set his sights primarily on Great Britain and Japan. In addition to their powerful navies, the two empires also shared a military alliance and boasted the biggest presence in China, in both leaseholds and investments. For Japan's leaders, naval limitation was an unusual inquiry, and issues related to China impinged upon the empire's increasing sense of regional responsibility. But they concluded that multilateral cooperation could best enhance their nation's status. As for Great Britain, by 1921, Pax Britannica was slowly coming to terms with the dawn of Pax Americana. The Great War had greatly accelerated America's world power trajectory. New York was on the cusp of usurping London as the financial capital of the world, and the US Navy rivaled Britain's in capital ships. America's political, economic, and military might—latent for three decades—was now unmistakable and doubtless informed Prime Minister Lloyd George's words at a commonwealth conference in 1921. "Friendly co-operation with the United States," said Lloyd George, "is for us a cardinal principle."[27]

The conference opened in Washington, DC, on November 12, 1921. It was no coincidence that the previous day marked the third anniversary of Armistice Day. Or that the opening invocation solemnly stated, "God forbid that the horrors of those years should ever again be revisited upon the earth." President Harding's welcome speech, meanwhile, produced "prolonged cheering" after he asked the assembled chamber, "How can humanity justify or God forgive?" This was a world still walking with trepidation in the shadow of the First World War. As part of the search for permanent peace, the conference produced three significant multilateral treaties: the Five-Power Treaty (naval disarmament), the Four-Power Treaty (termination of the Anglo-Japanese Alliance), and the Nine-Power Treaty (codification of China's territorial integrity, or the Open Door). The Five-Power Treaty and especially the Nine-Power Treaty figured prominently in US-Japan relations throughout the troubled 1930s.[28]

We think of arms control talks today as a normal component of international relations. This was not the case in the early twentieth century, which explains the shock that filled Memorial Hall after Secretary Hughes stated in businesslike fashion that what he had in mind was a ten-year naval holiday and hard caps on each nation's total tonnage of capital ships. For the American and foreign officials and some 300 newspaper correspondents who crowded the hall expecting to hear diplomatic platitudes about future naval building, what Hughes proposed bordered on radical. In some cases, the plan would require the destruction of existing ships in order to get under tonnage limits. In all, Hughes called for the three largest naval powers to scrap a whopping sixty-six vessels, mostly battleships: United States (30), Britain (19), and Japan (17). Finally, as a precondition to disarmament, Hughes called for the termination of the Anglo-Japanese Alliance, which had been in effect since 1902. The alliance was a thorn in US-British relations. Americans perceived the exclusive pact to be a relic of the old diplomacy, one that tilted power in the western Pacific and emboldened Japan.[29]

A reporter for the *London Daily Chronicle* declared the opening of the conference to be "one of the great days in modern annals" and Secretary Hughes's address "real, palpable, enormous." Hughes received a boisterous standing ovation that went on for several minutes. Wild cheering from the gallery also went up for French Premier Aristide Briand and Japanese delegate Tokugawa Iesato. Much of the exuberant response came from the fact that Hughes's speech, as the Associated Press (AP) asserted, was "more far-reaching than the most ardent advocate of disarmament dared to hope." A major catalyst for naval limitation was pacifist groups who argued that munitions makers had helped ignite the Great War by fueling an arms race. Partially because of their activism, the League of Nations had rekindled disarmament talks in Geneva, and powerful maverick senator William E. Borah (R-ID) had mounted an aggressive campaign in Congress.[30] In catching the pacifist wave, Hughes was suggesting that the five largest naval powers (Britain, Japan, the United States, France, and Italy) were overarmed—that they possessed more warships than what was sufficient for their security needs. The underlying assumption was that an oversized navy held within it the temptation for offensive war.

Then came the hard part. What constituted sufficient defense for each of the naval powers? Hughes's answer came in the form of a ratio system (5:5:3:1.75), with an eye on how much territory a nation's navy had to defend. This included national coastlines and overseas possessions. Great Britain and the United States, Hughes argued, required 525,000 tons of battleships, Japan, 315,000 tons; France and Italy, second-tier naval powers, were accorded 175,000 tons. Hughes's rationale was as follows: Great Britain had to defend a global empire (which, in itself, was becoming increasingly difficult to defend in principle under the lingua franca of liberal internationalism). The United States, meanwhile, had to defend two coastlines. Japan's coastlines were smaller and its possessions nearer. Italy's requirements were the Mediterranean; France's were more expansive, but pressure and veiled threats from Hughes brought the French into the fold.[31]

Despite a positive first impression, alarm bells went off among the Japanese delegation. Back in Tokyo, the Naval General Staff was apoplectic. The naval hard-liners (or "fleet faction") demanded absolute parity, explaining that a 5:5:3 ratio was meaningless in the event of a decisive battle, in which a belligerent would concentrate its entire battle fleet against an enemy. Japan's official delegation, meanwhile, argued for a 10:7 ratio. This proportion would give Britain or the United States a 43 percent advantage in Japanese waters, less than the 50 percent deemed necessary to defeat a defending navy. Japan's chief delegate, Navy Minister Katō Tomosaburō, maintained that anything less than a 10:7 ratio left the empire fearing "for her security and defense." Strategic concerns, however, were not the only thing that mattered to Japan. National pride was on the line as well. The psychological effect of parity—of *equality*—in the new era was important. In fact, Secretary Hughes was sensitive to bruised egos. At one point, the secretary considered using the term "relative national security" instead of "ratio" as a sop to Japan's pride.[32]

In the end, Japan accepted the 5:5:3 ratio on condition the United States not fortify its possessions in the western Pacific, including the Philippines and Guam. Japan also demanded unlimited construction of other vessels, including cruisers, submarines, and destroyers. These guarantees did not appease the fleet faction, but they nonetheless gave Japan's delegation confidence that the resultant Five-Power Treaty ensured the nation's security. Moreover, worldwide pressure for signing was immense. And so was American power. US officials were hardly equivocal about their nation's capacity to outbuild the Japanese navy. Essentially, the American position was that the treaty enhanced everyone's security at far less cost.

In the celebratory glow that followed, the Five-Power Treaty, the world's first disarmament treaty (the Hague Conventions of 1899 and 1907 had merely broached the idea), was hailed as another notch in the liberal internationalist totem. Along with the Four-Power Treaty—which both ended the Anglo-Japanese Alliance and obliged the United States, Japan, Great Britain, and France to "consult peaceably" on disputes in the Pacific—the Five-Power Treaty reflected the new diplomacy's emphasis on orderly processes and the belief that pledges of self-denial and sanction of public opinion could restrain the age-old demons of power politics. In the words of Minister Katō, the treaties represented "the new order of thought," underwritten by "the spirit of international friendship and cooperation for the greater good of humanity."[33] It was in this spirit that the conference turned to China and East Asia, believed by many observers to be world's new storm center.

China, the once proud and mighty hegemon, for centuries had fancied itself occupying "the middle of the universe." In fewer than one hundred years, however, it had fallen to the ranks of a "third-class" power—divided, depleted, exploited. This meteoric slide in great power status coincided with persistent territorial claims by the Western powers and Japan. The Qing dynasty, as we saw, met these demands in the form of long-term leased territories, stretching from port cities to the provincial hinterland. At this juncture, in 1899, an alarmed US Secretary of State John Hay sent a diplomatic note to the great powers, requesting equal economic opportunity (an "open door") in their respective leaseholds. Not surprisingly, his bid for fair play in a jungle of self-interest resulted in raised eyebrows and cold shoulders. A year later, after nationalist Chinese rebels ("Boxers") revolted violently against foreign interests, Hay amended his first note, urging the powers also to "preserve Chinese territorial and administrative entity."[34] Hay had injected a moral imperative into a zone of rapacious land grabbing. The perils were too great, Hay seemed to say. Carving up more territory would further

Figure 1.2. Delegates to the Washington Conference, 1921–1922. Pictured (L to R): Japan's chief delegate, Navy Minister Katō Tomosaburō, Shidehara Kijūrō (ambassador to the United States), and Secretary of State Charles Evans Hughes. (Library of Congress, Prints & Photographs Division, photograph by Harris & Ewing [reproduction number LC-DIG-hec-14440].)

destabilize China and heighten tensions between the great powers, possibly leading to war. Hay likely grasped the costs of modern warfare in ways others did not; he had been President Lincoln's personal secretary during the American Civil War.

Hay's second note, like the first, was a request. Again, the great powers gave evasive replies, though they did pay lip service to the Open Door in subsequent bilateral treaties with China. In retrospect, Hay's notes asked too much of imperialists at the height of the "age of empire." Predatory nations were not about to act selflessly in leaseholds they had independently acquired and begun to develop—particularly if they sensed that Hay was concerned more about American economic access than "territorial entity." Indeed, the United States was no innocent in China. In the 1840s, in tandem with European powers, Washington had negotiated "unequal treaties" with China, resulting in extraordinary rights and privileges in designated "treaty ports."[35] These rights included extraterritoriality, control over tariffs, and the creation of foreign-only zones called International Settlements. In 1882, meanwhile, the United States closed its door to Chinese immigration.

Despite the world's rebuff, the Open Door became entrenched as the official US policy in East Asia. The results over the next two decades, however, were modest. The leasehold spree abated, but the unequal treaties endured. The United States and Japan, in particular, butted heads over the meaning of the Open Door. This was especially true during the Great War, when Japan's sense of regional entitlement became more pronounced. In 1915, as noted, Japan presented China with the Twenty-One Demands. Some demands were specific to existing interests, such as extending the term of Japan's leased territory on the Liaodong Peninsula from 1923 until 1997, and control over the South Manchurian Railway until 2002. A series of claims in a "Group V," however, would have made China almost a protectorate of Japan. The Wilson administration refused to recognize the demands, which left the relationship between the Open Door and Japan's regionalism in a state of confusion. In 1917, Secretary of State Robert Lansing and Japanese envoy Ishii Kikujirō met to reconcile their nations' conflicting worldviews.

The Lansing–Ishii negotiations assumed an air of meaningful compromise, but they merely perpetuated the confusion. Reading sources on their conferences becomes a mind-numbing exercise in verbal gymnastics, with each side parsing the meaning of qualifying adjectives. Were Japan's interests in Asia "special" or "paramount"? Did Japan's geographical propinquity to China make its position "peculiar" and "unusual"? As it turned out, the final agreement's ambiguity was intentional; Lansing hoped opacity would convey a semblance of harmony.[36] Mostly, the agreement showed that the Open Door and Japanese regionalism could occupy the same room, albeit unpleasantly, as long as the Open Door remained solely an American principle in the old edifice of power politics. After the Great War, however, when the world began razing the old structure and building anew, double occupancy became untenable.

Secretary Hughes now sought to wind up the conflict between the Open Door and Japanese regionalism by turning American principles into universal law. Privately, he said he was willing to recognize Japan's "natural and legitimate economic opportunities" in China, but not its "political control." According to Hughes, the ensuing Nine-Power Treaty was intended to be "a substitute for all prior statements and agreements" (read: Lansing–Ishii). As Asada Sadao has made clear, such sweeping aspirations raised equally sweeping concerns among Japan's delegation. American delegate Elihu Root, a chief author of the treaty, proved to be a moderating influence. The Japanese respected Root for his fair-minded negotiations with Japan during the administration of Theodore Roosevelt; for this reason, Japan's delegates came to him unofficially many times to voice their concerns. Root's assurances and the inclusion of his "security" clause in Article I convinced the Japanese that the treaty recognized their "special position" in Manchuria.[37]

On its basic premises, the Nine-Power Treaty borrowed the language of both Hay's notes and Wilson's Fourteen Points, obliging the eight foreign powers with interests in China to respect the country's "territorial and administrative integrity." Similarly, the treaty sought to eliminate trade and investment barriers in China so that all nations could enjoy "the principle of equal opportunity of commerce." Though the most meaningful trade barriers in China were those of the still-existent foreign concessions, the Nine-Power Treaty targeted presumptions of perpetuity by requiring the contracting powers to respect China's independence and "provide the fullest and most unembarrassed opportunity to China to develop and maintain for herself an effective and stable government." In case of disputes, meanwhile, the signatories agreed to hew to the liberal imperative of "full and frank discussion."[38]

The Nine-Power Treaty (February 6, 1922) thus signified a solemn pledge to abide by expressed moral and legal principles regarding acceptable international conduct in China. That alone was significantly different from 1900, when not a single invited guest showed up at Hay's diplomatic table. Going forward, naked aggression in China was unacceptable and exclusive treaty rights should be discharged in the near future when certain legal conditions were met. Here again we see the Wilsonian emphasis on rules-based "orderly processes" and evolutionary change in the quest toward lasting peace. The status quo mostly remained, but the document's language and projection looked to a far different future.

To be sure, such assurances offered cold comfort to the Chinese, who demanded the immediate repudiation of all leased territories and foreign privileges. One is reminded here of African American civil rights activists in the 1950s being told by white moderates to be "patient." Moreover, the treaty was nonbinding; it was a promise made without any enforcement mechanism. If nations went back on their word, the violation would be transparent, but that was it. What happened next depended on the unknown power of world opinion. Looking back, it is clear such piecemeal promissory notes fell far short of the League of Nations' collective security and were good only as long as relations among nations remained tranquil and friendly.

When the conference concluded, the mood was optimistic and relations among nations were tranquil and friendly. Japan, as promised, retroceded its leasehold in Shandong; Britain vowed the same in Weihai. The good vibrations carried over to US-Japan relations. As historian Iriye Akira noted, the respective governments "were soon describing in glowing terms the coming of a new era of peace in the Pacific." Back in Tokyo, Navy Minister Katō told his compatriots he could "categorically state" there was no Anglo-American coercion during the talks. In Tokyo's Ueno Park, a peace bell rang out daily at a Peace Exposition for four months following the conference. Among Americans, the former assistant secretary of the navy in the Wilson administration, Franklin D. Roosevelt, said it was notable that Japan had begun carrying out the treaties in good faith. "American sympathies," he wrote in *Asia* magazine in 1923, "have been pro-Chinese rather than pro-Japanese. Perhaps, however, we are appreciating now a little more readily than formerly the Japanese point-of-view."[39]

Signs of America's new sympathies and improved relations with Japan became manifest in the fall of 1923 after large parts of Tokyo and Yokohama were destroyed by a massive 7.9 earthquake and subsequent fires. The American people responded with disproportionate generosity, making cash contributions totaling over fifteen million yen (about $98 million in 2018 dollars), compared to the rest of the world's combined total of six million yen ($40 million). Relations also remained on an even keel because of robust trade between the two Pacific powers. The United States purchased nearly 40 percent of Japanese exports. And starting in 1924, the Japanese ambassador to the United States and Washington Conference delegate Shidehara Kijūrō was appointed Japan's foreign minister. For much of the 1920s, Shidehara became the face of Japan's liberal internationalism and cooperative engagement, which earned the moniker, "Shidehara diplomacy." When he assumed office, Shidehara alluded to the Versailles and Washington treaties, saying, "Machiavellian stratagem and aggressive policy are now things of the past. Our policy must follow the path of justice and peace."[40]

DETOURS

Despite this budding optimism in US-Japan relations, there nonetheless were significant detours along the internationalist road in the 1920s. The most conspicuous one involved America's discriminatory immigration act of

1924. This nativist law arose out of widespread alarm at the influx of nearly 20 million immigrants between 1885 and 1920, mainly from southern and eastern Europe. The xenophobic backlash against some 200,000 Japanese residents was confined mainly to the West Coast. The legislation was designed to limit immigration from any nation to 2 percent of its representation in the 1890 US Census. Citizens from countries with nearly nonexistent populations in the United States in 1890, such as Japan, therefore, were effectively barred from immigrating once the law took effect.

In the case of Japan, however, Congress went even further. The proposed law categorically excluded Japanese immigrants by exploiting a recent Supreme Court ruling that identified Japanese as racially ineligible for citizenship. A section of the immigration bill thus simply stated that "no alien ineligible to citizenship shall be admitted to the United States." Almost immediately Japanese Ambassador Hanihara Masanao made clear to Secretary Hughes that the thing was anathema to his countrymen. In an era touting liberal internationalism, one in which Japan played a prominent role at world conferences and the League of Nations, the legislation would grant Great Britain an annual quota of 65,721 immigrants to the United States, while Japan would be consigned to a status below that of Albania.[41]

Groping for some way to stir Congress from what he believed were dangerously myopic impulses, Hughes asked Hanihara to write him a public letter outlining the efficacy of previous voluntary restrictions—namely, the so-called Gentlemen's Agreement of 1907. Hanihara had worked closely with Hughes at the Washington Conference and duly responded with a missive that included this infamous sentence: "I realize, as I believe you do, the grave consequences which the enactment of the measure . . . would inevitably bring upon the otherwise happy and mutually advantageous relations between our two countries." An outraged Congress took the statement as a veiled threat and passed the law with Japan's exclusion intact.[42]

Tokyo's official response to the National Origins Act was surprisingly muted, but public reaction was vociferous and indignant. Patriotic organizations announced a "National Day of Humiliation," and renowned internationalist Nitobe Inazō declared he would never set foot in America again. What incensed the Japanese was not the assertion of a sovereign nation to place limits on immigration, but rather legislation that discriminated against Japan solely on the basis of race. Elihu Root, who had negotiated the Gentlemen's Agreement, very bitterly blamed fellow Republican Henry Cabot Lodge, de facto Senate majority leader and a Washington Conference delegate. So, too, did Hughes, who wrote to Lodge shortly after the law's passage, saying, "I fear that our labors to create a better feeling in the East, which have thus far been notably successful, are now largely undone."[43] That was not the case, though the misguided law momentarily sullied US-Japan relations in the aftermath of the Washington Conference and Great Kantō earthquake relief—and provided nationalistic grist to Japanese hard-liners who derided liberalism as an Anglo-American ruse.

Another source of early tension with the liberal order stemmed from interpretive differences over the Nine-Power Treaty. To recall, the treaty privileged gradualism, with the signatories promising "to provide the fullest and most unembarrassed opportunity to China to develop." Chinese officials instead called for a prompt restoration of tariff autonomy and an end to extraterritoriality. The conflicting positions produced a catch-22: the Chinese said tariff autonomy was necessary to facilitate a stable government; the signatories wanted evidence of nationhood before granting tariff autonomy. The problem was complex. On one hand, China's political map represented a constantly shifting power grid. In the south, the Kuomintang, or Nationalist Party, struggled to consolidate power. Warlords dominated in other areas, including Manchuria and Beijing. The embryonic Chinese Communist Party (CCP) also began to play a role. The atomization of Chinese political power made it difficult for the Nine-Power signatories to trust the legitimacy and lifespan of any authority. On the other hand, the nominal Chinese government in Beijing could rightfully claim that foreign control over tariffs did not gibe with the promise of "unembarrassed opportunity." Over the next few years, the treaty powers sought bilateral accords with China, which minimized the need for consensus and maximized self-interest. This approach, of course, contravened liberalism's emphasis on multilateralism.

Worldwide, however, the liberal internationalist seeds sown at Paris and Washington continued to take root and develop. The League of Nations in Geneva became a hive of activity, settling several significant disputes; promoting disarmament; addressing human trafficking, narcotics, and health and labor standards; and sponsoring intellectual cooperation and cultural exchange.[44] Outside of the league, the largest naval powers carried on with the demolition of capital ships into scrap metal. At the same time, the world continued to be bound closer together through the ever-expanding processes of modernity, including transoceanic telephone lines, the advent of radio broadcasting and wireless news reporting, airmail service, sleek photo-illustrated weeklies, and still faster passenger steamships. On the near horizon were sound motion pictures.

Moreover, in 1925, specific to Asia and the Pacific, conscientious cosmopolitans from the United States, Japan, China, Canada, Australia, New Zealand, and the Philippines founded the Institute of Pacific Relations (IPR). Spearheaded initially by civic leaders and missionaries associated with the YMCA in Hawai'i, the IPR dedicated itself to the liberal goal of perpetual peace and prosperity in Asia-Pacific through multilateral cooperation. As Akami Tomoko has written, the IPR sought "to institutionalize Wilsonian internationalism" from a nongovernmental approach. Carried by the prevailing liberal winds, the first two conferences in Honolulu (1925, 1927) stood out for their communitarian spirit.[45] Conference papers broached myriad opportunities for cooperation among Pacific Rim countries—including immigration, education, disarmament, interfaith dialogue, racial understanding, and economic development.

Thus, for cosmopolitans in the 1920s who dreamed of a permanent peace by eroding national differences and cultivating mutual understanding through international organizations and cross-cultural networks, such aspirations seemed to be maturing rapidly within their own lifetimes. And yet there remained a yearning to say directly and simply what all of the conferences had implied: an unequivocal statement that outlawed war.

PARIS CONFERENCE (KELLOGG–BRIAND), 1928

In the 1920s, academics working within the Carnegie Endowment for International Peace, including Columbia professor James T. Shotwell, had kept in the public eye a proposal for the universal repudiation of war. In 1927, Shotwell and others—having impressed upon French Foreign Minister Aristide Briand that Americans were growing irritated by French posturing on the continent—suggested to Briand that bilateral relations could be repaired with a "no-war" pact. Briand was receptive. Consequently, with Shotwell's guidance, Briand floated the idea of a bilateral peace pact to US Secretary of State Frank B. Kellogg. Kellogg was concerned about such a treaty drifting into a security alliance, but he was intrigued enough to encourage an expanded pact. As a result, in August 1928, nine years after the Treaty of Versailles, fifteen nations, including Japan, gathered again in Paris to endorse a multilateral treaty that outlawed war.

The preamble of the ensuing Kellogg–Briand Pact read like a prospectus for liberal internationalism. With the purpose of perpetuating "peaceful and friendly relations" among nations, the delegates pledged themselves to "a frank renunciation of war," and that "changes in . . . relations with one another should be sought only by pacific means and be the result of a peaceful and *orderly process*." Thus the liberal mantra was stated verbatim. These principles were squeezed into a few succinct articles. In Article I, the signatories renounced war "as an instrument of national policy." When two nations went to war, therefore, either one or both must be at fault. This view also negated the idea that there ever again could be neutral bystanders to a conflict. The treaty's wording, however, allowed for military action in the name of self-defense. Article II, meanwhile, dealt with conflict resolution, obliging signatories to resolve "all disputes or conflicts of whatever nature or whatever origin" through peaceful measures.[46]

Significantly, the memory of the Great War, as well as the peace efforts of the now-deceased President Wilson, enveloped the signing ceremony on

August 27, 1928. Minister Briand proposed that the treaty be dedicated "to the dead" of the Great War; he then turned to German Foreign Minister Gustav Stresemann and intoned, "to all the dead." The moving gesture showed how far the new diplomacy had traveled in just nine years. In paying tribute to President Wilson, Briand called the new treaty "reinsurance" for the League of Nations. A key factor was reinsurance *with American participation*, which was crucial to European leaders. Taking stock of the profound symbolism of the day's events in the Hall of Clocks at the French Foreign Ministry (where the 1919 Peace Conference opened), a *New York Times* reporter wrote, "It would be a heartless man who did not feel that the spirit of Woodrow Wilson lived this afternoon." One political cartoon imagined Wilson's ghost peering over Secretary Kellogg's shoulder as he signed the pact, invoking the Wilsonian phrase, "And now they have all become too proud to fight."[47] By the end of the decade, the no-war vow included sixty nations.

On the critical question of its capacity to deter aggression, the treaty leaned on the liberal weapon of world opinion. Following Wilson's lead, Briand warned, "The nation which went on a warpath ran the risk of bringing against it all other nations." Back in the United States, President Calvin Coolidge asserted that a Kellogg Pact in 1914 would have prevented the Great War. In hindsight, such boundless faith in public opinion seems deeply naïve, but a preponderance of voices at the time believed aggressors could not long function in an interdependent world in which they were ostracized. There simply was too much to lose, which is why the pact's preamble declared that aggressors were to "be denied the benefits furnished by this Treaty." These unstated benefits implied the unimpeded participation in global society, what one scholar has called "a transnational economic society of free commerce and industry linking people across borders."[48] In reality, they seemed to confer little more than a stamp of good state-keeping.

For this reason, not all contemporaries were impressed with the new treaty. Japanese diplomat Ishii Kikujirō said the most striking thing about the pact was the absence "of any restraint on states violating its provisions." Here he blamed the Americans, who, he said, consistently opposed "the inclusion of a penalizing provision." On this point Ishii was correct. Similarly, journalist Henry Cabot Lodge Jr., grandson of the late senator, writing in *Harper's*, excoriated the treaty's promises of securing peace without sacrifice: "thousands of persons are being made to believe that something really has been done, when, of course, nothing has or can be until a price is paid. . . . Is it not apparent that the Kellogg treaty, with its many textual dangers, only thickens the haze, deepens the pitfalls, and once again postpones the day when some really clear thinking is done?" In light of such criticisms, one historian has labeled the Republican approach to liberal internationalism in the 1920s as "involvement without commitment."[49] It is important to remember, however, that critics of the pact tended to champion other multilateral measures. The apparent success of the Washington Conference, in particular, had kept pressure on governments to limit classes of ships omitted in the Five-Power Naval Treaty. Toward this end, at the invitation of Great Britain, the largest naval powers convened in London.

LONDON NAVAL CONFERENCE, 1930

In January 1930, officials from Great Britain, the United States, and Japan, amid the scrutiny of four hundred newspaper reporters, began work on what they believed would add yet another layer of protective coating to the interlocking treaty system.[50] The focus this time was on long-range, high-speed "heavy cruisers." In the spirit of Wilsonianism, US Secretary of State Henry Stimson, interviewed on newsreels before his departure, said he wanted to remove any "feeling of insecurity" among the naval powers, especially Japanese fears of Anglo-American collusion. Accordingly, upon arriving in London, the secretary met at once with the Japanese, in order, as he put it, to erase "any suspicion" about playing favorites at the conference. Despite this Wilsonian air, Stimson pursued a somewhat duplicitous diplomacy: two days before the start of the conference, he met privately with British Prime Minister Ramsay MacDonald and urged a united front against Japan's strategic ambitions.[51]

The American delegation subsequently returned to the 10:6 ratio agreed on at the Washington Conference, treating it as an established formula. Japan's delegates demurred, countering once again with a 10:7 ratio, which they considered the minimum requirement for maintaining naval superiority in the western Pacific. After intense negotiations, the Japanese accepted the 10:6 ratio with conditions that guaranteed a de facto 70 percent ratio in heavy cruisers until 1936. In Tokyo, the Naval General Staff was again livid, fueling a public backlash against the empire's allegedly weak-kneed delegation. Viscount Ishii said he was "astonished" by the virulent opposition to the treaty. Why, the Japanese asked, did Washington insist on a naval ratio that theoretically gave it the capacity to bring offensive war to Japan's home waters—unless it held some notion to do so?[52] The London Conference thus exposed a fierce undercurrent of dissent in Japan over perceived inequities and the supposed benefits of the new liberal order.

Not unrelatedly, Japanese complaints also had surfaced in Paris during the no-war talks. Japanese officials at that time had considered submitting reservations to the Kellogg Pact out of concern about the treaty's potential impact on Japan's freedom of action in its Manchurian leasehold. Although the Japanese balked, not wishing to challenge world trends, a year later, at the 1929 IPR conference in Kyoto, Japanese delegates gave expansive defenses of the empire's rights in Manchuria, thus shedding light on a persistent strain of regional entitlement. And yet, prominent internationalist James Shotwell's *War as an Instrument of National Policy*, published shortly after the Kyoto conference, makes clear that reading the prevailing ideological winds in Japan at the time was fraught with complexity: Shotwell devoted an entire chapter in praise of Japan's commitment to the liberal order.[53]

For the present, the London Conference concluded with participants outwardly buoyed by good feelings arising from cooperative action, and the belief they had further immunized the world against the scourge of global conflict. Japan's chief delegate, Wakatsuki Reijirō, for example, said he hoped their work would "fulfill the earnest desire of humanity, scarred by bitter ordeal, to earn appreciation of subsequent generations." Stimson, meanwhile, said the conference "increased our hope that civilization will be able to form the habit of settling peaceably the questions and controversies which arise between nations." In other words, a hope that the emphasis on "orderly processes" was becoming second nature. Such aspirations were repeated in a dramatic coda to the treaty, one that symbolized the interconnected global society the new peace structure aimed to preserve. In October 1930, the leaders of the three naval powers—Premier Hamaguchi Osachi, Prime Minister MacDonald, and President Herbert Hoover—participated in an international radio hookup from their home capitals to mark the treaty's significance. Premier Hamaguchi lauded the striking overhaul in diplomacy over the previous decade, which he referred to as the "growing consciousness of mankind." According to Hamaguchi, "a more generous spirit" was quickly replacing "the jealousies and suspicions of the past," resulting in "a new chapter in the history of human civilization."[54]

***

Considering the energy and scope of the postwar peace movement from 1919 to 1930, one is presented with the image of world leaders and diplomats deeply haunted by the Great War and uniquely committed to preventing another one. World War I left deep scars but also rejuvenated the international system. The experience opened up minds to novel methods of structuring relations between nations, especially the emphasis on so-called orderly processes. The postwar treaties—the League Covenant, Five-Power Treaty, Nine-Power Treaty, Kellogg Pact, and London Treaty—produced a sense of pride and budding confidence among the postwar generation, as if strung together like a set of gleaming pearls of peace. Indeed, as Iriye Akira has observed, the new era's emphasis on "peace" could rightly be described as a hegemonic ideology.[55]

What no one knew, of course, is that the London Conference would be the last great expression of cooperative diplomacy before the long and troubled road to World War II. Certainly, disturbing signs were in the air. For one thing, the London Conference had begun two months after the onset of the global stock market crisis. Yet most financial observers anticipated nothing more than a bad recession. Then, a month after his radio broadcast, Hamaguchi was shot in the abdomen by an ultranationalist (dying of complications nine months later). And yet, although Japan at the time was a fertile breeding ground for right-wing militants, its political system in the 1930s did not succumb to the cliché of "government by assassination."

It therefore was not entirely surprising that, almost a year later, on September 17, 1931, Japanese Ambassador Debuchi and Secretary Stimson agreed that US-Japan relations appeared more tranquil than in many years past. Debuchi remarked with satisfaction that he had just completed a long trip throughout the United States and "had found everywhere more marked evidences of friendliness towards his own country than he had ever before noted during his long stay as Ambassador."[56] Within twenty-four hours of this conversation, however, Japan's Kwantung Army began its move in Manchuria. The new liberal order was about to face its first real test.

NOTES

Chapter Two

Toward Two Worlds

The Manchurian Crisis (1931–1933)

On the day Ambassador Debuchi and Secretary of State Stimson agreed that US-Japan relations were more tranquil than in many years past, the ambassador had no idea Kwantung Army leaders were plotting aggression in Manchuria. To be sure, there had been intermittent rumblings from officers stationed in the leased territory; however, the detonation on the South Manchurian Railway on the night of September 18, 1931, was not the result of a grand conspiracy among Japan's leaders to make a hostile break with the international system. And yet, what began as an "incident" soon turned into a crisis, culminating in Japan's retreat from the postwar peace structure. A conversation that took place between Debuchi and Stimson just over a year later illustrates the stunning turnabout in international relations. Debuchi informed Stimson the United States "would have to recognize" the new circumstances in Manchuria. In response, Stimson reminded Debuchi "what the movement against war meant since the Great War and that we were trying to protect civilization, and if Japan wanted to live on a different basis than the one we had chosen with those peace treaties . . . we would consider ourselves living in two different worlds."[1]

As the first major test case for liberal internationalism, the Manchurian crisis (1931–1933) became the focal point of an exhaustive ideological drama, in which Japan, the United States, and the League of Nations debated the meaning and merits of the new diplomacy. The prized devices of the liberal machinery—the League Covenant, the Nine-Power Treaty, and Kellogg–Briand Pact—were duly carted out onto the world stage. Statements by government officials on all sides played to world opinion. Japan's case, as historian Sandra Wilson has shown, "was put regularly and vigorously in debates at the League of Nations, in diplomatic conversations, at international conferences, in public lectures to American audiences and in articles sent to American and European newspapers."[2] Initially the empire relied on liberal arguments of "self-defense" and "self-determination." When these failed to move world opinion in Japan's favor, officials turned to traditional claims of "special rights and interests" in Manchuria. In the process, a decidedly illiberal regionalist perspective, undergirded by a chauvinistic Asianism, began to propagate among Japan's political, military, and cultural elites.

This chapter explores the transformation of the Manchurian Incident into an ideological crisis and a turning point in world affairs and US-Japan relations. After a decade of unprecedented multilateral cooperation, the new world order suddenly teetered on the precipice of an uncertain future. Japan's belligerence in Manchuria violated tenets of the League Covenant, the Nine-Power Treaty, and the Kellogg Pact, and yet all the world could muster was a verdict affirming Japan's culpability. Although the liberal program's sanction of world opinion exhibited some resilience, internationalists learned the hard way that moral condemnation did little to deter belligerence. Most detrimental of all to the liberal cause was America's "halfway internationalism"—a self-centered presumption that the world's leading creditor nation with the second-largest navy could sit out the league and participate in world affairs with one foot in and one foot out. America's abandonment of the League of Nations proved to be a blow to both the institution's credibility and its capacity to contain its first major bout of naked aggression.

THE MANCHURIAN INCIDENT AND "SCRAPS OF PAPER" (SEPTEMBER–DECEMBER 1931)

Within a few days of the initial skirmish between Japanese and Chinese troops near Shenyang on September 18, 1931, the government of China appealed to the League of Nations' Council to take action on the hostilities. Japan's delegate on the Council, Yoshizawa Kenkichi, the empire's minister to China for much of the 1920s, maintained that his nation had "no territorial designs" on Manchuria; he also contended Japan had acted in self-defense, claiming Japanese troops were dispatched to protect Japanese interests. Before adjourning, the league adopted a resolution calling on Japanese forces to withdraw as rapidly as possible. Instead, a week later, Japanese planes bombed Jinzhou, a strategic city located 129 southwest of Shenyang on the Beijing–Shenyang railway.

When the League Council convened again in mid-October, the expansion of hostilities demanded a more substantial response. With an eye on greater American involvement, the Council invoked Article II of the Kellogg–Briand Treaty, which dealt with conflict resolution. The Council also brought up

Article X of the League Covenant and, over Yoshizawa's opposition, issued a deadline of November 16 for Japan to withdraw its troops back to the Kwantung Leased Territory. The decisions in Geneva, however, merely produced defiance within the Kwantung Army and, for the time being, opacity in Tokyo. Instead of returning to their barracks along the South Manchurian Railway, Japanese troops pushed northward toward Qiqihar (Tsitsihar), nearly 385 miles from Shenyang. Domestically, Japan's government faced challenges on multiple fronts. The Kwantung Army had defied its authority, the press strongly backed the army, and the campaign was very popular with Japan's highly literate and news-devouring public.[3]

In Washington, Secretary Stimson's anxiety deepened daily. On November 19, the secretary wrote in his diary that Japan's aggression "seems to me to be a flagrant violation of the spirit and probably the letter of all the treaties, the Kellogg Pact and the Nine-Power Treaty." He rehashed the global stakes and alleged power of moral sanction, informing Ambassador W. Cameron Forbes in Tokyo that Japan was lining up "against herself all the nations of the world." This assertion, however, coincided with the dawning realization that American options were limited. For one thing, Stimson's boss, President Hoover, disagreed with his secretary on the heart of the matter. The Manchurian conflict was regrettable, said Hoover, but it primarily involved China and Japan and did not pose a threat to US interests; moreover, the treaty system confined America to judgments of "moral reprobation."[4] On this point, Hoover was right.

Herbert Hoover's presidency often does not make it past the public caricature of the man who led the United States into the Great Depression. Whatever his failings in that regard, the president's unique international background arguably made him more prepared for foreign affairs than any president since John Quincy Adams (this is not to say he possessed rare judgment). Hoover, an orphaned child from Iowa, eventually parlayed a geology degree from Stanford University into a career as one of the most renowned mining engineers and consultants in the world. By the time he was forty, he had circumnavigated the world four times and lived abroad nearly twenty years. During and immediately after the Great War, he managed humanitarian relief programs for several countries, including the Soviet Union. And yet, in spite of his international experience, Hoover became a committed isolationist, wary of situations that might lead America into armed conflict, such as Japan and China's murky struggle in Manchuria.[5]

Stimson, in contrast, wanted to hold Japan's feet to the fire. Unlike many of his fellow Republicans, Stimson believed in the necessity of backing up the postwar treaties with at least the *threat* of American power, economic and military. He lamented that Hoover did not seem to realize what it meant to stand pat and "have Japan run amok and play havoc" with the treaties. Frustrated with holding just "scraps of paper," Stimson brought up economic sanctions. An alarmed Hoover later reflected "that my able Secretary was at times more a warrior than a diplomat." To Hoover, threatening a great power with economic sanctions was needlessly risky. It was like "sticking pins in tigers"; eventually, it "meant war."[6] Had the United States signed on to the League of Nations in 1919, of course, collective sanctions would have been a possibility. But Hoover and Stimson's own party had quashed the idea.

To Stimson's credit, as the scaffolding of the liberal peace structure began to creak and bend, he anticipated big problems on the international horizon. And yet, Stimson himself, from the start of the Manchurian Incident, had distanced the United States from the League of Nations, telling Senator Borah he did not want to encourage the world assembly to "drop their baby on my lap." The United States only went so far as sending an "observer" to Geneva. Thus, despite his grave concerns, Stimson wanted to have it both ways with the new liberal order. He wanted the United States to act, but he wanted the rest of the world to act first. It was a telling first response by the Americans, one that made clear just how significant the gap was between the country's Wilsonian rhetoric and imperatives of global leadership. In light of his own reluctance to lead, Stimson simply confessed he was worried about Manchuria but did not know what to do.[7]

An apparent answer came from Geneva. On December 10, 1931, the League Council approved sending a fact-finding commission to Japan and China, including Manchuria. Despite suspicion on both sides, Japan and China supported the initiative, a signal that each side believed it was in the right—though Chinese officials had wanted a concomitant deadline on the withdrawal of Japanese troops. Most important, the commission raised hopes the league was functioning as designed and could rein in the unwieldy incident. As one league officer affirmed, "before the World War, when a dispute arose between powers it often was regarded as infringing on the honor of one of the parties." The emphasis on peaceful processes, however, had "changed all that."[8] On the same day, President Hoover, in his annual message to Congress, more assertively recognized American obligations to uphold the Kellogg–Briand Pact and Nine-Power Treaty. He also cooperated with the league by agreeing to send an American representative to join the five-person commission, which included Italy, Great Britain, France, and Germany. (The commission arrived in Asia in late February.)

While the postwar "spirit of community" appeared to be ascendant, events in Tokyo lent themselves to more speculation. Facing a loss of confidence before a nationalistically roused Diet, the Minseitō Party cabinet of Premier Wakatsuki resigned on December 11. This cleared the way for a cabinet led by Inukai Tsuyoshi, the seventy-six-year-old president of the more jingoistic party, Seiyūkai, and vocal critic of "Shidehara diplomacy." The salient question for Stimson and the League of Nations was obvious: how would the new cabinet deal with hostilities in Manchuria? The initial response sent mixed signals. In late December, Japanese forces began massing for an apparent assault on Jinzhou, the main Chinese administrative seat in Manchuria and gateway to North China. On December 28, Inukai was quoted in American newspapers insisting that Japan did not want Manchuria. "If China would offer Manchuria to us," said Inukai, "we would decline the offer with thanks. If, for argument's sake, Manchuria were our territory today, we would give it to China and ask nothing in return. China can keep Manchuria with compliments."[9]

By New Year's Eve, however, Japanese forces from Shenyang had begun driving rapidly toward Jinzhou. Hallett Abend of the *New York Times*, reporting from Japan's leasehold city of Dalian, said Japanese officials revealed "an altogether open attitude" to eliminating Chinese authority from Manchuria. In an attempt to counter such statements, Premier Inukai penned a New Year's greeting to the American people, noting that "the confusion and excitement in Manchuria might be compared with a neighborhood fire which for the time being rouses all local inhabitants. The fire will soon be put out and peace and order restored." From the outside looking in, such contradictory signals from Tokyo cast confusion over the ideological composition of the new government and the degree to which it authorized or sympathized with army objectives. The truth is that Inukai had sought approval from Emperor Hirohito for more troops. Hirohito, in a halfway nod to the liberal order and growing world criticism, simply told Inukai to be cautious.[10]

Jinzhou fell without a fight to Japanese forces on January 3, 1932. The formal occupation of the city meant Japan had destroyed the last vestige of Chinese authority in Manchuria. Contrary to Japanese claims in Geneva of a localized self-defense, signs on the ground pointed to a military takeover of the whole of Northeast China, an area larger than France and Germany combined. Secretary of State Stimson now deemed the liberal apple cart upset. On January 3, after a self-described restless night, he continued work on a more vigorous American response.[11] The Manchurian Incident had turned into an international crisis.

THE GATHERING STORM: CHINESE NATIONALISM (1926–1931)

In reviewing the origins of what became the first major assault against liberal internationalism, we need to understand why events happened when they did, or what precipitated the Kwantung Army's initial aggression. The main stimulus leading up to hostilities on the night of September 18, 1931, was the gale force of Chinese nationalism and, specifically, the success of the Kuomintang (KMT, or Nationalist Party) to unify much of the country for the first time since the fall of the Qing dynasty in 1912. The KMT's assertion of national authority, however shaky, put added pressure on all nations with interests in China to recognize Chinese sovereignty.

Kuomintang forces under Generalissimo Chiang Kai-shek had begun their unification drive in July 1926, five years prior to the Manchurian crisis. From their base in the Guangdong province in southern China, the KMT's Northern Expedition, as it was called, aimed to destroy the power of regional warlords all the way to Beijing. In March 1927, Nationalist troops reached Nanjing, the old capital of the Ming dynasty (1368–1644), which the KMT designated as their own capital. The open wounds of history—the humiliation of the unequal treaties—led to random looting of foreign property, including the British and American legations.

In Japan, the Seiyūkai government under Tanaka Giichi assumed a more pugnacious posture toward China. The new liberal milieu, however, remained unforgiving to jingoism. In the spring of 1928, for example, as Chiang's armies progressed toward Beijing, the Tanaka cabinet sent troops to Shandong province with the stated intention of protecting Japanese residents. Another reason was to hinder the Northern Expedition and forestall the fall of the Beijing regime and a potential drive on Manchuria. Minseitō opposition and internationalist-minded voices in the Japanese press, however, condemned unilateralism over diplomacy, and nothing serious came of the deployment.[12] Then, on June 4, 1928—four days before Kuomintang troops took Beijing—Kwantung officers in Manchuria blew up the private rail car of Manchurian warlord Zhang Zuolin, who they feared was cozying up to the KMT. The army's goal of provoking Japan's control over Manchuria failed, however, because Chinese authority there transferred to the warlord's son, Zhang Xueliang, who, in late 1928, recognized the KMT as China's legitimate government. Zhang was not alone. Between July and December 1928, twelve nations with interests in China also recognized the Kuomintang government. The United States, the first nation to do so, also granted conditional tariff autonomy to China. Japan offered recognition in 1929 and tariff autonomy a year later under the Hamaguchi-led Minseitō government.

What suppressed a Manchurian Incident at this time? Three factors stand out: the liberal precept against naked aggression was strong (the Tanaka government had signed the Kellogg Pact in August 1928); the KMT regime was still in the early stages of consolidating power and thus did not pose a compelling threat to Japanese interests in Northeast China; and the world economy was not yet in crisis. By the end of 1930, however, the Great Depression had devastated global markets. All around the world unemployment levels soared and governments resorted to protectionism. In the United States, Congress passed the illiberal Smoot–Hawley Tariff, which increased duties on hundreds of American imports. The economic crisis also distracted world leaders. President Hoover, for example, was far more interested in employment rates at the Ford factory than upholding territorial integrity in

China. As Secretary Stimson remarked in 1931, "The president is so busy over his domestic and financial troubles that he is not thinking out ahead the problems of international relations."[13] The onset of the Great Depression plus surging Chinese nationalism combined to create a perfect storm in East Asia. Tension brewed and stewed until it finally boiled over in southern Manchuria.

Starting in the spring of 1931, the Nationalist government in Nanjing intensified its demands for the retrocession of all leased territories and the abolition of foreign privileges. Above all, Chinese officials demanded the immediate and complete end to extraterritoriality. The major signatories of the Nine-Power Treaty, however, lacked a consensus on the legal fulfillment and timing of KMT aspirations. The result was that multilateral processes devolved into on-again, off-again bilateral treaty negotiations, which were mostly inconclusive. On March 27, Nanjing halted talks with Japan. A month later, Kuomintang Foreign Minister Wang Zhengting criticized the United States and Great Britain for foot-dragging and threatened to suspend negotiations. Finally, on May 4, the KMT announced it would unilaterally abrogate all extraterritoriality rights by January 1, 1932.[14] The Nanjing government, however, was weak and increasingly preoccupied with destroying a new communist base in mountainous Jiangxi province led by Mao Zedong.

Relations between Nanjing and Tokyo, in particular, simmered through the summer of 1931. In July, Chinese gendarmes apprehended, and subsequently shot and killed, a Japanese army captain traveling undercover in Manchuria. Friction also stemmed from repeated Japanese claims of Chinese infractions against Japanese interests in the region. Amid these tensions, the Kwantung Army was growing restless for direct Japanese rule in Manchuria. Two Kwantung officers in their forties, Col. Itagaki Seishirō and Lt.-Col. Ishiwara Kanji, eventually plotted to take things into their own hands. Itagaki was chief of intelligence in the Kwantung Army. Ishiwara, a bright military theorist who held a key planning position, has been described as the "charismatic mastermind" of the Manchurian Incident. He was also a regionalist ideologue, someone who held apocalyptic views about a "Final War" between Japan and the United States. Much of Ishiwara's Manichean worldview flowed from the ethnocentric teachings of Nichiren Buddhism, a missionary sect that envisioned a Japanese-inspired regeneration of the world. To Asianists like Ishiwara, the Chinese Nationalists in Nanjing represented the "wrong kind" of Asian people, or those who failed to grasp the primacy of Japanese leadership in Asia.[15]

Itagaki and Ishiwara's Manchurian machinations did not remain entirely covert. In late June 1931, nobles close to the emperor caught wind of "considerable plans" for military action in Manchuria. In August, while in Tokyo for routine duties, Ishiwara obtained tacit sanction from the Army General Staff's operations and intelligence divisions for his contingency plans to seize Manchuria in case of a major incident. Then, at a press conference in early September, reporters grilled Premier Wakatsuki about rumors emanating from Manchuria, asking, "When will the war start?" Most tangibly, on September 12, Foreign Minister Shidehara received a top secret cable from his consul general in Shenyang warning of imminent action by the Kwantung Army.[16] Whether disbelief, sympathy, or fear—or a combination therein—was responsible for Wakatsuki and Shidehara's consequent inaction after the start of hostilities on September 18, the sources are incomplete. That the Kwantung Army manufactured an incident and defied the Tokyo government is undeniable. But defiance of civilian authority alone cannot account for the sustained military campaign that followed. The Manchurian Incident blew up into an international crisis because a wide swath of Japanese officials believed in the righteousness of the empire's cause.

SPECIAL RIGHTS, SPECIAL INTERESTS, AND SPECIAL RESPONSIBILITIES

In analyzing the Manchurian crisis and its connection to the winding road to World War II, it is tempting to fall into the conceptual trap of simple dichotomies. A standard dichotomy for what happened in Manchuria is that a small cabal of "militarists" hijacked power from a helpless civilian government in Tokyo and ran amok for the next fifteen years. There are many reasons for the tenacity of this historical interpretation, stemming from facile contemporary assumptions, the imperatives of America's postwar occupation of Japan, as well as influential popular histories like John Toland's *The Rising Sun*. The preponderance of evidence, however, makes clear that a broad coalition of Japanese elites—including Emperor Hirohito, members of the Privy Council and House of Peers, statesmen, intellectuals, and military officials—were responsible for Japan's subsequent retreat from liberal internationalism and the empire's expansionism in Asia over the next fifteen years (1931–1945).

From the beginning, as noted, the Kwantung Army had the tacit endorsement of the Army General Staff's operations and intelligence divisions. It also enjoyed support from "renovationist" politicians and intellectuals. Renovationists (sometimes called "reformists") carried with them a mash-up of resentment and indignation, particularly against Anglo-American liberalism and the international status quo.[17] In the wake of the Paris Peace Conference, renovationists swam in cynical currents, skeptical of a "rigged" treaty system. Renovationists like party politicians Nagai Ryūtarō and Mori Kaku and diplomat Shiratori Toshio held on to slights and injustices, including rejection of the racial equality clause, the unequal naval ratios, and US immigration laws. They bristled, not unreasonably, against the perceived hypocrisy of the British Empire and American supremacy in the Western Hemisphere. Moreover, the United States was not even in the League of Nations, and yet it leaned on the league to counter Japanese interests in China. In ideological proximity were statesmen and diplomats such as Hirota Kōki, Arita Hachirō, Shigemitsu Mamoru, and Matsuoka Yōsuke and aristocrat Konoe Fumimaro.

Far more surprising was the sympathetic support for Japan's cause by reputed internationalists, especially individuals who had been involved with the League of Nations and the Institute of Pacific Relations in the 1920s, such as Nitobe Inazō, Ishii Kikujirō, and Yoshizawa Kenkichi.[18] Unexpected apologists ultimately included Prime Minister Wakatsuki and Foreign Minister Shidehara, as well as elite members of Japan's business class, such as Gō Seinosuke and Dan Takuma. Shortly before resigning, Shidehara—seen by Americans as the paragon of moderation—penned a commentary published by the AP in which he assigned total blame to China. "The whole difficulty in Manchuria," wrote Shidehara, "originates from a long series of open disregard by China of treaties. . . . Its immediate cause is now well known to be the violent attack . . . made by Chinese troops." This was either intentional distortion or deft self-deception; Shidehara knew that events on the night of September 18 were more complicated. As for the role of Emperor Hirohito, the thirty-year-old sovereign who had ascended the throne in 1926, historian Herbert Bix has argued that the emperor displayed an "indulgent" attitude, one that amounted to "silent endorsement" of Japanese aggression.[19]

What bound this wide swath of Japanese elites together on the Manchurian issue, from the crown to statesmen, diplomats, scholars, and business leaders—and ultimately the mass of Japanese society—were three layers of "special" rationale: special rights, special interests, and special responsibilities. "Special rights" comprised a legalistic defense, based on "rights of possession" from previous wars and treaties. The transfer of leasehold rights in southern Manchuria that Japan won in the Russo-Japanese War (1904–1905) can hardly be overstated. Japan mobilized more than one million troops during the war; 81,455 of them lost their lives. This considerable sacrifice cultivated a keen sense of regional entitlement. Indeed, Manchuria became regarded as hallowed ground, an impression seared into the consciousness of a generation of Japanese who came into positions of political, military, and intellectual authority in the 1930s. Adding to this sense of entitlement was that the empire had sunk an enormous amount of capital into the leased territory. The South Manchurian Railway became Japan's biggest firm, with interests in rail freight, shipping, coal mining, soybean production, and tourism.[20] There remained as well a psychological hangover from the Twenty-One Demands of 1915—a belief, embedded into the fabric of historical truth, that China had freely accepted the demands. And now, China was going back on its word, violating treaties, and abusing Japan.

"Special interests," on the other hand, referred to national security interests that derived from "nature and geography." Japan's proximity to China, went this "realist" argument, gave Japan unique decision-making prerogatives on the continent. In modern diplomatic parlance, this meant that China and its frontiers were a vital interest, economically and strategically. During the Manchurian crisis, Japanese began to describe Northeast China as Japan's "lifeline." There was much talk about the need for raw materials and outlets for surplus trade and population. However inflated these claims, the important point is that Japanese officials and commentators at the time became convinced of their veracity.

A third factor is that Japanese officials became animated by a more chauvinistic strain of Pan-Asianist thinking, which posited that Japan had a "special responsibility" to rescue Asia from the West. Japanese grievance against the West thus was melded with superiority toward the East. Japan was now self-consciously cast as an exceptional nation, preordained to bring about the regeneration of Asia. Japan, after all, alone among Asian nations, had modernized, fought off unequal treaties, and stunned the world by defeating Tsarist Russia. This paternalistic strand of Pan-Asianism recalled the spirit of imperialism's "civilizing mission" from the late nineteenth century, in which a caretaker nation had a moral obligation—the "white man's burden"—to bring order and progress to allegedly less-enlightened peoples. In fact, during the Manchurian crisis, the American-based Japanese journalist K. K. Kawakami claimed that Japan's leadership in Manchuria was "one of the most significant developments in the century—a great experiment in the reorganization, regeneration, and rejuvenation of an ancient nation long wallowing in chaos and maladministration. . . . For the first time in history, a non-white race has undertaken to carry the white man's burden."[21]

Such expansive purpose required a profound sense of national uniqueness. In the 1930s, as scholars of Japan have made clear, strong currents of exceptionalism flowed through Japan's body politic from a multiplicity of influential tributaries, with some headwaters reaching back to the early twentieth century. A nationalist literary movement, the Japan Romantic School, for example, exalted the unique traits and importance of Japanese civilization. Particularly industrious was a group of philosophers from Kyoto Imperial University, led by Professor Nishida Kitaro, who extolled the uniqueness of the Japanese family state. Other significant sources included eminent academics who filled think tanks, Nichiren Buddhist millennialists, ultranationalists such as Kita Ikki, and Pan-Asianist ideologues like Ōkawa Shūmei.[22]

That the Manchurian crisis acted as a powerful ideological catalyst and coagulant in Japanese thinking can be deduced by comparing Kawakami's spirited piece above on Japan's mission with a commentary he wrote ten years prior, during the Washington Conference:

> All the Powers ... have bound themselves by agreements or resolutions not to return to the old practice of spheres of influence or special interests [in China].... This change is no shadowy thing. It is as definite as it is real. Twenty years ago the Powers were talking only what they could take from China. Today they are talking about what they can give her. Certainly that indicates a vast moral progress.[23]

Thus, what was once the "vast moral progress" of liberal self-denial now required Japan's civilizing intervention.

The rationale of special rights, special interests, and special responsibilities combined to create a powerful sense of legitimacy for Japan's actions on the continent. Japanese leaders routinely invoked the arguments, not only during the Manchurian crisis but throughout the 1930s. This can be seen in essays that perceived moderates Wakatsuki Reijirō and Viscount Ishii wrote for *Foreign Affairs*. "The Manchurian affair," claimed Wakatsuki, "was really a life-or-death struggle for Japan [special interests].... There accumulated between Japan and China more than three hundred unsolved questions [special rights].... I believe that Americans will soon come to comprehend correctly the Manchurian question, and to appreciate fully Japan's position in East Asia [special responsibility]." Ishii's apologia for Japan's cause, meanwhile, was striking for its indifference to the postwar diplomatic revolution and liberal principles.[24]

Eventually, Pan-Asianist-inspired "special responsibilities" developed into the principal justification for Japanese expansionism in the decade following the Manchurian crisis. The imperative of a Japanese rescue mission in Asia resonated with the imaginings of an alternative world order, unfettered by the liberal language of the Nine-Power Treaty and the Kellogg Pact. To be sure, for the present, Japan still sought to win over world opinion for its actions and maintain good relations with the United States. The distinction between liberal internationalism and Japanese regionalism, however, remained inherently antagonistic. From January 1932 until February 1933, the developing ideological crisis played out on the world stage. The battle occupied two fronts: the first involved Secretary of State Stimson's rhetorical campaign against Japan; the other was directed within the League of Nations.

IN DEFENSE OF LIBERAL INTERNATIONALISM: HENRY STIMSON'S WAR OF WORDS

After the Kwantung Army's occupation of Jinzhou, Secretary Stimson concluded that the "long-drawn out process" of trying to convince the Japanese to reach a peaceful settlement had been in vain. It was time to take a strong stand on behalf of the treaty system. On January 7, 1932, with President Hoover's cautious consent, Stimson announced a policy of nonrecognition. It amounted to a kind of preemptive rejection of whatever Japan had in mind for Manchuria. The United States, declared Stimson, did not intend "to recognize any treaty or agreement" made between Japan and China that compromised "the sovereignty, the independence, or the territorial and administrative integrity" of the Republic of China. Nor did the United States intend to recognize any agreement contrary to the no-war pledge. In other words, Stimson was defending verbatim the internationalist principles embodied in the Nine-Power Treaty and Kellogg Pact.[25]

Stimson's note was an explicit reminder to Japan's leaders that they had pledged to uphold the postwar treaties, with the implicit threat that breaking the pledges would lead to international isolation. Such was his faith in the power of world opinion to halt an aggressor. As Stimson later explained to Belgian politician Paul Hymans, president of the League of Nations, he wanted "to keep ever before the Japanese people the difficulty of the task they had undertaken . . . through the constant focusing of public attention on the violations of treaty obligations."[26]

In fact, the secretary's reach exceeded the treaties' grasp to do much of anything at all. Stanley K. Hornbeck, chief of the Far Eastern Affairs Division, opposed a formal statement, arguing that words were just that—words. Other critics complained the note left the United States on a diplomatic island. Indeed, far from nipping the crisis in the bud, the "Stimson Doctrine," as it came to be called, illustrated international inertia. The British Foreign Office thought the note excessive, an early sign that upholding liberal principles in Manchuria would take a back seat to safeguarding Britain's interests in China. The Inukai government, meanwhile, affirmed the Open Door as a "cardinal feature" of Japan's policy but claimed the Nine-Power Treaty did not apply in this case because Japan had acted in "self-defense." In support of this claim, an imperial rescript proclaimed in the name of Emperor Hirohito honored the Kwantung Army's courageous actions of "self-defense" against Chinese "bandits" (a popular euphemism that gave Japan's actions a gloss of curbing criminal elements). More sincerely, Foreign Minister Yoshizawa Kenkichi told Kwantung officers the Inukai government shared the army's aims.[27]

Perhaps the biggest effect of Stimson's nonrecognition statement was the bitter backlash that rumbled across Japan. The Japanese press excoriated the secretary, whose note was seen as sanctimonious lecturing. Yoshizawa, doubtless adding color, told the French ambassador he was uncertain whether "an outbreak" against the United States could be prevented. At the same time, a story made the rounds in Tokyo that Ambassador Forbes had told Stimson, "If you want to send any more notes, you had better send battleships to deliver them." The story was likely apocryphal, but it demonstrates just how strained relations had become between the two Pacific powers. The acrimony spread to government mouthpieces. When it was reported in Japan that Stimson said the Japanese army had run amok, Foreign Office spokesperson Shiratori Toshio tartly retorted it was Stimson himself who had run amok.[28]

Stimson, however, showed few signs of keeping quiet. And Japanese leaders gave him little respite to do so. Three weeks after Stimson's nonrecognition note, the Inukai government dispatched warships to Shanghai in response to widespread anti-Japanese boycotts in the city and an attack on several Japanese Buddhist priests (instigated, in fact, by Japanese agents hoping to divert attention from Manchuria). News of the arriving squadron

Figure 2.1. Henry L. Stimson, secretary of state (1929–1933) and secretary of war (1940–1945). (Library of Congress, Prints & Photographs Division, photograph by Harris & Ewing [reproduction number LC-USZ62-54011].)

and the burning down of two Chinese mills by Japanese agitators set the city on edge. On January 28, nearly two thousand Japanese marines landed in Shanghai, and a day later Japanese warplanes bombed the Chinese district of Chapei.[29] In the coming weeks, and technically in the name of the emperor, the high command sent two army divisions to reinforce naval units. Sporadic but fierce fighting lasted throughout February.

The Japanese advance on Shanghai shook the international community from inside out. Whereas Manchuria conjured up images of a dusty, lawless, remote frontier, the great port city of Shanghai evoked a bustling and cosmopolitan commingling of East and West. More than forty thousand foreigners lived and worked in the city's International Settlement, that ironic centerpiece of the imperial era. Many of these expatriates spent their leisure time as they would in the West—at dance halls, cinemas, pubs, cabarets, golf courses, polo grounds, and racetracks. The American presence was significant. In 1932, there were more than 250 American firms in Shanghai, including General Motors, Eastman Kodak, Goodyear Tire, Singer Sewing Machine, Ford Motor Company, and Marshall Field's. American direct investment in Shanghai alone was valued at $129,768,000 in 1930 (roughly $2 billion in 2018 dollars).[30]

Bold headlines blared across the front pages of the world's major dailies with news of hostilities in Shanghai. In the United States, Harvard University president A. Lawrence Lowell ignited a petition drive to impose an economic embargo on Japan. President Hoover told Thomas W. Lamont, a partner at J. P. Morgan who worked closely with Japan, that his administration had "now wholly lost confidence in the Japanese government." Secretary Stimson described the Japanese attack as "inexcusable barbarity," saying it created the same sensation as Germany's invasion of Belgium in 1914. That overstated things; nonetheless, such statements illuminated the era's pronounced memory of the Great War. Economic self-interest played a role as well. One merely needs to compare Britain's languid response to Stimson's nonrecognition note with its forceful warning to Japan about British interests in Shanghai. The large foreign presence also explains why the Inukai government sent out assurances that Japan's objectives were peaceful—that there was no intention of keeping reinforcements in Shanghai.[31]

Stimson, however, said he was through taking Japanese assurances at face value. After Shanghai, he wanted to find a way to let "Japan sizzle in a pretty sharp disapproval." This, again, pointed to Stimson's faith in the moral force of public opinion. What is increasingly clear at this juncture is that America's rebuff of the League of Nations in 1919 was starting to take its toll. The United States wandered paradoxically on the outskirts of Geneva. American internationalists at the time, such as members of the nonpartisan League of Nations Association (which pressed for belated US admission to the league), commended Stimson's individual persistence, but they savaged fellow

Americans for being "insufficiently informed" about the complexity of international affairs. One member held the United States partially responsible for events in East Asia on account of its empty seat in Geneva. Had the United States joined the world body, he asserted, the league "could now speak with a concerted voice that no power could possibly afford to disregard."[32]

International diffidence went both ways. Such was the case after Stimson came to the conclusion that the East Asian crisis could be resolved most emphatically through the Nine-Power Treaty. Almost immediately, Britain's Conservative-dominated coalition National Government pulled back. Stimson's repeated appeals by transatlantic telephone to Foreign Secretary John Simon went nowhere. The British remained, in Stimson's words, "soft and pudgy" on the issue. The British felt similarly about the Americans. One got nothing out of Washington, complained statesman Stanley Baldwin, but words—"big words, but only words." The result, as historian Christopher Thorne put it, is that at the peak of the Manchurian crisis, Whitehall and Washington held "a clear but exaggerated image of the other government as being timid, rigid, and uncooperative."[33]

Seeking some forward motion, Stimson decided to unilaterally criticize Japan's violation of the Nine-Power Treaty. The medium was a diplomatic contrivance known as an "open letter," typically addressed to a renowned person but sent to the press for maximum effect. Stimson addressed his two-thousand-word missive to Senator Borah, who chaired the Senate Foreign Relations Committee. It appeared in newspapers worldwide on February 24, 1932. Stimson reviewed the history of the Nine-Power Treaty and its goal of giving "the people of China the fullest opportunity to develop without molestation their sovereignty and independence." He then coupled the treaty to naval limitation, claiming that one accord could not be ignored without disturbing the other. The threat of a renewed naval race was thinly veiled. Stimson also pointed to the alleged linkage between the Nine-Power Treaty and the Kellogg Pact, especially their common touchstones of aligning the conscience of the world "in favor of a system of orderly development by the law of nations." Once again we see the American emphasis on orderly processes—of playing by agreed-upon rules and dealing with disputes multilaterally. What's clear is that Stimson hoped to further shame and isolate Japan, clarify policy to the American people, prod the British to be more openly vocal, and compel the league to endorse his nonrecognition policy.[34]

In Japan, a Foreign Office spokesperson blasted Stimson's "ignorance" of history for coupling the Nine-Power Treaty with naval disarmament. To the Japanese, no such linkage ever took place at the Washington Conference; on this point, the evidence favors Japan. More revealing was a statement by Japan's minister to China, Shigemitsu Mamoru, who said the world misunderstood Japan's aim "to remove the menace of irresponsible militarism" in China. Behind this assertion lay the chauvinistic strain of Pan-Asianist thinking, implying that Japan's military actions in China were meant to bring about regional order and enlightenment.[35]

Like receding galaxies, the ideological gap between Japan and the rest of the world was rapidly growing wider. The distance traveled in just two years can be measured by comparing Japan's incursion in Manchuria with Premier Hamaguchi's 1930 paean to the new peace principles. Extolling the spirit of the Kellogg–Briand Pact, Hamaguchi had said, "It is clear that any breach of that solemn agreement must rally the whole world against the aggressor."[36]

The monthlong hostilities in Shanghai ended with a truce in March at a cost of nearly 10,000 Chinese and 2,500 Japanese dead. Amid the attention-grabbing headlines, disquieting news continued to emanate from Manchuria. On February 18, an ambiguous "administrative committee" suddenly declared the "independence" of a new state, with a pledge to maintain the Open Door. Henceforth, the East Asian crisis began to resemble a relay race toward some indeterminate finish line, with Stimson passing off the diplomatic baton to the League of Nations.

JAPAN, THE LEAGUE, AND "MANCHUKUO"

The truce in Shanghai coincided with the arrival in Tokyo of the League of Nations' Commission of Inquiry, headed by Great Britain's Lord Lytton. The Lytton Commission's charge was seemingly straightforward: collect facts on the crisis so the league could make informed decisions for a settlement. The first stop in Tokyo, however, was mainly to make personal contacts with Japanese officials before returning for a longer stay in July. In addition to a luncheon hosted by Emperor Hirohito, the commission attended a banquet with renowned Japanese internationalists, including Ishii Kikujirō and Tokugawa Iesato. Ishii revealed Japan's strong national consensus on continental policy, telling the commission that Japan had been bearing the brunt "of a hostile challenge from China" for more than ten years. The implication was abundantly clear: Japan had acted in self-defense. Importantly, Ishii also provided clues about Japan's evolving worldview, saying the postwar treaties needed an updated interpretation.[37]

On March 9, as the Lytton Commission prepared to sail for Shanghai, insinuations turned to deeds as Japanese officials installed Henry Pu Yi, the last emperor of the Qing dynasty, as regent of "Manchukuo." Elaborate ceremonies took place in the new capital of Changchun (Hsinking), whose new, wide boulevards were festooned with the flags of both Japan and Manchukuo. There were good reasons Japan had moved quickly to create a puppet state. If the world were to become convinced that Manchukuo had been birthed out of the voluntary will of the local population, then Japan had not violated China's territorial integrity or any of the postwar treaties. On one hand, this suggests Japan's leaders were still sensitive to world opinion. On the other hand, it makes clear they were convinced of the justness of their actions, which, if put to the harsh light of historical interrogation, could be classified as nothing other than an imperialist project. In an example of this self-deception, diplomat Matsudaira Tsuneo, a perceived moderate, told Stimson how the Chinese denizens of Manchukuo had objected to a visit by a member of the Nanjing government, saying he would make political trouble. Matsudaira claimed that Japan had tried to "curb the new Manchukuo government" from doing so, but "found it very obstinate." In this case, a Japanese "liberal" depicted a supposedly sovereign Manchurian regime, over which the Japanese government was powerless.[38]

The rest of the world, however, remained skeptical. In Washington, Stimson brooded over the intensifying ideological conflict, telling a colleague that events in East Asia were "shaping up an issue between two great theories of civilization." In other words, a world order underwritten either by orderly processes or the point of a bayonet. On March 11, the clash became more stark after the League Assembly, represented by fifty nations, followed Stimson's lead and voted unanimously not to recognize any new situation in Manchuria that flouted the treaty system.[39] The key question now for Tokyo was whether it should officially "recognize" Manchukuo. As a result of the Seiyūkai's landslide victory in the recent national election, party hard-liners had been urging Premier Inukai to move toward recognition. Inukai was hesitant to do so, partially because acting before the Lytton Commission had finished its inquiry would likely isolate Japan further.

Terrorism temporarily shrouded possible outcomes. On May 15, junior naval officers and army cadets, many of whom were followers of ultranationalist groups, assassinated Inukai. (Extremists at the time were responsible not only for Inukai's murder but also for those of Mitsui head Dan Takuma in February and former finance minister Inoue Junnosuke in March.) The American reaction to these tragedies was informed by a prevalent assumption: that Japan's political system was besieged by a historic struggle between "mad dog" militarists and "moderate" civilian politicians. Almost overnight the American press transformed Inukai from a man who oversaw Japan's consolidation of Manchuria into a "foe of militarism."[40] Although it was not unreasonable for Americans to interpret the assassination of civilian authorities in dichotomous terms, such an oversimplified binary failed to separate the abstract motives of extremists from the consensus-driven, conservative orientation among Japan's civilian and military rulers. Members of ultranationalist societies were often animated by allegations of political corruption and nebulous notions of "domestic renovation" and "national reconstruction."[41]

In the immediate circumstances, Inukai's murder resulted in the formation of Japan's first nonparty cabinet since 1924, with the news of retired admiral Saitō Makoto's appointment as premier. The seventy-three-year-old Saitō had strong ties to Japanese regionalism, having served twice as colonial governor in Korea in the 1920s. So, too, did Saitō's selection for foreign minister, Uchida Kōsai. In June 1931, following his participation in nearly all of the major postwar conferences (his seal graced the Kellogg Pact), the Japanese government appointed Uchida president of the South Manchurian Railway. Unknown to outsiders, in the aftermath of the Manchurian Incident, Uchida had offered strong support for the Kwantung Army.[42] Such sympathies became apparent over the next eight months as the Saitō cabinet moved aggressively to convince the world of Manchukuo's legitimacy and Japan's mission in East Asia, culminating in a showdown with the League of Nations.

The Saitō government's campaign to normalize Manchukuo within the new liberal order began in earnest in July 1932, with the return of the Lytton Commission to Japan after nearly four months in China. This time the fact-finding group stayed in Tokyo for nearly two weeks and met twice with Foreign Minister Uchida. If facts were stubborn things, as John Adams once said, dueling interpretations of facts could be equally stubborn. Uchida responded to queries with stock replies that accorded with the liberal treaties: Japan had acted in self-defense; Manchukuo resulted from the voluntary will of the thirty million local (mostly Han) Chinese. Then, paradoxically, Uchida reiterated to Lord Lytton that Manchuria was Japan's "lifeline."

In response, Lytton tried to connect emotionally with Uchida, seeking to bridge the divide by comparing Japan's historical sacrifices in Manchuria with European remembrances of the Great War. Lytton's reply to Uchida warrants fuller expression:

> We know of your treaties, we accept what you have told us about your economic interests, we know from history of the wars you have fought, and we respect your sensitiveness on this subject. Will you allow me to tell you that there are some things about which other nations are also sensitive, some things in which they take pride, some things which they feel as strongly about as you do about Manchuria? There are some States who fought to the very death in the Great War, States that staked and lost everything. You say you have spent a billion yen in Manchuria; well, these States spent much more than that in the Great War and incurred debts which will cripple them for generations. You lost 200,000 lives [sic]; these people lost many millions. And they got nothing out of it except one thing. The only thing which these nations have saved from all their sacrifices in the War is their collective machinery for maintaining peace and preventing a repetition of such horrors. They are proud of it and sensitive about it. It is to them a lifeline, the lifeline of their civilization, and it counts for them as much as Manchuria counts to you. I ask you, therefore, to remember this. You are up against a very difficult task; do not make it more difficult by flying in the face of world opinion.

When Uchida insisted that the Nine-Power Treaty did not apply to situations involving self-determination, the commission cut short its visit and departed, in the words of one journalist, "intensely disappointed."[43]

The diplomatic baton then passed back to Stimson. In a diary entry on July 20, the secretary complained about "a flood of Japanese propaganda" dealing with the allegedly spontaneous rising of the Chinese population for a new state in Manchuria. Calling it "pure bunk," Stimson decided to return to the rhetorical fold. He told President Hoover he planned to develop the Kellogg Pact into "a living vital force, with a living vital public opinion behind it." Hoover was not in the mood for more public diplomacy; he was trying to get reelected in the middle of an economic depression. (The president's aloofness shone through in his postpresidential memoir, in which he erroneously referred to Japan's leader at the time as Konoe Fumimaro.)[44] Stimson went on with a planned speech anyway. On August 8, 1932, the secretary spoke about the significance of the no-war pact before the Council on Foreign Relations in New York City. The Republican statesman sounded utterly Wilsonian.

The Great War loomed large in Stimson's address. He described it as a turning point, the impetus for a new way of thinking about peace and war. "The treaties," said Stimson, "signalize a revolution in human thought . . . a consciousness that unless some such step were taken modern civilization might be doomed." The world's first step, the League Covenant, he praised for developing a "community of spirit" among nations. That spirit, he claimed, shone even brighter with the Kellogg Pact's no-war pledge. To critics who scoffed at the peace system's reliance on world opinion, the secretary said they had "not accurately appraised the evolution in world opinion since the World War." He maintained that public opinion could be made "one of the most potent sanctions in the world." All it took was the will of the people of the world to make it effective. "If they desire to make it effective," said Stimson, "it will be irresistible."[45]

Stimson's underlying assumptions, however, left a trail of nagging questions. What, for example, had shown moral condemnation to be "irresistible" as a deterrent? And who exactly were "the people"? With his eye perpetually on the British, one gets the idea that Stimson's view of the "public" was tiered in importance, with Anglo-Saxon opinion counting the most. Moreover, Stimson viewed public opinion as some sort of monolithic force, when, in fact, uniform agreement among the peoples and governments of the world did not square with history. And how could the succinct Kellogg Pact represent something "even more sweeping" than the expansive League Covenant? Finally, what exactly constituted "self-defense"? This important exception from the Kellogg Pact remained unrefined in international law. Stimson's concerns nonetheless were in the right place. He sensed the potentially profound consequences of Japan defaulting on the liberal order in a way that many of his contemporaries did not. Talking to Ambassador Debuchi, Stimson warned that Japan's conduct in Manchuria "was going to lead to years of anarchy and . . . perhaps a World War."[46]

And yet at the very moment Stimson was trying to keep the heat on Japan, Americans were opening up their newspapers to glowing depictions of Japan at the 1932 Summer Olympics in Los Angeles. Only Japan came close to the United States in number of athletes (250), or enthusiasm—a point underscored by the *New York Times*, which said the Japanese had gone in for the Olympics in "elaborate style." No other nation's athletes caused more of a buzz than Japan's swimmers, who obliterated several world records in the United States' traditional bailiwick. American spectators cheered on the Japanese swimmers; the press raved about them. Struck by the warm reception for Japanese athletes, the *Chicago Tribune* stated, "There has been astonishing sweetness in the demeanor of the native Californians toward the Japanese. . . . They undoubtedly are sincere in their admiration of the pluck, enthusiasm, and instinctive sporting courtesy which Japanese athletes have shown throughout the Games." Given the recent exclusion laws aimed at Japan and racist books like *The Rising Tide of Color*, the counterintuitive observations illuminated the potentially awkward relationship between global sports and international politics.[47]

As Japanese athletes won accolades and radiated the Olympic ideal of peaceful internationalism, Japanese envoys kept up a diplomatic offensive around the world. One of the most recognizable emissaries was Nitobe Inazō, who had embarked on a yearlong lecture tour of the United States in April 1932 in hopes of explaining Japan's cause. A renowned internationalist, Nitobe had married an American Quaker and was undersecretary-general of the League of Nations from 1920 to 1926. Despite these worldly credentials, Nitobe carried with him baggage from the old diplomacy, including a more chauvinistic Pan-Asianism. As historian Thomas Burkman noted, Nitobe believed in the inexorable advance of superior civilizations and the imperialist duty of the "civilizing mission." In the East, where Japan was "in the forefront of the civilization," that job belonged to Japan.[48]

On August 20, Nitobe offered a rebuttal to Stimson's address on the Kellogg Pact. Speaking to Americans on CBS Radio, Nitobe admitted that Stimson waxed eloquent on the "sanction of public opinion"; the problem was that the secretary wrongly accused Japan of violating the treaty. Japan's only crime, said Nitobe, was self-defense and helping a neighbor come into being. "Does the new dispensation," he asked Americans, "provide that if a new state is born, it must receive no help from a midwife?" Even though evidence suggests the key targets of Nitobe's speech—American political, academic, and religious elites—were mostly unimpressed with his arguments, the conspicuous takeaway was that Japan's brightest internationalist lights believed the empire's intentions were benign.[49] As such, it was clear that liberal internationalism faced troubled waters ahead.

The widening ideological divide became evident five days after Nitobe's broadcast. In a highly publicized address before the Japanese Diet, Foreign Minister Uchida offered the most candid explanation yet of Japan's view. Clearly mistrustful of the impending Lytton Report, Uchida said allegations of Japan's violation of the peace machinery were "incomprehensible" and that Japan's recognition of Manchukuo was only a matter of time. He also established a doctrinal template for Japan's foreign policy positions throughout the 1930s, which went something like this: (1) The outside world does not fully comprehend "actual conditions" in East Asia. (2) Japan must provide a correct understanding of actual conditions. And (3) Japan's just cause stemmed from special rights, special interests, and special responsibilities— especially the view that Japan had a special duty as "the stabilizing power in the Far East" to bring civilization and enlightenment to the region. More infamously, in response to a parliamentary interpellation, Uchida declared that Japan "would not yield an inch [on Manchukuo] even if the country turned to scorched earth."[50]

The world quickly learned the Japanese were not bluffing. On September 15, almost one year to the day after the "incident," the Saitō government preempted the Lytton Report and officially recognized Manchukuo. In a "bilateral" protocol, Japan affirmed that Manchukuo was created by the "free will of its inhabitants"; "Manchukuo," in turn, agreed to respect Japan's treaty rights and allow Japanese troops to guarantee "mutual security." At a surreal signing ceremony, Japan essentially shook hands with itself. Manchukuo's "foreign minister," Xie Jieshi, a Taiwanese colonial who received his law degree from Meiji University, pleaded with the Western powers to follow Japan's lead. Lifting language from the Nine-Power Treaty, Xie said it was their duty to "assist and encourage the fuller development of the new state." The world ignored the appeal and waited for the Lytton Report.[51]

The much-anticipated 100,000-word Lytton Report was distributed on October 2, 1932. It was an evenhanded account of the crisis but nonetheless critical of Japan's actions. It acknowledged Japan's economic interests and historical rights in the region but rejected the claim of self-defense. It also refuted the idea that Manchukuo was the organic creation of the local population. In fact, according to the report, the five-person commission received 1,550 letters during their visit to Manchuria, all but two of which were "bitterly hostile" toward the Japanese. As a result, the commission recommended the creation of a new administrative entity in the region "consistent with the sovereignty of China" but with sensible deference to local autonomy. The *Economist* opined that the report was "one of those documents which a Government can reject only at its peril."[52] Such a statement represented the grand threat of liberal internationalism. The outstanding question was whether the threat had any teeth to it.

SHOWDOWN IN GENEVA (NOVEMBER 1932–FEBRUARY 1933)

In mid-November, representatives of forty-four nations gathered in Geneva's Palais Wilson to debate the Lytton Report and decide whether or not to endorse its conclusions. The stakes were palpable: the singular postwar liberal institution was to make a decision that held potentially crucial consequences for its own credibility. Moreover, despite America's central role in world affairs and Secretary Stimson's omnipresence throughout the Manchurian crisis, the United States would be standing on the sidelines. That incongruity was palpable. It was also newly amplified, with American attention drawn overwhelmingly to domestic politics after Franklin D. Roosevelt trounced Herbert Hoover in the presidential election on November 8, 1932.

In Geneva, much of the world's attention focused on Japan's chief plenipotentiary, Matsuoka Yōsuke. Matsuoka was one of the most interesting and important Japanese statesmen in the interwar era. In 1893, when he was just thirteen years old, his once-wealthy merchant family shipped him across the Pacific to Portland, Oregon, in a program sponsored by the Methodist church. There he acclimated to American ways under the tutelage of a host family. He eventually entered the University of Oregon law school, graduating second in his class. In 1902, armed with a law degree and fluent in English, Matsuoka returned to Japan and carved out a career in the Foreign Ministry. Along with consular posts in China, he joined Japanese delegations to the Lansing–Ishii talks and the Paris Peace Conference. In 1921, he bowed out of the Foreign Ministry and took a position with the South Manchurian Railway. The Japanese government appointed him vice president of the company in 1927. Based on Matsuoka's diplomatic experience, fluency in English, and firsthand knowledge of Manchuria (he gave a stout defense of Japan's rights in Manchuria at the 1929 IPR conference), it is easy to see why the Saitō government tapped him to make Japan's case at the League of Nations.

Despite his short stature, the self-assured Matsuoka commanded attention. He departed Tokyo amid cries of *banzai* and arrived in Geneva, as one scholar noted, actively seeking occasions for informal tête-à-têtes and giving impromptu press briefings at the Grand Hotel de la Metropole.[53] Matsuoka prepared to explain Japan's case by cribbing the Saitō cabinet's policy template. Above all, Matsuoka's guiding premise was that the world did not fully understand "actual conditions" in East Asia. To rectify this information gap and prove that Japan's cause was just, Matsuoka unfurled layers of rationale

Figure 2.2. Matsuoka Yōsuke, Japan's chief plenipotentiary to the League of Nations (1932–1933) and foreign minister (1940–1941). (Courtesy of the *Oregonian*.)

based on special rights, special interests, and the evolving theme of Japan's special responsibilities in the region.

As a prologue to official proceedings—and a symbolic nod to the spirit of liberal internationalism—in early December, league officials allotted Matsuoka and China's lead delegate, Dr. W. W. Yen, fifteen minutes each to address the world at large on Radio-Nations, the league's new shortwave broadcast station in Geneva. Yen, a former English professor and premier and foreign minister of the Beijing government in the early 1920s, urged the league to act decisively and endorse the Lytton Report to avoid further bloodshed. Matsuoka, meanwhile, took the occasion to say he did not believe that Europe and America "understood conditions in the Far East." Countering Yen, he cautioned the world against acting hastily.[54]

Matsuoka's first chance to make a meaningful impression on league delegates came on December 6. In an address to the assembly, he accused Nanjing of craftily employing propaganda to shape world opinion against Japan "before the facts were fully known." He also covered the well-worn arguments of self-defense, self-determination, and the disorder of China.[55] Afterward, the assembly referred the Lytton Report to a special Committee of Nineteen (nations), charged with making recommendations for a final vote in February 1933.

Perhaps disappointed in his own performance on December 6, Matsuoka returned to the assembly two days later on a mission. He told newsreel men to get their cameras ready. Matsuoka spoke for nearly ninety minutes without notes. Seeking big gains, he took big risks. Instead of fighting public opinion, he turned it on its head. For the sake of argument, he joined in supposing "that public opinion was so absolutely against Japan as some of the [league delegates] try to make out." But, Matsuoka wondered aloud, was public opinion ever wrong? He kindly proffered an answer: "Humanity crucified Jesus of Nazareth two thousand years ago. And today? Can any of you assure me that the so-called world opinion can make no mistake?" However blasphemous the comparison was to some in the audience, Matsuoka was intent on discrediting a pillar of liberal internationalism and underscoring Japan's alleged victimization. His language was vivid, alive with metaphor. On treaty rights, he stated, "It is as if we [Japanese] were invited into the house of our neighbor, who began to abuse [us]. . . . we at last got mad and hit the neighbor, and straightaway our neighbor comes to Geneva and says the Japanese invaded his house and struck him down for no reason." In Japan, the speech was hailed as one of the greatest public addresses of the century. Whether it changed the minds of delegates, however, would not be known until the assembly reconvened after the New Year.[56]

During the holiday interlude, Matsuoka offered more evidence of Japan's deepening regionalist ideology. In an interview featured in the Sunday *New York Times*, he declared that Japan "held a unique position among Far Eastern countries" and had a moral responsibility to lead. And not just in East Asia. "In the future," said Matsuoka, "it is obvious [Japan] must have room in the South Seas." A decade before Japan's advance into Southeast Asia, here was arguably an embryo of the impulses that one day would evolve into the Co-Prosperity Sphere. Matsuoka's views also hinted at ethereal aims, saying, "Japan's mission is to lead the world spiritually and intellectually." Japan, he said, would be "the cradle of a new Messiah."[57] Even accounting for Matsuoka's characteristic bravado, his words signaled an emergent Japanese confidence about the empire's allegedly exceptional role in Asia—one decidedly at odds with the postwar treaties.

Japan's new confidence played out dramatically on the morning of February 24, 1933, when the heart and soul of the liberal peace system reconvened for the most important vote of its short existence. Events during the recess had only complicated things for Matsuoka. On January 3, Japanese troops launched an offensive into Rehe province (now part of Liaoning and Hebei provinces) in Northeast China. China's delegate, Yen, spoke first. Despite a momentary lapse of hyperbole—he called Japan's belligerence "the most wanton aggression ever recorded in the annals of human history"—Yen praised the league's "verdict of right and wrong" and effectively put the onus on Tokyo. Recalling events on September 18, 1931, he said even if Japanese troops "were under the delusion or 'belief' that they were acting in self-defense, it could not exonerate the Japanese Government of the responsibility for the consequences that followed."[58]

Matsuoka, anticipating a devastating tally, stepped to the podium for one last defense of Japan's cause. He argued passionately; he argued with forceful repetition. Three times he claimed the league failed to fully understand "actual conditions" in East Asia. But he betrayed a defensiveness born of imminent defeat. "Manchuria," he shouted, "belongs to us by right. Read your history." On Japan's special role in Manchuria, he asserted the Japanese "are a great civilizing and stabilizing force in that wild country." Casting a wider civilizing net, Matsuoka again offered a glimpse of the empire's changing view of world order, saying, "Japan has been and will always be the mainstay of peace, order and progress in the Far East." His statement presaged future tension with the new peace structure. Rather than regarding itself as one of the mainstays of peace in the region, Japan now viewed itself as *the* primary authority. Matsuoka concluded by warning the assembly that endorsing the Lytton Report would be a mistake.[59]

The vote was 42–1 in favor of the report, with Japan the lone dissenter. Afterward, Matsuoka read from a prepared statement. He explained how Japan had been a proud member of the League of Nations, but now it held greatly different views on how to achieve peace in Asia. The Japanese had "reached the limit of their endeavors to cooperate with the League." The assembly sat in silence, stunned, as Matsuoka, described by one reporter as "grim and determined," led his delegation out of the hall. "We are not coming back," he stated matter-of-factly.[60]

***

There is no way to dress up the fact that liberal internationalism failed its first real test. An aggressor had seized a vast expanse of territory by force and walked away with its spoils. The international community had spent more than seventeen months responding to the crisis, exhausting hundreds of thousands of words in speeches, cables, and reports—to no avail. Several reasons account for its failure. First, the crisis exposed the limits of "world opinion" as a deterrent to aggression. If public opinion were to carry any compelling weight, it would have to be united and free from state manipulation. And even then its deterrent power was questionable. Another weakness stemmed from residual ambiguity in the treaties. The Kellogg Pact, for example, may have outlawed war, but the meaning of "self-defense" remained fuzzy. As the new US ambassador to Japan, Joseph C. Grew, observed, "I doubt if one Japanese in a hundred really believes that they have actually broken the Kellogg Pact, the Nine-Power Treaty, and the Covenant of the League."[61] Most of all, the episode revealed a lack of will by the leading powers to uphold the letter of the new order. From 1919 to 1930, they had collaborated to craft a series of ennobling and groundbreaking agreements with the aim of stifling aggression, but when the time came to back words with deeds, their response did not rise to the majesty of their diplomatic creations.

Washington's ambivalent role was especially impactful. Although Secretary Stimson sensed the consequences of Japan's defiance, he seldom confronted the fallout of America's own self-centeredness in playing world affairs with one foot in and one foot out. As the Tokyo-based correspondent Hugh Byas had opined, the League of Nations without the United States was "one-eyed and one-armed." American delegations to the 1920s conferences, as we saw, had placed inordinate faith in the premise that global peace could be ensured with US participation limited to a latticework of multilateral treaties outside of the League of Nations. Washington Conference delegate Elihu Root had attempted a nuanced defense of this circumscribed American approach in the inaugural issue of *Foreign Affairs* in 1922:

> The "League of Nations" is merely a contract . . . by which [the signatories] agree to super-add to the existing usages, customs, laws, rights, and obligations of the existing community of nations . . . certain other rights and obligations. . . . Whether a country enters into that contract or not, its membership of the community of nations continues with all the rights and obligations incident to that membership.[62]

The Manchurian crisis left this American assumption shot through with uncertainty.

Imagining American participation in the league during the Manchurian crisis entails a series of ahistorical counterfactuals that lead down blind alleys. But supposing anyway that the United States was a league member and public opinion supported participation and action *as President Wilson envisioned it*. First, by November 1931, a unified international community would have issued a strong censure of Japan. Then, after the Inukai cabinet dispatched troops to Shanghai in January 1932, league members would have slapped economic sanctions on Japan. Failing that, after publication of the Lytton Report, the league would have begun preparations to guarantee China's territorial integrity through collective force. In the face of such incremental international pressure, it seems conceivable that Japan's leadership might have followed a different path. This scenario, of course, only leads to more counterfactuals, ad infinitum.

More fatefully, the Japanese government, by breaking its vows of self-denial on multiple multilateral treaties—by choosing unilateralism and force over cooperative diplomacy—inaugurated a decade-long ideological rupture between Japanese regionalism and liberal internationalism. Although the new American administration of Franklin D. Roosevelt steered clear of provoking Japan, it consistently affirmed the sanctity of the postwar agreements, while emphasizing the importance of rules-based "orderly processes." As one American diplomat put it, "We cannot renounce [the liberal principles] without self-stultification and falsity to our own fundamental conceptions of the proper relations among nations." At the same time, American leaders and commentators held out hope that one day Japanese "moderates" would return Japan to the ethos of liberal internationalism and its cooperative conduct of the 1920s. As the *New York Times* noted, "The nations who voted unanimously at Geneva must be as unanimous in hoping that Japan's self-imposed exclusion may yet be canceled by the assertion of her own better self."[63]

Japan's leaders certainly wanted to avoid protracted international isolation. The increasingly interdependent world was real. At the same time, the empire sought to make Manchukuo "ordinary and unexceptional"[64] among the so-called family of nations, and to establish that Japan was "the stabilizing force in the Far East." In reality, then, very little had changed since January 1932. These were the same foreign policy goals articulated by Uchida and Matsuoka, by Japanese diplomats all over the world. They also carried with them the same paradoxical double wish—of demanding acceptance from global society without accepting the demands of liberal internationalism. Japan's leaders, however, remained convinced the real problem stemmed from other nations "not understanding actual conditions in East Asia." As a result, in the aftermath of the Manchurian crisis, Japan set out to educate the world, but especially the United States, of Japan's "true intentions" in the region.

Chapter Three

Japan's Charm Offensive (1933–1934)

During his closing address at the League of Nations on February 24, 1933, Chinese delegate W. W. Yen summed up Japan's dilemma going forward: "Seventeen months ago, the world, including my country, was bound to admit of Japan's high place in the councils of nations." Now, he said, "Japan finds herself all alone." The *New York Times* similarly deemed Japan "morally isolated."[1] Indeed, although walking out of the league may have momentarily stimulated among Japanese a rush of muscular defiance, it nonetheless did not alter the fact that forty-two nations delivered a unanimous verdict against the empire. Or that US President-Elect Franklin D. Roosevelt had publicly affirmed the nonrecognition policy of the outgoing secretary of state, Henry Stimson.

And if Japan's leaders were hoping time would heal all wounds and compel the United States to accept new conditions in East Asia, immediate indications were not promising. In early 1933, for example, Ambassador Debuchi told the State Department's Stanley Hornbeck that "he wished the world would close its eyes and turn its back [on Manchuria], give Japan a chance to work the thing out her own way, let her demonstrate the wisdom and success of her policy." Hornbeck replied that such a request "amounted to asking the League of Nations to forget the Covenant, the whole world to forget the multilateral treaties; everybody to forget the efforts which have been made during recent years to substitute new methods for old in connection with the settling of international disputes."[2] From Hornbeck's perspective, Japan wanted to have its geopolitical cake and eat it too. And yet, American officials like Hornbeck also wanted to have their cake and eat it too. They routinely invoked the sanctity of the League Covenant despite America's absence in Geneva. A sympathetic view would say the Americans were channeling broadly the new international norms, with an emphasis on "orderly processes" and multilateral engagement.

For Japan's leaders, the prospect of prolonged international isolation was not an idle concern. As one observer in Tokyo noted, they had been "loath to relinquish" the prized permanent seat on the Council of the League of Nations.[3] They were also sensitive to the importance of good relations for global trade and investment. Nonetheless, as Emperor Hirohito's rescript on March 27, 1933, made clear, a "wide divergence of views" separated Japan and the rest of the world. So it was not surprising that Japan's leadership emerged from the Manchurian crisis as convinced as ever that the world's antagonism was due to ignorance about "actual conditions" in East Asia—ignorance about Japan's special responsibility, about the disorganized nonstate that was China, about the independent new state of Manchukuo. Any permanent solution therefore would not involve Japan's submission to the world's verdict; rather, the world would have to awaken to the truth about Manchukuo's sovereignty and Japan's primacy in East Asia.

Or so Japan hoped. In 1933, defiance still carried an asterisk. As Matsuoka Yōsuke told reporters on the eve of his departure from Geneva, "I am still hoping that someday Japan will be understood."[4] Besides a wistful regret in his voice that Japan was at odds with the world, Matsuoka's words bared a deeper truth. Despite Japan's new status *outside* the framework of the liberal peace system, it was clear some Japanese officials still believed it was important, even necessary, to obtain recognition for Japan's territorial gains by nations *within* the system. Like a planetary body dislodged from orbit but still under the gravitational influence of the system, Japan wobbled in the cold space of international isolation still beholden to the peace system's "laws" of legitimacy.

As a result, over the next few years, Tokyo continued to work actively and creatively to be "understood." Japanese officials were especially persistent in their efforts to influence American public opinion. Several factors explain Japan's singular focus on the United States. Not only did the United States pose the biggest strategic threat to Japan, it was also the originator of the Open Door policy and Nine-Power Treaty, and Japan's main nemesis during the Manchurian crisis. Perhaps most important, the United States was Japan's biggest trading partner. Japan purchased large quantities of cotton, oil, scrap iron, cars, machinery, and consumer products from the States.[5]

Japan's Ministry of Foreign Affairs, as noted, had expended an inordinate amount of energy during the Manchurian crisis trying to convince Americans of Japan's just cause. Despite this "diplomatic offensive," the sentiment meter did not move in Japan's favor. This raised questions in some Japanese circles about incorporating nontraditional forms of diplomacy to help foreigners understand Japan. In fact, even before the end of the Manchurian crisis, Nitobe Inazō had argued for a more nuanced strategy toward the

United States, saying Japan should avoid exclusively political discussion and instead emphasize Japanese "character." According to Nitobe, "When we explain Japan for the American audience, it is not necessary to confine our attention to current issues between Japan and the United States. An explanation covering Japanese history or a wide range of aspects of Japanese life would likely be of greater lasting value."[6]

What began as informal, bureaucratic discussions and a few pilot projects by Foreign Minister Uchida eventually blossomed into a vigorous and multifaceted diplomatic campaign comprising both standard diplomacy and subtler "soft power" strategies. By early 1934, under the guidance of Prime Minister Saitō and new foreign minister Hirota Kōki, the strategy approximated a coordinated charm offensive. Hirota took the lead with concerted, conciliatory gestures to the United States, emphasizing past friendship and downplaying discord over Manchuria as a "thing of the past." The foreign minister also attempted to promote amity through soft power channels of public diplomacy, in which eminent Japanese cosmopolitans were dispatched to the United States under the guise of autonomous goodwill trips. Finally, in a striking application of soft power, Tokyo inaugurated a comprehensive program of cultural diplomacy under the auspices of the Foreign Ministry. The Society for International Cultural Relations (Kokusai Bunka Shinkōkai, or KBS) aimed to promote a positive image of Japan abroad by foregrounding the nation's culture—with the implication that the greatness of Japanese civilization justified a paramount role for Japan in Asia. Above all, Tokyo's charm offensive was motivated almost single-mindedly with the goal of providing "correct information" about the empire's special responsibility as the "stabilizing influence" in East Asia. The change in Japan's diplomatic approach to the United States coincided with the inauguration in March 1933 of a new administration in Washington.

TEAM ROOSEVELT

Japanese officials could take comfort knowing that the American gadfly Henry Stimson was gone. But it was cold comfort, considering the newly elected president, Franklin D. Roosevelt, had invited Stimson to his Hyde Park home in January and publicly confirmed continuity in America's East Asian policy. At the same time, the American people did not elect FDR in 1932 on foreign policy issues. With nearly 25 percent of the workforce unemployed, economic recovery remained the nation's number one priority. Roosevelt's first one hundred days produced a tempest of governmental activity toward solving domestic problems—not foreign ones.

In ideological outlook, the fifty-one-year-old Roosevelt, like Woodrow Wilson, subscribed to nineteenth-century British liberalism. Historian David

Reynolds maintains that, in some ways, FDR's liberal convictions exceeded Wilson's, especially the exceptionalist notion that America was the "supreme exemplar" of democratic values. In foreign policy, however, Roosevelt pursued a more pragmatic liberalism. At times, his policies were decidedly illiberal, such as his decision in early 1933 to renounce global currency stabilization. Moreover, like his distant cousin Theodore Roosevelt, he championed naval theorist Alfred T. Mahan's ideas on the importance of sea power.[7]

Roosevelt assigned nearly full responsibility for US policy in East Asia to his sixty-one-year-old secretary of state, Cordell Hull. Hull had spent two decades in Washington as a Democratic congressman and senator from Tennessee. He was a staunch proponent of liberal internationalism, placing particular emphasis on treaty obligations and reducing trade barriers. Hull and Roosevelt first got to know one another during Hull's tenure as chair of the Democratic National Committee in the early 1920s. Temperamentally, the two men were worlds apart. The president exuded a spontaneous charm and loved an audience. Hull, on the other hand, exhibited reserve and "quiet good sense." In an era of apparently unrestrained backslapping, one of Hull's personal acquaintances remarked, "I have never seen Cordell Hull slap or get slapped on the back by anyone." Although Hull operated outside of Roosevelt's inner sanctum, he remained a "wheel-horse of the administration." FDR generally respected Hull's opinion, spoke to him in a complimentary way, recommended him several times for the Nobel Peace Prize, and kept him on as secretary almost for his entire tenure.[8]

Secretary Hull's point man in Tokyo was Ambassador Joseph C. Grew, whom Roosevelt had retained from the Hoover administration. Grew was a member of the Eastern Establishment and longtime diplomat. Like FDR, he had attended Groton and Harvard, graduating two years ahead of the president. To his credit, Grew had arrived in Japan determined to understand the country, which his wife's great-granduncle, Commodore Matthew C. Perry, had coerced out of its self-imposed samurai seclusion in the 1850s. Almost immediately, however, Grew fell prey to the simplistic dichotomy in which "liberal statesmen" struggled against a "hotheaded military clique." Grew's views suffered from limited perspective. He moved mainly in Japan's aristocratic circles, attracted by the rarified air of cosmopolitans who loved to play golf or a "bully" game of poker. And though he often tried to gauge public opinion through the native press with the help of talented embassy staffers, Grew's diary suggests that any insights gleaned about Japan's national temperament seldom prompted him to question preconceived notions. As America's ambassador in Japan for a decade—he served from 1932 to 1941—Grew thus propagated an imprecise picture of Japan's domestic politics and the theory that the country moved historically in pendulum-like extremes.[9] The

Figure 3.1. President Roosevelt (1933–1945) and Secretary of State Cordell Hull (1933–1944). (Everett Collection Historical / Alamy stock photo.)

implication was that the United States needed only to wait out the current storm.

Grew, however, was hardly alone in his one-dimensional discernments. Throughout the 1930s, American pundits routinely characterized Japan's political culture as an epic struggle between civilians and the military. As America's most popular mass-circulation magazine, the *Saturday Evening Post*, stated, "On one side [in Japan], convinced to the death that the sword is the only ultimate solution, is the military element. . . . On the other side are the politicians." Another magazine described the apparent conflict as "Sword People and Paper People."[10] The seduction of reductionism, of course, is its tidy package of explanatory lucidity. In this case, Japan's military played a prominent role in national politics with not a few outspoken officers, so it made sense that career military officers in khakis, rather than cosmopolitan civilians in striped pants, were the prime movers behind Japan's expansionism and repudiation of the liberal peace system. It was not an unreasonable assumption; it just happened to be misguided.

Figure 3.2. Joseph C. Grew, ambassador to Japan (1932–1941). (Courtesy of the US Embassy, Tokyo.)

The reality, as noted, is that a rough ideological consensus formed in the 1930s among Japanese political, military, and cultural elites regarding the empire's continental policy. According to historian Eri Hotta, a deepening chauvinistic regionalism acted as a powerful ideological glue and "promoted a consistent set of goals."[11] This is not to deny any policy differences in the aftermath of the Manchurian crisis *among* and *within* Japan's civilian leadership, military branches, and the imperial house. Indeed, factions racked the Foreign Ministry as well as the army and navy. But while different viewpoints inevitably arose among all government institutions regarding the empire's foreign policies, these mostly concerned variations on a hegemonic theme, such as strategic priorities (Northeast Asia vs. China proper) and paramount obstacle (Soviet Union vs. US-Britain). In other words, in the 1930s Japan's civilian leaders, military officers, and Emperor Hirohito did not disagree in the main about the empire's primacy in East Asia. As we will see, they collectively couched this presumption in commonly euphemistic Pan-Asianist phrases: above all, that Japan was the region's "civilizing and stabilizing force," and, increasingly, that the empire was engaged in a "holy mission" to save all of Asia.

A sympathetic explanation for the confusion of foreign observers is that Japanese politics was genuinely difficult to read. In 1889, the Meiji oligarchs had created a labyrinthine constitutional system in which power and responsibility were diffused in ambiguous layers. At the top was a "sacred and inviolable" emperor, who was the locus of power and yet politically undefined. The lawmaking side of government consisted of a bicameral parliament (the Diet), featuring a House of Representatives and a nonelected House of Peers. A twenty-four-member Privy Council formally vetted laws and treaties for constitutional compliance. A ministerial cabinet (with a murky selection process for prime minister) and powerful bureaucracy executed the daily functions of government. The General Staffs of Army and Navy, meanwhile, operated independent of the cabinet, with direct access to the throne. For this reason, it cannot be denied the Meiji charter gave the military disproportionate influence in decision making. Lastly, shuffling discreetly on the outskirts of government were Japan's elder statesmen, though their ranks, with the notable exception of Prince Saionji Kinmochi, had dwindled by the 1930s. Stitching together these disparate institutions was a political culture with a strong proclivity for consensus—one forged in the crucible of daily interactions at General Staff and ministerial offices and elite social venues like the Tokyo Club and Peers' Club.

The US official who proved to be the least prone to reflexive observations about Japan was Secretary Hull's most important advisor for policy in East Asia. This was Stanley K. Hornbeck, the chief of the State Department's Division of Far Eastern Affairs. The forty-nine-year-old Hornbeck had spent most of his adult life engaged in studying, teaching, or advising about East Asian affairs. In 1911, he received his Ph.D. in political science at the University of Wisconsin–Madison under China expert Paul Reinsch. In his twenties he was an eyewitness to major historical events in China, teaching at colleges in Hangzhou and Shenyang as the Qing dynasty collapsed. He later taught at Wisconsin and Harvard before joining the US State Department in 1927 as chief of its Division of Far Eastern Affairs. Despite Hornbeck's reputation as a "China Hand," as someone who interpreted East Asian relations with a sentimental bias toward China, his policy recommendations often contradicted assumed biases.[12]

In the aftermath of the Manchurian crisis, then, a diverse assemblage of new faces, new players, and new institutions in Japan and the United States merged with familiar ones to manage the increased complexity of the transpacific relationship. Japan stood outside the framework of liberal internationalism and sought to establish a Japanese-guided regionalist order, justified by a chauvinistic strand of Pan-Asianism. In an attempt both to avoid isolation and win recognition of this new framework, Japan launched a charm offen-

Figure 3.3. Stanley K. Hornbeck, chief, Division of Far Eastern Affairs (1928–1937), and special advisor to Secretary of State Hull (1937–1944). (Library of Congress, Prints & Photographs Division, photograph by Harris & Ewing [reproduction number LC-DIG-hec-19254].)

sive aimed at the United States, undergirded by friendly persuasion and cultural diplomacy. The extent to which Japanese officials invoked soft power tools as a way to influence Americans and leverage international power illuminates a most unusual crossroads in the mid-1930s between the new diplomacy and neo-imperialism. Essentially, Japan employed soft power to exploit a key component of liberal internationalism (public opinion), in order to legitimize an imperialist project on the continent.

In the United States, a Depression-focused administration neither encouraged nor provoked Japan. The new administration affirmed the nonrecognition policy and the "sanctity" of international treaties. US officials, however, remained intrigued by the Manichean narrative of competing Japans, in which moderates and militarists vied for power. This, in turn, engendered optimism that alleged moderates could, in the near future, stay the challenge from militarists and return Japan fully to the internationalist basis of the 1920s. Every so often American officials and commentators became entranced by signs from Japan that such a thing was happening.

THE PUBLIC DIPLOMACY OF MATSUOKA AND ISHII

Following the League of Nations vote in February 1933, Tokyo set out to revitalize US-Japan relations and provide "correct information" about the empire's "true intentions" in East Asia. The first sign came from Matsuoka. Instead of returning to Japan by way of a sensible eastward journey via the Trans-Siberian Railway, Matsuoka crossed the Atlantic for a monthlong transcontinental speaking tour of the United States. A primary goal was to meet the new American president. This he did on March 31, 1933, though Roosevelt limited Matsuoka to only a brief conversation with him and Secretary Hull. Hull remarked that Matsuoka was very affable, made a few complimentary references, and regretted that his country "felt obliged to quit the League." Before leaving, the Japanese diplomat handed Hull a pamphlet of his league speeches, the foreword of which became a recurrent theme among Japan's leaders in the 1930s: "It is because there is in Europe and America so little understanding of Japan . . . that the Western World has permitted itself to be misled with regard to the policies of my country." Conveniently ignoring the seventeen months the world devoted to the Manchurian crisis, Matsuoka asked that Japan be given time in which "to make herself better understood" to the world.[13]

Matsuoka then took Japan's case directly to the American people. Appearing before foreign policy groups and Japan-America Societies, he asked Americans to give Japan a fair hearing in Manchuria. In a *New York Times* op-ed piece, Matsuoka appealed to American vanity. "I think your heads are with us in spite of your prejudice," he wrote, adding, "I think your hearts are with China, in spite of your common sense." Matsuoka also revealed the deepening influence of Japan's regionalist ideology, maintaining that his nation's actions in Manchuria would be "a blessing to humanity." The chauvinistic strain of this worldview also came through: "We know and understand what we are doing [in China] better than Europe or America." He reprised these themes in broadcasts over NBC and CBS radio networks. Before his return to Japan, Matsuoka received a particularly warm welcome from his alma mater, the University of Oregon, which awarded him an honorary doctorate. In Portland, he had a red granite block inscribed with words of gratitude for his surrogate mother's gravesite. The *Oregonian* confidently claimed in an editorial that Matsuoka's visit was "not political" but rather "a sentimental pilgrimage of one of the world's foremost men back to the American state that mothered him."[14] Actually, it was both. That the good hosts got it wrong meant that Matsuoka had hit the right notes.

Like the continuous loop of a Japanese kite in a figure eight, no sooner had Matsuoka departed for Japan from San Francisco than another Japanese cosmopolitan, Viscount Ishii (of the famous Lansing–Ishii talks), arrived in the Bay Area. Ishii was on his way to the London Economic Conference—via a curiously elongated eastward journey across America. During his goodwill visit, the retired diplomat gave a series of speeches, some over national radio networks. In New York, he spoke to six hundred American dignitaries at a dinner hosted by the Japan Society. Under the theme of America and Japan's "traditional friendship," Ishii deftly presented subjective claims with an air of objective truth: recent events, he said, were "nothing more serious than such differences as may often occur even between good friends and loving brothers," and "more than ever the heart of either nation is in the right place." In Washington, Ishii and FDR issued a joint declaration, in which they referred ambiguously to an "unusual situation" in East Asia and placed hope in a "spirit of cooperation" to build peace and prosperity in the region.[15]

Even Emperor Hirohito got into the mini-burst of Japanese public relations. The emperor sent Roosevelt a telegram, thanking the president for his "kind hospitality" afforded Ishii, adding he was "convinced" the meetings would promote peace. Then, in June 1933, Hirohito granted an interview to Roy W. Howard, president of the Scripps-Howard newspaper chain—the first audience granted to an American journalist by the throne. It was a calculated choice, given that Howard was a noisy advocate for boycotting Japan during the Manchurian crisis. In a series of syndicated columns, Howard hailed Hirohito as a man of peace, saying the thirty-two-year-old sovereign showed a "keen interest" in Japanese-American friendship. "The cordial earnestness of his manner and the simplicity and directness of his statements," said Howard, "carried an inescapable ring of sincerity and conveyed a much more friendly feeling toward the U.S."[16] In constructing the image of a friendly Asian partner, a reasonable supposition is that the influential newspaperman had become an unwitting agent on behalf of Japan's foreign policy objectives.

Japan's embryonic campaign to charm American elites included a preliminary foray in cultural diplomacy. In March 1933, Ambassador Debuchi had recommended to Foreign Minister Uchida that Japan broaden its diplomacy to include cultural aspects as a way to improve relations. Toward this end, the Japanese consulate in New York organized a traveling exhibition of

Japanese modern art, which visited eleven cities, including Boston, Baltimore, Cincinnati, Milwaukee, and Los Angeles. Consul General Horinouchi Kensuke later reported to Uchida: "Despite the fact that the American public's feeling toward Japan got substantially worse due to the Manchuria and Shanghai incidents . . . the [exhibition] received an exceptional welcome at each place." The result, he asserted, is that the show "greatly contributed to easing up the [bad] feeling toward Japan." Horinouchi subsequently suggested that the Foreign Ministry stage large-scale exhibitions at Boston's Museum of Fine Art and New York's Metropolitan Museum.[17]

For the time being, however, resources for nontraditional diplomacy went toward the Chicago World's Fair, which opened in May 1933. On display in the Japanese pavilion was a subtle form of cultural propaganda aimed at legitimizing Japan's allegedly special role in Manchuria. Visitors entering the Japanese hall—more than three million did in 1933—first encountered a life-sized diorama of what supposedly represented the inside of a middle-class "Manchukuoan family" home. The exhibit also featured a large relief map of Manchuria, wired with a system of lights locating the coal, oil, and commercial areas. The fair's *Official Guidebook* noted, "The resulting development of the surrounding countries, due to the construction of the South Manchurian Railway, will represent the more serious industrial and engineering genius of the Japanese nation." According to the fair's director of operations, the Japanese pavilion did more than any other medium "to educate the great mass of the people in the U.S. as to what Japan really does mean."[18] Such a statement mimicked almost verbatim the Japanese government's aim to explain its "true intentions" and normalize an alternative order in East Asia.

"LET US CULTIVATE THE ROSES"

Tokyo's efforts to mend relations with the United States became far more persistent after Prime Minister Saitō reshuffled his cabinet in the fall of 1933. The most meaningful change was the replacement of Foreign Minister Uchida with Hirota Kōki. Hirota played a significant role in Japan's policy making in the mid-1930s, first as foreign minister for nearly two and a half years and then as prime minister, before reprising the part of foreign minister in June 1937. As a young man, Hirota had come under the influence of a right-wing group, Dark Ocean Society. The American press, however, came to perceive the fifty-five-year-old Hirota as a moderate, perhaps because his arrival coincided with the reassignment to Europe of blunt-talking Foreign Office spokesman Shiratori. In a full-page essay in the Sunday *New York Times*, for example, Sterling Fisher stated that "a new force of moderation entered Japanese political life when Koki Hirota walked into the Foreign

76   Chapter 3

Office." Photographs of the Diet juxtaposed with Japanese soldiers underscored the impression of mutually antagonistic elements. A caption read: "Rivals for the Supreme Power in Japan: The Lawmakers and the Military." Mass-circulation magazines were similarly disposed in their judgment. Hirota appeared on the cover of *Time*, which said the foreign minister "was popped into office before most Japanese militarists realized what was brewing."[19]

The American news media also looked favorably on the appointment in December 1933 of the affable Saitō Hiroshi as the new ambassador to Washington. Having spent fourteen years in the United States, the forty-seven-

Figure 3.4. Hirota Kōki, foreign minister (1933–1936, 1937–1938) and prime minister (1936–1937). (National Diet Library, Tokyo, "Historical Figures" website.)

year-old Saitō exuded an Americanized mien and liked to bandy about quips, bon mots, idioms, and baseball analogies. In a widely distributed AP article, Saitō described his appointment as a "cinch job," pointing out "there were no real differences between Americans and Japanese." He blithely declared his special mission was to "drink whiskey with good Americans." When an American newsman asked what he attributed his youthfulness to, Saitō replied, "Whiskey and soda—all afternoon—every afternoon." For his candid manner in talking to the press, he became known as the "indiscreet diplomat," a title in which he delighted. The *New York Herald Tribune* called Saitō's selection a "fortunate one," stating he was "one of the ablest and most modern-minded of the younger Japanese diplomats." Indeed, Saitō in suit and tie, casually dispensing colloquialisms, hardly cut the figure of a jingoist. And yet if this appearance were more deeply examined, one would have found a diplomat whose ideological bearings were consistent with his government's rough consensus regarding Japan's primacy in East Asia.[20]

Regardless, the appointments of Foreign Minister Hirota and Ambassador Saitō, combined with the reassignment of Shiratori and resignation of War Minister Araki Sadao (which Ambassador Grew described as "a victory for the liberals"), seemed to affirm that real change was taking place in Japan— change that boded well for the future of US-Japan relations and the postwar treaty system. As the influential nondenominational weekly *Christian Century* observed, "the signs multiply that conditions at Tokyo are undergoing a radical and fortunate transformation."[21]

Far Eastern Division Chief Stanley Hornbeck was not so certain about an overhaul, but he wanted to learn more. Shortly after Hirota was tapped as foreign minister, Hornbeck sent his assistant chief, Maxwell M. Hamilton, on a four-month fact-finding tour of East Asia. Hamilton, a Chinese language specialist, visited a host of major cities, including Tokyo, Osaka, Beijing, Shenyang, Harbin, Dalian, Tianjin, Shanghai, and Guangzhou. In Tokyo, Hamilton met with new Foreign Ministry spokesperson Amō Eiji, whom he knew from consul days in Guangzhou. Amō was especially curious about American attitudes regarding Manchuria. Hamilton reported, doubtless to Amō's delight, that the "Manchuria question" had disappeared from the front pages of American newspapers. Amō, in turn, explained that Japan was keen on improving bilateral relations and wondered aloud about goodwill visits. Hamilton was noncommittal, saying the "fundamentals of America policy with regard to Japan never changed." Certainly, Amō understood that to mean the Nine-Power Treaty and nonrecognition. The same day Foreign Minister Hirota also queried Grew about goodwill missions to America. Grew relayed the query to Secretary Hull, who responded that conversations were welcome but not goodwill missions.[22] From the start, both Hull and Hornbeck harbored a suspicion that goodwill visits reeked of propaganda.

Figure 3.5. Saitō Hiroshi, Japan's ambassador to the United States (1934–1939). (Library of Congress, Prints & Photographs Division, photograph by Harris & Ewing [reproduction number LC-DIG-hec-23873].)

Hamilton found the outward friendliness of Japanese officials and their desire for goodwill trips intriguing but not necessarily illuminating. He had traveled to Japan to make sense of the nation's political dynamics. Hamilton subsequently turned to longtime Tokyo resident Thomas Baty, a British legal scholar and advisor to Japan's Foreign Ministry, for some expatriate insight.

But even Baty, an inveterate defender of Japan, was uncommonly flummoxed. "Something less tangible and difficult to define" was taking place in Japanese politics, Baty told Hamilton.[23] In fact, it seems Baty was trying to comprehend for Hamilton (and himself) the evolving, somewhat inchoate, ideological justification for Japan's allegedly special role in Asia.

Hamilton received the clearest picture of Japanese thinking at the time from Vice Minister of Foreign Affairs and decided Pan-Asianist Shigemitsu Mamoru, who ironically had lost a leg the year prior in Shanghai from a bomb thrown by a Korean nationalist. The friendly Shigemitsu said the Japanese government believed relations with the United States were the most important among all nations, but that Japan's retreat from the postwar liberal system was irreversible. He dismissed the treaty system as "philosophy." Instead, Japan's policy in East Asia would be based on "practicalities," an analogue to the catchphrase "actual conditions." This perspective was consistent with Shigemitsu's recent comments to the editor of the American-owned *Japan Advertiser* that the Nine-Power Treaty "no longer responds to the realities of the situation" and that Japan's position in the region "is a special one."[24]

Shortly after Shigemitsu's comments, a Five-Ministers Conference (premier, foreign minister, and ministers of finance, army, and navy) gave policy substance to such views. For the first time, a Japanese cabinet articulated the outlines, however vaguely, of a regional order under Japanese leadership, involving not just Japan and Manchukuo but also China. The resultant "Foreign Policy of Imperial Japan" coincided with the rise of arguably the most influential Pan-Asianist group in Japan in the 1930s, the Greater Asia Association, whose membership included Foreign Minister Hirota. In an early tract, the GAA declared that "the heavy responsibility for Asia's reconstruction and reorganization rests on the shoulders of Imperial Japan."[25]

By the end of 1933, then, a more chauvinistic regionalism was strengthening among Japan's ruling elites even as the empire sought better relations with the United States. Over the next two years, under the stewardship of Foreign Minister Hirota, this contradictory trend congealed. Japan's charm offensive toward the United States intensified, and so did its illiberal declarations. Despite this contradiction, Japan's leadership remained convinced this circle could be squared through a campaign of friendly persuasion. Evidence suggests this approach was already making an impact, if not among cynics like Hornbeck, then among American journalists and foreign policy pundits. As a writer for *Forum* magazine observed, "We have had more than enough war talk [between Japan and the United States]. Now let us have some peace talk. . . . '[Goodwill] brings back a harvest of roses, instead of rows of bright bayonets and eyes glittering with hatred.' Let us cultivate the roses." One scholar of public opinion at the time claimed that "the great majority" of Americans concurred with that statement.[26]

Chapter 3

THE BOLD INCONGRUITY OF MR. HIROTA'S CHARM OFFENSIVE

On January 23, 1934, Foreign Minister Hirota fulfilled his parliamentary duty by presenting to the Diet an annual address on Japan's foreign relations. In retrospect, it was a remarkably forthright distillation of how Japan's leadership saw the world, and how it planned to conduct foreign affairs over the next several years. Consistent with efforts to recapture American sympathies, Hirota hailed the two countries' "traditional friendship" and dismissed tensions over Manchuria as a "temporary estrangement." At the same time, the foreign minister was uncommonly direct about Japan's conception for a new order in East Asia. In a dramatic salvo, Hirota referred to Japan as "the *only cornerstone* for the edifice of peace in Eastern Asia," and therefore it "bears the *entire burden* of these responsibilities." With more hope than conviction, Hirota said he was "confident the United States will not fail to appraise correctly Japan's position" in the region. Perhaps the most remarkable thing about the speech is that Hirota identified ideological divergence as the fateful breach between nations in the 1930s. "A conflict of ideas," Hirota stated candidly, "threatened to destroy international equilibrium at any moment."[27]

Ambassador Grew, who tended to see the world sunny-side up, focused on the friendlier aspects of Hirota's address. In a diary entry, Grew noted, "Hirota is genuinely doing his best to improve Japan's relations with foreign countries. . . . He has succeeded in creating a better atmosphere with the United States, mainly through keeping the military comparatively quiet." Shortly after, the ambassador observed that the "highest influences in the country are pacific" and that "a strong group of liberals in the country have been steadily working behind the scenes." Grew's analysis brimmed with unfounded assumptions. What did it mean at the time to be a Japanese moderate or a liberal? Steadily working behind what scenes? His conclusions seem to have been colored by conceit as well. "I can often plant ideas in Hirota's mind," wrote Grew, "and I find that some of these seeds readily take root."[28]

Nevertheless, in the early part of 1934, the bulk of evidence appeared to support Grew's views. Starting in February, Foreign Minister Hirota launched what must be described as nothing less than a full-blown diplomatic offensive to win over American hearts and minds, with the purpose of advancing Japan's foreign policy goals. The campaign had three facets: an exchange of "personal and informal" goodwill notes between Hirota and Secretary Hull, "unofficial" goodwill trips by Japanese cosmopolitans, and a state-sponsored cultural diplomacy.

On February 21, Hull received from Hirota a spirited pledge of friendship in the form of a personal note. "It is significant that ever since Japan and the United States opened their doors to each other exactly eighty years ago," remarked the foreign minister, "the two countries have always maintained a relationship of friendliness and cordiality." Hirota said Japan sincerely desired to establish peaceful relations with "her great neighbor across the Pacific." Hull subsequently returned the favor on March 3, though with the stipulation that the messages not be made public until March 21 (Hull wanted to distance the notes from the March 1 coronation of Pu Yi as emperor of Manchukuo).[29]

Editorials across the United States praised the goodwill notes as a promising break in tension, noting it was the first time since the fall of 1931 that Japan's foreign minister and the US secretary of state had communicated directly. Most conspicuous of all, observed foreign policy pundit T. A. Bisson, was a tendency to avoid talk about Manchukuo. Indeed, neither Hirota nor Hull mentioned the puppet state. From Bisson's perspective, Washington's nonrecognition policy may not have been discarded, but there also had been no "continued reiteration" of the doctrine. This was true, though State Department memos often assigned quotation marks to Manchukuo. Still, as Bisson and others noted, the exchange seemed to represent a general trend toward moderation in the Roosevelt administration's East Asian policy.[30]

A few weeks after the exchange of notes, Tokyo and Washington reaffirmed their friendly intentions in a transpacific broadcast over NBC Radio. Hull and Hornbeck offered goodwill greetings to Japanese listeners, and Ambassador Saitō spoke to American audiences. Hirota delivered a message through an American interpreter. The *New York Times* said the radio messages marked "another step in the rapprochement which began last month." The talk of a rapprochement must have been music to the ears of Hirota and other Japanese officials. It was a positive first step in a campaign meant to massage the American mindset into accepting a fait accompli in Manchukuo and appreciating Japan's "stabilizing influence" in East Asia.

A second layer of Tokyo's charm offensive involved dispatching eminent cosmopolitans to the United States on goodwill visits. The idea was to promote foreign policy objectives by employing individuals seemingly independent of the government, such as elder statesmen, business leaders, and academics. There was significant precedent in Japan for this form of public diplomacy, such as Baron Kaneko Kentarō's "unofficial" visit to America during the Russo-Japanese War.[31] The crucial difference in 1934 was that Japan's public diplomacy was conceived to justify its continental claims in the face of a novel liberal order.

Although Hirota had gotten the cold shoulder from Grew about such missions, the Saitō cabinet went ahead anyway in late February and sent Prince Tokugawa Iesato across the Pacific. Tokugawa's internationalist credentials were notable—delegate to the Washington Conference and president of both the Japanese Red Cross and America-Japan Society (AJS), a private organization founded in Tokyo in 1917 to promote mutual understanding.

For this reason, the amiable prince was known widely as "International Man." Tokugawa visited President Roosevelt, addressed a national radio audience from NBC's studios at the recently opened Rockefeller Center, and penned an op-ed in the *New York Times*, in which he asserted the United States and Japan were "overwhelmingly complementary." He also spoke at a dinner hosted by the Japan Society of New York, a pioneering analogue of the AJS, founded by American cosmopolitans in 1905. Although Japan-America Societies flourished in several American cities, the New York association was by far the most influential, enjoying greater access to political and cultural luminaries. Echoing Hirota, Tokugawa stressed that Japan desired peace and friendly relations with the United States. He also perpetuated the fiction of an independent Manchukuo, lauding its "rapid development" and, implicitly, Japan's civilizing mission. Tokugawa's dinner hosts responded in kind. Japan Society President Henry W. Taft believed that Japan and the United States were "increasingly making themselves understood to the other." Episcopal bishop James DeWolf Perry, meanwhile, flirted with an open sanction of Japan's regionalist ideology by recognizing "the heavy responsibilities which the Empire of Japan has undertaken for the promotion of peace on [her] own borders."[32]

As part of its informal diplomacy, the Japanese government also dispatched Matsukata Otohiko, a Harvard classmate and friend of President Roosevelt, and industrialist Asano Ryōzō, another Harvard graduate. Both men filled essential qualities to create an air of unsanctioned sincerity: private citizens with personal charm and some connection to the president. FDR met briefly with each of them; each repeated the theme of extolling bilateral friendship.

Hornbeck, however, had begun to smell a rat. In a memo to Undersecretary of State William Phillips, Hornbeck said he had been thinking over "the various communications made to us by Japanese officials" regarding the stream of goodwill visits. "For what purpose?" Hornbeck wondered. He told Phillips, "We ought not be surprised if it develops that the Japanese government is preparing to lay before the American government some definite project," which would indicate "to the world that there has been developed a new degree of cordiality or something in the nature of a rapprochement between their country and the United States." He recommended against goodwill missions.[33]

Despite Hornbeck's gift for sniffing out ulterior motives, Japan's Ministry of Foreign Affairs (MOFA) was already moving toward a form of soft power more nuanced than even goodwill visits. This was the ministry's determined venture into cultural diplomacy. Suggestions for a cultural demarche pointed to the expansion of cultural relations across national boundaries, which had sprung up in the late nineteenth century and blossomed in the 1920s. The Alliance Française (1883), which promoted French language and culture abroad, and the Carnegie (1911) and Rockefeller (1913) Foundations epitomized the private and voluntary approach in which the state remained a mostly peripheral bystander. In the aftermath of the First World War, international cultural relations boomed, aided by the organizational energies of the League of Nations. In 1922, for example, the league established the International Committee on Intellectual Cooperation, which promoted scholarly and cultural exchange. Toward these ends, Japan's Foreign Ministry inaugurated a league-affiliated committee on intellectual cooperation in 1926 and an independent Department of Cultural Affairs in 1927.[34]

What ultimately coalesced in Japanese official circles in the 1930s, however, was the creation of a state-sponsored organization employing unidirectional cultural tools for the express purpose of advancing foreign policy goals. Indeed, although the interwar years marked an increasing awareness among governments about the potential value of allocating resources to promote culture in foreign relations, what set apart MOFA's cultural strategy in 1934 was that it was conceived to overcome umbrage over the world's inaugural assault on the new liberal order.[35]

The result was the Society for International Cultural Relations (Kokusai Bunka Shinkōkai, or KBS), which opened its doors in Tokyo in April 1934 with a ceremony attended by Prime Minister Saitō. A diverse group of prominent Japanese politicians, business leaders, academics, and diplomats filled the society's roster. These included Prince Konoe (president of the House of Peers), Count Kabayama Aisuke (House of Peers), Baron Dan Inō (art professor and son of the late Mitsui head), Vice Foreign Minister Shigemitsu, Prince Tokugawa, and eminent scholar Anesaki Masaharu. Advisors included Foreign Minister Hirota and Viscount Ishii. Prince Takamatsu Nobuhito, the younger brother of Emperor Hirohito, became a key patron.

Despite residual historical confusion regarding the KBS's official association with the Japanese government, as best can be discerned by available evidence, the relationships and networks between government officials and KBS members in the 1930s were so intimate and cross-dutied that "semiofficial" and "state-sponsored" become blurred to the point of insignificance. At the same time, Japanese officials were not insensitive to the importance of creating the impression of institutional autonomy in order to maximize the efficacy of soft power strategies. As MOFA official Amō (Amau) Eiji later wrote in an official memo, propaganda should be as inconspicuous as possible (i.e., seemingly detached from state organs).[36] Congruent with this aim, MOFA stressed the KBS's "unofficial" orientation and favored cosmopolitan cultural ambassadors, especially those who had worked with league-related agencies.

From its inception, the KBS sought to legitimize the empire's regional primacy by providing "correct" and "accurate" views about Japan, especially to representative American elites. In other words, these were not just cultural dilettantes infatuated with art for art's sake. The lingering sting of world censure and political limbo of Manchukuo permeated the KBS prospectus, which delicately explained, "As international relations of the world grow in complexity," it was imperative for Japan "to promote the value and prestige of its own culture . . . so as to merit greater respect, affection, and sympathy on the part of other peoples." Comments by KBS officials echoed the conviction that the institutionalized use of culture could combat negative images abroad and advance Japan's foreign policy goals.[37]

Precisely how cultural charms could achieve such complex international objectives was addressed by KBS President Konoe Fumimaro. According to Konoe, "The culture of a nation [was] the key to an understanding of its people and their institutions." From Konoe's viewpoint, the apparent authenticity of culture signified "correct knowledge." When other peoples understood Japan "correctly," friendly relations would necessarily follow.[38] For the KBS, "correct understanding" meant appreciating Japan as a highly sophisticated civilization. Such an image not only contrasted with that of marauding militarists; on another level, it reinforced the more chauvinistic strain of Pan-Asianism—with its implication that the greatness of Japanese culture mandated an exceptional role for Japan in Asia. The KBS thus began laying the groundwork for myriad cultural projects, including art exhibitions, films, lantern slides for public lectures, a photo-illustrated magazine, and English-language publications extolling Japanese culture. Ironically, enough, however, on April 17, 1934—almost to the day the KBS opened its doors—an egregious lack of subtlety momentarily distracted from Japan's soft power strategy.

AMŌ'S "BOMBSHELL"

During one of his triweekly question-and-answer sessions with the foreign press, Foreign Office spokesman Amō casually dropped the illiberal "bombshell" that Japan was *wholly responsible* for peace in East Asia. Japanese officials in recent months had grumbled about proposed international developmental loans to the Nanjing government, but Amō now seemed to suggest that any foreign assistance would require Japanese authorization and that Japan would use force, if necessary, to implement its policy. As for the postwar treaties, "We must be the judges," he said. "[Treaties] will be respected, but there may be differences in interpretation of treaties."[39]

Foreign correspondents, interpreting Amō's comments as an assertion of Japanese hegemony in China, filed alarming reports back home. Questions abounded. For whom was Amō speaking? Was it an impromptu slip? American editorials were nearly unanimous in their condemnation of Japan. Foreign diplomats in Tokyo called the statement more "startling" than any declaration since the Twenty-One Demands. US and British officials avoided public comment, choosing instead to wait for a Japanese clarification. Prime Minister Saitō stated that Amō had "distorted" Japan's policy. Amid the confusion, Amō offered a supplementary statement on April 20, and the Japanese government released an "unofficial translation" of Amō's "unofficial statement." One week into the affair, uncertainty reigned; the government still had not commented officially on Amō's utterance.[40]

In private discussions with Grew, Hirota explained in confidence that Amō had indulged in "high flown language" without his approval, that the statement had been "mistranslated" and "misunderstood." In a subsequent report to Secretary Hull, Grew portrayed Hirota as a beleaguered statesman trying to stay afloat in chauvinist-infested waters, avowing that a public denial by the foreign minister "would have placed him in a thoroughly dangerous position." Grew was convinced that Hirota had not approved Amō's statement, which became known as the Amō Doctrine.[41]

The truth was far different. Amō, in fact, had orally summarized an Asianist-loaded cable that Hirota had written to Japan's minister in China only four days prior. As Hirota put it, "Japan has reached the point where it must endeavor with all its strength to carry out its mission in East Asia, regardless of whether or not other powers agree. . . . The maintenance of peace and order in East Asia . . . will naturally require Japan to act independently and on its own responsibility. Japan is resolved to realize completely this mission."[42] Moreover, on April 28, when the Japanese government officially clarified Amō's statement, it referred explicitly to Japan's "mission" and repeated that the empire was responsible for peace in East Asia. The clarification also referenced Hirota's forthright speech to the Diet in January. Hirota himself followed with a memorandum that, though softer in tone, nonetheless emphasized Japan's "special interests and responsibilities in Eastern Asia." And in Washington, Ambassador Saitō, while affirming Japan's commitment to the treaty system, repeated the mantra of Japan being "the stabilizing influence in the Far East."[43]

The Amō statement, therefore, was not a bombshell at all. Rather, it was the most candid expression in a series of recent statements in which Japan's leaders sought to gain acceptance of their vision for a Japan-guided order in East Asia. The episode also suggests that, despite a growing self-confidence about the empire's special regional role, Japan's civilian leaders remained cautious about frontal assaults on the new postwar system. This helps explain the motivation for Hirota's charm offensive at the time—to gain desired ends gradually through less abrasive means. In Hirota's words, he aimed "to conduct matters so as not to arouse diplomatic difficulties."[44]

On another level, Japanese officials continued to equate their regional ambitions with America's longtime hemispheric policy. The Asian Monroe Doctrine, as it was called, signaled that Tokyo's policy in East Asia paralleled Washington's claim of protective guardianship in the Western Hemisphere. As Viscount Ishii benignly framed it, "The United States has a special interest in the territorial integrity of South and Central America, but South and Central America do not suffer in any way from it. . . . Should not China likewise feel happy that her territorial integrity is guaranteed by the existence of Japan's special interest in her?"[45]

Japanese assertions of hemispheric parallelism, however, ran into a prickly American defensiveness. Henry Stimson, both as secretary of state and later outside government, expressed the representative American viewpoint, dismissing Japan's claim as "fantastic" and "ridiculous." According to Stimson, Japan's regional doctrine was aggressive while the Monroe Doctrine (1823) was proclaimed as a "defensive bulwark of local independence and self-government among the South American republics." But what about the recent history of American actions toward its neighbors to the south? In 1903 the United States had seized a canal zone in Panama, then followed that power play by sending troops into various Caribbean countries in the next two decades. The basis of these interventions had been Theodore Roosevelt's 1904 corollary to the Monroe Doctrine, by which the United States' self-proclaimed status as a "civilized" power gave it authority to intervene in the region in cases involving "chronic wrongdoing."[46] Was not Japan's version of the Monroe Doctrine, therefore, simply an updated reading of TR's paternalistic corollary, with emphasis on a great civilization's special responsibility in its respective region? It undeniably was. For Americans, however, the crux of the issue was temporal: that was then, this is now.

From the American perspective, the Great War had precipitated a genuine diplomatic revolution in the international system and rules of acceptable state behavior. As Stimson explained it, "In those days there was no Kellogg Treaty, no Nine-Power Treaty, and no Article X of the League of Nations." Similarly, Wilfred Fleisher, the American managing editor of the *Japan Advertiser* and correspondent for the *New York Herald Tribune*, while conceding comparisons between American actions in Panama and Japan's in Manchuria, maintained that the key difference was "the factor of time." When America intervened in Panama, said Fleisher, "there were no international commitments to stand in the way of the American Government." But now, "the peoples of the world have set their faith in a new order of which the treaties are a symbol." Which is why in December 1933 FDR had renounced his distant cousin's corollary and embraced President Hoover's Good Neighbor Policy toward Latin America.[47]

Despite these divergent views on hemispheric policies and international order, in the spring of 1934, Secretary Hull chose to follow Hirota's lead and pursue a calm exit from the Amō ruckus. Although the secretary reasserted American rights outlined in the Nine-Power Treaty, he nonetheless called attention to transpacific amity, asking American reporters, off the record, to refrain from writing stories that would irritate Japan. These were sensitive times, Hull seemed to say; Japan's government hung in the balance between moderates and militarists.[48]

The Chinese, meanwhile, were livid. Once again the Americans had invoked the sanctity of the Nine-Power Treaty only to treat it as a scrap of paper. In an essay in *Foreign Affairs*, former Kuomintang foreign minister Wang Zhengting blasted Washington and London for their limp responses to Japan's hegemonic pretensions, which he defined explicitly as "The Pan-Asiatic Doctrine of Japan." In disbelief, Wang wondered how the British and Americans could fail to grasp Japan's aggressive tendencies in the name of Asian leadership, calling it a "definite trend of Japan's continental policy." He predicted that Japan's "lifeline" would not "voluntarily stop at the borders of Manchuria." Remarkably, he unmasked Hirota's charm offensive, saying Japan would try to "consolidate her economic and military resources in 'Manchukuo' on the one hand, and, on the other, try to confuse world opinion by broadcasting benevolent intentions and her superficial achievements." Wang arrived at a prescient conclusion: "That which could have been nipped in the bud by a few firm actions in September 1931, was left to drift until it would have required sanctions to arrest it in 1933; and that which can still be stopped by sanctions today will be neglected to develop into a first-class war."[49] Wang's essay did not come out until October 1934. By that time Tokyo had been in damage control for almost six months to correct "misinformation" about Japan's intentions.

CHARM OFFENSIVE REBOOT

In Japan, evidence suggests a wide section of the press and political leadership believed the Amō incident had undone much of the good feeling brought about between Japan and the United States through Foreign Minister Hirota's systematic efforts.[50] Thus, almost immediately, Tokyo sought to recapture lost gains. Ambassador Saitō and the newly inaugurated KBS led the charge.

On May 16, Saitō, with an air of impending import, asked Secretary Hull to meet in secret at the latter's Washington residence, the Carlton Hotel. Hoping to engage in heart-to-heart discussions, Saitō asked Hull why the United States invariably tried to block Japan's "progress externally." Almost fifteen years Saitō's senior, Hull took the opportunity to go into a paternalistic lecture about progress. Hull told Saitō they were living in a "highly civilized age" and that Japan and the United States had a duty to work together as "trustees of the greatest civilization in history." Hull's point was clear enough. The postwar principles expressed the highest form of thinking about war and peace in human history—and Japan had spurned them. Come back to the fold, he seemed to say.[51]

Three days later, Saitō sought out Hull again. The ambassador offered felicitations from Hirota and then mostly endured another round of moralizing from Hull, who stated "there was considerable inquiry everywhere" whether Japan was trying to create "an overlordship of the Orient." During a third visit at the State Department, Saitō tried to sell Hull on a joint declaration in which each nation recognized spheres of influence in the Pacific. Hull was not buying. He told Saitō that in recent years Japan had acquired "a reputation for truculence and trouble making" and that it was "up to Japan to live down and remove these impressions."[52] Saitō expressed disappointment and departed. It was an inauspicious start in rebooting efforts to obtain American understanding for the legitimacy of Japan's claims in East Asia.

Removing truculent impressions, however, was the raison d'être of the Kokusai Bunka Shinkōkai. While Saitō reached out to Hull, the KBS hosted an informational reception at the Peers' Club in Tokyo, in honor of the foreign diplomatic corps. Ambassador Grew, noting the attendance of Prime Minister Saitō, Foreign Minister Hirota, and other important Japanese officials, informed Hull that "the prominence of the officers of the Society indicates the importance with which its program is regarded in Japan." Of significance, on May 17, KBS President Konoe Fumimaro embarked on a two-month journey to the United States to gauge American public opinion, clarify Japan's "true intentions," and lay the groundwork for cultural activities.[53] And he did so while creating the air of an unofficial visit by virtue of his attendance at his son's graduation from Lawrenceville, an exclusive preparatory school in New Jersey.

The forty-two-year-old Konoe (scion of the highest-ranked family within the illustrious Fujiwara clan of the old Kyoto court nobility) was a rising political star in a nation whose politics were built broadly and blandly around consensus making. Part of the attraction was Konoe's ancestry, another part was his rather tall height for a Japanese at the time (six feet), and yet another was his intellectual acumen and activity. Konoe had become involved in several prominent think tanks, authored a few noted essays on world politics, and was president of the House of Peers.

Like Matsuoka and Ishii before him, Konoe made stops in San Francisco, Chicago, Washington, New York, and Boston. It was an extraordinary visit. Konoe met with hundreds of prominent American political and business leaders, including an aged Edward M. House, President Wilson's close advisor at the Paris Peace Conference. The press described Konoe as a "liberal" who was "anxious for a real friendship between Japan and the United States." In Washington, Konoe and Ambassador Saitō attended a luncheon with President Roosevelt, Secretary Hull, and Hornbeck. Konoe also visited the House of Representatives, and Vice President John N. Garner introduced him on the floor of the Senate. Meanwhile, in Tokyo, in an attempt to parlay Konoe's amicable visit into something even grander, spokesman Amō said Foreign

Minister Hirota was open to meeting President Roosevelt in Honolulu to discuss bilateral relations. Nothing came of it, but it presaged a similar gambit by Konoe in the summer of 1941.[54]

In New York City, the Council on Foreign Relations hosted a dinner for Konoe, who later participated in a four-hour roundtable discussion with prominent journalists, including the managing editors of the *New York Times* and Scripps-Howard newspapers. Leading the discussion, and also interpreting for Konoe, was the US-based Japanese journalist K. K. Kawakami. Political scientist Rōyama Masamichi, a confidant and founding member of the influential public policy think tank Shōwa Research Association, also attended. Throughout the exchange, Konoe sought to instill in his American hosts a sense of Manchurian autonomy, with questions such as, "What do you think of the possibility that Mongolia may join Manchukuo?"—asked as if Japan were an innocent bystander to circumstances it categorically controlled.[55] Again, it suggests that Japan's brightest lights had become particularly deft at convincing themselves of geopolitical fictions.

The presumed benevolence of Japan's regionalist ideology is what prompted Konoe to report later that he had "endeavored to explain the truth" to financier Thomas Lamont. And that Japan had no desire to expand. Konoe doubtless meant every word of it. After all, was not Japan engaged in a noble mission in East Asia—managing uplift and delivering a positive good in the region, as only it could do? Still, the absence of doubt among Japanese officials about the more obvious contradictions in their worldview is striking. Perhaps the best answer is because the age of empire persisted. Despite the dawn of the new diplomacy, no critical thinker poring over world maps could miss the paradox of the still-sprawling British Empire. Or French rule in North Africa and Indochina. Or the Dutch in Indonesia. The same for US rule in the Philippines (though America's promise of eventual self-government for Filipinos came to fruition three months before Konoe's visit to the states).[56] The larger point, of course, is that Japan's contradictory aspirations were taking place in a world system that remained contradictory.

Konoe, in fact, in his late twenties, had eviscerated what he saw as the hypocrisy of an impending liberal order dominated by the Anglo-American powers. In 1918, before traveling to Paris as personal secretary to Prince Saionji (Japan's chief delegate to the Peace Conference), Konoe published an essay titled "Reject the Anglo-American-Centered Peace." The young Konoe blasted Wilson's internationalist agenda as a ruse for the United States and Britain to maintain the status quo in their favor. Although his postconference impressions tempered somewhat, Konoe never lost his indignation over what he perceived as a rigged system.[57] Six years after his visit to America, this paradoxically woven man would play a crucial role in hastening Japan's violent collision with the United States.

Despite his own confidence about Japan's "true intentions," Konoe found American perceptions of Japan sobering. In a "General Report" of his trip, shared with fellow KBS officials and distributed to the Japanese government, Konoe said Americans were mistrustful of Japan and sentimentally biased toward China. He was taken aback with how firmly "American public opinion" believed in the new postwar principles "formed at the Washington Conference and after," and the impression that Japan was a "violator of the Nine-Power Treaty." Believing tensions between Japan and the United States stemmed solely from misunderstanding, Konoe concluded that "greater efforts must be taken by Japan to make the American nation acquire a correct conception of Japan's standpoint."[58]

Konoe repeated his observations to a gathering in Tokyo of some two hundred leaders of Japanese public life. The prince also gave a flurry of high-profile newspaper interviews. The "American people," Konoe told the *Osaka Mainichi*, "are not well informed about the situation in the Far East," and therefore "misunderstanding results." He bemoaned American ignorance about "the real Japan." As for the underlying source of the problem, Konoe was unequivocal: Chinese propaganda had won over American hearts and minds. Accordingly, said the KBS president, Japan had to make its "culture and national ideals better known." The way to do this, said Konoe—whose gifts to Americans had included photo albums of Japanese gardens—was to "establish cultural institutions and libraries in large American cities."[59] Essentially, Konoe was advocating the use of "soft power" to sway public opinion and thereby win favor for what Japan had gained through "hard power." It was a curious inversion of Wilson's idealized belief in public opinion to prune power rather than reward it.

Shortly thereafter the KBS opened a branch office in New York City at the Consulate General of Japan on Fifth Avenue. In New York, the KBS could partner with an established network of transnational cosmopolitans, particularly the Japan Society of New York. With its roster of enthusiastic, internationally minded Americans, the Japan Society was uniquely situated to operate as a kind of KBS affiliate. In fact, consistent with the KBS prospectus, the Japan Society's annual report (1933) stated as axiomatic that "a knowledge and a study of the culture of a people tend toward better understanding and goodwill toward them." By promoting Japanese art and hosting cultural events, the Japan Society demonstrated an abiding faith in the idea that Japan's culture offered a window into the "true nature" of Japanese character.[60] The outstanding question, of course, was *what was that true nature?*

KBS Director Anesaki Masaharu, regarded as the father of religious studies in Japan, opportunely had answered that question in his book *Art, Life and Nature in Japan*—published, incidentally, by the Japan Society for its twenty-fifth anniversary in 1933. Not only did Anesaki make a compelling case for the singular beauty of Japanese aesthetics, he also argued that it suffused the nation *as a whole*. According to Anesaki, "To a remarkable degree Japanese art enters into the daily life of the people."[61] The true nature of Japanese character, then, was a uniquely cultivated people. Anesaki's thesis of pervasive refinement became an important KBS theme. Importantly, it implicitly bolstered Japan's metanarrative about the nation's mission as an enlightened civilization mandated to lead Asia. In June, Anesaki traveled to the United States on behalf of the KBS to discuss his book and promote Japanese culture. The KBS also distributed its first series of publications and in July welcomed eighty American college students to Tokyo for the inaugural American-Japanese student conference.

The appointment of former navy minister Okada Keisuke in July 1934 as Japan's prime minister further bolstered the KBS message that the nation's guiding influences were reasonable and respectable. Although Okada unequivocally endorsed the fiction of Manchukuo independence, he was hailed by American commentators as a political "moderate" largely because he was associated with the navy's "treaty faction." Perhaps the most popular endorsement of Okada came from the premier himself, via an interview in *Literary Digest*, a popular newsmagazine read by more than one million Americans. Leading questions resulted in utterly predictable replies, such as the following:

Q: You are democratic in political faith?

A: Yes, I believe in the people.

Q: Peace is Japan's uppermost political ideal?

A: It is our uppermost ideal and our most resolute practical purpose.

Q: Do you expect friendly collaboration ultimately among Japan, Manchukuo, and China?

A: We strive untiringly toward that end.

Hirota Kōki, retained by Okada as foreign minister, also was interviewed, with similar results:

Q: You deem Japanese-American peace impregnable?

A: I do.

Q: Do you expect another war?

A: No, I expect peace.

Q: Do you believe in democracy?

A: I do.[62]

Such uncritical engagement was especially striking because the interviewer was the highly respected Edward Price Bell, longtime correspondent for Frank Knox's *Chicago Daily News*. Perhaps the key point is that if the renowned Bell accepted Manchukuo as a fait accompli, if not a sovereign state, then Americans likely were warming up to the idea. If so, a reasonable assumption is that Japan's charm offensive was making an impact. As if sensing a positive correlation between soft power and better bilateral relations, the Okada cabinet boosted the government's share of KBS funding from 49 percent in 1934 to 61 percent in 1935.[63]

Of particular significance among new KBS initiatives was the society's sponsorship of a glossy propaganda quarterly, *NIPPON*. Launched in October 1934 by Natori Yōnosuke, a twenty-four-year-old wunderkind who had studied design in Germany, the Bauhaus-influenced *NIPPON* was a striking example of the new photojournalism. Attractive cover art opened up to cutting-edge photomontages and content that acclaimed Japan's traditional arts as well as its modern amenities. Articles on Japanese literature, painting, theater, gardens, and temples mingled with features on Japanese architecture, film, broadcasting, rail travel, and sports.[64]

In *NIPPON*'s inaugural issue, Prince Konoe introduced the KBS, saying the group aimed to provide "a correct grasp of Japan" through the "time-honored culture of which Japan boasts." Here, again, was the premise that a nation's innermost character was revealed through culture, with the attendant hope that readers would make critical connections; namely, that the refined splendor of Japanese civilization meant that East Asia was in good hands under Japan's leadership. If such ideological-geopolitical linkages seem like a stretch to modern readers, let us consider the remarks of KBS Director Count Kabayama Aisuke. Writing in the second issue of *NIPPON*, which Ambassador Grew forwarded to Secretary Hull, Kabayama declared that ignorance about Japan "is regrettable in as much as the world interest demands—especially since the outbreak of the Manchurian Incident of 1931—that Japan be known and understood." Such notions were made explicit on the cover of *NIPPON*'s fourth issue, which claimed to present "actual life and events in modern Japan and the Far East." Foreign Minister Hirota authored an article in which he encouraged readers to "study Japan more closely, more diligently, and more seriously" since Westerners had "so far failed to comprehend fully and correctly the character of our state."[65]

The eternal challenge for Tokyo was whether KBS programs and other soft power initiatives could compete with the blunt force of power politics. In October 1934, for example, the Japanese and American press focused their attention on the opening of preliminary naval talks in London. The Washington and London naval treaties were set to expire in December 1936, so these preliminary discussions among the three major naval powers were meant to lay the groundwork for renewal. In Japan, navy hard-liners reiterated that the 10:6 tonnage ratios humiliated Japan and imperiled its security. Moreover, from their view, the strategic calculations of the 1920s were no longer relevant—technological advances had increased the cruising radius of ships, and the carrier was emerging as an integral warship of the modern navy. For this reason, momentum grew for abrogation.[66] The Okada government subsequently dispatched chief delegate Rear Admiral Yamamoto Isoroku to London with the minimum demand of parity.

In the United States, President Roosevelt reprised the argument that every nation's security was best served by the treaty limits. In fact, for Japan, the thirteen years since the Washington Naval Conference had augmented the empire's security in an unexpected way: Japan had built up to treaty strength; the United States had not, thus creating an effective tonnage ratio of 10:8. And though the US Congress in March 1934 had granted Roosevelt's request to authorize monies allowing the administration to build up to treaty limits, fulfillment would not be completed until 1942.[67] America's delegation subsequently arrived in London urging the powers to renew the treaties with the same self-denying strictures in place.

The preliminary conference instead became a showcase for ideological estrangement. Although each side agreed to sever political questions from strategic considerations, the two were inextricably linked. Japan's regionalist ideology increasingly required preponderant power in the western Pacific, and Washington sought to limit such power and provide "adequate support" to the Nine-Power Treaty. Avoiding discussion about underlying ideological imperatives merely prolonged the inevitable—no deal would get done. Talks meandered until mid-December and then abruptly ended. On December 29, 1934, Ambassador Saitō informed Secretary Hull that Japan intended to terminate the treaties. Hull expressed "genuine regret," saying the naval accords had been achieved by a "community of effort."[68] In other words, they were evidence of the apparently salutary effect of liberalism's cooperative engagement and "orderly processes." If the parley's failure was not altogether unexpected, the resultant dour mood nonetheless hung in stark contrast to the standing ovations Hughes, Tokugawa, and Briand received in 1921 and the spirit of cooperation that MacDonald, Hamaguchi, and Hoover acclaimed in their radio hookup in 1930.

***

The intervention of power politics brought into sharp focus the complexity and tension inherent in the US-Japan relationship since the Manchurian crisis. For Japan, open discussions on contentious issues presented a formidable challenge to its program of friendly persuasion and aesthetic representation. For one thing, it was far more difficult to control the narrative of unwieldy power politics. Another challenge involved American reception, and neither side fully appreciated its ramifications. Specifically, a disconnect began to form between the desired goals of Japan's charm offensive and the ultimate impact on American perceptions. To repeat, Japanese officials engaged the United States with goodwill notes, emissaries, and cultural diplomacy in hopes of advancing the empire's foreign policy goals—namely, to gain acceptance of Manchukuo as a sovereign nation and Japan's primary role as the "stabilizing influence" in East Asia. Early indications suggest that Americans like Ambassador Grew were genuinely affected by Japanese geniality and impressed by the nation's high culture. But contrary to Japan's desired ends, Grew and other Americans were not therefore more likely to accept Japanese primacy in Asia.

Instead what happened is that Japan's contradictory signals between its charm offensive and aggressive policies like naval treaty renunciation tended to reinforce American assumptions of a great divide in Japan between cosmopolitan "moderates" and chauvinistic "militarists" on Japanese primacy in East Asia—with the consequent hope that moderates one day would return Japan to the cooperative diplomacy it practiced before the Manchurian crisis. This, of course, was the *opposite* direction Japan's so-called moderates were taking their nation. With neither Americans nor Japanese grasping the confusion between intention and reception, in 1935 Japan intensified its soft power initiatives, and American commentators looked for signs that "moderates" were in the ascendance.

·

Chapter Four

The High Tide of Cultural Diplomacy (1935–1936)

The impasse at the preliminary naval talks in London amounted to a partial tearing away of the veil of rapprochement that had begun to appear in US-Japan relations. With its stated intention of terminating the naval treaties, Japan delivered another blow to the liberal treaty system. And yet, the deadlock did not end in volleys of recrimination or angry retreat. Ambassador Saitō did his best to soothe anxieties in Washington by promising that Japan had no plans to embark on a naval building binge. To be sure, Division Chief Hornbeck, wary as ever, asserted in a memo on January 3, 1935, that there was a "more obvious possibility" (not probability) of war with Japan than any other country. Ambassador Grew, however, remained fixated on the alleged militarist-moderate dichotomy. Just before the new year, he stated to Secretary Hull that Foreign Minister Hirota would steer Japan "into safer and saner channels" if left unhindered by the military. Later he told Hull, "The cleavage between the liberal school of thought on one hand and the chauvinistic or military school of thought on the other is marked. . . . Hirota may be classed with the Liberals." In fairness to Grew, the stolid Hirota often spoke in benign generalities. In January the foreign minister perfunctorily described Japan "as the stabilizing force in East" and spoke of "a growing trend among the Chinese people to appreciate the true motives of Japan."[1]

By the start of 1935, relations between Japan and the United States could safely be described as guarded and uncertain, with each side holding out hope for encouraging signs. Again, for the Americans, this would mean signs of resilience among Japanese "moderates" and a turn toward cooperative diplomacy. For the Japanese, it would entail evidence that Americans recognized the legitimacy of Japan's paramount leadership in East Asia. As we have seen, in the wake of the Manchurian crisis, Japanese officials sought to finesse American opinion through soft power strategies. These efforts intensified in 1935, especially Tokyo's commitment to a vigorous cultural diplomacy. The Kokusai Bunka Shinkōkai (Society for International Cultural Relations) sponsored a number of expansive cultural initiatives aimed at American elites, including art exhibitions at the Metropolitan Museum of Art in New York and the Museum of Fine Arts in Boston, and organized an exclusive garden tour in Japan. American audiences greeted KBS programs with enthusiasm, and critical reviews and general-interest articles proffered images of a society imbued with a profound sense of artistic sophistication.

At the same time, a curious and complementary dynamic developed between the KBS-directed message of Japanese cultural refinement and American accounts of Japan as a vibrantly modern nation. Specifically, in the mid-1930s, American travel writers and correspondents in Japan commented self-satisfyingly on the proliferation of American-style department stores and automobiles, American fashions, Hollywood films, jazz clubs, and, perhaps most striking of all, a singular passion for America's national pastime—baseball. Such disarming images of Americanized mass consumerism and mass culture tended to reinforce the perception that there existed within Japanese society kindred spirits with whom the United States could find common ground and coexist peacefully.

In other words, the positive correlation between Japanese refinement and modernity lent credence to the moderate-militarist binary, which underpinned hopes among some American observers for an alternative course in US-Japan relations. Such dualistic perceptions were premised, however, on flawed assumptions about Japanese politics in the 1930s, especially an ignorance about the pervasive influence of regionalist thinking. The result was a topsy-turvy disconnect: on one hand, American diplomats and pundits pinned their hopes on individuals like Hirota, Konoe, Shigemitsu, Ambassador Saitō, and an inchoate group of Japanese liberals "working behind the scenes" to return Japan to 1920s internationalism; on the other hand, Hirota, Konoe, Saitō, Shigemitsu, and others hoped US officials would recognize the sovereignty of Manchukuo and Japanese primacy in East Asia. Until the summer of 1937, this geopolitical-cultural brew was as intriguing as it was deceptively hopeful. Japanese art, Nō robes, Zen gardens, baseball, jazz, and Hollywood films mingled peculiarly with Japanese militancy in North China and more overtly hegemonic declarations by Japan's government. A failed coup in Tokyo by the army's Imperial Way faction only magnified the seeming mystification of East Asian affairs.

The High Tide of Cultural Diplomacy (1935–1936) 97

"THERE WILL NEVER BE A WAR WITH JAPAN"

The intensification of soft power interactions between Japan and the United States in the mid-1930s can be traced to the end of 1934, when a team of major-league baseball all-stars toured Japan. Although the barnstorming tour was the brainchild of private American and Japanese promoters—and represented an unofficial form of *American* cultural diplomacy—the exhibition was most significant for its impact on American perceptions of Japan. In November 1934, Americans came face-to-face with a country in which the "All-American" sport appeared to be equally popular, if not more so, a country where Japanese fans revered major leaguers, Japanese players displayed keen talent, and youngsters played ball at six o'clock in the morning.

A distinguishing element of the 1934 exhibition was the participation of American icon Babe Ruth.[2] Despite having announced his retirement after the 1934 season (prematurely, as it turned out), the thirty-nine year-old Ruth maintained a mystical hold over the American public. The explanation was simple: Ruth had single-handedly lifted professional baseball to new heights with his proclivity for hitting home runs. As a result of Ruth's luster, the press covered the 1934 exhibition with special interest, thereby bringing far more Americans into close contact with a baseball-crazy Japan. The fourteen-member American squad, which included six future Hall of Famers, played seventeen games against a Japanese team of mostly college all-stars.

When the American ballplayers arrived on November 2, the *New York Herald Tribune* headline proclaimed, "100,000 Acclaim Ruth at Tokio [Tokyo], Halting Traffic to Pay Tribute." Most major dailies, such as the *Chicago Tribune*, *San Francisco Chronicle*, and *Cleveland Plain Dealer*, drew from the same AP story, which said Japan's "rabid baseball fans" jammed both sides of the Ginza, Tokyo's famous thoroughfare. Wire photos showed a grinning Ruth riding in an open car, holding American and Japanese flags, swarmed by Japanese fans. *Sporting News* said Ruth "autographed so many baseballs that he could no longer write."[3] The words and images that arrived from Japan and adorned the news kiosks in American cities or the breakfast tables of American homes looked more like a hero's ticker-tape parade down Broadway than Yankees in a land allegedly overrun by fascists.

It was widely reported that the first four games at Tokyo's Meiji Stadium, with a seating capacity of 65,000, were sold out three weeks in advance. According to the AP, the first contest, which Ambassador Grew and his wife attended, "opened with ceremonies akin to those that start a World Series." Throughout the tour, the press remained riveted on Japan's impassioned welcome for the visiting all-stars. A week into their visit, Ruth and other players paused to discuss events in a transpacific broadcast. Speaking to Americans from Tokyo over NBC radio, Ruth waxed on the warm reception and Japan's love of the American game. Nationally syndicated sportswriter

Figure 4.1. Babe Ruth with Japanese batboys in Osaka, Japan, 1934. (Associated Press.)

Jimmy Powers claimed Ruth's fame had spread throughout Japan. "In the newsreels," wrote Powers, "we see him walking the narrow streets of Tokyo, Osaka, and Nagasaki, and as he walks, round-headed children swarm in his wake. Their elders line the curbs with shining eyes." Connie Mack, baseball's elder statesman and tour impresario, later described to Americans what he called the "prize story of the lot." Mack recalled that when the team arrived in the city of Kokura it was "raining pitchforks," so the players settled down in their hotel for a quiet afternoon. Before long, they were told that seventeen thousand fans were waiting for them. In disbelief, off they went to the ballpark. "Lou Gehrig was in left field wearing rubber boots," said Mack, and "Babe and the other boys went to the plate with parasols over their heads. It was the strangest ball game I ever saw."[4]

The totality of mass media accounts told a poignant story of traffic-halting parades, elaborate pregame ceremonies, fans swarming Ruth—vivid, flattering images connoting cultural affinity. Baseball, as Elmer Berry's *Philosophy of Athletics* (1927) asserted, was "peculiarly American in its temperament and psychology." Sportswriters routinely propagated the notion that baseball was culturally particular—something *inherently* American. And yet here was the voice of Ruth, the most vaunted player in the history of professional baseball, singing the praises of Japanese fans on national radio. Here was *Literary Digest*, the popular weekly newsmagazine, proclaiming that the Japanese "eat, drink, and sleep" baseball.[5] Here was a seemingly significant segment of Japan in love with one of the quintessential symbols of the "American way of life." Was there not something significant to this?

Various American observers answered affirmatively, believing the United States could find common understanding with any people who had adopted the allegedly democratizing "national pastime" as their own. One popular sports monthly editorialized that Japan's exuberant reception ought to receive more attention than the "scareheads of Japan's increasing navy and *supposed* militaristic aims." And Powers wrote, "Psychologists say it is impossible for an Occidental to comprehend the involved superstructure of the Nippon Mind. I suppose that is all very true, but a common ground must exist somewhere. After all, the Bronx mechanic in the Yankee Stadium and the brass worker in the Meiji bleachers bask under identical suns and canonize the same outfielders." The most striking comment, however, came from Mack a few months after the tour. Japan's raucous welcome prompted the still-awestruck manager to go so far as to proclaim "there will never be a war with Japan."[6] Again, underlying such a claim was the notion that the "cult of the sword" and the "cult of the bat" entailed mutually exclusive fanaticisms.

In lockstep with American commentators was the KBS's ubiquitous Prince Tokugawa Iesato, who added official Japanese gloss to the narrative of cultural compatibility. In a popularly distributed AP news story, Tokugawa was quoted as telling American and Japanese luncheon guests: "Between two great peoples, able really to understand and enjoy baseball, there are no national differences which cannot be solved in a spirit of sportsmanship."[7] Tokugawa thus suggested that baseball, like art, represented a more authentic expression of national character. In that case, Americans could take comfort in Japan's leading role in Asia.

While Tokugawa was extolling the allegedly deeper meanings of US-Japan diamond diplomacy, he and his colleagues at the KBS also were preparing for the organization's first major art exhibition in the United States as well as an exclusive tour of Japanese gardens. Japan's program of soft power, with its goal of avoiding "international misconception of Manchurian-like incidents from happening again," was about to burst forth in full bloom.[8]

NŌ ROBES, ZEN GARDENS, AND "MR. AND MRS. AMERICA"

Before 1934 came to a close, KBS Director Anesaki Masaharu spoke at the Peers' Club in Tokyo. Anesaki wanted to clarify the methods and mission of the young cultural organization. He noted that some officials believed the promotion and flaunting of Japan's culture abroad risked being perceived as undignified. Anesaki disagreed. He said the goal of the KBS was "enlightened nationalism," which aimed to make Japan "exactly known" rather than merely admired. Also, for ultimate impact, Anesaki explained it was important that the KBS consider a country's "status and power in the world," and that the organization should target the "intellectual ranks, especially scholars and educators . . . [and] churches and women's clubs." The idea was to impress upon the pillars of American society the grandeur of Japanese civilization, including (per the era's gendered presumptions) the wives of powerful men.[9]

Anesaki's principles were deftly applied at the highbrow exhibition of Nō robes at the Metropolitan Museum of Art (Met) in New York. The KBS footprint was most conspicuous in facilitating privately loaned, rare artifacts. As the Met's *Bulletin* proudly announced, this was the first time private Japanese collectors had participated in any such exhibition in America. The KBS also donated a model of a Nō theater stage. The complementary relationship between the KBS and the Japan Society also shone through, with Baron Dan Inō working closely with Louis Ledoux and the curators at the Met. The art critic for the *New York Times* hailed the Nō robes as "exquisite," "incredibly beautiful," "brilliant," and a "gorgeous spectacle." Most important, for the purposes of the KBS, Baron Dan claimed that the show generated an "unforeseen degree of [American] sympathy and goodwill." KBS General Secretary Aoki Setsuichi, meanwhile, wrote to Vice Foreign Minister Shigemitsu and said the textile exhibition "received extremely good feedback." Aoki included a translation of a glowing newspaper review.[10]

With eyes on similarly propitious publicity, shortly after the Nō exhibition, the KBS organized what correspondent Hugh Byas called the "the most ambitious social experiment Japan has yet made in the cultivation of American friendship." In May 1935, KBS officials welcomed more than one hundred "socially prominent women" of the Garden Club of America to Japan for a three-week, all-expense-paid tour of the nation's most celebrated landscape gardens in Tokyo, Yokohama, Hakone, Nagoya, Kyoto, Nara, and Osaka.[11]

In addition to guided tours of gardens in private villas and public temples and shrines, the American guests were treated to a series of scintillating cultural events, including a Nō drama in Tokyo, a kabuki performance in Osaka, a bunraku puppet show and geisha concert in Kyoto, and a tea ceremony. The KBS also arranged a garden party hosted by Emperor Hirohito's younger brother, Prince Takamatsu (which Premier Okada attended), a reception by Foreign Minister Hirota, and afternoon tea at the homes of twelve distinguished families in Nagoya.

The KBS reception committee, it seems, spared no expense or detail to deepen the American visitors' experience: mayors welcomed the Garden Club members in nearly every city, hotel lobbies were "transformed into

Figure 4.2. Japanese Costume: Nō Robes and Buddhist Vestments, the Metropolitan Museum of Art, Wing D, Gallery 6, Floor II, February 19–April 14, 1935. (Image copyright © The Metropolitan Museum of Art. Image source: Art Resource, NY.)

gardens," menus were "attractively decorated," and American and Japanese flags fluttered conspicuously together throughout the trip. KBS officials also recruited seventy-two Japanese women to accommodate the American guests and edify them on the finer points of Japanese customs and gardening principles.[12] Additionally, the KBS presented each Garden Club member with the specially published *Art of the Landscape Garden in Japan* (a 245-page scholarly work, elegantly bound in hand-painted white silk) and reproduced the tour itself with a handsome photographic book comprising twenty-one high-quality plates and descriptions of the various gardens. Finally, in a magnanimous coda, the KBS compiled a photographic diary, chronicling every day of the visit.

Beyond the great lengths to which KBS officials went in hopes of making an indelibly favorable impression on Americans, what stands out about the privileged tour is again the society's targeting of select elites who were culturally predisposed to KBS charms. KBS officials regarded Garden Club members—many of whom had attended the Nō show at the Met—as women of "high cultural attainment," associated with America's ruling class. At a KBS directors' meeting, Kabayama Aisuke discussed this importance, saying the visitors were the "wives of super rich people who have jobs of great responsibility." He confessed that because of Japan's "strange feelings toward America lately," the KBS hosts were careful "not to spill even a drop of water."[13]

The exquisite gardens and carefully managed social events offered a compelling stage for national coiffing, in which a captive audience, generously attended to, drank deeply from Japan's cultural well. Prince Tokugawa hinted at Japan's larger designs, telling the visiting Americans "that through the study and appreciation of our gardens" they would come to know Japanese people "more intimately than in any other way." Doubtless, no small number of the American delegation, representing more than fifty garden clubs from nearly every state, returned home as newly minted emissaries of Japan's cultural diplomacy. Indeed, a few months after the visit, the *Bulletin of the Garden Club of America* published a glowing, forty-one-page summary, proclaiming that "one hundred enthusiastic pilgrims will carry a mes-

Figure 4.3. Garden Club of America members being welcomed by Japanese schoolchildren to Horyuji Temple in Nara, Japan. (A Photographic Diary of the Visit of the Garden Club of America to Japan, Cornelius J. Hauck Botanical Collection, Cincinnati Museum Center.)

sage of good will and friendship for Japan to the large organization of seven thousand members." Garden Club President Sarah Bulkley, speaking on behalf of the delegation, said the tour was "dreamlike and wonderful" and "one of the greatest experiences and privileges of our lives."[14]

From the KBS's perspective—based on "the piles of grateful letters received"—the visit was an unmitigated success. Kabayama called the results "superb." The KBS's official organ optimistically stated that "[the] visit of so many ladies representing the best of America's culture and society has contributed a great deal towards establishing better relations and friendship between the United States and Japan." Ambassador Grew, meanwhile, alluded to the Garden Club visit in a cable to Secretary Hull and, consistent with his binary analysis, referred to the KBS as "under the scholarly direction of a notably liberal tinge."[15]

At times, the breadth of Japan's soft power strategies went beyond the purview of the KBS. Certainly the most bizarre manifestation was that of the "Mr. and Mrs. America" visit to Japan, which followed in the footsteps of the Garden Club tour. On June 9, 1935, two life-sized, Caucasian-looking dolls named "Mr. and Mrs. America" set sail from New York for a two-month "guided" tour of Japanese cities. The doll tour was the brainchild of Japan's Board of Tourist Industry, which had connections with the KBS. After receiving a wild welcome at a jam-packed Tokyo Station, the dolls, according to the *New York Times*, "checked into" the bridal suite at the Imperial Hotel, received an official welcome from the city's mayor at Hibiya Public Hall (Tokyo's equivalent to Carnegie Hall), "bowed" at the gate of the Imperial Palace, and then "visited" Premier Okada and Foreign Minister Hirota. They returned to New York dressed in Japanese kimonos, their luggage bulging with gifts from Japanese officials, cities, and institutions. A letter from the mayor of Tokyo expressed hope that the "time-honored friendship" between the United States and Japan would be "further cemented by the dolls' goodwill mission."[16]

Although it is not easy to measure the impact of goodwill tours in which wax dolls call upon ministers of state, Japanese officials clearly embraced the tour as a meaningful gesture of amity that would enhance US-Japan relations. Ambassador Grew took note in his diary, saying he believed the trip, despite its gimmickry, would promote mutual understanding and spur American travel to Japan. In fact, from 1933 to 1935, Japan's collective efforts to recapture favorable world opinion seemed to be making a tangible imprint: Japan's Tourist Board recorded an annual 20 percent increase in foreign travel to Japan, with Americans topping the list.[17]

GIANTS AND JAZZ

Another cultural initiative outside the purview of the KBS, though not its core objectives, involved a touring squad of Japanese ballplayers to the United States. After Babe Ruth and fellow major leaguers visited Japan, *Sporting News* suggested that a Japanese team should tour the United States to show Americans a Japan that "wears the same clothes, plays the same game and entertains the same thoughts. In other words, that we are all brothers."[18] Japanese organizers were listening. In the spring of 1935, Japan's first ever professional baseball team, the recently established Dai Nippon Giants (Tokyo Giants), journeyed to the United States to play against minor league teams from California to Ohio. Over the course of four months and 104 games, numerous Americans had the rare opportunity to see Japanese ballplayers in action in their hometowns. Based on newspaper coverage of the tour, Americans came away with a decidedly positive image of the foreign barnstormers, one teeming with the spirit of cultural affinity. The press was unanimous in its praise: the Japanese loved the game, could play ball, and showed supreme sportsmanship. Baseball, it seemed, was not just the national pastime, but the transnational pastime.

The Tokyo Giants anchored in San Francisco in March 1935. There to greet them was the familiar face of Lefty O'Doul, manager of the Pacific Coast League's San Francisco Seals. O'Doul had participated in a previous tour to Japan and conducted a series of instructional clinics. Aided by O'Doul's cultural prompts, Japanese politeness—not militarism—became the talk of the town. In a preview story of the Giants' contest against the Seals, the *San Francisco Chronicle* featured Japanese civility under the curious headline "O'Doul Fears Politeness of Japanese Ballplayers." The *Chronicle* said there was some concern that one of the Seals' "uncouth hirelings" might interpret Japanese politeness as a sarcastic "rib." After much anticipation in the local press, the visitors made a sparkling debut, without incident, against the Seals and its star player, twenty-year-old local hero Joe DiMaggio. The *Chronicle* said a large and enthusiastic crowd "wildly applauded" every one of the Giants' good plays. The touring Japanese team extended this success—and attendant favorable press—throughout their trip.[19] Newspapers in places like Spokane, Pocatello, Salt Lake, Fargo, Kalamazoo, Flint, Milwaukee, and Madison drew attention to the Giants' incomparable sportsmanship and spirited play. (They also won nearly 70 percent of their games.)

Japanese sportsmanship—the embodiment of "fair play"—most enthralled American sportswriters and spectators, particularly the Giants' uncommonly polite habit of doffing their caps and bowing to umpires. A popularly circulated press photo of the gesture (actually, a conscious publicity stunt) prompted the *Salt Lake Tribune* to comment, "No wonder the umpire looks surprised. The poor maligned fellow who stands behind the plate gets nothing but courtesy." As for Japanese players' diamond skills, the paper stated the Japanese pitcher's fastball "was the best seen in these parts in a long, long time." A columnist for the *Milwaukee Sentinel* declared that the Japanese "play the game as well as we do in this country." In Madison, the *Capital Times* observed wryly that the record-breaking crowd was "distinctly partisan"—it pulled for the Japanese.[20]

Certainly a degree of underdog psychology informed that partiality; nonetheless, in light of historical claims that Japan's popularity among Americans declined rapidly in the 1930s, evidence from the tour suggests that perceptions of Japan in the mid-1930s were more complex. Stories that adorned the sports and society pages of newspapers and magazines often offered a portrait of cultural kinship and forces within Japanese society seemingly at odds with militarism. As one letter to the *Los Angeles Times* put it, the Tokyo Giants tour, together with many of the other cultural activities, was proof that Japan's "warlords do not have it all their way."[21]

American travel writers in Japan sent home the same message of kindred spirits. Indeed, some of the most striking cultural information received by American audiences about Japan in the mid-1930s was that of a nation both captivated and transformed by a vibrant, mass consumer society. Stories in middle-class slick magazines like *Saturday Evening Post* and *Collier's* described bustling Japanese cities with elegant department stores, Hollywood films, and jazz clubs. A writer for *Good Housekeeping* went so far as to tell readers that the Japanese "outmodern modern." Tokyo's bright lights played a decisive role in that surprise. Nearly seventy years before audiences were wowed by the neon-lit scenes in Sofia Coppola's *Lost in Translation*, J. P. McEvoy, writing in the *Saturday Evening Post*, said "Tokyo at night looks like an explosion in a match factory." *Scribner's* similarly remarked, "Not even Broadway achieves the chromatic splendor of the Ginza's neon signs." Moreover, Japanese modernity, it seemed, carried a distinctly American flavor. "Tokyo," marveled one writer, "is crammed with motor-cars, nearly all American." Indeed, 90 percent of automobiles in Japan came from the United States.[22]

But it was the living and breathing side of modernity that presented the most conspicuous surprises. *Fortune* magazine said "the Japanese takes to Metropolitan existence like a duck to soup." An article in *Harper's* claimed the Japanese are "the world's coming cosmopolites." The nation's younger generation, reported American writers, had gone head over heels for modernity. McEvoy correctly explained that the Japanese had coined abbreviated words—*mobo* (modern boy) and *moga* (modern girl)—to describe young devotees of the new era. "The girls have their bobbed hair," he said, "wear snappy dresses copied from the latest movies, and every last one of them can foxtrot as any American girl. The *mobos* have their hair plastered down slick, their shoulders padded out, and swoop all over [dance floors]." Japanese women, in particular, said American commentators, were exceedingly fashion conscious. The *Washington Post* remarked that young Japanese women were "completely and often quite becomingly, outfitted in American-style clothes."[23] The emergent portrait was that of a young generation devoid of *kimono*, *kabuki*, and *kakemono*, where the American Dream appeared to be eclipsing the Rising Sun.

American jazz music and Hollywood films figured prominently in Japan's appetite for the modern. McEvoy said Japan went for American jazz like catnip. *Fortune* said the country had caught "jazz fever" and never looked back. One could find jazz, it reported, at dozens of urban bars or dance halls—live on stage or on phonographs. As for cinema, *Time* stated that Japan imported three hundred American films a year. The *Herald Tribune* noted that all of the major American film studios had offices in Tokyo. Hollywood actors, Americans learned, had become household names in Japan. The *Washington Post* said Japanese women swooned over Clark Gable, Gary Cooper, Robert Taylor, and Robert Montgomery and idolized Norma Shearer, Kay Francis, Claudette Colbert, Jean Harlow, and Myrna Loy. Hollywood's influence, declared the *Post*, was changing Japan's "style of clothing, mode of life and habit of thought."[24]

In the face of such selective, self-flattering depictions, it was hardly surprising that some American observers construed modernity in opposition to Japanese militarism. *Fortune* asserted point-blank that the *moga* lifestyle was "anathema to the Japanese patrioteer." Robert K. Reischauer, a lecturer at Princeton, wrote in *Harper's* that Americanization had created a "chasm" in Japanese society between "reactionaries" and "progressives." Militarists, he asserted, "view with deep dislike everything that even faintly smells of America." It is true that Japanese nationalists, including a gathering storm of intellectuals and politicians, bristled against Americanized modernity, sometimes violently. The Japanese promoter of the Babe Ruth tour, for example, barely survived an attack by an ultranationalist who believed the exhibition was unpatriotic. To be sure, the harshest anti-American backlash came after right-wing reforms in 1940. The important point, however, is that it made sense for Americans to pit modernity against militarism and surmise that the future of Japan flowed toward America, not against it. As one writer stated, "These great Japanese cities tell one an interesting story of the interrelationship and interdependence of the modern world. Cosmopolitanism carries the day."[25]

The luxury of historical hindsight makes clear, of course, that cosmopolitanism did not carry the decade. Nonetheless, the mere expression of such optimism—as well as remarks by KBS officials in mid-1935 that US-Japan relations were "better"—presents an atypical storyline from the standard "road to war" narratives. In fact, American travel to Japan had surged, Americans bought more Japanese goods than any other people in the world, and commentaries in the American press increasingly suggested greater tolerance toward Manchuria. The dean of Harvard's Business School, for example, writing in the *Saturday Evening Post*, said, "[Japan's actions in Manchuria] irritate and disturb us, but irritation is a bad foundation for sane public opinion or national policy. . . . Though I look upon her activities . . . with deep anxiety and regret, I understand enough to make me both respect and admire her." An essay in the *New York Times*, meanwhile, gave tacit recognition to "the new state of Manchukuo" while raving about the modern makeover in Manchuria's cities, including the "2,000 American-style homes" in the capital of Changchun.[26]

Officially, Washington's nonrecognition of Manchukuo held firm. At the same time, the Roosevelt administration acquiesced to a policy of nonprovocation toward Japan—with the hope, again, that the empire's perceived "moderates" one day would change course. A writer for the *San Francisco Chronicle* summed up the evolving perspective, writing, "[Washington] is making no protests about [Japanese expansion]. The explanation is given that it will merely . . . wait until Japan becomes reasonable. The intimation is put out that we may not have a long time to wait."[27]

The most cited case in support of American acquiescence is a memo written in 1935 by John V. A. MacMurray, a senior US diplomat, in response to a request by Hornbeck to make a comprehensive study of US relations in East Asia. As America's minister to China in the late 1920s, MacMurray had fulminated against what he viewed as the Kuomintang's willful disregard of legal procedure. Lasting impressions subsequently informed his conclusions in 1935 that the Chinese were partly responsible for Japan's aggression in Manchuria. And that the United States should resign itself to the new geopolitical realities in East Asia. "Yield nothing of [the liberal] principles," wrote MacMurray, but refrain from "crusading in furtherance of them." This did not mean official recognition of Manchukuo, but rather American officials should privately accept Japan's claims it was the "stabilizing influence" in the region. Hornbeck disagreed about acknowledging Japanese hegemony, but he did caution against "needless friction [with Japan] by seeking to guarantee abstractions."[28] But that was before Japanese militancy began to rumble through North China.

INTIMIDATION IN NORTH CHINA

In May and June 1935, officers of Japan's North China Garrison Army based in Tianjin issued a series of coercive demands to Nanjing, the most significant of which were the elimination of Kuomintang party organs in Hebei province (which included the cities of Beijing and Tianjin) and the transfer of central armies to the south. Tokyo's explanation was that it could no longer tolerate "anti-Japanese activities," a euphemistic phrase for anything that undermined Japanese interests. A weak Nanjing government, no match for Japanese strength and still focused on annihilating the armies of the CCP, chose appeasement and submitted to the humiliating conditions.[29]

In reportage strikingly reminiscent of the Manchurian crisis, Tokyo correspondent Hugh Byas gave the impression of a rogue Japanese military running amok. The *Christian Century* similarly argued that "the recent action of [Japan's] army in presenting a series of new demands on the Chinese . . . can be understood only as evidence of the division between the Foreign Office and the War Office in Tokyo." Ambassador Grew also remained tethered to the thesis of army-civilian struggle. On June 24, Grew advised Secretary Hull that any protest against Japan "would almost certainly tend to solidify sentiment in favor of the Army's actions" against civilian leaders. A protest would be particularly detrimental at the time, Grew suggested, given that "the thinking men of the empire" (men like his friend KBS Director Kabayama) believed Premier Okada was in a stronger position relative to the military than any premier in recent years.[30] Again, American hunches and hearsay resulted in myopic perspectives and wishful thinking.

Some of the American confusion stemmed from the almost symbiotic relationship between Ambassador Grew and Hugh Byas, the Tokyo correspondent for both the *New York Times* and *The Times* of London, who had resided in Japan for nearly two decades. Byas's observations mattered. Not only did the sixty-year-old Scotsman write for arguably the most influential newspaper in the United States, his articles were often cited by other news sources. Byas routinely plied the American ambassador with "insider" information that reflected his own conviction about a moderate-militarist schism in Japan's ruling circles. Grew alluded to the importance of the relationship in his diary, stating, "As [Byas] is probably the soundest and most brilliant of all the correspondents in Japan, discussions with him are well worthwhile." Not surprisingly, Grew sometimes specifically referenced Byas's articles in his correspondence to Washington. Stanley Hornbeck similarly alluded to Byas's reportage in memoranda, and President Roosevelt received the *New York Times* on his desk every morning. Clearly, Byas played an important auxiliary role in the matrix of America's East Asian policy.[31]

In the end, Hull agreed it would be counterproductive to protest Japan's demands in North China; nonetheless, the secretary was becoming increasingly pessimistic about events not only in East Asia but around the world. In Italy, Benito Mussolini persistently rattled his saber toward Ethiopia (Abyssinia). In Germany, in violation of the Versailles Treaty, Adolf Hitler announced in March 1935 that the Reich would build a standing army of 550,000 men. Rumors also circulated about imminent Nazi laws denying Jews citizenship (the repressive Nuremburg Laws were passed in September). Hull expressed his growing concerns in commencement speeches at the

University of Michigan and the University of Wisconsin in June 1935. In Madison, Hull told the audience it was "high time that every human being should inquire where the world is going." The secretary returned to the theoretical problem of world order that the peacemakers faced in 1919: "How shall the world as a whole," he asked the audience, "be administered?" The stakes were high, said Hull, including the preservation of democracy and "our present high order of civilization."[32] But while Hull, in his speeches, returned to the liberal answers of 1919, Congress chose to return instead to what it believed were the literal lessons of 1917, the year the United States intervened in the Great War.

NEUTRALITY ACT OF 1935

Placing the Wilson administration and munitions-makers squarely in its crosshairs, in August 1935, Congress passed neutrality legislation aimed at preventing the United States from ever again getting drawn into war beyond the defense of its own territory. Guiding the isolationist law was the assumption that the country had been manipulated into entering the First World War. The Neutrality Act prohibited the export of arms to belligerent nations and reasonably warned American citizens who traveled in war zones that they did so at their own risk. (A 1936 provision banned loans to belligerents, while a "cash and carry" clause in 1937 mandated that belligerents pay for goods with cash and transport them in their own ships.) As one historian has noted, "these misnamed acts *relinquished* neutral rights."[33] Indeed, the measures also flouted the Kellogg Pact's premise that there never again could be innocent bystanders to a conflict.

In some ways, the Neutrality Act was the first admission by Americans, contrary to their British cousins, that avoiding war was more important than curbing aggression. In Great Britain, results from the "Peace Ballot," an unofficial questionnaire about League of Nation principles, showed that British citizens overwhelmingly supported the liberal peace system. FDR opposed the neutrality legislation because it gave the president no discretionary power to single out an aggressor; however, facing a brick wall of isolationism, he relented. Roosevelt was taken aback by some of the more histrionic attacks by congressmen responsible for what he called the "wild-eyed" law. In a letter to Col. House, with whom he maintained regular correspondence, FDR stated, "The trouble is that [isolationists] belong to the very large and perhaps increasing school of thought which holds that we can and should withdraw wholly within ourselves.... They imagine that if the civilization of Europe is about to destroy itself through internal strife, it might just as well go ahead and do it and that the United States can stand idly by."[34] Roosevelt's comments represented an early expression of what evolved into one of his principal foreign policy themes: technology had shrunk the globe, and thus the two oceans no longer provided immunity from a world increasingly at odds with liberalism.

Col. House agreed the United States could not unilaterally "innocent" itself in a complex world. But his answer to global discord, expressed in complementary essays with Prince Konoe in *Liberty* magazine, was surprising: the elderly internationalist now preferred appeasement. Accepting Japan's claims as a "have-not" nation and "the dominating influence in the Far East," House suggested, "Why not allow the Japanese to make [new territory] productive and add to the wealth and happiness of mankind?" He did add that Tokyo was "choosing the wrong time and the wrong methods" of righting wrongs. But he nonetheless held out hope. Reflexively invoking America's dualistic perception of Japanese politics, he stated, "There are two opposing groups in Japan, one led by the younger militarists, and the other [by civilian moderates]." The implication, of course, was that wiser, moderate, cosmopolitan Japanese officials were waiting to make their move and return Japan to the cooperative basis of the 1920s. If so, one of those presumed figures, Prince Konoe, suggested that cooperation depended first on rectifying Japan's victimization. "There are some peoples," wrote Konoe in *Liberty*, "which are, under the existing world order, denied the opportunity to develop their native capacity and to fulfill their mission as independent nations."[35] It is unclear from this article what Konoe meant by "mission" or how American readers interpreted it. But the loaded word progressively became a central premise of Japan's paternalistic Asianism.

SOFT POWER EXPANSION

Konoe's essay in *Liberty* pointed to yet another pillar of Tokyo's soft power strategy aimed at influencing foreign public opinion. This involved efforts to gain greater control of overseas information. By far, the most significant component of this propaganda initiative, as Akami Tomoko has detailed it, was the creation of the state-funded national news agency Dōmei. Despite the existence since 1926 of a state-subsidized, AP-modeled news cooperative (Rengō), in the aftermath of the Manchurian crisis, and in the new era of shortwave wireless, a consensus emerged in government circles of the need for a stronger state-directed news agency—in particular, one that could effectively counter Reuters's news dominance in East Asia with "correct information." The Okada government subsequently announced plans for a national news agency in mid-1935. Foreign Minister Hirota, quoted in the *New York Times*, delineated the perceived high stakes—and Tokyo's increasingly grandiose regionalism—saying the proposed agency would "foster a correct appreciation of Japan's . . . mission in the Far East." Dōmei officially began operating in January 1936, including bureaus in New York City and Washington, DC.[36]

In tandem with Dōmei, the Japanese government continued in its efforts to shape foreign opinion through established media networks, such as the English-language daily *Japan Times* (its content sometimes picked up by American dailies). The government also continued the practice of using Japan's consulates in the States to co-opt leaders of the Japanese American community and respective newspapers to help explain the empire's cause. Similarly, the consulates employed sympathetic American journalists to write newspaper and magazine articles that cast Japan in a favorable light. Tokyo also invited American editors from influential magazines and newspapers on all-expenses-paid visits to Japan, Korea, and Manchuria. Finally, starting in 1935, the government began reaching American radio sets when NHK, its national broadcast corporation, launched overseas shortwave broadcasting. Consonant with standard Japanese claims about the source of US-Japan tensions, in NHK's first broadcast to the States, its president told listeners he was overjoyed to tell them what Japan "really is." NHK subsequently aired programs such as *An Introduction to Japan*, which sought to explain unique qualities of Japan and the Japanese to Americans. One program, for example, focused on Japanese haiku and asked American listeners to send in their own creations, some of which were read on air.[37]

Outside of regular media channels, meanwhile, the Japanese government continued to pump out a variety of English-language literature heralding Japan's mission in Asia. This included the Foreign Affairs Association's *Contemporary Japan*, which covered political, social, and cultural topics, as well as the South Manchurian Railway Company's quarterly magazine and artful advertisements, which branded the firm in a Pan-Asianist glow as the "Carrier of Light and Civilization."[38] At the same time, the KBS persisted in its cultural propaganda efforts. In the fall of 1935, KBS officials Count Kabayama and Baron Dan spent three months in America, making new cultural contacts and marketing Japanese refinement. Fanning out across the country, they conferred with thousands of American educators, museum officials, businessmen, and politicians. In Washington, Kabayama made a point to call on Hornbeck, likely because Konoe, in his visit the previous year, had identified the Far East chief as a thorn in Japan's side—someone who held an "unflinching conviction" about Japan's violations of the liberal order. Hornbeck later received a cordial letter from Kabayama on KBS stationary, expressing appreciation for a warm welcome, with hopes that their meeting marked the "beginning of cordial relations of mutual assistance and cooperation through cultural activities." A subsequent package contained the first three issues of *NIPPON* and KBS publications on Japanese gardens and dolls.[39]

As Kabayama and Dan made the rounds in the United States, the Okada government welcomed Vice President Garner and a large delegation of senators and representatives on a stopover visit to Japan; the Americans were en route to the Philippines for the inauguration of the commonwealth's first president. Although the trip could have been used as a subtle lesson in liberal internationalism by contrasting the impending independence of a former colony to Japan's land grab in Manchuria, that is not how the delegation discussed it, or how the press reported it. Instead, Americans learned from AP reports that Japanese officials and "surging crowds" greeted the delegation at the pier in Yokohama with a "cordiality of unprecedented proportions." Vice President Garner met with Emperor Hirohito and later attended a luncheon with Okada and Hirota. Prince Tokugawa, meanwhile, hosted the entire delegation for a dinner at the Peers' Club. The Americans also mingled with two thousand eminent Japanese at an embassy reception, doubtless sharing toasts to mutual understanding. The American press depicted a country whose leading figures were genial and gracious. In all probability, noted isolationist Gerald Nye (R-ND) spoke for the entire delegation when he asserted that the "finest" of Japan were, at heart, friends of the United States.[40]

In this case, "finest" clearly referred to educated, well-traveled, cosmopolitan statesmen, business leaders, and scholars—men like like Hirota, Amō, Shigemitsu, Konoe, Tokugawa, Saitō, Kabayama, and Rōyama. On standard judgments of character, doubtless these were fine men; cordial, considerate, cultivated. And, at heart, desirous of friendship with the United States. That said, seeking American friendship and believing in Japanese hegemony in East Asia were not mutually exclusive. Evidence to this effect had already trickled out over the previous year. Official speeches and statements, especially by Hirota and Amō, bared imperialistic ambitions antithetical to the liberal order. In October, additional evidence began trickling out.

HIROTA'S THREE PRINCIPLES

In a cloud of intrigue, reports emanating from Tokyo and Nanjing indicated that Foreign Minister Hirota had presented the KMT ambassador to Japan with three irreducible demands: the suppression of anti-Japanese activity in China, respect for the existence of Manchukuo, and cooperation in containing communism. Nanjing replied that the demands—later termed Hirota's "Three Principles"—were too vague. The Chinese knew, of course, that "anti-Japanese activity" meant boycotts of Japanese commerce, while "respect for Manchukuo" referred to recognition of the puppet state. Japan's Foreign Office spokesman Amō subsequently clarified that Hirota had made "protests" to China but not demands. He added, however, that Tokyo hoped the warning would be sufficient and that force would not be necessary.[41]

But no sooner had Hirota declared his Three Principles than North China started heating up again. With the world engrossed in Italy's invasion of Ethiopia, Japan began encouraging a separatist movement in the very region from which it had previously evicted KMT officials. When encouragement failed, the Japanese relied on intimidation as well as propaganda that painted the appearance of a popular Chinese movement against Nanjing's authority. In November and December, Japanese pressure resulted in the creation of two autonomous governing entities in North China—one that included the major cites of Beijing and Tianjin and ran north into Mongolia ("Hebei-Chahar Political Council"); the other, a smaller nugget on the southern border of Manchukuo ("East Hebei Autonomous Council"). Thus, by the end of 1935, Japan had effectively evicted KMT power from North China and erected a long-sought buffer zone between Manchuria and Chiang Kai-shek's Nationalist government in Nanjing. According to pundit Nathanial Peffer, who lectured on East Asian affairs at Columbia University from 1929 to 1935, North China was following Manchuria "into a political twilight zone."[42]

Stanley Hornbeck, sensitive to the futile history of diplomatic notes during the Manchurian crisis, recommended to Secretary Hull restraint; nonetheless, Hornbeck still believed it was important for Washington to go on record and reiterate its rights and principles. This the secretary did. In a statement to the press, Hull described events in North China as a struggle that was "unusual in character," saying an effort was being made "to bring about substantial change in the political status" of the region. Then, pointing an unnamed finger at Japan, Hull declared it was of utmost importance for governments and peoples to respect the postwar pledges and principles, which, he claimed, were "essential to orderly life and progress."[43] Despite such affirmation of the liberal mantra, it was becoming clear that the administration's East Asian policy was caught in a diplomatic no-man's-land, with Hull clutching treaties and principles that were quickly losing relevancy. Indeed, Foreign Office spokesperson Amō intimated that Tokyo would view the Nine-Power Treaty as obsolete if applied to North China, saying, "circumstances have changed since it was signed."[44] As 1935 came to a close, unsettling challenges to the liberal order were developing on both sides of America's oceanic frontiers.

President Roosevelt did not hide his concern. In his State of the Union address on January 3, 1936, Roosevelt said "a point has been reached" in which Americans needed to "take cognizance of growing ill-will, of marked trends toward aggression, of increasing armaments, of shortening tempers—a situation which has in it many of the elements that lead to the tragedy of general war." He, too, condemned unnamed countries for running roughshod over the new peace principles, for reverting "to the old belief in the law of the sword, or to the fantastic conception that they, and they alone, are chosen to fulfill a mission and that all others among the billion and half of human beings in the world must and shall learn from and be subject to them." In the spirit of Wilson, he said "reasonable and legitimate objectives" could be attained by peaceful negotiations. Still, as Roosevelt told William Dodd, his ambassador in Germany, he was not expecting "much of a response within the autocratic nations," saying Wilson's faith in appealing "to citizens over the head of their government" was no longer tenable. The reason? Such governments tightly controlled "real news."[45] The reference pointed to the increasingly Orwellian degradation of language, and its pernicious impact on the Wilsonian reliance on public opinion to restrain aggression.

Roosevelt's caustic allusions to "nations chosen to fulfill a mission," moreover, left the president open to charges of hypocrisy, since the United States had built its own national mythology on exceptionalism.[46] Count the Japanese in the pack of critics. Although Amō and others took refuge in the statement that they had not read the speech, in fact they had pored over it. In an address before the Diet on January 21, Foreign Minister Hirota responded to Roosevelt with thinly disguised defiance. Hirota criticized statesmen abroad "who seem determined to impose upon others their private convictions as to how the world should be ordered." Casting aside Roosevelt's reproof, Hirota called for a "new" East Asia, embodied in his Three Principles of October 1935. For the first time he openly called for Nanjing's recognition of Manchukuo. Most significantly, Hirota once again heralded his nation's regional primacy, saying "the world is being brought . . . to recognize Japan's . . . whole-hearted endeavors toward the stabilization of East Asia." And he implicitly tied this primacy to presumptions about the grandeur of Japanese civilization. Referencing the KBS prospectus, the foreign minister declared it was time for Japanese "to introduce our arts and culture to other lands and thus contribute toward international good understanding and to the enrichment of world civilization and the promotion of the peace."[47] Doubtless few outsiders grasped the geopolitical linkages underlying such benign words.

Instead, the American press understandably focused on Hirota's demands on Nanjing. In a front-page *New York Times* article, a fairly shocked Hugh Byas remarked that "Japan's grandiose aims toward China have not been expressed so bluntly before by a responsible member of the Japanese government." Nathaniel Peffer wrote in the same paper that "notwithstanding the supposed schism between the civil and military authorities in Japan . . . China must acknowledge submission to Japan's ambitions." Peffer was one of the first observers to suggest that the perceived political polarization in Japan between hawks of the military and doves of the Foreign Ministry had been overblown.[48]

A week later, as if adding emphasis to Hirota's address, Ambassador Saitō dropped a few bombshells at the Japan Society of New York's annual dinner. Beyond reprising Japan's alleged just cause in Manchuria, the ambassador told the eight hundred guests that his nation was defending itself against "Occidental aggressions." This recalled Saitō's complaint to Hull that the Americans were obstructing Japan's external progress. Perhaps more shockingly, he applauded European dictators for their "patriotism and sincere purpose." Where others saw aggressive tendencies in Hitler and Mussolini, Saitō saw in them "higher motives, however much their own frailties."[49]

A transpacific war of words ensued when Key Pittman (D-NV), chairman of the Senate Committee on Foreign Relations, stepped into the rhetorical ring. In a widely reported speech on the Senate floor, Pittman assailed Saitō for asserting that Japan's actions in China resembled America's Monroe Doctrine.[50] When asked about the speech, Secretary Hull neither condoned nor condemned it. The larger point, of course, is that tensions between Japan and the United States were beginning to escalate over marked ideological differences concerning global governance. Then, in the proverbial blink of an eye, American perceptions tumbled again in the opposite direction and bilateral tensions diminished. The source of the perceptual U-turn was an attempted coup in Tokyo.

"2/26 INCIDENT"

On February 26, 1936, around five o'clock in the morning, some 1,500 troops of the army's First Division in Tokyo, led by twenty-two junior officers, rebelled against their government. In the dark, snow-muffled capital, the mutinous troops seized several strategic buildings and murdered several officials, including Finance Minister Takahashi Korekiyo and ex-premier Saitō Makoto. Premier Okada was also a target, but the assailants killed his brother-in-law in a case of mistaken identity. Failed attempts were also made on the lives of Prince Saionji and Count Makino Nobuaki, while Admiral Suzuki Kantarō was badly injured.

The American press defaulted to a narrative of militarists against liberals. Foreign policy pundit Sterling Fisher Jr. warned that the future of East Asia hung in the balance between two groups: those who sought to "bridle the wild trend on the continent" versus "the rabid and specious patriots." The reality was more complicated. The cabal of instigators were loyal to the army's Imperial Way faction and motivated principally by a slew of perceived domestic injustices, including economic inequality, incestuous corruption between politicians and business, "evil elements" around the throne, and an institutional bias toward the army's "Control" faction. They sought to establish an emperor-centered regime under Imperial Way leadership.[51]

Following initial government paralysis and halting negotiations, Emperor Hirohito stepped in with atypical resolve and ordered the rebels to stand down, which they did after eighty-one hours. (The ringleaders were subsequently charged with uncharacteristic swiftness—court-martialed in April and later executed by a firing squad.) Then, given Okada's close brush with assassination, Prince Saionji arranged the formation of a new cabinet, this time under Foreign Minister Hirota.

In assessing the significance of the 1936 coup, contemporary diplomats and commentators interpreted the outcome as an unequivocal victory for Japanese "liberals." The American press portrayed Prime Minister Hirota in both pastoral and cosmopolitan hues. Americans learned he was the "son of a poor stone cutter." *Time* noted that he had seen many parts of the world as opposed to insular and fanatically blind army men. In Byas's generous words, Hirota illustrated "the force of democracy and opportunity in Japan." He described the new prime minister as having brought hostilities in North China "to a tame end before irreparable changes had occurred." Grew told Secretary Hull that Hirota would "tranquilize Japan's foreign relations." The chorus of uncritical analysis continued unabated. Sterling Fisher wrote in the *New York Times* that Hirota's selection as premier "carried Japan back a long step toward the liberalism that grew up there before the outbreak of the Manchurian affair four and a half years ago." (Fisher's optimism at least made sense—he was on the payroll of the Japanese government.) *Christian Century*, meanwhile, melodramatically declared, "February 26, 1936, may prove to have been for Japan her blackest hour just before a newer and glorious dawn."[52]

Again, the habitual problem with such analysis is that it embraced a skewed ideological taxonomy, one that failed to question rigorously the meaning of constitutionalism in Japan and the degree to which "liberals" and "militarists" diverged on the critical issue of regional hegemony. Postwar interpretations, meanwhile, have tended to swing to the other side of the political pendulum, arguing that the rebellion resulted in the army's supremacy over civilians. One historian, for example, has written that in the incident's aftermath, "the military gained an even heavier hand over terrorized civil politicians and the foreign ministry." Another argues that "The terrorization of the civilian establishment by fanatical young army and navy officers made objections risky."[53] In contrast, the preponderance of evidence instead suggests that the 2/26 uprising—while enhancing the prestige of the army's Control faction—represented no meaningful departure from the empire's consensus-oriented politics and policy of Japanese primacy in Asia.

A comment by the incoming prime minister is instructive for its emphasis on consensus, in contrast to contemporary American opinion. According to Hirota, there were "no differences in thinking" between the military and himself. "We are in complete agreement," he said. And contrary to historical interpretations, Ambassador Saitō, in an address over NBC radio, confidently asserted that Japan's form of government would not be changed and her foreign relations would not be disturbed. "I do not foresee," said Saitō, "a rise of domination of any militarists or group of them who will chart a new course for our country.... [Military rule] will never occur in Japan."[54]

In many respects, Ambassador Saitō seemed a lot like Mr. Moto, the fictional creation of John P. Marquand. In 1933, the *Saturday Evening Post* hired Marquand to write a serial of "oriental" intrigue to replace the late Charlie Chan series. Marquand's first Moto story, "No Hero," appeared in 1935. "Thank You, Mr. Moto" and "Think Fast, Mr. Moto" followed in 1936. Like Ambassador Saitō, Moto whimsically drops colloquialisms, dresses impeccably, and enjoys American whiskey. To the *Saturday Evening Post*'s three million subscribers, Moto, like Saitō, came across as the paragon of moderation and reasonableness. In "Thank You, Mr. Moto," for example, Moto differentiates himself from Japan's militaristic troublemakers, telling the American protagonist Tom Nelson, "There is, Mr. Nelson, a disturbing, radical element in my country . . . somewhat bigoted and fanatical. It feels our nation is not moving fast enough. Frankly this group has been a source of very bad annoyance. My mission [in North China] has been to curb its activities." In another story, Moto laments to an American, "Army officers are so very, very crass. So many factions in Japan . . . The army faction is so very hard to deal with."[55] It seems reasonable to conclude that readers of the *Saturday Evening Post*, after confronting the suave and levelheaded Mr. Moto, likely came away reassured by the prospect of a Japan in the hands of its "real Motos," such as Ambassador Saitō and Prime Minister Hirota.

Every so often a perceptive mind worked through the moderate-military maze and gap between competing ideas of world order. In June 1936, for example, a reviewer of an anthology of speeches by Ambassador Saitō critiqued the ambassador's recurring thesis that any friction in US-Japan relations simply boiled down to "a lack of understanding." Pointing out the clash with liberalism, the reviewer wrote, "What our Japanese friends fail to realize is that one may accept, for purposes of argument, the full Japanese claim as to grievances, provocations, economic and strategic interest in Manchuria . . . without seeing how these things lessen the solemn obligations of [the postwar] treaties." The State Department increasingly parried in the same way. When Japanese diplomat Yoshida Shigeru, perceived by Americans as a moderate, called on Secretary Hull and Division Chief Hornbeck to lament the lack of bilateral understanding, a miffed Hull told him there was a growing impression that Japan sought "domination, first of eastern Asia, and then, of other portions as she might see fit."[56]

As the summer of 1936 beckoned, US-Japan relations cut deeper into their zigzag pattern, in which expressions of friendship and cultural affinity circulated with expressions of power politics and opposing ideas of world governance. Increasingly, the varying downslopes in the transpacific relationship were amplified by the militancy of Europe's revisionist powers. In March, for example, Hitler remilitarized the Rhineland in violation of the

Versailles and Locarno Treaties. Despite the Führer's own anxieties about a backlash from Britain and France, a broken League of Nations looked on impotently. Then, in July, right-wing nationalists in Spain ignited a violent revolt against a popularly elected government.

By mid-1936, as the League of Nations moved into its striking new home, the Palace of Nations, in Geneva, Switzerland, the postwar peace system was dying a slow death, born of multiple, unanswered strikes to its core principles. Revisionist foreign policies—underwritten by unilateralism, regionalism, and saber-rattling—were becoming normalized. Indeed, in August 1936, just five months after German troops crossed the west bank of the Rhine, fifty-three nations and 6,800 athletes arrived in Berlin to participate in the eleventh Olympiad, a spectacularly produced pageant of Nazi propaganda. In some ways, the lighting of the Olympic flame in the capital of a racist and militarized dictatorship symbolized the passing of liberalism into an uncertain future. So, too, did the news that the International Olympic Committee awarded the 1940 games to another illiberal power—Japan. The IOC's announcement made clear that a preeminent global institution founded on pacific ideals would not punish Japan for militarism in Manchuria and North China.

While the Japanese people "went wild with jubilation" with the news of landing the Olympics, Prime Minister Hirota convened one of the most significant cabinet conclaves in prewar Japan. The Five-Ministers Conference in August 1936 formulated national policy directives on East Asia, long-range strategic goals for the army and navy, and eventual expansion into the South Seas. In many ways, the conference realized as government policy what officials had intermittently thrown up as trial balloons, such as the Amō statement. On August 7, for instance, the conference completed a highly ideological document, "The Fundamentals of National Policy," which aimed to establish Japan "as the stabilizing power in the Far East." As noted, this loaded phrase prefigured a Japan-guided order with Manchukuo and China. Another document, the "Basic Administrative Policy toward North China," outlined plans to consolidate Japanese gains in North China—where the empire now stationed ten thousand troops. Two weeks after the conference, the Hirota cabinet revealed that nearly 70 percent of the 1937 budget would go toward the military.[57] A massive naval building program included plans for super-battleships of the Yamato class.

Taken together, the new policy initiatives and rearmament left little doubt that Japan's civilian and military leaders saw the empire's future entwined with the revisionist powers rather than the liberal powers. Indeed, despite the Five-Ministers Conference's professed desire for peace, it is difficult to avoid the conclusion that it increased the probability for future conflict with Great Britain and the United States.

Japan's cultural initiatives, meanwhile, ran in lockstep with the empire's foreign policy. KBS Chairman Count Kabayama, for example, reminded fellow officers of the "urgent" goal to "make foreign peoples understand our national conditions and culture and plan for cultural cooperation with them in order to resolve our difficulties in the areas of foreign policy, diplomacy, and economics." That such goals involved operational duplicity becomes clear from Kabayama's summary report on his visit to the United States, which noted that he explained to Americans that KBS programs had no political purpose. As for impact, Kabayama said American audiences warmly welcomed programs on Japanese culture. Baron Dan concurred but added that Americans still possessed "many mistaken ideas concerning Japan and the Japanese." The antidote, prescribed Dan, was "proper knowledge and information," a course of action that naturally privileged the KBS's cultural serums—like the ensuing full-court cultural press in Boston.[58]

THE DIPLOMACY OF ART

On September 10, 1936, amid background chamber music provided by the Boston Symphony, an audience of three thousand dignitaries gathered for the opening of the Special Loan Exhibition of Japanese Art at the Museum of Fine Arts (MFA) in Boston. The exhibition was deemed "special" because it featured more than one hundred Japanese artifacts loaned by private Japanese citizens, the national government, and even Emperor Hirohito. It was also breathtaking in scope, offering a panoramic retrospective of twelve centuries of Japanese treasures, including sculptures, screens, and scrolls.

The exhibition owed its happy occurrence to the crossroads of circumstance and history: Harvard was celebrating its tercentenary, and the MFA was the nation's preeminent authority and collector of Japanese art. With ten thousand Harvard alumni, including President Roosevelt, descending on Cambridge for what the *Washington Post* called the "Greatest Reunion in U.S. history," the tribute guaranteed the Japanese exhibition an elite audience pool as well as prime publicity.[59]

Indeed, the exhibition's opening night brimmed with the surrounding excitement of the tercentenary. Among those in attendance were Ambassador Grew and hundreds of fellow Harvard alumni, including Harvard President James B. Conant and Langdon Warner, curator of Oriental art at Harvard's Fogg Museum. Representing the Japanese were leading members of the KBS, including Prince Takamatsu, Dan Inō, Kabayama, Anesaki, and Yoshizawa Kenkichi (foreign minister during the Manchurian crisis). Both Takamatsu and Dan had contributed artifacts from their private collections. Meanwhile Ambassador Saitō was honored at an opening-night dinner hosted by MFA President Edward J. Holmes. Newspapers played up the opening-night attendance as well as the "who's who" patina of the guest list. Over a period of seven weeks, more than one hundred thousand visitors attended the show, along with a fawning American press.[60]

The KBS's cultural strategy can be seen in Ambassador Saitō's opening-night speech, which masterfully indulged assumptions about the larger meaning of Japanese aesthetics. Saitō asserted that his country's art, so extolled for its civilized essence, was also Japan's future:

> In such times as these, when social changes and confusion are rife, bewildered people will seize impulsively upon some emotional prejudice and hold to a concept that is without any validity [a reference to Japan's perceived militarism]. But by identifying themselves with the past and with men of another time they may gain an understanding of life and a power for effective action for human welfare and international peace. Japan, whose faith in the past is the strength of her civilization, delights on this occasion to share with America her realization that our future indeed is our past.[61]

Saitō thus urged Americans to view Japan through the lens of history—to construe Japan's civilized past as the soul of the nation and to superimpose that past onto the present and future. Again, the implicit message was that Asia was in good hands under a Japanese-guided regional order.

"Civilization" became an exhibition mantra, as American art critics gushed over Japan's aesthetic sensibility. In a full-page Sunday Arts section review, for example, the *Washington Post* said the show revealed Japan's "high artistic civilization, where . . . beauty is nearest to divinity." Royal Cortissoz, the prominent longtime *New York Herald Tribune* art critic, said the show "richly illustrates the genius of Japanese art," which he called "amazingly beautiful," "invariably exquisite," and "nothing less than miraculous." The influential *American Magazine of Art* devoted thirty photographs to the exhibition and a fifteen-page review by Japan Society official Louis Ledoux, who asserted that "any lover of art would have been amply rewarded for crossing a continent and an ocean to see [the exhibit]." The *New York Times*, meanwhile, published three stories on the exhibit, including two celebratory pieces by critic Edward Jewell. Jewell claimed the "radiantly beautiful" works emitted "the perfume of innate artistic rightness." In a follow-up piece, he declared rather dramatically that Japanese aesthetics were "the loom on which art's deathlessness is woven."[62]

Another message transmitted to Americans was the spiritual values embodied in the Japanese art. The *Washington Post* associated the Buddhist-themed aesthetic with pacific intent, stating, "We must visualize it as a longing for the peace—as an awaiting for the peace of the Most High." In light of the underlying geopolitical tension, that was suggestive language—especially if a reader embraced the implicit syllogism: Japan's soul was its art; its art longed for peace; therefore, Japan longed for peace. On another level, such views evoked the victimization of a cultivated people at the mercy of ultranationalists. As political analyst Eugene J. Young opined in his 1936 book on world affairs, "the most devoted lovers of sheer beauty in our modern world [had shown] a threatening, even arrogant, face to its neighbors and everyone else. A fantastic Oriental mask seemed to have been put over a countenance that wanted to be smiling."[63]

For the purposes of the KBS, certainly the most significant outcome was how commentators, such as the *Washington Post*, said the exhibition expressed the "solidarity of mankind." Ledoux reached a similar conclusion, calling the exhibition "a peculiarly notable example of international cooperation in that universal world which endures beyond the ephemeral changes of political and economic interests." The *Boston Herald* also viewed the exhibition as a beacon of hope, noting, "While Europe prepares for war, Japan and America clasp hands in the friendliest of international gestures." Like a page from the KBS prospectus, Langdon Warner asserted, "If we foreigners can but begin to comprehend the art of Japan, we shall know a spiritual kinship that treaties and trade fail to inspire." The *Herald Tribune*'s Cortissoz, mean-

Figure 4.4. Visitors attending the opening reception of the Special Loan Exhibition of Japanese Art at the Museum of Fine Arts, Boston, September 1936. Displayed center is a six-panel folding screen from sixteenth-century artist Kanō Motonobu. ("Art Treasures of Japan Opening Reception," Museum of Fine Arts, Boston. Photograph © 2021 Museum of Fine Arts, Boston.)

while, became downright Shakespearean, saying the show made for a "loftier internationalism, weaving the invisible strands that best bridge the salt, unplumb'd, estranging sea."[64]

It is hard to imagine those who attended the exhibition, or those who read about it, not being struck by Japanese amity and generosity. As MFA President Holmes noted in his opening-night speech, the Japanese loan represented "the most beautiful tribute that one nation can pay to another." Director George Edgell, meanwhile, recalled the trip he took to Japan to organize the show, telling the three thousand guests, "No words could ever paint the courtesy and hospitality with which I was received. No treasure was too precious to show me; no trouble too great if it straightened my path. . . . These are not only my friends but our friends." The diplomatic corps held similarly sanguine views. Ambassador Grew wrote to Edgell, saying he believed one of its main purposes "was to help our international relations [read: improve US-Japan relations]." An enthusiastic Grew and his wife attended the exhibition seven times between them; he later informed Prime Minister Hirota and Emperor Hirohito that the show had made a big impression on Americans.[65]

That the exhibition cultivated positive feelings toward Japan becomes evident in light of a Chinese intellectual's conscious attempt to counteract such feelings. In an essay published in the *New York Times*, renowned writer Lin Yutang argued that Japan owed its entire civilization to China, adding tartly, "so many Japanese things are pretty, and so few beautiful." The defensive and dismissive tone suggests a reeling combatant in a war of public opinion, threatened by what he viewed as a persuasive piece of Japanese propaganda.[66]

***

The Boston show was compelling. Critics expressed an emotional affinity to the "civilizational" sublimity of Japanese culture. *Atlantic Monthly* later claimed that Japanese aesthetics "appeal to the inner soul, and are the lamps to lead us to the higher culture which belongs to art and civilization." This view of Japan presented an unavoidable contrast with the image of marauding militarists, evoking mutually exclusive tropes of "civilization" and "barbarism." Perhaps.this is why prominent Japanese feminist Katō Shizue believed at the time that American understanding of Japanese art was "a more powerful factor in the promotion of goodwill between our two nations than all the diplomatic speeches of empty formality lumped together." Still, for those who attended the Boston exhibition, was it simply a momentary sanctuary, an ethereal escape from the material world, in which ink and wash paintings by fifteenth-century artist Sesshū took one's breath away—until one went home and woke up to the morning paper's accounts of the rough-and-tumble world of power politics?[67]

On November 25, 1936, for example, Americans learned that Japan and Nazi Germany had signed a treaty aimed nominally at the Communist International (Comintern). Mostly, the so-called Anti-Comintern Pact was a vehicle to express common antagonism against the Soviet Union—made clear by the fact that Soviet leader Joseph Stalin in 1935 had marginalized Comintern in favor of the so-called Popular Front. Americans generally were not troubled by consultation pacts against communist Russia; Japan's finding common ground with Nazi Germany, however, was problematic, symbolically and literally. It sent a strong message to Americans of *non*affinity, of alienation with all the civilizational bonds the KBS programs hoped to instill. In fact, even before the pact, such an association was coalescing. In late September, Nathaniel Peffer enumerated the "fateful parallels" between Japan and Germany in a *New York Times* Sunday feature. Peffer said both nations "chronically complain that they are willfully 'misunderstood'" and that each "overrides treaties, contracts and commitments. Neither concedes any obligations at international law." To those who doubted any association, he granted that "affinity" may be too strong a word but that "there is at least a kinship between them that transcends diplomacy and politics."[68]

By the end of 1936, the lines of affinity and nonaffinity between Japan and the United States—and their relations with other nations—were becoming more clearly drawn. The zigzag pattern between 1934 and 1936 had told a story of both friendly overtures and ideological tension, with alternate hopes for an "understanding" or a "moderate" resurgence—and a turnaround in bilateral relations. Although some signs in early 1937 still pointed to areas of potential cooperation, such hopes were dashed beyond repair starting in July 1937, with Japan's all-out invasion of China. The outbreak of war—the directed attention on power politics—once again crystallized ideological differences and diminished the efficacy of Japan's soft power strategies.

Chapter Five

A New Order in East Asia (1937–1938)

Four years after Matsuoka Yōsuke departed Geneva with the hope that one day the world would understand Japan, many of the nation's civilian and military leaders still believed that "misunderstanding" was the main cause of Japan's tensions with the United States. A weighty "if only" mindset fueled Japanese frustration: if only Americans would grasp "actual conditions in the Far East" and Japan's "special responsibility," they would come to see that the empire's objectives landed on the side of peace, order, civilization, and progress. Japan's leaders lent a friendly face to bilateral relations, and cultural programs were conceived to make clear to Americans the greatness of Japanese civilization and that the empire's regionalist ambitions were reasonable and valid. Instead, Japan's efforts tended to reinforce American perceptions of antithetical forces within Japanese society and hopes for a resurgence of political moderates. This incongruous interplay, as we have seen, resulted in a diplomatic quiescence between 1933 and 1937—as each side waited in hope for signs of change in the other. In 1937, the quiet imploded. Emboldened by the brashness of Europe's revisionist powers, Nazi Germany and Fascist Italy, Tokyo confronted Chinese nationalism—and, in effect, the Nine-Power Treaty—with a violent intolerance.

This chapter explores a critical juncture in the United States and Japan's competing visions of world order. After hostilities erupted in North China in July 1937, Japan's military successes precipitated even bolder ideological pronouncements and regional claims. Japan's leaders issued strongly worded Pan-Asianist statements and set out to realize an illiberal order on the continent. Following a massive mobilization of troops and terrific bloodshed, the Japanese government declared a "New Order in East Asia" and ruled nominally over two hundred million Chinese. Despite the inexorable deterioration in US-Japan relations, Tokyo persisted in its efforts to both explain and extol the empire using soft power strategies. Toward this end, the Kokusai Bunka Shinkōkai established a cultural institute in New York. Not surprisingly, the society's publicized objective to contribute to the culture and welfare of humankind "in happy unison with other nations" rang increasingly hollow.[1] Consistent with recent scholarship outlining the limits of cultural diplomacy, by 1938 the negative images of warfare and atrocity made Japan's carefully constructed representations of cultural refinement ineffectual. Such contradictions also contributed to a gradual unraveling of America's dualistic view of a meaningful civilian-military split in Japan.

For the United States, the volatile international climate over the next two years made Secretary Hull's diplomatic leverage with Japan even weaker than Henry Stimson's had been during the Manchurian crisis. Hull was limited to issuing a series of sober Wilsonian statements on the importance of "orderly processes." More substantially, as neither Japan nor China declared war on one another, President Roosevelt refrained from invoking the Neutrality Law. This allowed American military aid to continue to flow to the Chinese, though it also permitted American firms to sell war materials to Japan. At the same time, facing an isolationist Congress committed to neutrality, Roosevelt delicately sought to awaken Americans to the threat "of international anarchy . . . from which there is no escape through mere isolation or neutrality."[2] Three months after those words were uttered, however, the House of Representatives brought to a vote a resolution for a constitutional amendment that would require a national referendum for going to war. Thus, despite a major war in Asia and saber-rattling in Europe, Roosevelt trod carefully in his battle for global awareness. Having learned from the miscues of the president he served from 1913 to 1921, Roosevelt was cautious to nudge public opinion but not get too far ahead of it.

"IF JAPAN IS A GREAT NATION"

"The New Year for Japan, so far as her international relations are concerned, opens in an ominous key." So began Ambassador Grew's diary entry for January 1, 1937. The reason for Grew's dour assessment was Japan's anomalous position in North China and the country's signature on the Anti-Comintern Pact. Although Japan, like Germany, tried to sell the pact as a call for global unity against the "red menace" (à la Reich Minister Joseph Goebbels's shrill plea, "Europe, Awake!"), many of the world's foreign offices interpreted it in more foreboding terms, suspecting a concealed military alliance.[3] For US-Japan relations, the pact lent apparent credence to an ideological camaraderie between Japan and Europe's fascist regimes. If the adages "birds of a feather" or "the company you keep" were not as yet applicable, the pact certainly planted seeds.

But, as had so often been the case in US-Japan relations over the previous four years, just when some sense of ideological clarity about Japan, for "good" or "worse," seemed to present itself to interested American observers, ambiguity blew in like a zephyr. So it was again in February 1937, when the Hirota cabinet resigned. Beyond intraministerial squabbling, the government had failed to resolve lingering tensions in China. From a twenty-first-century perch, it is difficult to grasp why it did not dawn on Japan's leadership that the coercive formation of two autonomous governments, incorporating two of China's most populous cities, likely would not translate into stable, pro-Japanese zones. Perhaps the answer is as simple as the blinding arrogance of dogma. Japan's hegemonic strain of Pan-Asianist ideology in the 1930s was fueled by a heady brew of racial superiority and a profound exceptionalism. Japan, as one scholar from the Kyoto school of philosophy wrote in 1934, was an "unparalleled beautiful jewel" whose splendor was "incomparably greater than the pyramids of Egypt." The Education Ministry's stunningly chauvinistic *Fundamentals of Our National Polity*, a 156-page pamphlet written by prominent scholars and published in March 1937, similarly rammed home the alleged significance and uniqueness of Japan's heaven-ordained family-nation. According to postwar scholar Maruyama Masao, this family system was propagated "not as an abstract idea, but as an actual historical fact."[4] Was it therefore not reasonable for an Asian civilization like China, which had humiliated itself before the West, to heed Japan's "special responsibility" to lead Asia?

The ideological cloud enveloping Japan at the time is what makes it all the more surprising that the new prime minister, Gen. Hayashi Senjurō (February–June 1937), selected Satō Naotake as foreign minister. A member of the Foreign Service for thirty years, Satō aligned most closely with Shidehara diplomacy of the 1920s and its watchwords of cooperation, compromise, and Japanese expansion through trade. In a widely reported speech before the Diet on March 12, 1937, Satō said the crises in Sino-Japanese relations "were of Japan's own making." In reply to an interpellation, the foreign minister said he had no intention of linking the question of Manchukuo to negotiations with Nanjing and that relations with the United States would improve if Japan's policy toward China were fair and one of which Japan "need not be ashamed." In a stunning conclusion, Satō asserted that Japan, if it is a great nation, should "walk openly on the broad high road." The critique implied, of course, that Japan had not been behaving honorably—and that until his country did so, its claim to regional leadership was quixotic.[5]

The *New York Times* described the new developments in Tokyo as "unusually significant and encouraging" and published a stream of related articles between March 12 and March 28. To be sure, Satō was a fascinating outlier, a genuine departure from the rough policy consensus of the 1930s. That consensus, however, was not about to be radically altered. Almost immediately, pressure from within the Hayashi cabinet compelled Satō to walk back his most provocative statements. He thus affirmed the "inseparable relations" between Japan and Manchukuo and that Japan should not be submissive "if China trampled upon international justice or damaged the prestige of Japan."[6] Still, the fact that Satō was not dismissed suggests Japan's leadership at the time was open, albeit narrowly, to novel ways of dealing with China.

By April 1937, as the cherry blossoms in Japan burst forth in their annual pink-and-white explosion, a noticeable calm once again descended on US-Japan relations. The perception of a moderate cabinet and a break in disturbing news from North China guided American thinking. A spurt of goodwill trips added to the momentary glow. For example, Konoe Hidemaro, the younger brother of KBS President Prince Konoe, had just returned from a historic trip to the United States, where he guest conducted the Philadelphia Orchestra in a series of concerts in Philadelphia and Washington, DC. Konoe's performances won him unanimous acclaim in the press and a warm reception by American audiences, not to mention an invitation to conduct the NBC Symphony Orchestra for a national radio audience. Henry Luce's *Time*, no fan of Japan, said the maestro "made cultural face for his country such as no Japanese had ever made before."[7]

Even more poignantly, in April, deaf-blind social activist Helen Keller arrived in Japan for a highly publicized three-month visit. KBS advisor Prince Tokugawa, Prime Minister Hayashi, and Foreign Minister Satō welcomed Keller, who was honored at a banquet attended by nearly six hundred people, including "many of the highest people in the country." Keller swept through twenty cities and attracted more than one million Japanese admirers. Stories in the American press told how the beloved activist aroused "the Japanese people's sympathy and enthusiasm as hardly any other visitor has ever done." Keller must have thrilled KBS officials when she paid poetic tribute to Japan's cultural refinement, saying, "I cannot take in all the beauty, the grandeur and exquisiteness of the country. Japan is a big bouquet of loveliness over which my fingers wander in delight." Keller's comments and Japan's outpouring of affection for a person with a disability contrasted sharply with the image of villainous militarists overrunning North China. President Roosevelt likely ruminated on Keller's benign view of Japan, having received a letter with the quotation from Keller's personal secretary. A KBS directors' meeting, meanwhile, alluded to a renewed sense of momentum and plans for more activities and greater coordination with the Foreign Ministry, scholars, and Japan's corporate conglomerates.[8]

The perceived calm in the spring of 1937 was enough to compel *Christian Century* to allege that "Japan turns toward peace," while *Business Week* confidently declared, "The period of Japan's major political aggression in China is over." From an official angle, Ambassador Grew informed Secretary Hull that Count Makino, an eminent elder statesman and KBS advisor, had stated categorically that Emperor Hirohito "regards good relations with Great Britain and the United States as the primary objective of Japan's foreign policy." This development, Grew stated with the import of an insider, represented a "highly significant new trend in Japanese foreign policy."[9]

A more concrete trend was America's robust tourism and trade with Japan. Ocean liners from the United States to Japan were booked to near capacity for the approaching summer holidays, and the *New York Times*, without any apparent sense of political discomfort, noted that "Tokyo can be reached in fifteen days, with an opportunity of seeing the new state of Manchukuo." A vote of confidence for the likely continuation of pacific relations came from internationally renowned silent film star Harold Lloyd, whose horn-rimmed glasses had become exceedingly popular in Japan. According to *Scribner's Magazine*, Lloyd booked an entire floor of Tokyo's Imperial Hotel for the 1940 Olympics. American goods, meanwhile, continued to pour into Japan at a record clip.[10]

The most momentous news coming out of Japan in the spring of 1937, however, was the formation of a new cabinet under Konoe Fumimaro, following the failure of the Hayashi cabinet. The Japanese people responded enthusiastically to the popular prince, who was president of both the House of Peers and the KBS. The forty-five-year-old Konoe defied conventions of stodgy and reticent Japanese politicians—he was youthful, poised, and eloquent. As one young Japanese person remarked, the new premier "uses simple language and speaks as if he were your friend." The State Department's Joseph W. Ballantine noted in a memo that Konoe was "inclined toward liberalism." Hugh Byas wrote that Konoe brought "an atmosphere of reasonableness to the government" and possessed a "practical middle-of-the-road mind." The influential journalist called Konoe a "natural democrat." News reports also noted that Konoe's son was elected captain of Princeton's golf team and affectionately nicknamed "Butch" by his classmates. And that the premier's younger brother, Hidemaro, had returned to the United States for a second conducting tour. For Americans, the name "Konoe" (typically written as "Konoye" at the time) doubtless conjured up the promise of fruitful transpacific relations.[11]

In this case, looks were deceiving. Konoe carried with him a consistent and rather severe ideological outlook. This was conveyed in essays and speeches going back to his famous diatribe against the Anglo-American powers just before the Paris Peace Conference. An honorable but gloomy sensitivity to injustice colored his worldview, owing to his reading of Tolstoy and other European writers during his college years. "I felt oppressed," he confessed to Byas, "by the injustice of the world." Increasingly, Konoe's indignation became filtered through a prideful nationalism. Indeed, Prince Saionji,

Konoe's mentor, observed with concern in the 1930s that Konoe gravitated toward men who held "extremist opinions."[12]

The new premier offered clues about his convictions in a radio address shortly after taking office. "Our external policy," said Konoe, "will seek peace based on justice, which is not the same thing as the mere maintenance of the status quo." The implication, of course, was that Japan remained a victim of an unjust liberal order. His cabinet appointments, meanwhile, reflected strong currents of nationalism and expansionism, including Hirota's return as foreign minister.[13] Konoe's influence on Japan's foreign policy in the late 1930s can hardly be overstated. From the spring of 1937 until the fall

Figure 5.1. Konoe Fumimaro, prime minister of Japan (1937–1939, 1940–1941). (National Diet Library, Tokyo, "Historical Figures" website.)

of 1941, three different Konoe-led cabinets dominated Japanese politics for a total of 1,033 days. The premier's troubled legacy began with a collision between Japan's chauvinistic regionalism and Chinese nationalism.

"DUE REPENTANCE" AT THE MARCO POLO BRIDGE

The agreements forced upon Chinese authorities in North China in 1935 gave the Japanese extraordinary privileges and a buffer zone between Manchukuo and the Nanjing government. It did not give them, however, a magical wand to turn Chinese nationalism into pro-Japanese sentiment. As a result, Tokyo struggled in vain to drive a wedge between Nanjing and Chinese authorities in North China (especially Gen. Song Zheyuan). Japanese frustration with Chinese recalcitrance became clear a few days after Konoe took office. Tokyo received a top secret cable from the Kwantung Army's chief of staff, Tōjō Hideki, who recommended delivering a "blow" upon the Nanjing regime.[14] Konoe instead dispatched his ambassador to Nanjing with an offer to return the nugget of East Hebei back to KMT authority in exchange for Nanjing's recognition of Manchukuo. KMT officials showed the Japanese ambassador the door.

Amid the diplomatic impasse, on the night of July 7, 1937, Japanese and Chinese troops exchanged gunfire near the eight-hundred-year-old Marco Polo Bridge, about ten miles southwest of Beijing. (Japan's troops were stationed in the Beijing area by rights stemming from the 1900 Boxer Rebellion; Chinese troops were attached to the Hebei-Chahar administration.) Byas reported that "the affair was one of those unforeseen quarrels which flare up when soldiers of unfriendly armies are in too close contact." Indeed, unlike the Manchurian Incident in 1931, the bulk of evidence suggests the skirmish was a spontaneous affair. Still, as James Crowley has argued, "The consistent expansion of Japanese power in north China and the growing intensity of Chinese nationalism provided a historical context which rendered some type of open conflict highly probable, if not inevitable." Konoe's right-hand man at the Shōwa Research Association, Rōyama Masamichi, similarly asserted of the outbreak of war that "even if it had been averted at that particular time, it would have occurred at some time later."[15]

On the morning of July 8, the atmosphere was still tense. Tokyo sent word that it expected a "local settlement" between Japanese troops on the ground and local Chinese authorities. The last thing the Japanese wanted was meddling from Nanjing and attempts to reclaim legitimacy in the area. Japanese officers in Beijing thus demanded an apology, punishment of the Chinese instigators (thereby establishing a presumption of Japanese self-defense), and a withdrawal of Chinese troops from the vicinity. Secretary

Hull, struggling to see through the "confusion and fog," urged each side to exercise prudence and circumspection.[16]

Both the Konoe cabinet and the Nationalist government, however, made decisions that led to escalation. On July 11, after Japan's General Staff received reports that Chiang Kai-shek had mobilized four divisions to drive north toward Hebei-Chahar, the Konoe cabinet swiftly approved the army's request for three more divisions (about forty-five thousand troops) and additional troops from Manchuria and Korea. Emperor Hirohito gave the dispatch his official blessing. Over the next few days, "day and night," according to a longtime correspondent in China, "soldiers and artillery, horses and munitions, trucks and airplanes, ambulances and vast food supplies poured into North China from Manchuria by rail."[17]

In an unprecedented show of national unity, Konoe summoned his cabinet and invited the press, politicians, and business leaders to his official residence for a press conference. The premier condemned what he called China's unwarranted attack on Japanese soldiers, and announced the decision to mobilize more troops. According to the press, Konoe intimated a need to "facilitate due repentance" from the Chinese. Above all, Konoe's statement made clear Tokyo was committed to preserving Japanese hegemony in North China. Ambassador Grew, in an early confrontation with his thesis of a civilian-military split, informed Washington that there seemed to be "complete unanimity of opinion between the Cabinet, the military, the Foreign Office, the press, and the businessmen to resist any weakening of Japan's position in North China."[18]

Secretary Hull officially stepped into the East Asian fray on July 16 with a statement that urged self-restraint. Hull, however, framed the statement in Wilsonian terms, addressed to the whole world. It read like a Nicene Creed of liberal internationalism:

> We advocate abstinence by all nations from use of force.... We advocate adjustment of problems in international relations by processes of peaceful negotiation and agreement.... We advocate faithful observance of international agreements.... We believe in modification of provisions of treaties... by *orderly processes*.... We believe in respect by all nations for the rights of others.... We stand for revitalizing and strengthening of international law. We advocate steps toward promotion of economic security.... We advocate lowering or removing of excessive barriers in international trade. We seek effective equality of commercial opportunity.... We believe in limitation and reduction of armaments.... We avoid entering into alliances... but we believe in cooperative effort.[19]

In sending his statement to the fifty-plus nations of the world, it was as if Hull was requesting that nations renew their Kellogg Pact vows. His moral appeal recalled Stimson's powerlessness during the Manchurian crisis. Japan, Germany, and Italy perfunctorily sanctioned the statement.

On July 17, a day after Hull's declaration, both Tokyo and Nanjing gave indications that compromise was unlikely. Konoe demanded an end to what he called Nanjing's provocations (i.e., mobilization) and again warned that his government only would accept a settlement among local representatives. On the same day, Chiang Kai-shek gave a gritty speech entitled "The Limit of China's Endurance." At the time, Chinese leaders were gathering at a mountain retreat in Jiangxi province for a summer conference aimed at bolstering a nascent United Front. (Six months earlier Nationalist officers had "kidnapped" Chiang and demanded he accept solidarity with the CCP.) The Jiangxi gathering therefore included CCP representative Zhou Enlai, whose meetings with Chiang in March and June 1937 had forged a working reconciliation and subsequent "legalizing" of the Red Army. In his keynote address, Chiang said events in Beijing had thrown the Chinese people into "a state of profound indignation." The Chinese would accept a truce in North China but not at the expense of national humiliation. He famously declared, "If we allow one more inch of our territory to be lost, we shall be guilty of an unpardonable offense against our race."[20]

The skirmish at the Marco Polo Bridge, a symptom of profound discord between Chinese nationalism and Japanese regionalism, could not be papered over easily with a truce. This became clear on July 27, after Emperor Hirohito sanctioned an imperial order for Japanese forces to "chastise the Chinese army in the Beijing-Tianjin area." All-out war ensued. Prince Takamatsu, Hirohito's brother and patron of the KBS, gave insight into Japan's contempt for the "puffed up" KMT, writing in his diary, "the mood in the army today is that we're really going to smash China so that it will be ten years before they can stand up straight again."[21] One could hardly find a more stinging rebuke of the ideals embodied in the Nine-Power Treaty.

"UTMOST PATIENCE AND RESTRAINT"

By the end of July, Japanese troops occupied large parts of North China. On August 8, they rolled into Beijing. Leaflets dropped on the city informed the Chinese denizens that "the Japanese Army has driven out your wicked rulers." Including Manchukuo, Japan now controlled territory that ran from Tianjin all the way to Harbin, near the Soviet border—a distance of nearly eight hundred miles. Konoe released a statement that radiated benevolent paternalism, declaring, "In sending troops to North China . . . the Government has no other purpose . . . than to preserve the peace of East Asia." In an early sign of cracks in America's dualistic perception of Japan, the *New York Times* skewered both "the military and political leaders of Japan" for their "barefaced imperial arrogance."[22] In Washington, the Roosevelt administration, armed with little more than statements of moral reprobation, resigned itself to a wait-and-see approach.

An impending sense of "now what?" hung in the air. Evidence suggests Japan hoped to contain the conflict to North China and assume control of all territory north of the Yellow River. Reporters described the mood as "grave and delicate." Because Chiang ordained it, the conflict abruptly shifted south, to Shanghai, where the generalissimo kept his crack, German-trained troops. A Chinese militia, the Peace Preservation Corps (PPC), also operated in the bustling port city. Tensions peaked on August 10 after a Japanese officer and sailor were killed, along with a PPC member. Two days later, thirty-two Japanese warships and two thousand marines massed at Shanghai, and Nationalist troops prepared barricades and gun emplacements. The *New York Times* observed that Shanghai, the world's fifth-largest city with three million people, was on the "brink of tragic developments."[23]

Sporadic sniping on August 13 turned into a steady thunder of heavy guns the next day, and an expansion of hostilities that would embroil China and Japan in one of the mostly costly wars of the twentieth century. Tragic evidence came on the first day of major fighting when the Chinese air force, in its effort to destroy Japan's flagship, the cruiser *Izumo* (not hit), mistakenly dropped 550-pound bombs on Shanghai's busiest shopping and hotel district, killing more than eight hundred people and injuring 1,100. Three Americans were killed, including thirty-one-year-old Princeton lecturer Robert K. Reischauer, who was guiding students on a summer tour of East Asia. The aerial bombing, which came four months after the infamous fascist attack on Guernica, Spain, portended not only Japan's indiscriminate bombing campaign against Chinese civilians but also the normalization of terror bombing throughout World War II.

After the attack on Japan's warships, the Konoe government released a statement saying it had exercised "utmost patience and restraint" but that the Chinese had assumed an "increasingly arrogant and insulting attitude" and "committed acts of unpardonable atrocity" against the Japanese. It put the blame for hostilities squarely on Nanjing, with the implication that the gloves were coming off. Fighting quickly spread throughout Shanghai. On August 23, the Konoe cabinet approved sending another fifty thousand troops to the battle zone to offset the KMT's numerical advantage. Japanese military officials envisioned a quick victory within two to three months. Ambassador Grew presciently demurred. Writing to Hull, he said the Japanese seemed "incapable of pausing to consider . . . the possible effects of endless guerilla warfare" and financial drain.[24]

The fighting in Shanghai became a slog. Based on conversations with Japanese authorities, Wilfred Fleisher of the *Japan Advertiser* remarked that the Konoe cabinet never imagined the scale of the war into which it was taking the nation. On September 5, Emperor Hirohito appeared before the Diet in the dress uniform of a field marshal and blamed China for the hostilities. Shortly after, he sanctioned sending three more divisions to Shanghai. By the end of September, comparable to fifteen divisions had been dispatched to China, depleting almost the entire strength of the regular Japanese Army. Amid the shouts of "banzai," an endless stream of reservists left railroad stations bound for China. Soon pink postcards from the War Office were going out to young men all over the country in a massive conscription campaign. Japan's mission, the government repeatedly stated, was "the stabilization of East Asia," the ideological catchphrase articulated by a succession of ministers going back to Foreign Minister Uchida.[25]

Former secretary of state Stimson, in a personal letter to Hull, urged the secretary to take a tougher stand against Japan, calling its leaders' justifications "a mere farce." Hull was stymied. A boycott was at present out of the question, and a public protest, as Stimson knew full well, could be easily disregarded. Instead, Hull, relying on Wilsonianism's grand threat, instructed Ambassador Grew to impress upon Foreign Minister Hirota that Japan's belligerence was "laying up for herself among the peoples of the world a liability of suspicion, distrust, popular antipathy and potential ostracism." Grew further warned Hirota that the goodwill each of them had "been building up during these past years was rapidly dissolving." According to Grew, Hirota listened "gravely and silently."[26] Was Hirota's silence an expression of defiance? Or perhaps a tragic recognition that US-Japan relations were about to go off the rails? We will never know, of course, but very likely the foreign minister was discouraged that Washington still did not grasp Japan's "true intentions" in East Asia.

American outrage stemmed, in particular, from stories and photographs of indiscriminate aerial bombings of Chinese cities. The attack around Shanghai's South Station, for example, produced an iconic—albeit slightly staged—photograph in *Life* magazine of a crying, blackened Chinese baby, sitting alone amid wreckage. A commentary in the *New Republic* at the time provides a vivid example of American attitudes. Under the title "On Hating the Japanese," the author ominously enumerated what he had personally heard as desired outcomes for the war, including "that the Japanese army now in China should be destroyed to the last man, that Japan herself should be invaded and conquered, and that her great cities should experience the horrors of aerial bombardment such as have lately been inflicted upon Shanghai and other Chinese communities." The outpouring of sympathy also stemmed from the sentimental attachments of writers and children of missionaries, such as Pearl Buck (author of *The Good Earth*) and media mogul Henry Luce (owner of *Time*, *Fortune*, and *Life*), who were either raised in China or spent considerable time there. Chiang Kai-shek and his Wellesleyeducated wife, Song Meiling (Madame Chiang), graced the cover of *Time* as "Man and Wife of the Year" for 1937.[27]

LOOKING FOR OPTIONS

After front-page news stories described how eighty Japanese planes bombed the capital of Nanjing for several hours and killed a reported two hundred people, an outraged Roosevelt told aides he wanted to make "a dramatic statement" about the world trend toward militarism; he did not want to make "simply another speech." The goal was to awaken the American people to what he believed were unique threats to liberal "civilization" and delicately broach the concept of denying trade to an aggressor.[28] This seemed to imply imposing sanctions. The word the president used was "quarantine." The place he used it—carefully scripted—was in Chicago, home of a virulently isolationist press, including Robert McCormick's *Tribune* and William Randolph Hearst's *American* and *Herald-Examiner*. On October 5, 1937, amid great fanfare, including a ticker-tape parade and thousands of well-wishers, FDR pulled into Chicago to dedicate a new bridge. He spent most of his time talking about the emergent threat to the postwar order.

The president began by assaulting isolationism's "cake and it eat too" mentality, saying the American people "under modern conditions . . . must give thought to the rest of the world." Turning to that world and the ideology of liberal internationalism, Roosevelt lamented that the "high aspirations" expressed in the Kellogg Pact had "given way to a haunting fear of calamity." He resurrected the deepest fears of the Paris peacemakers, declaring that "the present reign of terror and international lawlessness" had "reached a stage where the very foundations of civilization are threatened." In a dig at an unnamed Japan, Roosevelt said, "Without a declaration of war and without warning or justification of any kind, civilians, including vast numbers of women and children, are being ruthlessly murdered with bombs from the air." In conclusion, he urged upholding the liberal order, saying, "the peace-loving nations must make a concerted effort in opposition to those violations of treaties which today are creating a state of international anarchy and instability." Comparing the specter of global militarism to an epidemic, the president suggested that this opposition take the form of a "quarantine."[29]

Though isolationist newspapers slammed the address, the overall reaction was surprisingly favorable. The *New York Herald Tribune*, for example, a bastion of Eastern Republicanism, more explicitly advanced the president's thesis, saying the Nine-Power Treaty was "no mere expression of pious sentiment. It was a business contract, and Japan knew it when she signed it, and knows it now." Still, at a follow-up press conference, reporters pushed for a clarification: did the president have sanctions in mind? "'Sanctions,'"

FDR replied, "is a terrible word to use." And yet, what else, beyond moral censure, could a quarantine amount to? The president said he was "looking" for options. It was as if a record had been skipping on the same song since 1931—with US administrations grappling with "scraps of paper" and groping for alternatives. Journalist Ernest Lindley told the president, "You say there isn't any conflict between what you outline and the Neutrality Act. They seem to be at opposite poles to me and your assertion does not enlighten me." A frustrated Roosevelt replied, "Put your thinking-cap on, Ernest."[30]

Roosevelt expressed these frustrations in a letter to his former headmaster at Groton, Endicott Peabody, saying, "I am fighting against a public psychology of long-standing—a psychology which comes very close to saying, 'Peace at any price.'" To Col. House, the president revealed an underlying compulsion to awaken Americans to a changing world, writing, "As time goes on we can slowly but surely make people realize that war will be a greater danger to us if we close all the doors and windows."[31] But he was cautious not to move ahead of public opinion.

The "quarantine speech" deeply distressed Ambassador Grew, who told an embassy staffer, "There goes everything I have tried to accomplish in my entire mission to Japan." Perhaps not without coincidence, the State Department appeared to have grown weary of Grew's redundant analysis of Japan's political dynamics. In a private letter to Grew, Secretary Hull told the ambassador it was impossible to keep him fully informed of "the many developments which affect our attitude and influence our course." Shortly thereafter Grew wrote in his diary, "Lately I have been rather reluctant to make recommendations to Washington, having felt that my recommendations fell on somewhat stony ground." The State Department, indeed, agreed with the president's view. As Stanley Hornbeck, now Secretary Hull's special advisor, stated in a department memo, "If we mean business [in East Asia] and if we intend to be realistic, we must consider earnestly whether we are willing to do anything beyond and further than express opinions."[32]

SOFT POWER DAMAGE CONTROL

The outbreak of war in China created publicity nightmares for the Kokusai Bunka Shinkōkai. In an attempt to combat the sudden increase of anti-Japanese sentiment in America, on October 7, KBS officials convened a meeting with scholars, artists, journalists, imperial house ministers, military officials, and business leaders. Baron Dan, acknowledging the new challenge, said the KBS somehow had to reach "the whole United States." Dan, however, offered few fresh ideas, mechanically declaring that the society needed to prove the sophistication of Japanese culture to the American people. The government, meanwhile, favored sending more emissaries on goodwill visits, such as KBS advisor Viscount Ishii. But when Ishii announced he wished to visit the United States to commemorate the twentieth anniversary of the Lansing–Ishii treaty, renowned journalist Oswald Garrison Villard, who had hosted a dinner for Ishii in 1917, leveled a warning in the *New York Herald Tribune*: "If you come, your first talk will be to explain away your own words and to attempt the impossible, that is, to reconcile your statement of just twenty years ago. . . . May I suggest that until you can do that it would be well for you to postpone your proposed propaganda trip to the U.S.?" Ishii visited Great Britain instead.[33]

Ishii's planned visit and Villard's retort show that *differences in perceptions* among Japanese and Americans of the ideological divide were nearly as wide as the divide itself. Comments by conductor Konoe Hidemaro, who had just cut short a second tour in the United States, confirmed this. Konoe told the *Asahi Shimbun* that "opinion in America is much worse than the people here know." Decrying "clever and artistic" Chinese propaganda in the United States—and indirectly criticizing the apparent impotence of the KBS—the maestro said he had urged his older brother to "get a hold of a man with a nose for propaganda." Premier Konoe chose to write President Roosevelt a personal letter. Konoe reminisced warmly about his 1934 visit and, hoping to tap residual goodwill from Japan's soft power initiatives, told FDR he was certain he was expressing the views of the vast majority of his countrymen by stating "our traditional sentiments of friendship toward your country are particularly strong and universal of late years." For this Konoe applauded individuals in both countries (read: Grew/KBS types) who were "contributing to the development and the maintenance of mutual friendship through sympathetic understanding and through reciprocal respect and confidence." At the same time, yet another government-sponsored soft power institution, the Japan Pacific Association, began printing English-language pamphlets that sought to explain Japan's aims in China. The back of one pamphlet showed Japanese soldiers playing baseball in the Chinese countryside with the title "How about Giving Japan a Break?"[34]

The gap between official Japanese statements and realities on the ground, however, conspired against Japan receiving the benefit of the doubt from Americans. Konoe's communications minister, Nagai Ryūtarō, for example, called Japan's actions in China a "Holy War for the Reconstruction of Asia." Nagai's point cut to the heart of how the Japanese had come to view and justify its actions in China. What Japan sought in China, said Nagai, was not territory but "partnership." More precisely, the Japanese "desire dearly that the Chinese people return to their true Asian mind." Although such Pan-Asianist idealism emboldened the Japanese nation throughout the war, its persistent paradox emboldened Chinese resistance. The critical leap was not great, for how would indiscriminate bombings help the Chinese return to their true Asian mind? Perhaps for this reason, Ambassador Saitō emphasized self-defense. In a CBS Radio address, Saitō told Americans that the fighting in China had been "forced upon Japan." One wonders how the affable ambassador would have responded if presented with the answer he gave in Chicago two years prior, on whether Japan intended to take control of China: "To us Japanese that seems like asking, 'Are you mad?'"[35]

A belated Nine-Power Treaty conference in November, meanwhile, showed why the liberal order was collapsing. Despite an excess assemblage of nineteen nations in Brussels—minus Japan, which said the treaty did not apply to the conflict in China—the conference turned out to be a fiasco lacking in leadership and resolution. Great Britain, in particular, expected greater American leadership, and Roosevelt, for domestic reasons, was reluctant to provide it. The president told his envoy to tell the British "there is such a thing as public opinion in the United States." A commentary headline in the *New York Times* skewered the gathering: "Brussels Conference in Bathetic Impotence." The writer added, "If [the conference] does not adjourn quickly it risks becoming pathetic." In the end, the meeting settled on a statement urging reliance on the liberal shibboleth of "peaceful processes," even as the current state of Shanghai made a mockery of such measured ministrations: the city's Chinese sections suffered frightful destruction while the foreign settlements functioned mostly unscathed. Given the explicit application of the Nine-Power Treaty to China proper, the tepid statement was a strikingly weak response. And yet "statements" was all the treaty accorded. In Tokyo, Premier Konoe, emboldened by news that the Japanese Army had broken the deadlock at Shanghai, responded to the Brussels meeting by intimating that Japan eventually would have to abrogate the Nine-Power Treaty.[36] Fifteen years after its birth, the liberal treaty was an empty vessel.

THE *PANAY* CRISIS AND THE NANJING MASSACRE

Shanghai fell on November 9. Chiang's best-trained troops were defeated; China's largest city was in Japanese hands. A whirlwind of activity ensued. Remaining Chinese forces began withdrawing west along the Yangtze River, toward lines protecting the capital of Nanjing; three columns of Japanese troops followed in pursuit. On November 20, Chiang said government agencies would move from Nanjing to cities farther west along the Yangtze—to Wuhan and Chongqing. Secretary Hull responded to the fast-changing events with a memo to American ambassadors in Asia and Europe in which he described Japan's ambitions in China as a "monstrous program." He called on his diplomats to rally other nations in opposition.[37] In Tokyo, the Konoe cabinet began preparing the nation for a longer conflict.

Japan's offensive moved quickly, with some units reaching the outskirts of the capital by December 7, the same day Chiang and his wife departed for

Wuhan. Chiang's generals prepared to hold Nanjing with a defensive ring of about three hundred thousand troops and hastily built barricades and trenches. But lacking planes, the KMT struggled to pinpoint Japanese troop movements and routinely were outflanked. While Japan's commanders consolidated their attacking forces, the empire's planes pounded Chinese positions. Japan's air corps also created a momentary crisis with the United States. On December 12, in broad daylight, Japanese warplanes attacked and sunk the American gunboat USS *Panay*, which was anchored on the Yangtze River, about twenty-eight miles upstream from Nanjing. Newsreel footage and photographs from onboard cameramen offered irrefutable proof, not only of the bombing, but also the strafing of survivors. Two American sailors were killed and thirty other people injured.

Americans, not surprisingly, were livid. The fact that a huge American flag had been freshly painted on the boat's awning suggested the attack was no accident. The usually composed Hull decried Japan's attackers as "wild, runaway, half-insane." An outraged Roosevelt demanded an apology, compensation to the victims, and guarantees against another attack. To emphasize the gravity of the situation, the president also asked that Emperor Hirohito be advised of how "deeply shocked" he was. This may have been simply a sincere gesture, but one observer described it as a "master stroke of diplomacy" since it forced Japan's statesmen to feel personally responsible for sullying the honor of their emperor. The administration also revisited punitive measures. Returning to the gist of his Chicago speech, Roosevelt insisted, "We don't call them economic sanctions, but call them quarantines." The combative secretary of the interior, Harold L. Ickes, went further and contemplated a preemptive war. As Ickes noted in his diary, "Much as I deprecate war, I still think that if we are ever going to fight Japan, and it looks to me as if we would have to do sooner or later, the best time is now."[38]

American indignation, however, soon subsided. The Konoe government was embarrassed by the incident and moved quickly to meet FDR's demands. Foreign Minister Hirota apologized, promised it would not happen again, and negotiated compensation. Premier Konoe, meanwhile, sent Roosevelt another cordial letter and, in a curious gesture that spoke volumes about personal convictions, attached a Pan-Asianist pamphlet, *Plea for Peace and Reconciliation*, whose author argued that the Japanese were fighting in China to "establish a United States of Asia."[39]

By Christmas Eve, the *Panay* crisis was over. The two-week affair was significant mainly for deepening America's conflicted double wish: it simultaneously intensified American sympathies for the Chinese and a desire to avoid war. Few newspapers recommended a strong response. Most pointedly, Rep. Louis Ludlow (D-IN), after several previous attempts, successfully introduced a vote in the House for a constitutional amendment requiring a national referendum whenever Congress declared war (except in case of invasion). The measure had been bottled up in committee for several past Congresses, but the *Panay* war scare finally brought it to the floor. Roosevelt put up vigorous opposition, marking his first real effort to stem the isolationist tide. On December 18, the *New York Times* noted that FDR "without hesitation, and with a sharpness not characteristic of him," quickly snapped in the negative when asked by the press whether the Ludlow measure was consistent with representative government. A few days later the president rejected "peace at any price."[40] In January 1938, the House defeated the Ludlow resolution by a comfortable margin, 209 to 188 (it required 290 votes to pass, or a two-thirds majority).

While Americans debated boycotts and compensation and Ludlow's resolution, Japanese forces seized Nanjing. The city capitulated on December 13, one day after the *Panay* sinking. A news blackout and eerie silence followed. Three American correspondents, F. Tillman Durdin of the *New York Times*, C. Yates McDaniel of the Associated Press, and A. T. Steele of the *Chicago Daily News*, were in Nanjing, which still contained more than four hundred thousand people, when the Japanese army entered the capital. The most detailed reports first reached Americans on December 18. Durdin's page-one story in the *New York Times* spoke of "wholesale atrocities and vandalism," with the prevalent killing of civilians. "Some of the victims were aged men, women and children. . . . Many Chinese men reported to foreigners the abduction and rape of wives and daughters. . . . [Nanjing's] streets were littered with dead." In January, Durdin's long summary of the massacre corroborated earlier reports of "unrestrained cruelties." McDaniel, meanwhile, said his last remembrance of Nanjing was "Dead Chinese, dead Chinese, dead Chinese."[41]

Most Americans, however, knew little about the massacre until well into the new year. A pair of articles published by the popular periodical *Reader's Digest* as well as a compendium of contemporaneous accounts, *Japanese Terror in China*, edited by H. J. Timperley—a foreign correspondent for the *Manchester Guardian* who was close to the Chinese government—eventually brought the massacre into the mainstream. Japan responded with *Behind the News in China*, authored by hired journalist Frederick V. Williams, who claimed that American missionaries had manufactured atrocity stories. Still, the cumulative effect of incendiary raids, the *Panay* affair, and continued aggression took a grievous toll on American perceptions of Japan.[42]

"WE WILL NOT DEAL WITH THEM"

Strict censorship prevented ordinary Japanese from hearing about atrocities committed by the emperor's army. But what they did hear was momentous: the Imperial Japanese Army had captured Chiang Kai-shek's capital. Celebrations took place all around Japan, marked by lantern parades. A newsreel distributed worldwide showed Gen. Matsui Iwane—a founding member of the Pan-Asianist group Greater Asian Association—entering Nanjing on horseback and proclaiming, "The dawn of the renaissance of Eastern Asia is about to take place." An indication of this deepening ideological rationale came from Konoe's new home minister, Adm. Suetsugu Nobumasa, a hardliner. Drawing from the "liberation" strand of Asianism, Suetsugu described the empire's mission in China as a race war, with the ejection of "white peoples" from Asia as the only path to justice. Suetsugu's assertion caused a sensation in the United States.[43]

Considering Japan's aggression against fellow East Asians, Suetsugu's race argument was mostly illogical obfuscation; nonetheless, it also contained a kernel of truth: whites had colonized vast territories in Asia and ruled over tens of millions of nonwhite people. As one expatriate American put it, "I had never liked my Occidental people's attitude in the East. There were many I knew personally who were models of exemplary conduct.... [But] there was the predatory class.... The East had a right to be rid of the white race in privileged position." The writer had touched upon the source of transcendent power in the idealized strand of Asianist ideology, but also one that could be easily exposed as duplicitous and self-serving.[44]

The surrender of Nanjing, in any event, tilted diplomatic leverage emphatically toward Japan. A month prior, both China and Japan had accepted mediation by Germany, which sought to maintain good relations with both belligerents.[45] The Konoe government now prepared to issue harsh terms. On January 9, 1938, a "Liaison Conference" (premier, foreign minister, army and navy ministers, and General Staffs) produced the "Fundamental Policy for the Disposition of the China Incident." It was a stunning unveiling of Tokyo's more grandiose regionalism, obliging Chongqing not only to recognize Manchukuo, but also to accept Japanese hegemony in North China; demilitarized zones in Central China; a political-economic bloc between Japan, Manchukuo, and China; as well as reparation payments. These were old-fashioned, punitive terms of peace by an imperialist power.

Surprisingly, opposition to the harsh terms came from the Army General Staff, which, fearing a protracted conflict, advocated instead for a negotiated settlement with the Nationalist government. Ultimately the staff relented. Although such dissent could be construed as representing a missed opportunity, this begs the question: missed opportunity for what? Over the previous six years, the Army General Staff had either ordered or tacitly sanctioned war making and intimidation in East Asia, all of which culminated in a million Japanese troops fighting in China by the end of 1937.[46] Thus, tactical differences among Japan's decision makers about "how" to deal militarily with China require distinction from the widely held Asianist worldview that envisioned Japanese supremacy in the region. In any case, Konoe promptly conveyed the surrender terms to Emperor Hirohito with a request to convene an Imperial Conference.

Imperial Conferences were called only on occasions of the utmost importance. This peculiarity in Japan's monarchical system was, according to Herbert Bix, "*the* device for legally transforming the 'will of the emperor' into the 'will of the state.'" At Imperial Conferences, the emperor sat quietly, surrounded by his highest military and civilian officials, offering not a single word. By virtue of the emperor's august presence, policy decisions were given imperial sanction. Imperial Conferences allowed the emperor "to perform as if he were a pure constitutional monarch" but without "bearing responsibility for his action." And, curiously, as Eri Hotta has shown, because policy decisions at once became divine and apolitical, they also relieved political leaders of any personal responsibility.[47] It thus was a shrewd device for cementing consensus and diffusing responsibility—no one, yet everyone, affirmed policy.

Hugh Byas's secondhand account of the Imperial Conference in the *New York Times* depicted an atmosphere of solemnity, majesty, and power. At the Tokyo Palace on January 11, reported Byas, the emperor, in khaki, and his generals, ministers, and admirals, sat before tables "draped with priceless brocades." Foreign Minister Hirota, surrounded by gilt screens and a massive painting, *The Thousand Sparrows*, read aloud the terms of the "Fundamental Policy," which was duly affirmed. It subsequently was announced to the world that the conference had approved a fateful ultimatum: if Chiang's regime did not submit entirely to Tokyo's terms, the Konoe government would no longer recognize it; instead, Japan would have no choice but to "annihilate" the Kuomintang and promote a new regime in China. The Nationalist government was given three days to respond. When no word arrived, Konoe released a statement teeming with the chauvinistic strand of Asianism, declaring that Nationalists had been given "a final opportunity to repent" but had failed to "appreciate the Empire's true intention." As a result, in order to create "peace and tranquility" in East Asia, the Japanese government "will not deal with" the KMT. Instead, Tokyo looked forward to the establishment of a "new Chinese government."[48]

"A WAVE OF ANTI-JAPANESE FEELING"

The capture of the Kuomintang capital was feeding a dangerous bravado. Konoe and other Japanese leaders spoke in the language of a playground bully, in which the targeted victim is expected to "understand" what the bully demands—and act accordingly—or else. The problem for Japan was that the playground was filled with four hundred million people. By refusing to recognize any Chinese regime that rejected its demands, Japan's leaders were painting themselves into a corner of outright colonial rule or more puppet regimes. Further, not recognizing the Nationalist government did not make it magically disappear—Japan would have to continue to fight it. In light of such challenges, including the prospect of endless guerilla war, pundit Nathaniel Peffer believed that Japan's rulers, deep down, must have realized they were "harboring a delusion." The evidence, however, suggests otherwise. Konoe, in fact, chided the Chinese for being "hopelessly deluded." And Rōyama Masamichi, a key member of Konoe's brain trust, wrote that the Chinese should forsake the "ideas of perverted xenophobic nationalism." Grew, meanwhile, informed Hull that Hirota recently had twice lost his temper to the British ambassador and that he was "steadily becoming harder and more intransigent as regards foreign interests in the Far East."[49] A human calamity was reaching a point of no return.

By February 1938, Japan held all of North China and the central coastline, territory that included the cities of Beijing, Tianjin, Qingdao, Shanghai, Nanjing, and Hangzhou. At the same time, the empire's regionalist ambitions received a welcome affirmation when Hitler's new foreign minister, Joachim von Ribbentrop, closed the gap between the German Foreign Office and the Nazi leadership and steered the Reich closer to Japan. In May, Germany recognized Manchukuo, followed soon after by the withdrawal of Hitler's ambassador from China and all military advisors.[50] For Japan, adding Germany's name (and Italy and Spain) to Manchukuo's backers shored up a heretofore anemic list of El Salvador, the Dominican Republic, and Costa Rica.

The quick succession of military victories combined with Germany's moral support stimulated further rhetorical flourishes from Tokyo. In a cynical replication of Chiang Kai-shek's Jiangxi speech after the clash at the Marco Polo Bridge, the AP reported that Premier Konoe insisted that Japan "would never give up an inch of the areas already occupied [in China]." Concurrently, Tokyo announced plans to install a new regime in central China, with its capital at Nanjing. According to Foreign Minister Hirota, military operations would continue until "friendly" regimes in North China and central China could be consolidated into a unified Chinese government. Hirota added that the Nine-Power Accord was only of "nominal existence."[51]

In Washington, the Roosevelt administration remained a mostly ineffectual bystander to Japan's progressive demolition of the Nine-Power Treaty, but it nonetheless had become encouraged by a spike in editorials supporting stronger measures against Tokyo. Recent commentary in the *New York Times*, *Philadelphia Inquirer*, *Baltimore Sun*, *Washington Times*, *Washington Star*, and *New York Herald Tribune*, for example, showed "considerable editorial sentiment" in favor of depriving Japan of war materials. Perhaps most conspicuously, prominent chain stores—including Woolworth, Kresge, Kress, and McCrory's—announced they would temporarily suspend purchase orders of Japanese products. Pro-China groups, meanwhile, flooded the country with boycott buttons and posters. An emboldened Roosevelt subsequently returned to the issue of punitive measures, informing Hull, "I think we should start to lay the foundation for holding Japan accountable in dollars. . . . Enough said!" In fact, much more would have to be said—and happen—before the administration felt confident enough to go down that road. But the first indications of a bolder response appeared in June.[52]

Day after day, as Japan's military campaign advanced down China's southern coast toward Guangzhou—the Nationalist's last access to the sea—the American public read about ferocious incendiary raids that set the city ablaze. For example, a story distributed on June 9 by the Associated Press, a cooperative serving one thousand newspapers, claimed, "Unrelenting Japanese bombardment of this once-prosperous South China metropolis has started huge fires, crippled the city's utilities and pushed the toll of dead and injured above 8,000." *Nation* magazine opined that "never in history has the civilian population of a city been subjected to such merciless bombings." And Ambassador Grew called the Guangzhou firebombings "one of the worst episodes in modern warfare," adding, "Japan's reputation can never recover from these things."[53] As a result of the bombings, President Roosevelt made his first foray into sanctions, calling on American firms to comply with a voluntary "moral embargo" on the sale of aircraft to nations engaged in indiscriminate raids on civilian populations.

The president had the public behind him. Eighty-four percent of Americans now said they would favor even a discretionary arms embargo against Japan. The *New York Times* noted approvingly that "American opinion today is openly and overwhelmingly on the side of China as against Japan: so openly and so overwhelmingly that it has winked at and approved a flagrant violation of the whole spirit of the Neutrality Act." According to Columbia scholar Jacques Barzun, "a wave of anti-Japanese feeling" had swept over America. "Everywhere," said Barzun, "in high circles and low, condemnation of the Japanese for their war on China is to be heard." Secretary Hull sent Grew a long cable summarizing American press coverage of Japan's aggression in China, instructing his ambassador to apprise Japanese officials of "the growing and widespread criticism in the United States" toward their country.[54]

Roosevelt's call for a "moral embargo" and rising anti-Japanese sentiment coincided with the formation of a prominent pro-China lobbying group—the American Committee for Non-Participation in Japanese Aggression (commonly known as the "Price Committee," after the surname of it founders). Its core members were American citizens who had spent considerable time in China, especially educators, journalists, and missionaries. Although not under the auspices or payroll of the Chinese government, informal linkages between the New York–based Price Committee and the KMT's information apparatus were nonetheless strong. The group focused on raising public awareness about the connection between US exports and Japanese aggression—with the goal of rallying Americans to compel Washington to embargo the sale of strategic resources to Japan. In the summer of 1938, the Price Committee disseminated its first publication, *America's Share in Japan's War Guilt*, and soon after announced Henry Stimson as its honorary chairman. The State Department's Stanley Hornbeck supported the group's publicity campaign but also tempered its expectations, as the administration juggled the war in Asia with saber-rattling in Europe, while contending with the ever-present force of domestic isolationism.[55]

THE KBS'S JAPAN CULTURE CENTER

The Japanese government, meanwhile, continued to place faith in soft power to assuage American antagonism and counter pro-China lobby groups. As Japanese bombs rained down on Guangzhou, the KBS's Kabayama arrived in New York City to lay the groundwork for the opening of a ten-thousand-square-foot "Japan Culture Center" at the Rockefeller Center—financed by the Konoe cabinet with four hundred thousand yen from MOFA's budget. Guided by the unrelenting Japanese contention that America's "bad feelings toward Japan [were] due to ignorance," in a KBS memo, Kabayama described the center as a "facts" institute that would inform about Japan "accurately" and correct "mistakes" in the American press. Indeed, KBS officials saw their role as more important than ever. According to the *K.B.S. Quarterly*, the Sino-Japanese War had "stimulated foreign interest in Japan and resulted in ever increasing requests . . . for information about Japan and Japanese culture." Toward this end, American visitors to the Japan Culture Center would have access to some seven thousand books and information on Japanese culture. Also in the works was KBS sponsorship of a special book-length issue of *NIPPON*, titled *The Nation in Panorama*, motivated by the Japanese expression that "one seeing is worth more than a hundred readings." The book's sleek photographic compositions, one scholar has observed, "took the use of montage aesthetics to a new crescendo."[56]

Notably, essays in the KBS-funded *NIPPON* magazine now blended the cultural with the political. Issue 14 (1938), for example, which devoted five articles to the Sino-Japanese War, declared that "men of understanding" would appreciate Japan's "plight." The author suggested that China's decrepit state had propelled the Japanese into the historically vital role as "cultural crusaders . . . entrusted with a holy mission to renew the life of the spiritual civilization peculiar to the Orient." Whereas China was failing to preserve its cultural riches, the Japanese army had been taking "every precaution to save [cultural artifacts] from damage even at the cost of some strategic disadvantages." Consistent with Asianist propaganda, the author stated the Japanese regarded it as " a great honor to be entrusted with such an important cultural mission." *NIPPON* also depicted a Japan whose intervention had normalized daily life in China. Captioned photographs in issue 15 included "Common people in peace-restored [Nanjing] watching juggling in the street" and "The parks [in Beijing] are always crowded with strollers." Tokyo's soft power apparatus additionally sponsored a four-hundred-page almanac, issued in the United States, titled *America and Japan in Amity and Trade*. Premier Konoe, who was enamored with soft power, wrote an introductory essay for the book, which was filled with *NIPPON*-like articles and photographs extolling Japan. Its stated mission repeated the nearly decade-long cause "to interpret Japan's true intentions in Asia."[57]

Given the seemingly irreversible slide in US-Japan relations, it is difficult to avoid wondering what KBS officials were thinking, plunging might and main, as it were, into a futile campaign to win over American hearts and minds. Indeed, when the KBS attempted to launch a traveling library in the United States, the State Department denied its request on concerns that "some person or group, carried away by feelings against Japan, might seek to do damage to the truck and its occupants." Even Americans most likely to become seduced by KBS programs—artists themselves—showed little ambivalence in the face of naked aggression. After the fall of Nanjing, for example, the American Artists Congress adopted a resolution condemning Japan's belligerence. And Pablo Picasso, shortly after delivering his painting *Guernica* to the Paris Exposition, sent a message to the group, stating "artists who live and work with spiritual values cannot and should not remain indifferent to [global conflict] in which the highest values of humanity and civilization are at stake." It was an abstract affirmation of the liberal principles presently under siege. Significantly, such responses revealed the inherent limits of KBS programs. As Joseph Nye and other scholars have indicated, soft power strategies are compromised by dissonance between a projected, desired image and a country's actual foreign policies.[58]

Despite these obvious limits, one also gets the sense that Japan's leaders, by the summer of 1938, while *preferring* American recognition of Japanese primacy in Asia, were becoming less disposed to that end. Self-assuredness flowed principally out of the barrel of hard power—from the one million Japanese under arms on the mainland, and offensives on the cusp of seizing both Guangzhou and Wuhan. In commemorating the first year of war, for example, Premier Konoe confidently claimed that, among the four hundred million Chinese, "there is quite a number . . . who really understand the true intentions of Japan." Konoe repeated Japan's "historic mission" to "lay the foundation of East Asian peace" and commended Germany and Italy for supporting the empire's cause—yet another sign of Tokyo's growing bond with Europe's revisionist powers.[59]

The interconnectedness between events in Asia and Europe became more marked in the fall of 1938. Following Germany's absorption of Austria in March, Hitler began angling for the cession of Czechoslovakia's German-speaking borderlands of Sudetenland. In hopes of resolving the crisis, British Prime Minister Neville Chamberlain flew to Germany in September for a series of meetings with the Führer at the latter's mountain chalet in Berchtesgaden. At a final conference in Munich—also attended by Mussolini and France's prime minister, but absent Czech officials—the two democracies agreed to Hitler's demand. Roosevelt's treasury secretary, Henry Morgenthau Jr., in a letter to FDR, eviscerated Britain and France's weakness and urged greater action against aggressor nations. He also imagined a parallel scene in which the president flew to Tokyo and humbled himself before the Japanese emperor.[60] Roosevelt, however, joined in the worldwide pacifist sentiments, thankful that war had been averted. Indeed, although the Munich Conference later became regarded as the apotheosis of appeasement, at the time it seemed to have preserved peace in Europe at a reasonable geopolitical price. Hitler promised that Sudetenland was the last of his territorial ambitions; Chamberlain arrived back in London showered with praise. In Tokyo, Konoe responded to the accord by promoting his military attaché in Berlin, the Hitler-admiring Lt. Gen. Ōshima Hiroshi, as ambassador, and launching a new military campaign that cut close to Britain's colony of Hong Kong. On the horizon was a bold Pan-Asianst declaration.

"A NEW ORDER IN EAST ASIA"

While Britain and France worked to prevent a spiral to another major war in Europe, a flummoxed Secretary Hull was trying to stitch back together a tattered Nine-Power Treaty. Over the previous year, Ambassador Grew had made innumerable protests to the Konoe government regarding violations of American commercial and property interests in China. And repeatedly, the Americans were told that Japan respected the Open Door and would look into the complaints. These were two nations dancing to dissonant realities. The Americans proceeded as if the war in China had not altered the status quo, when it had; Japan proceeded as if the Open Door was still in place, when it was not. The dance came to a halt in the fall of 1938.

On October 6, Grew presented Premier Konoe and Japan's new foreign minister and longtime diplomat Arita Hachirō with an extensive protest from Hull. The secretary contrasted the history of violations to American interests in China against Japan's "categorical assurances" to respect these interests. Hull demanded a prompt end to Japan's discriminatory practices. A cynical view might conclude the State Department was only interested in American commerce in China. That made outward sense in the face of a brutal war in which more than a million Chinese had been killed. In fact, however, the secretary was struggling to force the issue on the Nine-Power Treaty, which covered both Chinese sovereignty and American commercial interests. With the treaty's clause on China's "territorial integrity" already shot to pieces, any protest would amount to target practice using blanks. That left respect for the Open Door: was Japan prepared to guarantee American rights? "An early reply," Hull stated, "would be helpful."[61]

An early reply would not be forthcoming. Japan's army was on the march, overwhelming Chinese defenders at Guangzhou and Wuhan, which fell within days of one another. On October 24, Chiang Kai-shek abandoned Wuhan for Chongqing, situated one thousand miles west of Shanghai. All of China's major cities were now under Japanese authority. Fortified by these fresh military successes, on November 3, 1938, the Konoe government announced to the world the creation of a "New Order in East Asia." The declaration was an eloquent evocation of Japan's chauvinistic brand of Asianism, with Premier Konoe proclaiming peaceful and collaborative intentions behind a veil of an exclusive regional order. Despite an ongoing war that had effected untold suffering on the Chinese people, Konoe maintained that "Japan sincerely desires the development and not the ruin of China" and aimed "to build up a stabilized Far East by cooperating with the Chinese people." Fulfillment of this goal, he said, required "a new peace fabric." Excoriating the liberal order, Konoe argued there was "no denying the fact that various principles in the past have forced the maintenance of the status quo marked by an unbalanced state," adding, "that the covenant of the League of Nations has lost its prestige is fundamentally due to this irrationality." The premier concluded with a dramatic air of selfless sacrifice, saying Japan's "moral mission is heavy," while warning nations with interests in Asia to "adapt their attitude" accordingly.[62]

Thus, after years of prevailing upon the world to realize Japan's "special responsibility" and primacy in East Asia, Tokyo essentially made it official. To Konoe, the declaration was deeply personal, influenced by his close associates at the Shōwa Research Association. As historian W. Miles Fletcher has noted, the New Order declaration embodied the SRA premise that the war in China "now entailed a universally important moral purpose and creation of a new stage in world history." Indeed, the grandiose phrase "world-historical moment" became a key corollary to Japan's regionalist ideology. This view of an imminent overhaul in world affairs was given further illumination the day after Konoe's pronouncement, when the AP quoted Foreign Office spokesperson Kawai Tatsuo, who had authored a deeply mystical apologia for Japanese hegemony in Asia, as saying the Japanese deemed the Nine-Power Treaty "obsolete." Moreover, Foreign Minister Arita officially responded to Secretary Hull's October note, saying the "new situation, fast developing in East Asia" meant that "ideas and principles of the past" were no longer applicable to the present. References to "the past" made the liberal principles sound ancient; doubtless to many contemporaries, by the end of 1938, the postwar treaties seemed ancient.[63]

The New Order declaration, in particular, dominated headlines in the American metropolitan press, whose coverage made clear that, despite sixteen months of Japanese aggression and various regionalist statements, American observers were taken aback by Tokyo's bluntness. The *Los Angeles Times* announced "Tokyo Prepares to Rule China," the *Chicago Tribune* said Japan declared a "Guardianship over East Asia," and the *New York Times* stated "Japan Admits Aim to Dominate China." The *Washington Post* similarly declared that Japan had finally revealed its hand in its bid "to Rule China as Manchukuo." The vituperation was widespread. An analysis at the time of seven hundred American newspapers reported that Japan's regionalist presumptions had "unloosed a torrent of indignant editorial comment," with only ten papers voicing opposition to stronger measures from Washington. If anything, the collective surprise toward the Konoe declaration shows how America's dualistic perceptions of Japanese politics, shaped partly by soft power over the previous years, had bred a quiet optimism for an eventual reversal in the empire's continental conduct. Apart from Ambassador Grew, that bifurcated view and attendant cautious optimism now began to dissolve.[64]

***

With the proclaimed establishment of a New Order in East Asia, Japan's leaders believed they were embarking on a profound, world-changing, historical mission. Official statements increasingly embraced the sublime, with allusions to a "reconstruction" and a "renaissance" in Asia. On December 22, for example, after an Imperial Conference endorsed the New Order, Premier Konoe vigorously reaffirmed Tokyo's expansive regionalism, exclaiming that "the spirit of renaissance is now sweeping over all parts of China, and enthusiasm for reconstruction is mounting ever higher." Toward these ends, Konoe said, "China should cast aside all narrow prejudiced views of the past and do away with the folly of anti-Japanism and resentment regarding Manchukuo." The premier reiterated Japan's vow to "exterminate" the Kuomintang government. This was a leadership strongly convinced of its own moral authority (even with the pride-swallowing announcement that Tokyo had decided to cancel hosting the 1940 Olympics). Konoe's assertiveness was mirrored in the Japanese press, which, according to Byas in the *New York Times*, leveled "torrents of denunciation" against Britain and the United States, calling the latter a tool of the former. A *Japan Times and Mail* special supplement, meanwhile, described Foreign Minister Arita's regionalist proclamations "as a bold, flashing shaft from the heavens."[65]

At the same time, Japan's soft power apparatus continued to blend the cultural with the political. NHK overseas programming, for example, began to extol "The Japanese Spirit" and the creation of a New Order in East Asia, along with a new "Japan Culture Series." KBS Chairman Count Kabayama, at an America-Japan Society luncheon, hailed Japan's "reconstruction projects" in North China. And KBS officials began to anticipate more purposeful outreach to the prospective beneficiaries of Japan's regionalist vision. Diplomat Minowa Saburo, for example, stated that the Sino-Japanese War had helped his people "to become aware of our status as the successors and creators of the most powerful culture among East Asian nations, and upon that awareness, as pioneers of the Eastern nations." Cultural projects in Asia, he argued, would cultivate "spiritual awe and affection" toward Japan. Consonant with global trends, Tokyo also moved into closer cultural relationships with Europe's revisionist regimes. In 1938 the Konoe government signed a cultural agreement with Germany. A nationalistic ethos permeated the agreement's preamble, which said the two peoples were "deeply conscious" of "the intrinsic Japanese spirit on one side and in the German national life on the other side." Japan's Office of International Tourism subsequently began featuring Hitler and other Nazi officials in its publications, and the KBS participated in exhibitions in Leipzig and Berlin.[66] Contrary to the one-sided programs aimed at the United States, the new initiatives appeared more as genuine exchange and solidarity. A cultural agreement with Italy followed in 1939. Soon after, the flags of Nazi Germany and Fascist Italy became fixtures on the Ginza in central Tokyo.

Across the Pacific, the Roosevelt administration grew ever more concerned about the fast-changing international environment—unilateralism, autarky, and militarism—so antithetical to the precepts of the treaty system. Secretary Morgenthau, concerned about the seeming "slippery slope" beyond America's frontiers, told Roosevelt, "Japan at first wanted only Manchuria, then Northern China; now she will not be content with less than the whole of China. Italy wanted only Ethiopia; now she wants control of North Africa. Germany wanted only equality in armament, then the remilitarization of the Rhineland, then Austria, then Czechoslovakia, now colonies."[67] As always, such observations left a nagging question: how should the United States respond to these illiberal trends? In 1939, sensing dangerous points of no return in both Asia and Europe, the administration began to address that question directly with Congress and the American people. Twenty years after the Paris Peace Conference, signs everywhere suggested a great ideological divide was bringing nations closer to the great fear that inspired the peacemakers at the end of the Great War.

Chapter Six

"This Mad World of Ours" (1939–1940)

As the 1930s drew to a close, a perilous clash of ideologies—of core values among nation-states—loomed large. Fascism, Nazism, communism, and liberalism tumbled about in a global struggle of competing ideas, encompassing widely divergent assumptions about human nature and systems of world order. The liberal democracies, with their lingering, albeit faltering, commitment to liberal internationalism, increasingly seemed like the odd man out. Leaders in Fascist Italy, Nazi Germany, and Imperial Japan, with their confident pronouncements and regionalist claims, gave the impression of being on the right side of history. A strongly nationalist mythos, enveloping politics, religion, and culture, and a domestic economy geared toward the "total mobilization" of society added to a sense of collective forward motion toward some greater justice.

Japan's leaders anticipated a new era in East Asia. All liberal contrivances like the hypocritical Nine-Power Treaty would be consigned to the ash heap of history. A Japanese-dominated regional order seemed to be within grasp. With one million men under arms in China, and another five hundred thousand in Korea and Manchuria, Tokyo looked to annihilate the Kuomintang and precipitate an Asian renaissance. But therein lay the ideological-geopolitical rub. Evidence of challenges to Japan's aspirations appeared almost every day in Japanese cities in the form of wounded soldiers in white uniforms accompanied by Red Cross nurses. Or little white boxes unloaded at train stations that held the ashes of fallen soldiers. And if exhilarating military victories came fast and furious in 1938, the fact remained that Chiang Kai-shek's Nationalist government in Chongqing was still standing. Japan's policy makers thus faced the challenge of waging indefinite war while occupying and winning over a hostile population of two hundred million Chinese, in territory covering nearly one million square miles. Then there was the nagging issue of future relations with Germany. Should Japan extend and deepen relations with Hitler's Reich? A closer relationship would act decidedly as a bulwark against the Soviet Union on Manchukuo's northern border, but it could also provoke the liberal democracies and needlessly draw Japan into hostilities in Europe. Tokyo's soft power strategies toward the United States, meanwhile, dwindled amid the inexorable contradiction between presentation and aggression.

Across the Pacific, President Roosevelt began to emphasize the interconnectedness between ideology and national security, a correlation made all the more significant by the administration's tendency to perceive an ideological convergence of Japan, Germany, and Italy as a major threat to the "American way of life." Increasingly, Roosevelt enlarged the parameters of liberal internationalism by incorporating self-described foundational values, what Roosevelt later would call the "Four Freedoms." Famously sensitive to public opinion, Roosevelt became vigilant in what became a kind of personal mission to awaken Americans to the perceived threat of ideological encirclement and an antagonistic world order.

Ever so gradually the American people receded from their isolationist cocoon and came round to the president's worldview. By mid-1939, the administration, confident of public support, notified Japan that it intended to terminate the US-Japan Commercial Treaty of 1911. And shortly after an expansion of hostilities in Europe, Congress moved toward revising the Neutrality Act's arms embargo. Still, even with greater public support and a more pliant Congress, the administration was left reacting to the snowballing events thousands of miles away, from which there were no obvious "good" choices. Operating on a kind of hemispheric island, Roosevelt swiveled between two wars, across two oceans, struggling to fulfill America's conflicting double wish: help the "good guys," but don't leave the island.

***

In January 1939, two months after declaring a New Order in East Asia, Premier Konoe resigned. Historians tend to interpret his resignation as a sign of frustration with the stalemate in China.[1] This view, however, fails to explain the palpable sense of confidence coursing through Konoe's "renaissance" statement just two weeks before his departure. Though he might have feared a coming quagmire, very probably Konoe, plagued by an infirm constitution, simply grew fatigued by the immense responsibility of managing a nation during wartime (his colleagues, after all, said he made a cult of languor). Konoe subsequently repaired to the less stressful post as president of the Privy Council. In a political swap, taking Konoe's place was the man who held the privy presidency, seventy-three-year-old Hiranuma Kiichirō. The taciturn Hiranuma—whose résumé included prominent posts in the judicial system and Ministry of Justice and the founding of a conservative political organization in the 1920s—led the country unremarkably for eight months.

Tokyo correspondent Hugh Byas, with rare bluntness, called Hiranuma a "fascist." Scholars continually debate whether Japan in the 1930s should be classified as fascist. On one hand, the empire lacked a dictator shrouded in a personality cult as well as a single mass party that fetishized the vitality of male youth. Moreover, its constitutional system remained intact. On the other hand, Japan's leaders showed a pronounced admiration for Europe's dictators and embraced a corporatist state model, a rejection of both materialistic Marxism and finance capitalism. They also cultivated a nationalistic cult—albeit one centered on an emperor mystically descended from an "unbroken imperial line." As historian Carol Gluck has noted, "The Japanese were said to be imbued with the notion that Japan was the land of the gods, inhabited by a people uniquely superior in the world, who lived together, the whole nation as a single family, under the benevolent guidance of a divine emperor." Reto Hofmann says Japan's leaders at the time became fixated on this notion of "national uniqueness." And that, overall, fascism "was integral to interwar thought." Congruent with this conclusion, but with an eye on causality, other scholars suggest that Japan's expansionism on the continent, first in Manchuria, followed by total war in China, inexorably radicalized its domestic polity. According to this argument, the state-directed imperialist project in Manchukuo, in particular, acted as a "hothouse" for Japanese-styled fascism, with the ideology of Asianism as a core component.[2]

Premier Hiranuma's subsequent policy speeches certainly affirmed the centrality of Asianism in Tokyo's pursuit of an alternative regional order. Two weeks after his appointment, for example, the premier addressed the Diet and, as reported in the *New York Times*, insisted that all nations must find their "proper place"—a reference to Japan's allegedly special position among nations and primacy in Asia. Then, in a radio address, Hiranuma equated Japan's "sacrifices" in China to a great rescue mission, one that would bring about China's "rebirth," "renovation," and a "bright and cheerful new order." The result would be "a Utopia of everlasting peace" in Asia. Hiranuma urged the Anglo-American powers "to understand the real intentions of Japan" as the "cornerstone of Far Eastern stability."[3]

Looking back over the previous five years, the consistency among Japan's leaders in their regionalist rhetoric is striking. The difference in substance between Hiranuma's speech and that of Hirota in January 1934, for example, was negligible; the principal change was that geopolitical realities had moved more concretely toward Tokyo's worldview. Navy Minister Yonai Mitsumasa offers a good illustration of Asianism's potency as an ideological adhesive among Japan's ruling class. Typically labeled a moderate on naval relations with America, Yonai proved to be significantly less mild in his view of Japan's role on the continent. *New York Times* correspondent Hallett Abend noted that Yonai, in a speech before the Diet, asserted, "The construction of a New Order in East Asia is uppermost in the minds of Japanese naval authorities." More remarkably, he added that "Japan should advance toward [this goal] despite international conflicts that might take place."[4] The exact meaning of "conflicts" left plenty of room for interpretation, but it took little imagination to insert Britain and the United States as the unwelcome foes.

American commentators, meanwhile, became more cynical about Tokyo's justifications. Abend said Japan's leadership had ignored the fact that its invasion had made "at least 30,000,000 Chinese civilians into homeless refugees" and that Japanese air raids had "laid waste to scores of cities." And scholar Robert T. Pollard, in an address before the American Historical Association, downplayed Japan's "have-not" or realist motivations. "It seems apparent," argued Pollard, "that not a little of the driving force behind the Japanese expansion stems less from population pressure and industrial needs than from delusions of grandeur, a messianic complex." Without labeling it, Pollard had delved into the psychological contours of Asianism and its influence on Japanese policy. Nathaniel Peffer similarly asserted that "more than the requirements of its industrialization and its poor [natural] endowment," Japan's aggression was spurred by "an intoxicated chauvinism."[5] The "have-not" claim nonetheless remained a vexing issue.

TO HAVE AND HAVE NOT

Invoked almost mechanically by the revisionist powers in the 1930s, the "have-not" catchphrase shimmered with a kind of immediate and irreproachable logic. It conjured up imagery of powerful nations abundantly endowed while others were left with scraps. This stark dichotomy was exaggerated, but it was hardly without merit. Even a cursory look at the leading producers of the world's commodities could not hide the fact that two liberal powers, Great Britain and the United States, commanded disproportionate control over resources.

The expansive British Empire, where the sun still never set, contained resource-rich colonies in Southeast Asia, South Asia, and Africa. Ninety-five percent of the world's tin, for example, came from British colonies. The United States, meanwhile, produced 62 percent of the world's oil. Japan, which ran a small trade deficit in the 1930s, had to import the following percentages of strategic commodities: petroleum (95%), copper (75%), rubber (100%), manganese (95%), nickel (100%), tungsten (95%), and tin (100%). Such percentages explain why Secretary Hull, in numerous speeches, showed sensitivity to grievances about access to resources. But he also argued that expanding equal access was possible "only on the basis of peaceful international cooperation."[6] In other words, liberalism's "orderly processes" via multilateral engagement offered the best hope for resolving the have-not crisis.

Some American commentators, however, put Japan's "have-not" lamentations through a critical gauntlet, claiming they were overstated. Prominent journalist John Gunther, known for his *Inside* books on global perspectives, assailed Japan's—and Germany's—have-not claims in a piece for the *Saturday Evening Post*. The "so-called Have-Not powers," said Gunther, "have agitated for a more equitable distribution of world raw materials . . . and the return of colonies. But the colony issue is subterfuge. All the colonies of all the nations of the world produce only two important raw materials in great quantity—tin and rubber. . . . The fact is that any of the Have-Not nations can buy raw materials anywhere they please."[7] That also overstated matters, but Gunther's point was well taken.

Japan, for example, before the Manchurian Incident, held colonies in Taiwan and Korea, leasehold rights on the Liaodong peninsula, and mandates in the Pacific—all of which the world recognized. The South Manchurian Railway's assets in 1930 exceeded one billion yen, including control over six hundred miles of track. And Japan sold more goods to China than any other nation. According to historian Peter Duus, "by almost every quantifiable indicator, Japan had displaced Great Britain as the paramount foreign economic power in China." A broad view thus made clear that by 1930, Japan held a highly favorable position in East Asia. Evidence for this ascendant status sometimes came from unexpected sources, such as a nationalistic Japanese writer at the time, who, in an apologia for Japan's takeover in Manchuria, inadvertently described how well Japan had been doing in Manchuria *before* the incident. Though his point was that Japanese control of the region would guarantee its progress and development, that begged the question: would that not have happened by peaceful means as well? Viscount Ishii also offered an unintended argument for peaceful prosperity, writing, "The different countries of Europe and America require from one and-a-half to two months to deliver their products to the China market, whereas Japanese goods usually can reach this market in a day or two, or in one week at the most." Indeed, so why bungle such a favorable position with aggression?[8]

In fact, a paucity of natural resources seldom slowed the Japanese empire. Going back to the Meiji modernization in the late nineteenth century, what Japan lacked in resources it made up for in industrial efficiency, niche industries, and cheap labor. By 1890, a country that only thirty-five years earlier remained shut off from the world, and which relied entirely on horses and palanquins for modes of transport, suddenly evoked all the industrial clamor, smoke, and steam of a Turner painting. Factories began to sprout in its populated cities. Railroads and telegraph and telephone lines crisscrossed its rugged landscape. Its steamships plied the oceans carrying goods made in Osaka and Tokyo. As Nathaniel Peffer observed at the time, Japan had made "successful inroads into the market of almost every country in every part of the world." That success had been reaching the White House in a stream of panicked letters from American makers of toothpicks, twine, matches, pencils, toys, textiles, glassware, flyswatters, fish netting, cigar lighters, wool felt hats, handkerchiefs, umbrellas, sunglasses, and zippers—all of whom competed against resourceful Japanese manufacturers. Such success, however, depended upon peace.[9]

It thus was not difficult to grasp for Americans or Japanese that Japan's brisk trade with the United States and lack of strategic resources made it especially vulnerable to American economic pressure. In fact, by 1939, with war still raging in China, momentum began to build in the Roosevelt administration for a more aggressive East Asian policy. Secretary Hull's special advisor, Stanley Hornbeck, called "for a comprehensive and thoroughgoing program of measures of material pressure which might be applied, beginning with some one step and proceeding as the situation may unfold to other steps." And both Hornbeck and Morgenthau pushed Roosevelt to provide economic aid to China. In lobbying the president, Morgenthau argued that a loan to the KMT government would go far in deterring Japanese aggression. Hornbeck similarly asserted in a memo to FDR that a loan would help "halt Japan's predatory advance."[10] Roosevelt balked on tightening economic screws, but he agreed to float a twenty-five-million-dollar loan to Chiang's regime. This minimal credit represented a mere baby step toward a more active American policy, but it carried symbolic import. It sent a message that the administration rejected Tokyo's pretensions that government in Chongqing no longer represented the Chinese people.

Hornbeck's successor as chief of the State Department's Far Eastern Division, Max Hamilton, meanwhile, suggested that the demise of the Nine-Power Treaty had been greatly exaggerated. In a lecture at the Army War College, Hamilton performed ideological CPR, reminding his audience that each of the treaty's signatories was "under the obligation to respect the integrity of China." If the United States were to abandon the Nine-Power Treaty, he said, it would face an unsavory choice: either it would have to withdraw from China or "alter the fundamental principles of its Far Eastern policy." The latter, he insisted, would be "ignominious in its implications and psychologically impossible." Hamilton thus preached the impregnability of America's liberal principles with the same verve as Japan's leaders did with their regionalist ideals. Neither nation was giving ideological ground. And yet firm ground was elusive, certainly for the Japanese, whose aggression in the name of Asian solidarity had resulted in the deaths of millions of Chinese. And although the Americans had stood up for the Chinese, all too often it amounted to sanctimonious words. This was largely because, as Michael

Barnhart has pointed out, the liberal principles were important to Washington "for global reasons, not anything specific to China." That may be overstating things; nonetheless, President Roosevelt, at minimum, could have recalled Ambassador Grew from Tokyo in protest of Japan's aggression.[11]

As for holding out hope for a moderate resurgence in Japan, Hamilton was as pessimistic as Hornbeck. Differences of opinion between Japanese "moderates" and "reactionaries" on fundamental questions of policy, he asserted, were superficial. Any difference was in "point of method and of degree." And not just within the government. "A large majority of those who make up public opinion in Japan," he claimed, fully supported the government's program on the Asia continent. Hamilton's bleak assessment left little doubt the window for reconciliation between the two Pacific rivals was closing. In that case, bigger existential questions loomed on the horizon, ones that Americans were not accustomed to addressing. Hamilton suggested these were unique times, with unique ideological threats, requiring a new awareness. Could the revisionist states, "which believe in and practice aggression and international lawlessness," he asked, "in the long run exist side by side in the same world with states which, like the United States, believe in totally different principles?"[12] Hamilton's rhetorical question illuminated the era's intensifying divide along ideological lines.

"THE TENETS OF THEIR FAITH AND HUMANITY"

Hamilton was channeling FDR. Two days earlier, in his 1939 State of the Union address, the president made his most impassioned appeal since the "quarantine" speech for a more dynamic foreign policy. In particular, Roosevelt began to address the nexus between geopolitics and ideology, and the threat to the American "way of life." The president's view of that life was mainstream, if not a little storybookish, but it was sincere, and it aligned with the mass of his listeners. "There comes a time in the affairs of men," explained the president, "when they must prepare to defend not their homes alone but the tenets of their faith and humanity upon which their churches, their governments, and their very civilization are founded." Alluding to the Manchurian crisis as a turning point, Roosevelt said, "Since 1931, world events of thunderous import have moved with lightning speed. During these eight years, many of our people clung to the hope that the innate decency of mankind would protect the unprepared who showed their innate trust in mankind. Today we are all wiser—and sadder." That was nice talk, aimed at isolationists, whom FDR believed were not wiser at all but instead grossly naïve. But the message was clear enough: wise people, when facing existential threats, act to preserve their country and way of life. It was time, FDR argued, to modify the nation's neutrality laws. "At the very least," stated

Roosevelt, "we can and should avoid any action, or any lack of action, which will encourage, assist, or build up an aggressor."[13]

So-called isolationists were not inveterate appeasers, but they drew a line of defense at the nation's borders. Isolationists would fight like hell to repel any invading force and preserve national sovereignty, but they would fight with equal vigor to avoid involvement in wars beyond the nation's borders. The crux of the disagreement thus centered on a very personal view of the world; it was psychological, perceptual. It entwined views of geography and ideology, security and liberty. In terms of geopolitics, in early 1939, where did the nation's interests extend to? Isolationists tended to view the oceans like protective moats around America. From Roosevelt's perspective, technology had so shrunk the globe that the nation's security had become threatened from a much farther distance. Waiting until carrier task forces, troop transports, and bombers appeared from over the horizon was waiting too long. Moreover, the *kind* of threat was unique. Ideologically, Hitler was not the kaiser, and Imperial Japan was not just implementing an Asian Monroe Doctrine. The aggressors in the 1930s, in the president's view, thus posed an unprecedented threat to an interdependent global society. Isolationists remained unpersuaded. Senator Arthur H. Vandenberg (R-MI) acknowledged that technology had foreshortened the world, but he "still thank[ed] God for two insulating oceans."[14] He and other isolationists held firm in their opposition to the president.

New evidence of the perceived menace to a liberal order came suddenly in March 1939 when German troops occupied the remaining Czech territory.[15] A bitter Prime Minister Chamberlain declared that the British government would never again trust any assurance from Hitler and promptly recalled his ambassador from Berlin. British appeasement ended two weeks later, when Chamberlain told a hushed House of Commons that Great Britain would pledge full assistance to Poland if Hitler attacked his eastern neighbor. In Japan, Foreign Minister Arita congratulated his German counterpart, Ribbentrop, saying Germany's action would "contribute much toward the stabilization of Europe and the cause of world peace."[16] Arita's calculated reference to "stabilization" reinforced a catchword for Tokyo's regionalist ambitions and intimated an affinity of aims with Berlin.

A LETTER AND A FAIR

Germany's breach of the Munich agreement made Roosevelt "jittery" about the world situation. His answer was to reach out to Hitler and Mussolini personally—with a letter. Roosevelt's missive evinced the spirit of liberalism and the belief in direct talks and arbitration as a way to avoid conflict. It approximated the principles of the Kellogg Pact. Characterizing himself as a "friendly intermediary," Roosevelt began by noting that "hundreds of millions of human beings are living today in constant fear of a new war." He reminded Hitler and Mussolini that they had both insisted they did not want war; in that case, would they be willing to offer assurances that they would not attack thirty-one specifically named countries for a period of ten years? Most of the cited countries were in Europe, but, reflecting liberalism's moral confusion, Roosevelt also included the British colony of Egypt and French and British mandates in the Middle East. For his part, Roosevelt pledged he would strive to guarantee equal access to the world's resources for all nations.[17]

Hitler and Mussolini made great hay out of Roosevelt's olive branch. The Italian government said the letter "was the most incredible document in the whole history of diplomacy," something absurd and pitiful. Hitler, over the next ten days, basked in the pageantry and idolatry of his fiftieth-birthday tribute and asked Europe's "little nations" whether they feared Germany. In doing so, he shrewdly built up anticipation of his reply to Roosevelt, to be delivered in an address before the Reichstag at the Kroll Opera House and broadcast live in the United States. Newsreels of the speech, now a staple of historical documentaries, depict a bemused Hitler who, with mock earnestness, carefully reads each of Roosevelt's questions, followed each time with the Führer barking out "*Antwort*" (Answer) before responding with one. Each of the named thirty-one nations, he said, would have to promise not to attack Germany as well. With fawning regularity, party members burst into giddy laughter. As one observer noted, the audience "worked itself into a frenzy of approval." Hitler assailed Roosevelt for forty-five minutes and told him to fulfill President Wilson's promises to Germany—a reference to "peace without victory."[18]

The European dictators had made Roosevelt look weak and irrelevant. Leaders of most liberal governments had supported the president's letter, but critics noted that Hitler had broken his Munich pledge—so how credible would a positive response from the Führer be now? It was a good point, but as things turned out, it was also moot. Despite a lingering sense of democratic impotence, the note nonetheless had induced personal responses from Hitler and Mussolini that laid bare, in a novel way, their arrogance and lack of earnestness. Hitler had responded with puerile scorn and sarcasm on the profound issue of war and peace. Any residual hope of a negotiated peace for Europe dissolved; the norms of diplomacy, it was clear, no longer applied.

Which is why the grand opening of the New York World's Fair in Flushing Meadows, Queens, and its opening day slogan, "Dawn of a New Day," on April 30, 1939—the day after Hitler's mocking address—could not have seemed more out of sync with world trends. So, too, did the fair's optimistic view of the "World of Tomorrow," with its diorama of a utopian metropolis named "Democracity." Some thirty-five thousand guests of honor gathered at the fair's "Court of Peace" to hear President Roosevelt's dedication and, no doubt, his response to Hitler. But FDR ignored the German dictator, whose country had opted out of the fair. Invoking Ralph Waldo Emerson, the president told the large crowd that the United States had "hitched its wagon" to a "star of peace." Though both isolationists and interventionists could take solace in Roosevelt's poetic ambiguity, an address two days later by the president's agricultural secretary, Henry Wallace, at the opening of the League of Nation's pavilion clarified the administration's globalist bent. Speaking near the main entrance of the league's one-hundred-foot-high pavilion, whose first room highlighted Woodrow Wilson's "Fourteenth Point," Wallace paid tribute to Wilson's liberal vision and reminded the gathered observers and national radio audience, "We are closely associated with the whole world, whether we know it or not and whether we like it or not."[19]

"ADVANCING JAPAN"

For Japan's leaders and the KBS, the World's Fair represented a golden opportunity for self-representation and the promotion of Japanese exceptionalism. To this end, the Shinto-shrine-inspired Japanese pavilion stood out from other national displays because its planners chose to celebrate traditional architecture instead of the fair's modern motif. Fringed by a tenth-century Heian-period garden, the pavilion opened up to a dazzling depiction of a highly cultivated people. Its several halls displayed a variety of paintings, pottery, and sculpture, as well as tea ceremony and ikebana demonstrations. The pavilion's Diplomatic Room, meanwhile, celebrated the "Eternal Peace and Friendship between America and Japan." A photographic mural of happy, flag-waving American and Japanese schoolchildren provided the backdrop to historical documents and other artifacts spanning the two nations' eighty-six-year relationship. Nearby stood a striking eleven-foot-high and thirty-foot-wide gold lacquer screen depicting a map of the Pacific Rim. Bookending the room were massive murals of the sixteenth-century Himeji Castle and the Washington Monument. At the pavilion's dedication, Japanese officials introduced an Olympic-styled "Flame of Friendship," transported from the "sacred fires" of the ancient Izumo shrine.[20] Japan's contribution to the fair was remarkable, not the least because it was organized and assembled during wartime. But that was also its problem.

The sunny slogans and soft power aura of cultural refinement could only mildly minimize the ideological divide in US-Japan relations. Mayor Fiorello La Guardia in his dedication address implored the Japanese people to be "more considerate and kindly" to weak nations. La Guardia was kind enough not to mention China. The pavilion thus conveyed a strange ambivalence, where beauty and brightness collided with underlying discord. For the Japanese, what was there to gain? Initial motives, revealed two years prior when the Konoe cabinet first accepted the American invite, had connected cultural performance to a benevolent regionalism. Yoshino Shinji, minister of commerce and industry, was quoted in the *New York Times* saying his nation's participation would compel the world to approve "the constructive work Japan has been doing in Asia." In other words, the theatrical display of Japanese cultural refinement would obliterate any doubts about the empire's regional authority and peaceful intent. The fair's commissioner similarly stated, "Japan sees in the World's Fair a great opportunity to show she can justify [its continental policy] and her claim to leadership in Asia." But that was before two years of war. As things presently stood, according to James R. Young, a foreign correspondent for Hearst's International News Service, "All the flood of English-language literature from Japan, and tea ceremony and cultural exhibits only antagonize the American public, the reaction being that the effort is to becloud the real issue and cover up the facts."[21]

And yet, if such cultural efforts now fell mostly on deaf American ears, it was equally true that Tokyo's more muscular regionalism, concomitant with the rising collective confidence among the revisionist powers, had diminished the impetus for American approval. Indeed, the self-satisfying notion that Japan was in the vanguard of new global trends permeated KBS Director Baron Dan Inō's dedication speech for the Japanese pavilion. Although Dan extolled bilateral friendship, he also made gauzy allusions to Konoe's "New East Asian Order," telling the audience that Japan was entering "a new era of creation ... with a renaissance of the East." Dan's assertive vision was given further expression at Japan's exhibit at the collective Hall of Nations, which featured five Bauhaus-inspired photomontage murals, using work from the talented stable of the KBS's *NIPPON* magazine artists and photographers. Each of the panels measured fourteen feet high by nine feet wide and highlighted modern Japanese industry under the title "Advancing Japan."[22]

Six thousand miles away from Flushing Meadows, on the northwest border of Manchukuo, it was as if the Kwantung Army took the "Advancing Japan" slogan as its marching orders. In May and June 1939, the Manchurian-based army was on the move again, this time trying to expel Soviet troops from the vast border region of Outer Mongolia (present-day Mongolia), where the two sides had skirmished in previous years. To the rest of the world, the remote fighting near Khalkin Gol (Nomonhan), nearly seven hundred miles from Beijing, was a sideshow to rising tensions in Europe. To the Japanese, it turned out to be a costly sideshow. If Outer Mongolia seemed ripe for territorial aggrandizement, the area nonetheless was a Soviet protectorate—and the Russians were committed to the status quo. Fighting throughout the summer resulted in a significant Russian counteroffensive under commanding officer Georgy Zhukov, which included more than five hundred tanks and five hundred planes. By the time fighting ended in September, the Kwantung Army had suffered more than sixteen thousand killed and wounded.[23]

An undeclared border war with Russia, questions about an alliance with Germany, an ongoing war of annihilation against the Kuomintang, the need for a puppet Chinese government in Japanese-controlled China—the summer of 1939 proved to be challenging on many fronts for Japan's leaders. Also reaching critical mass was the problem of the foreign concessions in Chinese cities, illiberal detritus from nineteenth-century imperialism. The concessions were an irritating hindrance to Tokyo's neo-imperial ambitions, particularly those of Great Britain, which boasted the most extensive commercial holdings and personal networks in China. Not surprisingly, they became bases of anti-Japanese activity, including sabotage and boycotts. According to the Tokyo-based *Hōchi Shimbun*, as reported in the *New York Times*, the settlements "point[ed] like daggers at Japan's holy enterprise of building up a new order in Asia." Japan's ambassador to Britain, Shigemitsu Mamoru, meanwhile, informed a British official that Whitehall should recognize that the league system "was now virtually dead."[24]

More concretely, the Hiranuma government used the murder of a pro-Japanese Chinese collaborator in Great Britain's concession in Tianjin to force a showdown with the Nine-Power Treaty. The Japanese military set up a blockade of the British concession and demanded ever-widening curbs on foreign privileges. News reports told of humiliating strip searches when British residents entered or exited their settlement zone. The crisis dragged on into late July, when a parley between Foreign Minister Arita and Britain's ambassador to Japan, Robert Craigie, resulted in a diplomatic settlement favoring Japan. A humbled Whitehall agreed not to obstruct Japan's military efforts; Hiranuma went further and said Britain had agreed to withhold all financial aid to the Chinese Nationalist government. Whatever the fine print, Britain had yielded to greater Japanese authority in China. It was yet another sign the Nine-Power status quo had collapsed.[25] It was not yet clear, however, whether Japan's New Order was its irrefutable replacement.

While Arita and Craigie were negotiating, Japanese planes again pounded the Nationalist capital at Chongqing, resulting in numerous civilian deaths. US Ambassador Nelson T. Johnson's dispatches to Secretary Hull repeatedly contradicted Arita's claim that the assaults were limited to military targets. "I have personally witnessed," Johnson told Hull, "some 66 raids by Japanese planes. . . . I have learned to distinguish between a raid made upon a military objective and one that is made merely for the purpose of terrifying and killing unarmed and innocent civilian population." An angry Hull summoned Ambassador Horinouchi and told him the "facts" of the indiscriminate attacks "speak for themselves" and that he had been "earnestly pleading with and urging [upon Tokyo] the view that there is enough room on this planet for fifteen or eighteen great nations like his and mine." The big question now, continued the secretary, was whether all of China was to be "Manchuria-ized by Japan." Hull did not let on that the Americans were nearing the end of tepid replies to Japan's revisionist assault in East Asia.[26]

TOKYO'S TWIN TREMORS

If the successful Tianjin blockade and increasingly sequestered Nationalist government gave Japan's leaders a sense of being in control of their own destiny again, events over the next month quickly upended such notions. A pair of shocking "messages" on July 26 and August 23, 1939, sent the Hiranuma cabinet into a tailspin. The first came from Secretary Hull. Two weeks after his meeting with Horinouchi, Hull gave Tokyo notice that the Roosevelt administration intended to abrogate the US-Japan Commercial Treaty of 1911. The treaty provided most-favored-nation treatment and legal protections for trade and property rights. The required six months' notice meant that economic sanctions against Japan could commence on January 26, 1940. It was the first time Washington indicated it intended to defend the premises of the Nine-Power Treaty and Kellogg Pact with something more than words. As writer K. K. Kawakami noted, for almost ten years since the Manchurian crisis, Japan had received nothing from the United States "but brickbats—complaints, lectures, protests, scoldings and spankings." Abrogation of the commercial treaty, he asserted, represented a turning point.[27]

The Japanese, indeed, were stunned. One spokesperson said Washington's announcement was "unbelievably abrupt." The Foreign Office denounced the action as "unfriendly and hardly intelligible." Although the first official statement from Tokyo held the ideological line about a New Order—that a "new situation is fast developing in East Asia" and the government had "long been hoping that other countries would frankly recognize this fact"—such seeming matter-of-factness could not conceal the grave threat posed by economic sanctions. The United States supplied Japan with 70 percent of its scrap iron and steel, nearly 80 percent of its oil and gasoline, 41 percent of its pig iron, 92 percent of its copper, and 91 percent of its autos and trucks. At the same time, the United States purchased 80 percent of Japan's raw silk and accounted for nearly 17 percent of its exports, first among all other nations.[28]

Such lopsided data explains why Treasury Secretary Morgenthau stressed Japan's vulnerability to sanctions and the restraining influence he believed they would have on Japanese expansionism. In a memo on July 31, Morgenthau reported that Japan was frantically trying to increase its exports to reverse a severe lack of foreign exchange. Sanctions therefore would exacerbate an economic situation that was "becoming more desperate every month." Journalistic evidence reinforced the picture of a challenging environment. East Asian correspondent Hallet Abend described an increased austerity in Japanese daily life, including strictly rationed gasoline, general stores lacking foreign goods, and a ban on nightlife. "Dance halls are closed, and even private dances or charity balls are forbidden," wrote Abend. Tokyo, a city of seven million people, was "dead and quiet by 10 o'clock at night." The obvious implication was that such daily woes would only worsen following an American embargo.[29]

Polls showed that a large segment of the American public was on board. In a Gallup survey from July 1939, 75 percent of Americans said they favored some kind of action against Japan, with 51 percent supporting an embargo of all war materials.[30] These numbers included many isolationists, though their support was conditional on negotiating a new, more limited commercial treaty. Hardened isolationists remained firmly opposed, believing termination was a Roosevelt ploy for war. The Hearst newspapers called it a "reckless deed." Historian A. Whitney Griswold, author of *The Far Eastern Policy of the United States* (1938), similarly asserted that American interests in China were not worth increased antagonism with Japan. The thirty-two-year-old scholar speculated that "Japan and China may only have entered the second quarter of a modern Hundred Years' War." In contrast to the internationalist view that liberalism faced unique threats, Griswold's assessment was like peering into a snow globe and seeing world conflict as a remote curiosity. Nathaniel Peffer defended the administration's position in a piece for *Harper's*. "With unimpeachable logic it has been demonstrated," wrote Peffer of hard-line isolationists, that "America has no vital interest in the European or Far Eastern conflict." Even accepting such narrow regionalism, he suggested, still left the problem of ideology, and a weighty question: could the United States "remain a democratic island surrounded by fascist states?"[31] For the time being, Americans could afford the luxury of extended debate.

The same was not true for the Japanese. While the Hiranuma cabinet processed the shock of a potential American embargo, it experienced a second bolt from the blue. On August 23, Hitler and Stalin startled the world with a nonaggression pact. The treaty occurred three days after the Russians launched their counteroffensive in Outer Mongolia. Tokyo was awash in disbelief and new insecurity, prompting the Hiranuma government to resign. For Hitler and Stalin, the Machiavellian treaty gave the archenemies a slice of security relief in central Europe, but it turned Asian affairs upside down. Japan's motivation for considering a formal alliance with Germany was to neutralize Soviet power in Northeast Asia. The Nazi-Soviet Pact augmented it. Thrown into question also was the Anti-Comintern Pact. As historians have noted, if the letter of the treaty was not breached, certainly the spirit was compromised.[32]

War clouds quickly gathered over Europe amid a rumble of rumors. The thunderclap came on September 1, just nine days after the signing of the

Nazi-Soviet Pact. Germany invaded Poland; Great Britain and France followed with a declaration of war on Germany. German troops, in coordination with armored units and dive-bombers, tore through western Poland in two weeks. On September 17, in accordance with the secret protocol of the Nazi-Soviet Pact, the Red Army invaded eastern Poland. In short order Poland was subdued and divided. Twenty years following the signing of the Treaty of Versailles, Europe faced the prospects of another catastrophic war. As President Roosevelt mused to his cabinet, "I was almost startled by a strange feeling of familiarity." Having been through it all before, FDR said it seemed more "like picking up again an interrupted routine."[33]

The rapid transformation of European relations and outstanding questions about the war's course dominated the Japanese Foreign Office and US State Department over the next several months and pushed US-Japan relations temporarily to the sidelines. Ambassador Grew's extended leave in the States added to the sense of interruption. Amid the topsy-turvy state of world affairs, Interim Army Minister General Abe Nobuyuki was selected to head a new cabinet. The sixty-two-year-old Abe, following a fairly nondescript military career, proved to be an ineffectual transition figure, lasting just four months. Americans, meanwhile, became consumed by the question of whether or not to revise the Neutrality Act.

CASH-AND-CARRY CONTROVERSY

Throughout the fall of 1939, a tense drama unfolded in the United States between isolationists and the Roosevelt administration and its allies. On September 15, famed aviator and anti-interventionist Charles Lindbergh addressed the nation from the Carlton Hotel in Washington, DC, where Secretary Hull resided. (Lindbergh's 1927 solo transatlantic flight from New York to Paris had vaulted him into the stratosphere of universal reverence.) In his radio address, Lindbergh urged Americans to stand above the European fray, to be "as impersonal as a surgeon with his knife," in what was "a quarrel arising from the errors of the last war." But Lindbergh proved that he himself was not above the fray. His sympathetic references to the Nazi program prompted renowned syndicated columnist Dorothy Thompson later to make the sensational assertion that Lindbergh was pining to be "the American Fuhrer." President Roosevelt similarly told Secretary Morgenthau he was "absolutely convinced" Lindbergh was a Nazi.[34]

Six days after Lindbergh's speech, with political temperatures rising, Roosevelt addressed Congress. Isolationist obstructionism was gnawing at the president. Privately, on one occasion, he had sardonically suggested that his administration should propose a bill to erect statues in Berlin of Republican senators Arthur Vandenberg, Warren Austin, Henry Cabot Lodge Jr., and

Robert A. Taft—and to "put the swastika on them."[35] Suffice to say, his speech before Congress was more sober. He regretted, he said, that Congress had passed the Neutrality Act and, equally, that he had signed it. The president asked Congress for immediate repeal of the law's arms embargo, saying America could best avoid war by arming those fighting aggressors. The straightforward speech paid immediate dividends. Sixty-two percent of the public now favored allowing Britain and France to purchase war supplies in America on a cash-and-carry basis—pay cash and carry the munitions away in their own cargo ships. That percentage, incidentally, mirrored the president's approval rating, which had returned to the highs of his 1936 landslide victory.[36]

On October 27, after four weeks of debate—amid a perplexing idleness in the European war—the cash-and-carry revision received a two-thirds majority in the Senate. Several days later, the House passed the measure by a vote of 243–181. President Roosevelt signed it into law on November 4, 1939. A somber Senator Vandenberg said he "did not believe we can become an arsenal for one belligerent without becoming a target for another." He amplified this view in his diary, writing, "My quarrel is with this notion that America can be half in and half out of this war." But as the administration saw it, such a view equally could be turned on its head: one could also quarrel with the notion that America could be half in and half out of this world. FDR nonetheless sought to calm political nerves, telling congressional leaders he hoped world events would not necessitate another extraordinary session.[37] Based on his evolving worldview regarding new ideological threats, however, the president doubtless knew that to be unlikely.

Despite the temporary marginalization of US-Japan relations, Washington never lost sight of the ongoing war in China. Ambassador Grew became keenly aware of this fact during his five-month hiatus in the States. Returning to Tokyo, he told his staff, "Our position in the Far East is regarded as an important factor in our position in world affairs at large and not at all an isolated problem," adding that President Roosevelt and Secretary Hull "seem determined" to support the Nine-Power Treaty.[38] This was consistent with Roosevelt's increasing tendency to discern ideological convergence among the revisionist powers and its geopolitical implications. When the State Department informed Grew of its plans to send Japan another strong note, the ambassador suggested instead that he be allowed to give a public speech. The department approved, but in a sign of growing distrust of Grew, it had the Far Eastern Division write a rough draft.

THE "HORSE'S MOUTH" SPEECH

On October 19, Ambassador Grew addressed a gathering of Japanese dignitaries at the America-Japan Society in Tokyo in what became known as the "horse's mouth" speech. Forsaking extended pleasantries, Grew conveyed America's hardening opinion of Japan and growing demand for sanctions—and the underlying reason for these things. Americans, he said, were "shocked" by the bombing of Chinese cities and disturbed by the presumption of a "new order in East Asia." And that, contrary to Japanese protestations, Americans had good reason to believe that Japan sought complete domination in East Asia. More reflectively, the ambassador peddled the liberal cause, saying the world was complicated and interdependent, and wars could not easily be confined to belligerents. As a result, said Grew, Americans believed world peace was dependent on "orderly processes," as articulated in the postwar treaties.[39]

Time called Grew's speech "unprecedented," saying he gave the Japanese an "earful" of "shockingly frank words." The main shock was that it had come straight from Grew's mouth. The ambassador was seen as a friend to the Japanese, as someone who chose words carefully, without harsh tones. Moreover, Japanese officials knew that Grew had been trying to placate his government by saying things like, "There are two distinct elements in Japan: the extremist right and the neutral pacifists." But although the speech was uncommonly candid by Grew's standards, it did not break any new ground in US policy. Again, the Americans were relying on what Hamlet referred to as "words, words, words."[40]

Not long after his speech, Grew presented Admiral Nomura Kichisaburō, foreign minister in the Abe cabinet, with a long list of alleged Japanese violations of the Nine-Power Treaty. Nomura reminded Grew that both the United States and Japan were "stabilizing influences in their respective regions," an allusion to the Monroe Doctrine and Japan's New Order. Then, in a stunning illumination of the core paradox of Japan's chauvinistic regionalism—considering more than two million Chinese had been killed or wounded in the Sino-Japanese War—Nomura said "Japan's paramount object is to convert an anti-Japanese China into a China sympathetic to Japan." Journalist Hallet Abend made plain Japan's challenge, writing:

> The great obstacle to the establishment of the desired "New Order" is the ingrained arrogance with which the Japanese reveal their feeling of racial superiority over the other peoples of the Asiatic mainland. . . . In their homeland the Japanese will rank among the most polite people in the world. . . . But put a Japanese upon the Asiatic mainland, put him in any kind of uniform—soldier, sailor, police, customs examiner, passport official—and for some reason he is a changed person.[41]

Washington's new candor prompted Premier Abe to excavate ex-premier Hirota's diplomatic tool kit and send a "private," unofficial envoy to America. He selected former KBS director Kabayama. Abe's reason for choosing Kabayama stemmed from a report the latter had submitted to the Foreign Office after his trip to the United States the previous year. In it, Kabayama had puffed up his own influence on high officials in the Roosevelt administration as well as the efficacy of the KBS's cultural diplomacy. Unknown to the Japanese, Secretary Hull had received a copy of a related article in the Tokyo *Nichi Nichi*, which described the singular effect Kabayama supposedly had on the secretary of state:

> Secretary of State Cordell Hull highly praised the work of the [KBS] and said: "the international cultural [programs] being conducted by Japan at present is the best means of promoting international goodwill and constructive world peace. All false propaganda must be defeated in the face of justice and truth. I have great admiration for Japan as a cultural builder." Mr. Hull gripped Count Kabayama's hand and incited him to fresh effort for the sake of American-Japanese goodwill.[42]

At the same time, Hornbeck received a detailed, twelve-page report on Japanese propaganda activities in the United States, sent to him by Earl Leaf, a former United Press correspondent in China. Leaf headed an information office in New York City funded by the Chinese government and was briefly involved with the formation of the Price Committee. The report he shared with Hornbeck, originally drafted for authorities in Chongqing, described an "enormous propaganda machine" consisting of Japanese goodwill missions, cultural diplomacy, news outlets, and "secretly paid" American agents who failed to register with the State Department as required by law. Leaf enumerated the activities of the KBS's Japan Institute and identified its key officers. And he claimed that Japan's Board of Tourist Industries and Chamber of Commerce had recently joined the Japan Institute at the Rockefeller Center in order to coordinate cultural propaganda under one roof. Leaf also commented on all-expenses-paid American junkets to Japan, saying, "it is simply amazing what an American will swallow when he gets a free trip [to Japan], and how zealous he is to tell others about the beauty, peaceful intentions and artistry of Japan." He estimated—albeit with dubious empiricism—that the Japanese government was spending eight million dollars on propaganda in the States. Despite that assessment, Leaf concluded overall that Tokyo's robust propaganda efforts had failed to "acquire American sympathy for Japan's 'manifest destiny' in Asia."[43]

As a result of having been sent the *Nichi Nichi*'s curious account of the Kabayama-Hull meeting as well as Leaf's propaganda report, when the State Department learned about Kabayama's proposed trip to the United States, the trio of Hull, Hornbeck, and Hamilton were quick to see through it. Kabayama's subsequent visit was predictably uneventful and revealed Washington's present low regard and suspicion of Japan's cultural ambassadors.

HORNBECK VERSUS GREW

By the end of 1939, the world had arrived at a strange crossroads. Following Hitler and Stalin's conquest of Poland, the war in Europe slowed to the point of mystification. Britain and France were officially at war against Germany, minus any fighting. The Wehrmacht and Red Army were busy consolidating control in Poland. The Russians, to be sure, were about to mount a misguided winter war against Finland, but all was quiet on the Russo-Japanese frontier. Japan's foreign relations remained in flux, still blindsided by Germany's pact with the Soviet Union and America's abrogation of the commercial treaty. In Washington, Roosevelt dispatched Undersecretary of State Sumner Welles to Europe to take the pulse of Rome, Berlin, Paris, and London; at the same time, his administration was gearing up, if need be, to employ its economic might against aggressors—munitions for cash for the British and French, and material pressure against the Japanese. In the process, the rift between the State Department and its embassy in Tokyo widened.

Over the next few months, as Stanley Hornbeck urged economic pressure on Japan, Ambassador Grew, from afar, often urged restraint, believing economic coercion would dangerously exacerbate already taut relations between the two nations. At times, Grew seemed spun around like a top, as if becoming unsure of his own recommendations. His cables became more contradictory. On December 1, 1939, for example, Grew sent Hull a bleak assessment of US-Japan relations, writing, "Japan is not going to respect the territorial and administrative integrity of China, now or in the future, has not the slightest intention of doing so and could be brought to do so only by complete defeat." Remarkably, the ambassador also revised his thesis about Japan's political dualism, asserting that the whole of Japan believed in the righteousness of the "new order in East Asia." And then, just as remarkably, two weeks later, Grew again flip-flopped and repeated his dualistic impressions to Washington, arguing, "The simple fact is that we are dealing not with a unified Japan but with a Japanese Government which is endeavoring courageously, even with gradual success, to fight against a recalcitrant Japanese Army."[44]

The State Department had heard enough. The next day Hornbeck shot back in a departmental memo that "the thought the 'civilian' element in the Japanese nation may gain an ascendancy over the 'military' element and, having done so, would alter the objectives of Japanese policy can lead to nothing but confusion and error in reasoning. . . . Practically the whole of the Japanese population believes in and is enthusiastic over the policy of expansion and aggrandizement of the Japanese empire." Hornbeck's use of quotations around "civilian" and "military" indiscreetly conveyed a caustic doubt in the utility of such terms. State Department Japan expert John K. Emmerson later attested that Hornbeck "found Grew's arguments unpersuasive and red-penciled [the ambassador's] dispatches and diaries with bold dissents."[45]

The American public's perception of Japan indicated increasing congruence with that of Hornbeck. Despite the sensation surrounding Germany's invasion of Poland, Americans viewed Imperial Japan nearly as menacing as the Third Reich. Thirty percent of polled Americans believed Germany "was most likely to threaten the peace of the United States," while 28 percent said Japan. As the new year unfolded, the divergence of opinion between Washington and its Tokyo embassy continued to widen. Ambassador Grew, still under the reassuring influence of Byas and Japanese cosmopolitans, wrote that he foresaw a "steady and progressive moderation of [Japan's] scope and methods [in China]." Hornbeck again issued a prompt reply, charging that any change in "scope and methods" would apply only to field operations rather than broad objectives. A few months later, Hornbeck described Japan in terms antithetical to ideological coexistence, saying it was "in the hands of a quasi-fanatical leadership just as Germany is."[46] Fanatical or not, Japan's leadership was once again new.

"IF ONE BROTHER SHOULD BECOME DEGENERATE"

In January 1940 the short-lived Abe cabinet gave way to one headed by Navy Minister Yonai Mitsumasa. Yonai's cabinet would also be short-lived as it tried to reconcile Japan's grandiose claims of a New Order in East Asia with the reality of a static war in which Chiang Kai-shek's government remained upright. Close to 1.5 million Japanese soldiers were stationed in China; more than one hundred thousand had been killed. Moreover, as Abend explained, although Japan's War Office claimed to occupy one million square miles of Chinese territory, "occupied" was an elastic term. "In no single province that the Japanese claim to 'occupy,'" noted Abend, "are they actually in control of anything more than the towns and cities which their troops garrison.... Japan's mandate, literally, does not run any farther into the Chinese countryside than her guns can shoot."[47]

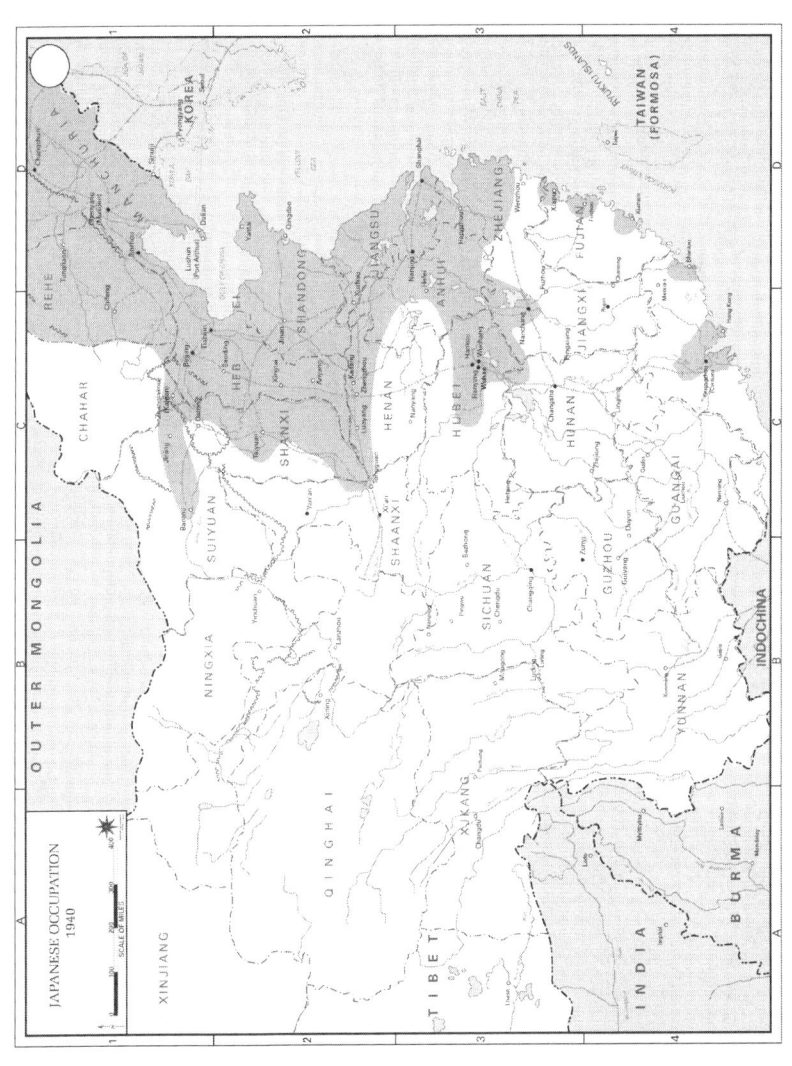

Figure 6.1. Map of Japanese-occupied territory in China, 1940. (Courtesy of the United States Military Academy Department of History.)

The Yonai cabinet also had to deal with the fact that the US-Japan Commercial Treaty expired on January 26, 1940. Japan's old nemesis, Henry Stimson, in a full-page letter in the *New York Times*, urged the Roosevelt administration to impose sanctions. Among both American and Japanese officials, rhetoric became increasingly curt and testy. Yonai warned that economic sanctions "would result in an extremely grave situation." Arita Hachirō, back as foreign minister, said the United States simply did not understand Japan's "Holy War" in China—yet another pan-Asianist code phrase by which Japan was to reorder East Asia under its civilized leadership.[48]

Secretary Hull, in turn, gave Ambassador Horinouchi another dressing-down, drawing almost verbatim from the one he gave following Ambassador Nelson's report on the Chongqing raids. The United States, said Hull, "was under no illusion" that the whole of China was going the way of Manchuria. But the secretary was mum on sanctions. At another meeting, an exasperated Hull told Horinouchi the difference between the Monroe Doctrine and Japanese objectives in Asia was "black and white." According to Hull, Japan could trade "on absolutely equal terms . . . in every port of every nation" in the Western Hemisphere. Trade statistics tended to support the secretary's claims. On the other hand, trade statistics alone failed to convey fully the United States' asymmetrical power and influence in Latin America—the result of which, some historians have argued, derived from so-called "informal" or "free trade" imperialism.[49]

When Hull said the United States was under no illusion about Japan's aims in China, he was anticipating what eventually transpired on March 30, 1940. As cold spring rains battered Nanjing, Japan unfurled its long-planned collaborative government under disillusioned Nationalist and Chiang rival Wang Jingwei. Even the normally restrained Byas called Wang's inauguration, which took place amid the heavy presence of Japanese troops, "merely the curtain-raiser for another puppet play." It was a startling moment in the Sino-Japanese War. For nearly twenty years, the charismatic Wang had been one of the most prominent leaders and personalities within the Kuomintang. Now the Nationalist-turned-collaborator was conceding Japanese hegemony. At a press reception, Wang recited Japan's Pan-Asianist platitudes, saying his government would "share the responsibility for building up a new order in East Asia." He claimed the Chongqing government—whose inner circle he had been a member of until late 1938—was nothing more than a "regional refugee regime."[50]

In Washington, Secretary Hull said Wang's regime violated the Nine-Power Treaty; recognition thus was out of the question. As if to add emphasis, the administration sent an additional twenty-million-dollar credit to Chongqing. Tokyo denounced the loan, while an essay in an English-language government mouthpiece condemned the United States as a hypocritical moralist seeking to dominate East Asia. "America should realize," said the *East Asian Review*, "that the Chinese people are paying hardly any attention to the so-called Nine-Power Treaty. In fact, they hate the one-sided Open Door Policy, which they regard as an insult to the Chinese nation." Another essay, however, belied Japan's superior attitudes toward Chinese. "Westerners may argue," said the author, "If China and Japan are brothers, why has Japan gone on this rampage in China? A perfectly reasonable question, with a perfectly reasonable answer. If one brother should become degenerate and sully the good name of his house or family, it is up to the other brother to chastise the wrong-doer and restore the honor of the house or family."[51]

More sober assessments came from the KBS's floundering Japan Institute in New York, which reported to Tokyo that Americans were asking "more complex questions" about Japanese ambitions in China. A KBS "business plan" for the institute thus emphasized building credibility with American visitors. Japanese officials, it stated, needed "to make an effort to . . . avoid giving subjective opinions, and try to sustain and improve the inquirer's trust in our center." NHK, meanwhile, inaugurated a Japanese language course for English speakers, but faced unique struggles with other programming, especially musical entertainment. Although it appears Japanese Americans in Hawai'i and on the West Coast enjoyed traditional Japanese music, evidence suggests songs like "Nihonbashi in the Edo Period" did little to move American audiences in general. NHK ultimately settled on heavy doses of classical music, all the while, ironically, attempting to "raise the consciousness of people abroad as to the greatness of the Japanese empire." In any case, by early 1940 such soft power objectives had become irrelevant. The three-year war in China had damaged Japan's image beyond cultural repair.[52] Moreover, aggression in Europe once again sucked the air out of the global room. And this time, it was soon apparent that Germany's rapid advances profoundly augmented Japan's regionalist aspirations, thereby intensifying the ideological clash and raising the geopolitical stakes to a breaking point.

"LIFE-GIVING SWORD"

On the morning of April 9, 1940, Hitler's armies invaded Denmark, and subsequently, Norway, thereby putting to rest notions of a "phony war." Germany defended its surprise invasion as an act of "protection" against British "encroachments" on Scandinavia. The abrupt shift of the war to Western Europe caused immediate alarm among the Japanese. The occupation of Scandinavia meant a move closer toward the Netherlands, the imperial overlord of Indonesia. Having already experienced the Reich's capriciousness, Japan's leaders were newly concerned about Hitler's intentions. Might not German warships steam into Jakarta (Batavia) following an invasion of Holland? On April 15, Foreign Minister Arita gave Hitler notice, saying the extension of hostilities to the East Indies "would give rise to an undesirable situation from the standpoint of peace and stability of East Asia." It sounded like a defense of the Nine-Power Treaty. Indeed, Secretary Hull concurred nearly verbatim, saying alteration of the status quo in the Dutch East Indies "would be prejudicial to the cause of stability, peace, and security" in the region.[53] It had been a long time since the two rivals had agreed on anything, superficial as it was.

As it turned out, Arita and Hull's concern about German encroachment in Southeast Asia was undue. On May 10, German troops, as anticipated, invaded the neutral Netherlands and Belgium and also crossed into French territory; shortly afterward, however, the Yonai cabinet received assurances from the German ambassador in Tokyo that Hitler had no designs on the Dutch East Indies.[54] That created new concerns for the Americans but precipitated a geopolitical realization among the Japanese that bordered on euphoria. Behind German panzers and dive-bombers, the attack on the Netherlands and France had opened up heretofore only imaginary southern vistas. Suddenly, both the Dutch East Indies and French Indochina had become militarily vulnerable—all of which carried profound ramifications for fighting the Kuomintang. The Yonai cabinet pounced on the new possibilities. On June 19, two days after France notified Germany of its intention to surrender, the Japanese government handed the French ambassador in Tokyo an ultimatum demanding a halt in the transport of oil and weapons across the Indochina border into China. A supine France agreed. Meanwhile, Great Britain, which was bracing for a cross-channel invasion, also sought to limit losses in its distant colonies. Though now led by a more pugnacious prime minister, Winston Churchill, Britain promised Japan it would close for three months the Burma Road, a key supply route to the Nationalist government in Chongqing.[55]

Foreign Minister Arita followed the ultimatum to France with the most significant geopolitical-ideological pronouncement since Premier Konoe's "New Order" declaration. Addressing the Japanese people on June 29, 1940, in a nationwide broadcast, Arita said it was only natural that Japan should extend the "new order" into the South Seas. Speaking in the benevolent tones of an idealized Pan-Asian order, Arita said, "Peoples who are related closely with each other geographically, racially, culturally, and economically should first form a sphere of their own for co-existence and co-prosperity." Arita's speech, which dominated the front pages of American newspapers, was the first iteration of what eventually culminated in the coming months as the Greater East Asia Co-Prosperity Sphere. The address positioned Japan as a heroic liberator setting out to slay Western exploiters. As Arita put it, Japan was brandishing "a life-giving sword that destroys evil and makes justice manifest."[56]

"FOR GENERATIONS YET UNBORN"

In Washington, the spread of war to Western Europe and its potential for stimulating Japanese expansion into greater Asia jolted the Roosevelt administration into unprecedented action. It began with a fireside chat, in which Roosevelt spoke as a confidant, as a commonsense explainer. "Let us sit down again, together, you and I," the president invited fellow Americans, "to consider our own pressing problems that confront us." This was an argumentative speech posing as a conversation. The president zeroed in on isolationists. "There are many among us," he said, "who in the past closed their eyes to events abroad—because they believed in utter good faith what some of their fellow Americans told them—that what was taking place in Europe was none of our business . . . that the many hundreds of miles of salt water made the American Hemisphere so remote." Eschewing that mindset, the president maintained the country needed to prepare itself against unprecedented dangers and assume a new global leadership.[57]

To move Americans off the fence, Roosevelt returned to his ideologically loaded "way of life" theme. Borrowing from the political rhetoric of the nation's founders, but painting in broad strokes, the president said, "We build a life for generations yet unborn. We defend and we build a way of life, not for America alone, but for all mankind." This one sentence contained a revolution in thought for the United States in the world. It asked a reluctant America to step out from the wings and move to the center of the world stage—and, in fact, that the United States had no choice if the American system was to survive. Global interdependence, global society, as Americans knew it, was at stake. The president's words therefore could just as well have been inverted: defending *all of humankind* meant defending America. The speech anticipated Churchill and Roosevelt's Atlantic Charter of the following year and portended a new global responsibility for the United States in the postwar world. It also represented a direct ideological challenge to Japan and Germany, depicting a future built on liberal values rather than Nazism and Japanism. From this global perspective, Roosevelt said he prayed day and night "for the restoration of peace in this mad world of ours."[58]

Congress was not about to defend all of humankind, but it had no qualms about preparedness at home. And so between May and July 1940, like a constant and forceful release of dam water, Congress let loose funds that substantially overhauled the US military. Starting even before the president's "let's build" speech, Congress had appropriated monies to rebuild the relatively anemic US Army. FDR had requested and received one billion dollars for a 750,000-man army and an annual production of fifty thousand planes. The new emphasis on planes revealed the era's shifting realities about airpower and the speed and range of modern weaponry.[59]

New funding for a two-ocean navy came next. On June 17, Congress began work on increasing the fleet by 70 percent, or 1.325 million tons. The preliminary price tag of four billion dollars was earmarked for seven battleships, eighteen aircraft carriers, twenty-nine cruisers, 115 destroyers, and forty-two submarines. The new appropriations vaulted the United States over the Washington Conference's mandated tonnage limits for the first time. Roosevelt, meanwhile, ordered the Pacific Battle Fleet, which had sailed to Hawai'i for its annual exercises, to remain at Pearl Harbor and not return to its home bases at San Pedro and San Diego, California. Admiral James Richardson, commander-in-chief of the US Fleet, demurred, arguing the decision left the navy overly exposed to the Japanese. But both Roosevelt and Hornbeck believed the saber-rattling would act as a deterrent to Japanese ambitions in the Dutch East Indies.[60]

Finally, in a move laden with both politics and the imminent demand for bureaucratic leadership, Roosevelt announced the appointments of two Republicans as secretaries of the War and Navy Departments, Henry Stimson and Frank Knox, respectively. Doubtless the Japanese were none too thrilled to hear about the return of Stimson. As for Knox, he was publisher of the anti–New Deal *Chicago Daily News* and had joined Alf Landon on the 1936 Republican ticket. But he had praised Roosevelt's "quarantine" speech in 1937, and the president took notice. Amid dangerous times, with a general election approaching in November—and with Roosevelt breaking from the two-term precedent—the appointment of two nonisolationist Republicans to important cabinet positions revealed both FDR's shrewd politicking and nose for administrative talent. Their goals would be to keep the United States out of war while preparing for war, keep Great Britain free, and keep Japan from advancing into the Southeast Asia.[61]

Tokyo was also undergoing political change. Germany's spectacular blitzkrieg victories in western Europe, including the startling inducement of a French surrender within two months, revived talk about a Japanese alliance with the Nazi regime. But despite the Yonai cabinet's muscular Asianist proclamation, it reacted tentatively to an Axis alliance, fearing premature hostilities with the liberal powers. In response, Prince Konoe and his political allies, particularly in the army, engineered a political move to undermine Yonai, starting with the unilateral resignation of the premier's war minister. When the army refused to submit a new minister, a new cabinet had to be formed, leading to Konoe reprising his role as premier. For the important post of foreign minister, Konoe tapped a familiar face—the self-assured Matsuoka Yōsuke. Big plans were soon in the making that would put Japan and the United States on to the path of a fatal collision.

***

Germany's invasion and rapid occupation of western Europe upended the global status quo. News reports described hostilities that were stunningly one-sided. Defeated Allied troops massed vulnerably around the French port of Dunkirk (avoiding certain destruction only by a remarkable evacuation across the English Channel). Rotterdam lay in ruin from air attacks; the Battle of Britain soon commenced. The decisive Nazi offensive instilled a palpable sense of shifting geopolitical plates, of a new chapter in world history. In Japan, there were excited visions of a new world historical era, in line with the empire's regionalist aspirations. The German assault left European colonies in Southeast Asia particularly vulnerable, like imperial fruit ripe for picking off a pan-nationalist tree. It also exposed the liberal paradox of white domination over Asian peoples. In the United States, factories furiously began fulfilling requisitions for planes, tanks, ships, and bombs. The Roosevelt administration also took steps to impose sanctions against Japan. To this rising enmity was added the return of statesmen who had played prominent roles in US-Japan relations in the 1930s—especially Matsuoka, Konoe, and Stimson—and who now would play even bigger roles amid bigger stakes in the turbulent ideological waters that separated the two nations.

Chapter Seven

"So Many Unexplainable Things Are Happening" (1940–1941)

Taking stock of the electric atmosphere in Tokyo, Ambassador Grew reported to Secretary Hull that the German victories in the spring of 1940 had gone to the heads of Japan's leaders "like strong wine." The lightning speed and seeming invincibility of Hitler's invading forces mesmerized the Japanese. The quick victories appeared to affirm the Führer's bold rhetoric—and that the Japanese were, in fact, witnessing a momentous turning point in world history. It was only a matter of time before Germany would conquer Great Britain, leaving a lone democracy, the United States, on an ideological island. Henceforth, the revisionist powers no longer would be hamstrung by liberal moralizing and geopolitical hypocrisy. A golden opportunity to fulfill Japan's mission in Asia must not be missed, as announced by the slogan heard around Japan: "Don't Miss the Bus!"[1]

Hitler's invasion of western Europe thus almost immediately aggravated the tension between the United States and Japan. It incited the two Pacific powers into more aggressive and mutually antithetical policies. Ironically, the aim of both nations was to contain the actions of the other side—and the results were opposite. While Japan envisioned a closer relationship with Germany in order to arrest American bellicosity, the United States ratcheted up sanctions in hopes of containing Japanese bellicosity. In both cases, the core ideological antagonism informed respective policies and accelerated the two countries down the slippery slope to transpacific war. Protracted bilateral negotiations in the spring of 1941 merely punctuated the yawning ideological gulf. Eleventh-hour negotiations similarly failed to reconcile the fundamental principles that separated the two nations, thereby making any genuine accommodation ultimately unattainable. The tragic tumble toward war also served to discredit the skeletal remains of Japan's cultural diplomacy in the United States.

***

The second Konoe cabinet entered office on July 22, 1940, with an urgency and confidence matching the perception that world historical change was in the offing. More than anyone, Foreign Minister Matsuoka became the face and voice of this apparent forward motion. Following his dramatic walkout of the League of Nations in 1933, Matsuoka had wandered in the political wilderness until 1935, when the government appointed him president of the South Manchurian Railway Company. There he periodically wrote about Japan's purported mission in Asia. His resignation in 1939 hurled the diplomat back into the wilderness. Clearly, Konoe thought the time was right for Matsuoka's brand of bold diplomacy. Matsuoka's immodesty, so contrary to customary Japanese respect for humility, was excused on grounds of his Americanization, and also deemed an asset for the times. As one confidant noted, the Japanese believed Matsuoka would be successful in dealing with Americans because of the impression that he thought and conducted himself like one. If so, Secretary Hull still believed Matsuoka was "as crooked as a basket of fishhooks."[2]

In a bombshell interview with the *New York Herald Tribune* on the day the Konoe cabinet took office, the sixty-year-old Matsuoka stated matter-of-factly that the democracies were "bankrupt and finished" and that the "totalitarian system is going to win out the world now." More pointedly, the foreign minister declared there was not enough room in the world for two different political and economic systems. By aligning Japan openly with the fascist/expansionist camp, Matsuoka's comments revealed that he shared the Roosevelt administration's increasing doubts about coexistence.[3]

Premier Konoe echoed Matsuoka's convictions. In a highly publicized national broadcast a day after his inauguration, Konoe intimated a closer alignment with the Axis powers going forward, saying, "Japan must be determined to cooperate in the establishment of a new world order." He added that Japan's dependence on (unnamed) foreign nations would necessitate an advance into the South Seas and that the "total strength" of the nation would be mobilized. That Japan's ideological-geopolitical course had never been so clearly stated before reveals the depth of Tokyo's altered perceptions in the summer of 1940.[4]

Perceptions among the newly shuffled Roosevelt administration were in an altered state as well. The rising optimism in Tokyo corresponded to rising alarm in Washington. Two objectives quickly coalesced in the White House: keep Great Britain afloat and contain Japanese expansionism. The two goals were connected, given Britain's strong presence in Asia. The result was an opening shot over Japan's bow in the form of sanctions. It had been six months since the expiration of the US-Japan Commercial Treaty, and yet there had been no sign of economic pressure. The combination of Hitler's westward thrust and Tokyo's stated ambition to expand southward changed everything. Treasury Secretary Morgenthau, with the support of Stimson, Ickes, and Hornbeck, pushed for a total embargo of oil and scrap iron. When Undersecretary of State Sumner Welles objected, fearing it would embolden Japan, not contain it, Roosevelt told the two sides to "go off in a corner" and find agreement. The resultant compromise, issued on July 26, 1940, banned the sale of high-octane aviation fuel and scrap metal.[5]

The *Asahi Shimbun* called the sanctions "intolerable"—perhaps a subtle reference to Britain's Coercive Acts against the American colonists in 1774. When Tokyo complained it was being singled out for discriminatory treatment, the State Department said the sanctions were issued "in the interest of national defense" and therefore a protest by any foreign government was "unwarranted."[6] Truth be told, the new Japanese government was less focused on formulating a protest to sanctions than it was on preparing for bold moves of its own.

THE GREATER EAST ASIA CO-PROSPERITY SPHERE

Just before officially assuming the premiership, Prince Konoe had called a policy meeting with three of his top cabinet picks at his Tekigaiso villa in Tokyo's western suburbs. Joining the newly appointed premier were Matsuoka and soon-to-be war and navy ministers General Tōjō Hideki and Vice Admiral Yoshida Zengo. Consistent with current debates in Tokyo and notions of a new world order, two policies took precedence: the first aimed at "strengthening ties" with the Axis powers, with an additional nonaggression pact with Russia; the second dealt with incorporating the Asian colonies of Britain, France, and the Netherlands into Japan's empire. Relatedly, but paradoxically, the four leaders sought to "avoid an unnecessary clash" with the United States. Admiral Yoshida, representing a navy faction of strategic pragmatism, was wary about an Axis alliance triggering a premature naval engagement with the United States. This "Tekigaiso template" nonetheless informed Japanese policy making throughout the summer and fall of 1940. For the Japanese, it was a heady period of seemingly endless forward motion.[7]

The first bold stroke of official policy came on August 1. In a virtual corollary to Konoe's New Order declaration of 1938, Matsuoka announced to the world that Japan aimed to establish a "Greater East Asia Co-Prosperity Sphere." The newly coined phrase now anticipated subsuming all of Asia into a Japanese-guided economic, political, and cultural bloc. This implied a promise of liberation from white overlords—a powerful message that resonated throughout Asia, including within Japan. As Ethan Mark and others have noted, the widespread reversal among Japanese intellectuals at this time from left wing to right wing can be traced, in part, to the "profound appeals of the Asia-Pacific [struggle] as a world-historical 'war of liberation' against Western imperialism."[8] In symbolic evocation of the new era, St. Luke's Hospital in Tokyo, founded by the American Episcopalian Church, was renamed the Greater East Asia Hospital. Still, however exhilarating the newly imagined regionalist vistas, Japan's actual experience in China presaged the challenge of reconciling the promise of "co-prosperity" to all of Asia with Japanese occupation armies and assumptions of racial superiority.

At a press conference after his declaration, Matsuoka warned would-be opponents of the Greater East Asia scheme that Japan was "through with toadying." Proving his point, Matsuoka summoned the Vichy ambassador, Charles Arsène-Henry, and requested that French authorities grant Japan the right to use air bases and station troops in northern Indochina for incursions into China. Arsène-Henry protested that such an authorization would amount to a French declaration of war on China. That did not matter, suggested Matsuoka. "In the world today," said the foreign minister, "so many unexplainable things are happening." Matsuoka's request turned into an ultimatum. In late August, the French yielded to Japan's demands after Matsuoka accepted the token gesture of affirming a liberal oxymoron, "the territorial integrity of French Indochina." Japan had acquired its first foothold in the embryonic Co-Prosperity Sphere. One Japanese writer explained the empire's new imperatives, saying, "If Japan confines itself within its old shell of morality and ideals, it will never be able to gain a place in the sun."[9] That place was both literal and figurative—calling for Japanese primacy in sunnier Asian climes, and also in the ranks of nations, one commensurate with its inherent greatness to regenerate Asia. Tellingly, just twenty years after the Paris Peace Conference, Wilsonian ideals were deemed "old."

THE AXIS PACT AND "JAPAN'S TRUE INTENTIONS"

Most important of all, the Konoe cabinet moved briskly toward formalizing an alliance with the Axis powers. Matsuoka, on that historic day of August 1, in addition to announcing the Co-Prosperity Sphere and presenting demands to the Vichy ambassador, also met with German Ambassador Eugen Ott. Over tea, Matsuoka intimated to Ott that Japan desired an alliance. As David Lu has pointed out, Matsuoka, in fact, had become obsessed with negotiating an alliance with Germany. Hitler's bold leadership, German military success, and the seeming imminence of a new world order all fed Matsuoka's urgency. Army and navy policy papers also advocated sealing an alliance, though

Navy Minister Yoshida, out of strategic pragmatism, remained opposed. Reflecting official trends was the Reich's general popularity in Japan, where Hitler's *Mein Kampf* and Goebbels's *Diary* continued to be best sellers.[10]

Germany was interested. At the end of August, Foreign Minister Ribbentrop dispatched to Tokyo a special envoy, Heinrich Stahmer, for further discussions. Unknown to the Japanese, Hitler was growing anxious about Britain's resilience in the ongoing air war. Keeping the United States out of the Atlantic, therefore, was crucial, and Japan could help by keeping the Americans on edge in the Pacific. Stahmer and Matsuoka proceeded diligently; negotiations concluded in mid-September, and Italy subsequently was asked to join. The final accord—eventually referred to as the Tripartite or Axis Pact—set its sights squarely on an unnamed United States, with the signatories agreeing "to assist one another with all political, economic, and military means" when one of the contracting parties was attacked by a power "not presently involved in the European War or the Sino-Japanese conflict."[11]

Technically, this was a military alliance. More precisely, it was an ideological alliance, backed by ambiguous military support. As stated in the treaty's preamble, because Japan, Germany, and Italy had been denied their "proper places" in the world, they had decided to "co-operate with one another in their efforts in Greater East Asia and the regions of Europe respectively" in order "to establish and maintain a new order." From the perspective of the signatories, these were similarly aggrieved great nations wielding a righteous sword. This often-overlooked rush of ideology helps explain a realist riddle, in which none of Japan's leaders during the many debates about the Tripartite Pact "pointed to the folly of Japan, a sea power, aligning with Germany, a land power." A seemingly lone critique of this anomaly came from the Washington-based Japanese columnist K. K. Kawakami, who wondered if Konoe and Matsuoka were "hypnotized" by Hitler and Ribbentrop. Suppose, said Kawakami, Japan's actions in Southeast Asia provoked the United States to move its fleet toward the British naval base at Singapore. "What could Germany do to help Japan?" he asked. Kawakami's answer: "Absolutely nothing."[12]

Support in Japan nonetheless was widespread. Before the official signing in Berlin on September 27, an Imperial Conference approved the agreement. Leadership looked forward to a new world order comprising massive, exclusionary pan-nationalist spheres among the revisionist powers. As Privy Council member Viscount Ishii remarked, Japan, Germany, and Italy were bound together by their "common interests." At a celebration in Tokyo, Premier Konoe reportedly broke into tears. His emotion carried over into public comments. In a message to the Japanese people, Konoe echoed Ishii, stating, "Germany and Italy share with our empire the same ideals and aspirations." At a press conference, as reported by Hugh Byas in the *New York*

Times, Konoe promised that the Japanese, Germans, and Italians "would be remembered with admiration in the history of mankind."[13]

Japan's leadership also flirted with belligerence. In a highly publicized statement, Konoe infamously warned, "if the United States refuses to understand the real intentions of Japan, Germany, and Italy, and persists in challenging those Powers, there will be no other course open to them but to go to war." Matsuoka likewise said Japan was "firmly determined to eliminate any nation which will obstruct our order. . . . We must be prepared to fight with the German and Italian people." These were stunning statements, attributed not to the cliché of Japan's "controlling warlords" but rather to the country's best and brightest civilian statesmen—to a premier who had sent his son to Princeton and a foreign minister who had earned his law degree from the University of Oregon. Doubtless it was the countervailing allure of the latter that could still commit Ambassador Grew to report, despite Konoe's central role in establishing the Axis alliance, that he was told on "excellent authority" that Konoe was "dead against" the pact.[14]

Contrary to Grew's "insider" information, the KBS's *NIPPON* magazine celebrated Konoe and Matsuoka—not generals and admirals. A special issue on the pact included an imposing cover headshot of Konoe (emblazoned with a golden hue), photographs of the signing in Berlin, a feature article that lionized Matsuoka, and six pages of congratulatory advertisements by Japanese firms. This overt promotion of the Axis Pact by Tokyo's cultural apparatus was corroborated at the time by a young American college student who attended a KBS-sponsored student conference in the summer of 1940 and reported in his diary, "we're hearing much of regional blocs led by Japan." Perhaps most astonishing was that the KBS put effort into hosting a small number of American students, including paid visits to Korea and Manchuria, in hopes of still shaping public opinion. (Such efforts aligned with Earl Leaf's second report to Stanley Hornbeck, which claimed that "Japanese propagandists" at the "swank" KBS offices at the Rockefeller Center were "working overtime." Leaf also exposed numerous Americans alleged to be doing Japan's bidding.)[15]

If there is a single most important marker on the proverbial road to Pearl Harbor, the Axis Pact may have been the one. What is remarkable is how Japan—and Germany—misjudged the United States. Japan's leaders genuinely believed the pact would paralyze the United States into inaction—that Roosevelt would realize he had more to gain in the recognition of pan-nationalist spheres than through war. This view all but ignored Roosevelt's expressed doubts about coexistence with the revisionist powers. As one State Department official remarked at the time, the Japanese seemed not to have realized that the United States was guided by principles "to which it held quite as tenaciously as any totalitarian government." Above all, the Axis Pact sent a message of ideological affinity, that Japan was officially *one of them*.

Indeed, 60 percent of Americans now believed Japan posed a "serious threat" to the United States, and a whopping 90 percent supported a more comprehensive embargo against the empire. As Warren Cohen has observed, "nothing the Chinese or their friends in the United States could have done could have convinced Americans of their stake in the outcome of the Sino-Japanese war as effectively as Japan's decision to ally with Nazi Germany." The Tripartite Pact essentially melded two wars into one.[16]

In the face of such illiberal momentum, Roosevelt stepped up preparedness measures. On September 2, by executive order, he completed a "Destroyers-for-Bases" deal with Great Britain, whereby the United States gave the British fifty old destroyers in exchange for more than ten air bases in the Western Hemisphere. Congress also passed the Selective Service Act, culminating in the republic's first peacetime draft. Just as conspicuously, speeches by Roosevelt and his cabinet members became increasingly Manichean, approximating a "clash of civilization" theme. On October 5, Navy Secretary Knox said the Axis Pact threatened the "American way of life" as never before. On October 12, Roosevelt referred to "the dictator countries of Europe and Asia" as the "forces of evil," in contrast to the British, described as "the last free people now fighting to hold them at bay." And Secretary Hull warned that the aggressor nations would "transform the civilized world as we have known it into a world in which mankind will be reduced again to the degradation of a master-and-slave relationship." Present in these speeches was a foreboding sense of ideological encirclement, in which the light of democracy would be dimmed and ultimately extinguished. Ironically, this fear of encirclement was mirrored in Japan, where the empire's propagandists described the country as being surrounded by hostile "ABCD" powers—American, British, Chinese, and Dutch.[17]

A TOTALITARIAN PLAN AND AN UNPARALLELED POLITY

Two weeks after signing the Tripartite Pact, the Konoe cabinet offered Americans further evidence of ideological congruence with Germany and Italy with news it was creating a one-party system in Japan. More precisely, the proposed national scheme, which went by the grandiose moniker the Imperial Rule Assistance Association (IRAA), was not so much a political party as a national organization. The idea was to rally the nation toward the goal of the New Order in Asia. To do this, the government dissolved all political parties and organized "neighborhood associations," which structured the daily lives of Japanese people, politically, economically, and culturally. This "total mobilization" included a crackdown on Americanization, including Hollywood films, dance clubs, and women's dress, and shutting down the *Japan Advertiser*. Eventually, complaints by big business watered down the organization. Ambassador Grew called the new national structure "an awful mess."[18] Whatever its troubles, the IRAA clarified the ideological direction the Konoe cabinet wished to take the nation.

The nationalistic spirit sought by the IRAA was more deeply felt in November when the nation celebrated the purported 2,600th anniversary of Japan's founding and "unbroken imperial line." The Japanese government, culminating a yearlong buildup, orchestrated a lavish two-day program intended to enhance the nation's imperial cult and Japanese exceptionalism. As reported in American newspapers and captured in newsreels, more than fifty thousand dignitaries attended an outdoor ceremony near the palace grounds, which Premier Konoe opened with studied reverence. Konoe acclaimed the uniqueness of Japan's national polity, asserting "the sacredness of our national structure is naturally unparalleled in all the world." Once again the premier soldered the infallible throne to the legitimacy of Japan's Asianist ambitions, saying, "His Highness has dispatched forces to a foreign land [and] concluded an alliance with friendly Powers . . . in an effort to establish the stability of East Asia and thereby promote the peace of the world." One contemporary Western scholar of Japan concluded that the "ingenious sophism" of Japan's Asianist ideology had "captivated the public mind and conformed to the ideals of the majority of people."[19]

In the aftermath of the imperial celebrations, Japan and the puppet Wang regime formalized the alleged new order in East Asia with a bilateral treaty. The two governments pledged cooperation for sublime-sounding but hazily construed objectives, such as "cultural harmony, creation, and development." Perhaps the most curious thing about the accord was the lip service paid to the principles embodied in the Nine-Power Treaty, with Japan promising to respect China's sovereignty, abolish extraterritorial rights, and relinquish its settlements.[20] No Western power had gone this far. Truth be told, with 1.5 million Japanese troops in China, neither would Japan. Nonetheless collaborators like Wang felt compelled to invoke the principles in order to provide the gloss of Chinese sovereignty to the Chinese people and soft-pedal Japanese hegemony, none of which, of course, augured well for Japan's occupation. As if calling out such ideological mirages, the Roosevelt administration countered by announcing new loans to Chongqing worth one hundred million dollars, calling Wang a "puppet," and doubling down on liberalism's most hallowed shibboleth, saying it was "opposed to the use of force as an international instrument."[21]

Ignoring American opposition, Japan's main rationale for its actions on the continent remained grounded in claims of a benevolent regionalism. Foreign Minister Matsuoka made this premise clear in a talk at the America-Japan Society in Tokyo. Matsuoka described Japan's objectives in Asia as a "moral crusade." He rehashed the empire's Asianist platitudes, declaring, "We are endeavoring to initiate an era of enduring peace and unlimited prosperity, based on justice, equality, and mutuality, in Greater East Asia where we firmly believe we have a great mission as the civilizing and stabilizing force." The phrasings nearly replicated Matsuoka's defense of Manchukuo in 1933. Matsuoka further reminded Americans that the liberal status quo had crumbled, implying there was no turning back except through war. He suggested it would be prudent for Americans "to think twice, thrice, nay, ten hundred or thousand times before they take the leap that may prove fatal to all humanity." It was a chilling speech in front of a group established to build lasting friendship between Americans and Japanese. The repetition of such brash talk among Japan's leadership was enough to prompt even Ambassador Grew to sense a point of no return. To President Roosevelt, Grew wrote, "This, indeed, is not the Japan we have known and loved." He lamented that Japan had become "openly and ashamedly one of the predatory nations and part of a system which aims to wreck about everything the United States stands for."[22] Grew's thinking had caught up to the State Department and White House.

"ALL PARTS OF A SINGLE WORLD CONFLICT"

In Washington, President Roosevelt, buoyed by a landmark third consecutive electoral victory, went on an oratory offensive. In a span of eight days, the president gave two prominent foreign policy speeches, both of which drew the relationship between ideology and strategic considerations in stark terms. On December 29, hoping to rally material support for Great Britain, the president again described world affairs as a clash of civilizations between forces of good and evil. "Never before since Jamestown and Plymouth Rock," Roosevelt warned, "has our American civilization been in such danger as now." And once again he ripped isolationists. To those who believed the Axis powers would never attack the Western Hemisphere, Roosevelt chastised them as engaging in a "dangerous form of wishful thinking." To meet the new threats—and keep out of a "last-ditch war"—the president said the nation needed to build up its defenses and become "the great arsenal of democracy." And not just in the Atlantic; again, to Roosevelt, the perceived ideological threat was global. "The democratic way of life," the president explained, "is at this moment being directly assailed in every part of the world." As he told Ambassador Grew, "We must recognize that the hostilities in Europe, in Africa, and in Asia are all parts of a single world conflict. We must, consequently, recognize that our interests are menaced both in Europe and in the Far East."[23] The president's thesis was now absolute: coexistence with the revisionist powers was impossible.

Not content to let up, Roosevelt hammered home this thesis in his State of the Union address on January 6, 1941. In "no previous time," asserted the president, "has American security been as seriously threatened from without as it is today." Once again, there was no separating American core values from a peaceful world order. He looked forward, he said, to a world founded on "Four Freedoms," calling them the "very antithesis of the so-called new order of tyranny." These were freedom of speech, freedom of religion, freedom from economic want, and freedom from fear or the menace of war. He punctuated each freedom by envisioning their spread to "everywhere in the world."[24] Roosevelt's America no longer would be a reluctant power with one foot in and one foot out of world affairs. The United States would lead; it would promote liberal values. And at the present time, the president argued, the ideological contest was clearly drawn.

The Japanese could not have agreed more. Their regionalist framework, as noted, was similarly construed as creating a more just world order in contrast to an Anglo-American liberal order. As Matsuoka told the Diet two weeks after Roosevelt's Four Freedoms address, "It is our avowed purpose to bring all the people of Greater East Asia to revert to their innate and proper aspect, promoting conciliation and co-operation among them, and thereby setting the example of universal concord." And whereas Roosevelt still swam against strong domestic currents and must have wondered if his nation would rise to the occasion, Japan's leaders in early 1941 were still brimming with confidence. Premier Konoe pledged to Diet members he would stay premier until the war in China was concluded. The assembly, observed Hugh Byas, "cheered wildly."[25]

H.R. 1776

By early 1941, a sense of inevitable clash began to gather force across the Pacific. Matsuoka claimed a new world order was only a matter of time and that it was "useless to talk further with the Americans." The minister branded Roosevelt and Hull as "warmongers" and said the Japanese "were not dreaming empty dreams." Grew noted that Matsuoka, at a luncheon address, "practically threatened the United States with war." The ambassador reported to Secretary Hull that "the general anxiety over the worsening of relations with the United States ... has been more intense than at any time of my observations during the past eight years in Japan." Even the emperor, he was told, was caught up in the more belligerent temperament of Japan's leaders. Then, on January 27, Grew relayed to Hull that a Western diplomat had heard from many sources that the Japanese navy was planning "to attempt a surprise attack on Pearl Harbor" if relations worsened. It seemed too fantastic to take seriously. Meanwhile, in the United States, nearly 40 percent of Americans now believed the United States should *risk war* with Japan in order to keep the empire from seizing the Dutch East Indies and Singapore. For a nation repeatedly subjected to the isolationist message that distant conflict was "none of our business," the support for such a risk showed a remarkable swing in public opinion.[26]

Another distinct sign of a changing American mindset was Congress's approval of the White House's "Lend-Lease" scheme. Symbolically numbered H.R. 1776, Lend-Lease gave the president the authority to "lend" military supplies to Britain and other friendly nations. The program's genesis were the limits of cash-and-carry: Britain's cash reserves had dried up. To sell the plan, FDR presented Americans with the questionable analogy of lending a fire hose to a neighbor whose house was on fire. It took little critical thinking to deduce that the probability of getting back military supplies or deferred payments from the British and Chinese was a lot lower than getting a hose back from a neighbor. But most Americans looked the other way. Despite isolationist opposition, the House passed the measure 317–71; the Senate, 60–31. Key support for Roosevelt came from media mogul Henry Luce, who played the anti-Lindbergh. In a long commentary in *Life* magazine titled "The American Century," Luce admonished Americans for their "halfway hopes and halfway measures" in the global conflict, telling them to accept the fact that the United States was already in "the war"—and that it was time to act.[27]

Following his signing of the Lend-Lease bill in March, Roosevelt's spirits soared. In an address at the White House Correspondents dinner, the president's confidence was unmistakable. "Let not dictators of Europe or Asia," he said, "doubt our unanimity now. . . . We, the American people, are writing new history today." He made clear that help was on the way to allies:

> The British people . . . need ships. From America, they will get ships. They need planes. From America, they will get planes. From America they need food. And from America they will get food. They need tanks and guns and ammunition and supplies of all kinds. From America, they will get tanks and guns and ammunition and supplies of all kinds. China, likewise, expresses the magnificent will of millions of plain people to resist the dismemberment of their historic nation. China . . . asks our help. America has said that China shall have our help.

With uncommon directness, Roosevelt had lumped Japan's rulers with Europe's dictators and condemned their new order in Asia as the "dismemberment" of a great nation. Hugh Byas reported that the Japanese press collectively skewered the president. The *Asahi* portrayed Roosevelt's speech as "rabid" and opined, not inaccurately, that the United States had at last "come forward on the active stage of the World War." Communication within the US Navy captured the building tensions between the two Pacific powers. Admiral Harold Stark, chief of naval operations, wrote to Admiral Husband

E. Kimmel, commander-in-chief of the Pacific Fleet, that "the question as to our entry into the war seems to be *when*, and not *whether*."[28]

MATSUOKA'S TOTALITARIAN TOUR

If passage of Lend-Lease poured sunny optimism into the Oval Office, the mood in Tokyo was similarly sanguine. At the vanguard of Japan's confident posture was the Konoe cabinet's media celebrity, Foreign Minister Matsuoka. On March 12, the day after Roosevelt signed the Lend-Lease bill, Matsuoka left Tokyo for a six-week journey that would take him to Moscow, Berlin, and Rome. In the ensuing global splash, Matsuoka basked in the big crowds and met with Stalin, Hitler, and Mussolini. He noted proudly that great leaders were "disposing quickly the affairs of state."[29] In other words, great men (including himself)—not the wishy-washy encumbrances of liberal institutions—were making history. The goals of the trip were twofold: to cement Axis unity, and to follow Hitler's lead and reach a nonaggression treaty with the Soviet Union. An agreement with the Russians, it was assumed, would provide Japan with double-bolt security: plug a strategic dike on the empire's northwest frontier, and induce hesitancy and pliancy in the Americans. The combined effect would open up opportunities for a southward advance.

Matsuoka's first stop, following a week of travel on a Trans-Siberian Railway luxury sleeper, was Moscow. The weather was cold and snowy, but the politics were warm. The Russians had guessed correctly Matsuoka's aims; the Konoe cabinet had first reached out to the Soviets in the summer of 1940 about a nonaggression treaty. In meetings with Stalin and Prime Minister/Foreign Minister Vyacheslav Molotov, Matsuoka found the Russians receptive. Like Japan's leaders, Stalin could not afford volatility in Northeast Asia. A stable frontier would allow him to focus on the Baltic and eastern Europe and keep an eye on Germany. Matsuoka would not commit to a treaty, however, until visiting his Axis partners. As if creating the aura of a patient rainmaker, Matsuoka departed Moscow for Berlin, with the intent of returning afterward to negotiate a treaty with the Russians.[30]

During the ensuing week in Berlin and Rome, diplomacy blended with festive banquets and appearances on balconies before large crowds. In the German capital, as reported in the *New York Times* and shown in newsreels, Matsuoka and Ribbentrop rode in an open car along the city's main thoroughfares, which were lined by three hundred thousand "lustily cheering" Berliners and festooned with swastikas and Rising Suns. Matsuoka assured the German people that the Japanese nation "is with you in joy or sorrow." In three meetings with Ribbentrop, including one with Hitler, Matsuoka was told repeatedly of Britain's imminent defeat. "Each bomb which falls on England," said Ribbentrop, "brings the island empire nearer to its final doom, and with each ton of shipping sunk, there sinks a piece of Great Britain." So now was the time for Japan to attack the massive British naval base at Singapore and deliver a knockout blow—and, so hoped the Germans, keep the Americans out of the Atlantic. Matsuoka hailed Hitler as a "man of genius" but said he had no power to pledge his government to action against Britain. Thus, despite the air of bravado and ideological camaraderie, self-interest was fully present as well. It was an early sign that the fanfare of the Tripartite Pact exceeded its promises and that the Axis powers lacked the same kind of solidarity that bound the liberal powers, the massive British empire notwithstanding.[31]

Matsuoka subsequently traveled to Rome for another round of Axis celebrations, followed by a brief return to Berlin, before heading back to Moscow for a week of treaty negotiations. In talks with Stalin and Molotov, Matsuoka pushed for a nonaggression treaty in which Russia and Japan pledged never to attack one another. The Soviets, however, replied that such an agreement required the restoration of Russian territory seized during the 1904–1905 Russo-Japanese War (southern half of Sakhalin Island). Matsuoka was in no position to surrender the spoils of Japanese sacrifice and glory,

Figure 7.1. Foreign Minister Matsuoka's motorcade and welcoming throngs in Berlin, March 1941. (US Holocaust Memorial Museum, courtesy of Perquimans County Library.)

and so the two powers settled on a neutrality pact, signed on April 13. Both sides promised neutrality in the event that a third power attacked either Japan or Russia. The Soviets also agreed to respect the "territorial integrity" of Manchukuo. With rare deference, Stalin saw Matsuoka off at Moscow's Yaroslavskaya railway station, where the two embraced. In Tokyo, Premier Konoe called the pact "epoch-making."[32]

As a result of the Soviet-Japanese Neutrality Pact, the main goals set forth at Konoe's Tekigaiso villa in July 1940 were on the road to realization: treaties with the Axis powers and Soviets and the pronouncement of a Greater East Asia Co-Prosperity Sphere. The final pillar in the construction of the hegemonic edifice, it will be recalled, was the paradoxical aim of avoiding war with the United States. For the job of getting through to the United States, using the Tripartite Pact as a fulcrum, Matsuoka appointed ex–foreign minister Admiral Nomura as Japan's new ambassador. Not surprisingly, new faces could do little to bridge the two nations' ideological divide, especially at a time of peak tensions. The diplomatic impasse surrounding the so-called Draft Understanding in the spring of 1941 drove the point home.

A MISUNDERSTOOD UNDERSTANDING

Ambassador Nomura, six feet tall and physically strong with a warm personality, had enjoyed a successful career in the navy. And as Japan's naval attaché in Washington during the First World War and a member of Japan's delegations to the Paris and Washington Conferences, he had built personal relationships with US navy officers. Oddly, despite appointing him, Matsuoka dismissed his sixty-three-year-old ambassador as "an awfully nice guy, but not a bright one." It was another example of the foreign minister's egotism. In fact, Nomura had graduated second in his class from the Japanese Naval Academy. If only Matsuoka knew that FDR had described the foreign minister's instructions to Nomura as "the product of a mind which is deeply disturbed and unable to think quietly or logically." The administration was now regularly reading Japan's diplomatic correspondence, thanks to American cryptanalysts, who in the fall of 1940 had cracked Japan's diplomatic code machine (PURPLE) with their decrypting machine (MAGIC).[33]

To his credit, Nomura seemed to grasp the grave divide in US-Japan relations with greater awareness than many of his Japanese contemporaries, telling an interviewer at the time, "What is responsible for the long list of [bilateral] divergences dating from the Manchurian Incident is not so much 'misunderstanding' as it is fundamental differences in policy."[34] What he did not appear to wholly grasp, however, was that respective policies flowed from fundamental differences in ideology. The result is that Nomura almost immediately perpetuated misunderstanding. Soon after his arrival in Washington, Nomura initiated private talks with Hull, often meeting in the evening at the secretary's residence at the Wardman Park Hotel, with the hope of minimizing tensions. Discussions in mid-April, however, triggered confusion, requiring further clarification, resulting in greater ideological lucidity—and deeper tensions.

On April 14, Secretary Hull, in close consultation with his East Asia advisors, queried Ambassador Nomura about a curious peace proposal that a small group of interested Japanese and Americans—including a pair of Maryknoll Catholic clerics—recently had presented to the State Department. The proposal, which became known as the Draft Understanding, consisted of seven broad categories affecting US-Japan relations, including the wars in Europe and China. Some points were general enough to satisfy multiple interpretations. The group had reached out to Nomura, who supported it. Hull wondered, did the ambassador intend to present the proposal "as a first step" in talks between Japan and the United States? Nomura was favorably inclined. Hull was not opposed, but he hung on the word "preliminary." Before the document was introduced, *preliminary discussion* was necessary to ascertain whether formal discussions were worthwhile. Hull did not elaborate, but he wanted to know beforehand if any ideological common ground existed between the two governments. This aim became clear two days later.[35]

Meeting again with Nomura at his hotel apartment, Hull handed the Japanese ambassador a piece of paper on which was written "Four Principles." Japan's acceptance of the principles, said Hull, would satisfy Washington's precondition for further talks. The four liberal points amounted to a compressed version of the Nine-Power Treaty and Kellogg Pact, with their emphasis on orderly processes. These included respect for the territorial integrity and sovereignty of all nations, noninterference in the internal affairs of other countries, and the equality of commercial opportunity. The fourth point declared that the status quo in the Pacific could not be altered except by peaceful means. Nomura, not surprisingly, was more interested in the Draft Understanding: was the secretary ready to approve the proposal? Certain ideas, replied Hull, the United States could agree on—but others only with considerable alteration. Hull asked Nomura to present the Four Principles to his government, stressing that, at this point, the two governments were exploring talks "in a purely preliminary and unofficial way." The two sides were talking to each other while talking past each other.[36]

On April 18, Nomura cabled *only* the Draft Understanding to Tokyo—with the impression of it being an official US proposal. Premier Konoe immediately called a Liaison Conference to discuss the document. Excitement grew over what was perceived as American acceptance of Japan's fundamental foreign policies, including the Axis Pact (provided it was a defensive measure), the Wang regime (to be combined with Chiang's), and recognition of Manchukuo. Nomura had pointed out to Hull the Draft Understanding's explicit recognition of Manchukuo; the secretary's oblique response perhaps could have been interpreted as positive. But the fact that Hull on April 14 had used the Soviets' recent recognition of Manchukuo to reaffirm American *nonrecognition* should have made clear that Washington had not changed its position.[37]

Nomura had either misunderstood Hull or understood him all too well and knew the ideological divide would lead to an impasse. So he had sent his government the good stuff and the result was a gross misunderstanding and unrealistic expectations for an entente. This can be seen in Konoe's succinct postwar memoir (more like a hurried defense brief), which dedicated excessive attention to the Draft Understanding. Firm American objections to the Axis Pact and demands for troop withdrawal in China were skimmed over. Indeed, Emperor Hirohito praised the Axis Pact as *bringing about* the Draft Understanding and America's alleged about-face. "In the end," he told his chief advisor Kido Kōichi (Lord Keeper of the Privy Seal), "it is all about being patient and persistent, would you not say?"[38]

"BETWEEN HUMAN SLAVERY AND HUMAN FREEDOM"

Nomura's incomplete communication aside, one can only wonder why Japan's leading statesmen, attuned to American foreign policy, would interpret the proposal as the Roosevelt administration's word, especially one whose "vague and hortatory language," as Waldo Heinrichs pointed out, conveyed an amateurish quality. It took Matsuoka to prick the balloon of Japan's delusion. The foreign minister had first caught wind of the proposal on his way back from Europe. His initial impulse sprung from ego: Matsuoka's great diplomacy had forced American pliancy; there was talk of him traveling next to Washington. Upon reading the understanding, however, Matsuoka privately scoffed in disbelief to a colleague, "Clearly, that's not a U.S. document. That thing has been written by Japanese."[39] But Matsuoka wanted something even stronger. It was like three trains running in different directions: Hull insisting on the Four Principles, Konoe clinging to the Draft *Mis*understanding, and a pugnacious Matsuoka agitating to set things straight with America.

Matsuoka believed his journey to Europe had "killed five birds with one stone" (a reference to the alleged impact on relations with Russia, China, the United States, French Indochina, and the Dutch East Indies). Mostly, as the *New York Times* suggested under the headline, "Matsuoka Visions Axis 'Millennium,'" the trip to Berlin and Rome was fueling an ideological fever dream. Following a luncheon given for Matsuoka by Emperor Hirohito, the Japanese foreign minister paid a full-throttled tribute to Hitler and Mussolini at a "mass meeting" in Hibiya Hall, "which was often interrupted by thunderous applause." The fascist parallels drawn by the paper's new Tokyo correspondent, Otto Tolischus, were unmistakable. Esteemed British diplomat and historian George Sansom, meanwhile, wrote in *Foreign Affairs* that it was "a mistake to suppose that there is a split between military and civilian opinion in Japan."[40]

Matsuoka's swagger subsequently carried over into Liaison Conferences, with the foreign minister exhorting his colleagues to back a naval attack on Singapore. On May 12, he cabled Nomura a firmer revision of the Draft Understanding. A month had passed since Hull and Nomura's key exchange. The ideological sticking points—the war in China and alliance with Hitler—only stuck more. Japan's ties to "barbaric Hitlerism" baffled Hull. Matsuoka's exchanges with Grew only deepened this astonishment. Matsuoka, not inaccurately, remarked that Hitler had shown "patience and generosity" in not declaring war on the United States. If the US Navy were to attack U-boats in the Atlantic, Matsuoka said Japan would regard it as an act of aggression, triggering the Tripartite Pact. In that case, he saw little chance of avoiding war with America. Impulsively, he told Grew the "manly, decent, and reasonable" thing to do was for the United States to declare war on Germany.[41]

Not surprisingly, in light of the ideological gulf, talks between the State Department and Japan's Foreign Ministry stalled. On June 21, Hull formally replied to Japan's revision of the Draft Understanding, restating the necessity of agreeing to the Four Principles as a basis for formal talks. He added an oral statement that singled out Matsuoka without naming him. "Some Japanese leaders in influential official positions," said Hull, "are definitely committed to a course which calls for support of Nazi Germany and its policies of conquest." As long as this was the case, inquired the secretary of state, was it not "illusory" to expect the current proposal to precipitate an entente? In the end, the best one could say about these "Spring Talks" was that Hull desired an understanding with Japan—but not at the expense of American core values; and Japan's leadership desired an entente with the United States—but not if it meant compromising its exclusive regionalism. There simply was no way to paper over such polarized positions. This fact became more palpable in the summer of 1941, as ideology became more firmly entwined with strategic considerations and the expanded war in Europe again raised the geopolitical stakes in Asia.[42]

In Washington, FDR was working somewhat duplicitously, "finessing democracy," so to speak, to make certain that liberal values triumphed in the global struggle. In the weeks preceding the 1940 election, the president had promised that American boys would not be sent into any foreign wars. Then, in April 1941, he denied there were plans for naval convoys in the Atlantic. A month later, however, US warships began protecting Atlantic supply routes, though FDR used the less belligerent-sounding term "patrols." The evidence does not suggest a calculated plotting for war but rather another example of FDR's strategic scaffolding, employing measures to meet challenges as they appeared—cash-and-carry, sanctions against Japan, destroyers-for-bases, Lend-Lease, and now convoys. Still, it is hard to avoid the conclusion that, within the administration, the realization was growing that war would come.[43]

Roosevelt explained his position on May 27 in a fireside chat from the East Room of the White House. The president's main point was consistent with previous speeches: the global conflict was ideological and existential. Put simply, the "American way of life" was on the line. That such a sweeping phrase contained contradictions is a given (exhibit A: the "Jim Crow way of life"); nonetheless, it contrasted sharply with German and Japanese aggression and their respective occupations. In his "protecting the Atlantic" chat, Roosevelt laid it on thick:

> Today the whole world is divided between human slavery and human freedom—between pagan brutality and the Christian ideal. We choose human freedom.... We will accept only a world consecrated to freedom of speech and expression—freedom of every person to worship God in his own way—freedom from want—and freedom from terror. Is such a world impossible of attainment? ... the Declaration of Independence, the Constitution of the United States, the Emancipation Proclamation, and every other milestone in human progress—all were ideals which seemed impossible of attainment—and yet they were attained.... Shall we now, with all our potential strength, hesitate to take every single measure necessary to maintain our American liberties?[44]

This was Roosevelt as preacher and prophet, sounding his gravest warning yet: America's actions in 1941 would either preserve or surrender the liberal achievements of 1776, 1787, and 1863. Shortly after his address, a stunning expansion of the war in Europe gave new life to Great Britain, but augmented tensions between Japan and the United States in Asia.

SOVIET RUSSIA AND SOUTHERN INDOCHINA

In the early hours of Sunday, June 22, 1941, German armies invaded Soviet borderlands and occupied territories along a wide front. In one of the great conundrums of World War II, Stalin had ignored a stream of rumors about an imminent German attack, dismissing them as capitalist propaganda. As a result, "with sudden fury," observed the *New York Times*, "the two great revolutionary regimes of modern times [had] now been thrown into mortal combat." A strange and violent world had taken another strange turn. In Tokyo, an ineffable déjà vu suffused Japan's leadership—Hitler's unpredictability had struck again. Japanese officials were stony silent; still, the attack had not been a total shock. Premier Konoe's ambassador in Berlin, Lt. Gen.

Ōshima, had sent Tokyo several messages about a critical deterioration in German-Soviet relations. And on June 5, two weeks before the invasion, Ōshima informed Tokyo, "I think that the Rubicon will be crossed in a short time." Officials discussed the report, but Matsuoka doubted its veracity.[45]

Matsuoka first heard about the attack while attending a kabuki performance with the visiting Chinese collaborator Wang Jingwei. His first impulse, and one he would stick to, was a kabuki-like plot twist, recommending that Japan join Hitler by attacking Russia's rear. Acting as if the invasion was expected, Matsuoka told the press, "Something must be wrong with the brains of those who are surprised." He added philosophic ambiguity, saying, "When the Western wind blows, fallen leaves are piled in the East." An innocuous deduction suggested that turbulence in the West carried repercussions in the East; a more loaded interpretation was that Nazi victories provided expansionist opportunities in Asia.[46]

What is clear is that Germany's invasion of the Soviet Union put Japan's leadership at an immediate crossroads. As a result, over the ensuing week, the Japanese government hunkered down in a series of continuous conferences—Liaison, General Staff, and private meetings between Konoe and Hirohito. In the eyes of one American observer, Hitler's aggression constituted "a flagrant betrayal" of the Axis Pact, which "could have been taken by the Japanese as a reason for changing their foreign policy." In fact, on the day of the attack, Hull asked Nomura whether Berlin's declaration of war might not alter Japan's diplomacy. The ambassador replied perfunctorily that Japan was bound by its obligations. Matsuoka, meanwhile, continued to argue for a northern offensive against the Russians, before an advance south. "Great men," he said, "will change their minds." Matsuoka was still enthralled with Hitler's boldness and seduced by Ribbentrop's entreaties. The Reich foreign minister now urged Japan to attack Vladivostok instead of Singapore. German enticement included recognition of the Wang government in Nanjing.[47]

Matsuoka's view lost out, but Japan's policy remained aggressive. A Liaison Conference consensus eventually congealed around a southern advance while preparing for action in the north. Thus, despite rejecting Matsuoka's advice, the Japanese government was not disavowing Hitler or delinking German aggression from its foreign policy. It still sought to exploit the invasion of Russia, but with the intention of fulfilling the Greater East Asia Co-Prosperity Sphere. The reasons for this decision stemmed from several factors. From a broad perspective, the premises of Japan's "holy mission" invariably included expansion into Southeast Asia. Also, besides the memory of the 1939 Nomonhan debacle, the fact remained that the Soviet-Japanese Neutrality Pact still protected Japan's northwest frontier. Finally, key strategic resources—especially oil—lay toward the South Seas.[48]

On July 2, in the presence of Emperor Hirohito (resplendent in a navy uniform), Japan's highest civilian and military officials gathered for a fateful Imperial Conference to sanction the southward policy, titled the "Outline of National Policies in View of the Changing Situation." It was a succinct and bold document. The Japanese government was determined, it stated, to establish the Greater East Asia Co-Prosperity Sphere and world peace, "no matter what changes may occur in the world situation." Similarly, it declared that the "Empire [was] determined to remove all obstacles" to settle the "China Incident," which would "involve taking steps to advance south." Most ominously, it stated the empire would "not be deterred by the possibility of being involved in a war with Great Britain and the United States." German aggression, once again, had stoked Japan's expansionist appetite.[49]

Despite the expansionist policy, Prime Minister Konoe tried to have it— or play it—both ways. There was always a slightly wishy-washy abstraction to Konoe's personality, one that would intensify as tensions became critical with the United States. As one Japanese official remarked, Konoe was intelligent and perceptive, but he exuded "an atmosphere in which something somewhere is lacking." In a widely published interview, Konoe stated that Japan was "very anxious to maintain good relations with the United States." He believed there was no reason why the two powers could not remain friendly, emphasizing that the Tripartite Pact was purely defensive in nature. A few days later, however, in ceremonies commemorating the fourth anniversary of the war in China, the prime minister founded a new greater Asia group, whose members took an oath to eliminate the "evil" of Anglo-American encroachment in Asia. Konoe also led a group of five hundred prominent Japanese to the Meiji Shrine in Tokyo, where, he asserted, in opposition to Roosevelt's defense of the liberal order, that Japan was fighting in China to "realize peace and security for the whole world . . . for all time."[50]

Amid these conflicting signals, on July 16 came the surprising news that Japan's objectives in Asia would be pursued without Matsuoka's bombastic leadership. Konoe, it was announced, had resigned his post in order to form a new cabinet with a new foreign minister. A personality and tactical clash, not ideological differences, had estranged Matsuoka from his colleagues (northern advance versus southern advance, and the usefulness of seeking accommodation with the Americans). In particular, Matsuoka found Hull's June 21 reply to his May 12 draft—and especially the secretary's oral statement— "outrageous" and "absurd." At a series of Liaison Conferences in July, Matsuoka recommended rejecting the oral statement and essentially ending talks with the Americans. Surprisingly, it was the war and navy ministers—Tōjō and Oikawa Koshiro—who voiced opposition. Tōjō wondered, "If we sincerely convey to the Americans what we, as Japanese, believe to be right, won't [the Americans] be inwardly moved?"[51] Informing Tōjō's view was a common blind spot—that misunderstandings, rather than incompatible ideologies of global governance, were the main stumbling block, that Americans simply had not yet grasped Japan's "true intentions." It was the same kind of selective thinking that lulled the Konoe cabinet into embracing the Draft Understanding as a product of the Roosevelt administration.

In reference to these summer conferences, historians have described Matsuoka as unbalanced or myopic; another perspective, however, is that his position was ideologically grounded. He grasped the reasoning behind America's antagonism, which had been laid out in speeches and policies ad nauseam. Indeed, Matsuoka pressed Tōjō, "What concessions are you willing to grant [the United States]?"[52] There is no evidence that Japan's leaders and military were willing to concede anything substantial in China (where Japan had fought a four-year war sanctioned by the emperor) or the Axis Pact (a ten-year alliance sanctioned by the emperor). In contrast to Matsuoka, then, Konoe, Tōjō, and others remained seduced by the paradoxical double wish of a hegemonic sphere without US interference (though they still held out hope the United States would interfere just enough to induce the Kuomintang to accept a negotiated settlement with Japan). Japan's occupation of southern Indochina and America's response, however, revealed the scope of their delusions—and proved to be a critical marker on the slippery slope to transpacific war.

ASSETS AND OIL

In mid-July, MAGIC intercepts revealed that the Konoe government had handed the French Vichy regime an ultimatum, demanding the use of eight air bases and two naval ports in southern Indochina. Shortly after the ultimatum, news services reported that a Japanese naval squadron of sixty-five warships and thirty troopships was heading in that direction. The reports confirmed that Japan was expanding military operations while engaging in negotiations with the American government. To Secretary Hull, who was convalescing in White Sulphur Springs, West Virginia (he suffered from diabetes and tuberculosis), the mobilization came almost as a betrayal. On July 23, he instructed Acting Secretary of State Sumner Welles to inform Nomura that the United States saw no basis for continuing negotiations with Japan.[53] More gravely, the administration began plans to freeze all Japanese assets in the United States, an action that essentially would cut all trade ties with the empire.

Despite the apparent rupture in negotiations, Roosevelt himself made a rare foray into US-Japan talks, hoping to reverse the Indochina mobilization. The fact that Roosevelt let Hull handle Asian affairs almost unilaterally while he dealt with Europe makes clear the president saw Nazi Germany as the biggest immediate threat to liberal civilization and American interests. More than ever, however, he viewed the world conflict as profoundly interrelated. Meeting with Nomura in the Oval Office, FDR proposed a plan to "neutralize" French Indochina. If Japan refrained from occupying the southern half of Indochina, the president would "do everything in his power" to get Britain, the Netherlands, and China to join with the United States and Japan to regard Indochina as a "Switzerland" of Asia—as neutral and off-limits to aggression. It was hoped that Japan would perceive the plan as enhancing its security. Instead, it fully contradicted the premises of the Greater East Asia Co-Prosperity Sphere.[54]

American appeasement subsequently ended on July 25. Concluding that Japan's advance into southern Indochina (located about eight hundred miles from the Dutch East Indies) was intended primarily for the purposes of further conquest, Roosevelt issued an executive order freezing all Japanese assets in the United States. The British and the Dutch government-in-exile in London followed America's lead. Such a stern rebuttal, it was believed, would contain Japanese expansionism and prevent a premature clash in the Pacific. But as a confidant of Nomura noted, "the effect upon Japan was a staggering blow, psychologically as well as materially." Observers at the time were under no illusions about the far-reaching implications of the freezing action—it all but guaranteed that export licenses would be revoked and that Japan and America's expansive trade would come to a standstill. This included the presumption of an oil embargo. (Japan used nearly forty million barrels of oil annually but produced only three million barrels.) Despite a moment of bureaucratic confusion, the administration announced the expected oil ban on August 1, shortly after forty thousand Japanese troops began landing in southern Indochina and pouring into Saigon.[55]

Tokyo correctly viewed the oil embargo as a hostile act. The Japanese press blasted it as further proof of "ABCD encirclement," and a government official claimed "the current international situation is so tense that a single spark would be sufficient to cause an explosion."[56] For this reason, the embargo often leads the list of usual suspects in explaining the slide to Pearl Harbor. But therein lies the danger in not seeing the ideological forest for the tactical trees. The embargo was merely one more effect, albeit a significant one, of the ideological/geopolitical divide—like the China war, the Axis Pact, and decision to deploy troops to southern Indochina, which, in turn, triggered the freezing of assets and oil ban. In the wake of these accruing effects came yet another thickening of the ideological forest.

SOMEWHERE IN THE ATLANTIC AND SOMEWHERE IN THE PACIFIC

Following his strong response to Japan's advance into southern Indochina, Roosevelt turned back to the Atlantic. Between August 9 and 12, 1941, aboard naval vessels in Placentia Bay, Newfoundland, Roosevelt met secretly with Prime Minister Churchill to discuss the global conflict and a new postwar order. Their so-called Atlantic Conference resulted in a joint declaration of principles that became known as the Atlantic Charter. The eight-point plan was a liberal paean to Wilson and a conspicuous ideological repudiation of the Axis Pact. The failings of Versailles cast a long shadow, with pledges against war spoils and support for self-determination for "all peoples." Such universal language, however ambiguous, carried fateful implications for Britain's vast colonial empire. But the Americans argued anything less would expose the liberal powers to a postwar hypocrisy. Reactions by Japanese firebrands showed why. Nagai Ryūtarō said the British and Americans should begin immediately implementing the Atlantic Charter by withdrawing from Asia, where they "had been for a long time uninvited and unwelcome guests."[57]

Premier Konoe, meanwhile, had been taken aback by America's sanctions. But even though he ruminated about Japanese "miscalculation," his concerns pertained to tactical missteps and not desired ends. This was consistent with Japan's double wish—and Konoe's policies since 1937. He was premier at the start of the China war. It was his government that aligned with Hitler, declared a new order for greater Asia, and sent troops into Indochina. All of this was promulgated and justified with muscular rhetoric. Thus, the term *miscalculation* clouded the cabinet's calculated ambitions. In August, this same blind spot convinced Konoe that Japan and America's conflict still boiled down to "misunderstanding." Taking a page from Hitler's Munich script, the premier believed US-Japan relations could be resolved only by face-to-face talks between himself and Roosevelt. He thus set about trying to organize a conference somewhere in the Pacific.[58]

Nomura broached the topic with Hull twice in August. A wary Hull referred the matter to Roosevelt, who agreed to meet with the ambassador. FDR's response to Nomura on August 17, three days after his liberal declaration with Churchill, was double-edged. First came a sober warning: if Japan used Indochina as a stepping-stone for further conquest, the United States would "be compelled to take immediately any and all steps" to safeguard American interests. Next, the president said he was not, *in principle*, opposed to meeting Konoe but that Japan's recent actions were "directly the opposite" to the premises of the Hull-Nomura talks. Any "informal, exploratory discussions" thus would be dependent on proof of a peaceful Japanese foreign policy. Roosevelt's equivocation spurred Konoe to reach out directly to the president. On August 28 he asked FDR to meet with him "as soon as possible" to discuss bilateral relations "from a broad standpoint." The Americans, however, were not interested in generalities. Hull, Hornbeck, and Stimson objected to a meeting as "merely a blind spot to try to keep us from taking definite action." In the end, the administration stayed true to Hull's Four Principles as a precondition for a summit.[59] And Japan stayed true to its regionalist ambitions.

September to December 1941 witnessed an inexorable spiral to war. Each side prepared for war while keeping lines of communication open for a settlement. Avoidance of war, however, required ideological concessions—and the two sides had become entrenched in their respective visions of world order. Doubts about coexistence had crystallized. Because of the US oil embargo, the Japanese faced a particular dilemma: barring Japan's acceptance of a liberal settlement, the empire either would have to persuade the Americans to see Japan's side of things or strike south and seize oil fields in the Dutch East Indies. On September 6, an Imperial Conference sanctioned plans for both scenarios, stating that Japan would go to war with America if talks did not yield positive results by mid-October. America would need to restore trade and curb aid for Chiang Kai-shek; in return, Japan would withdraw its forces in Asia, albeit under an ambiguous timetable and method. Troops would leave Indochina, for example, "following the establishment of a just peace in the Far East." It matched the ambiguity of Hirohito's surprise reading of a poem written by his grandfather, Emperor Meiji, whose allusion to universal brotherhood nonetheless could not shroud Hirohito's complicity in Japan's expansionism.[60]

The Konoe cabinet submitted its revised offer for a settlement on September 25. Hull dismissed it a week later, rejecting its "broad assurances," especially troop withdrawals. He reiterated America's insistence on the Four Principles as a framework for talks. The secretary had the American public behind him. A Gallup poll showed that 70 percent of Americans now believed the United States should "take steps now to keep Japan from becoming more powerful, even if it means risking war." This was up from 40 percent in March. Doubtless this high percentage reflected the belief among some people that the Japanese would back down in the face of American strength. And doubtless such an attitude derived partly from a racist sense of superiority, but to what degree is uncertain.[61]

Faced with Hull's rebuff, on October 12, a concerned Konoe convened a Five-Ministers Conference at his Tekigaiso villa. It was Konoe's fiftieth birthday. The conference represented a last-ditch effort by the premier to avoid a calamitous war with the United States. One wonders if, at this moment, Konoe paused to peel back time, to consider the dramatic change in atmosphere since his meeting at Tekigaiso in July 1940, at the start of his second cabinet. At that time, Japan's leaders were riding a wave of momentum and swagger among the revisionist powers: Konoe's government hitched Japan's wagon to the Nazis and foresaw an extensive Japanese empire throughout Asia. Now, in October 1941, Konoe still wanted the empire; he just did not want the war. The ministers framed their meeting as a choice between war or diplomacy. Prospects for war against the United States were grim, but America's demands were unacceptable. And that returned the conclave to the original impasse. War Minister Tōjō assumed a fatalistic view, embodied in a recent statement in which he had said, "Once in a while it is necessary to close one's eyes and jump from the veranda of [Kyoto's] Kiyomizu Temple." It was time to take a daring leap. Konoe instead dropped out, resigning his premiership. He could not face the tragic consequences of his own decisions.[62]

"NOTHING NEW"

A new cabinet was organized with Tōjō as premier on October 17 (the same day German U-boats torpedoed a US destroyer, the *Kearny*, off the coast of Ireland, killing eleven sailors). Largely because he was a military man and Japan's wartime premier from 1941 to 1944, Tōjō has come down in American World War II lore as a caricature, as Japan's Hitler. But Tōjō's policies were not substantively different from Konoe's: prepare for a Japanese offensive against the United States while seeking a last-minute settlement with Washington.

To lead this effort, Tōjō tapped longtime civilian diplomat Tōgō Shigenori as his foreign minister. From October 23 to November 2, Tōjō and Tōgō convened Liaison Conferences nearly every day. At a seventeen-hour session on November 1–2, which extended the empire's deadline for an accord with the United States to November 30, Tōgō presented two different proposals, labeled Plan A and Plan B. Plan A was comprehensive, like the Draft Understanding; Plan B involved a more circumscribed modus vivendi, focused on the recent source of friction in southern Indochina. An Imperial Conference sanctioned both proposals on November 5.

Tōgō's presentation before the emperor, meanwhile, underscored the persistent paradox. The foreign minister said Japan must be ready "to sweep away any and all obstacles" to create the Co-Prosperity Sphere, and that the United States and Britain had obstructed Japan's "holy war" in China. He and Tōjō followed with similarly dogmatic speeches before the Diet on November 17. Indeed, nothing in Tōgō's comprehensive Plan A changed the ideological equation between Japan and the United States. To the Japanese, the Axis Pact was tangential and the ongoing war in China was Japan's problem. A full troop withdrawal from the continent, meanwhile, relied on an ambiguous "suitable interval." If the Americans asked what that entailed,

Tōgō instructed Nomura to "answer vaguely that such a period should encompass 25 years."[63]

The Americans would not be seeking clarification; Secretary Hull quickly learned about the whopping twenty-five-year interval from a MAGIC intercept. Most importantly, the Roosevelt administration still saw all three issues as interrelated. This was made clear on November 17 when Roosevelt and Hull met with Nomura and Kurusu Saburō, a special envoy appointed by Tōgō to assist with negotiations. The Axis Pact remained prickly. Kurusu emphasized self-defense; FDR and Hull parried. What did Hitler's "invasion across the earth with ten million soldiers and thirty thousand airplanes," they asked, have to do with self-defense? Above all, for the Americans, the pact had become a touchstone for Japanese intent—*who your friends were said a lot about who you were*. As for the Co-Prosperity Sphere, Hull told the Japanese envoys that was "but another name" for military domination. In his notes on the meeting, Hull said he saw "nothing new" in Japan's proposal. The door nonetheless was left open for further talks.[64]

On November 20, Nomura and Kurusu officially submitted to Hull the more limited Plan B, whose main Japanese concession was the transfer of troops from southern to northern Indochina. A full withdrawal from Indochina would come once peace in China was established. In return, the United States was to restore trade and refrain from aiding Chiang. What the Japanese saw as a reasonable compromise, the Americans saw as more of the same. A follow-up telegram from Tōgō to Nomura on November 22 (intercepted by the Americans) punctuated the deadlock: Tokyo viewed Plan B as Japan's "absolutely final offer." More ominously, Tōgō informed Nomura that after November 29, things were "automatically going to happen." Roosevelt's war cabinet met on November 25 to discuss the threatening telegram. FDR's allusion to the importance of maneuvering Japan into "firing the first shot" has become a staple of conspiracy theories. But all this meant was that the president knew Japan was priming to attack, likely in Thailand (Siam) or the East Indies, and that it was important not to give the Tōjō government any excuse of self-defense.[65]

Hull responded to Plan B on November 26. It was an uncompromising brick wall. The administration continued to see all outstanding disputes as interrelated—China, Axis Pact, Indochina, everything. As Undersecretary of State Welles told the Japanese, focusing on Indochina "was very much like asking" whether *Hamlet* could be staged without the character of Hamlet. And so Hull's Four Principles were in the document as well as ten additional demands—including the immediate withdrawal of all Japanese troops from Indochina *and* China and a nonaggression pact among Japan, Britain, Holland, the Soviet Union, the United States, and Thailand.[66]

The Japanese were livid. Tōgō derided America's "fantastic principles and rules" and invoked the decade-long mantra that the Roosevelt administration did "not understand the real situation in East Asia." In his postwar memoir, Tōgō said he was "blinded by utter disbelief" and that the American reply "stuck in the craw."[67] The Japanese viewed the "Hull Note" as an ultimatum. In fact, each side's position carried finality. Above all, the Japanese offer on November 20 and the American reply on November 26 showed that the two sides remained ideologically a decade apart. Japan's offer would return relations to June 1941, before southern Indochina; America's reply would return them to June 1931, before the Manchurian crisis. Professor of East Asian history Tyler Dennett, sensing the approaching war, wrote wistfully on what might have been, had Japan given liberalism a chance before aggression in Manchuria:

> If Japan had been content to make use of the orderly processes of international relations, if she had been willing to utilize the opportunities for conference which had been expressly provided in the Washington treaties and in the Covenant of the League of Nations, she could have presented to the other interested powers a case sufficiently strong to win ready support from many friends. . . . Having failed to seize this advantage, Japan lost her case, not because it was wholly lacking in merit, but first because she was not content with orderly processes.[68]

In sporadic conversations through the end of November, FDR and Hull impressed upon Nomura and Kurusu that Japan's interests would be better served with the United States than with Germany. Simultaneously, a Japanese carrier task force steamed toward Hawaiʻi, outside of common shipping lanes in the North Pacific and without radio contact. On December 1, an Imperial Conference sanctioned war against the United States, Great Britain, and the Netherlands. Six days later, on the afternoon of Sunday, December 7, Nomura and Kurusu met with Secretary Hull to deliver a long, fourteen-part cable, explaining that Japan was severing diplomatic relations with the United States. Hull, having already seen the MAGIC intercepts, feigned to read a few pages and then said he had "never seen a document that was more crowded with infamous falsehoods and distortions . . . on a scale so huge that I never imagined until today that any government on this planet was capable of uttering them."[69] Nomura and Kurusu left without saying anything, or knowing that their nation's carrier-based torpedo planes had been wreaking death and destruction at Pearl Harbor for well over an hour.

***

In their convictions about foundational political and cultural values, and ideas of world order, Japanese and American officials had come to a point in which coexistence was deemed impossible. For the Americans, the irreconcilable worldviews spanning the Pacific were profoundly reaffirmed in July

1941. Both through words and deeds, Japan had made its intentions clear that it was bent on further expansion—all before the US oil embargo. Moreover, the empire remained committed to its alliance with Nazi Germany. The impact of this on American perceptions can hardly be overstated. It reinforced time and again Roosevelt's conviction that the aggression in Europe and Asia were all parts of the same conflict. For the Japanese, despite their nation's formidable disadvantages (America's population, share of strategic resources, and industrial capacity dwarfed those of Japan), the emperor and civilian and military leaders chose war—and not impulsively, but after hour upon hour of countless conferences. Their decision tells us something profound about the deep-seated, regionalist convictions among this generation of Japanese leaders. As Navy Minister Adm. Shimada Shigetarō wrote in October 1941 while pondering the US-Japan stalemate, "no matter how hard I try to avoid war, it is impossible."[70]

Epilogue

The Asia-Pacific War began and ended as a fierce ideological conflict between competing ideas of world order. The Japanese and American governments reminded their citizens and the world of this point on December 7, 1941, and on August 15, 1945—and many times between. The Japanese government's fourteen-part message delivered to Secretary Hull on December 7, for example, asserted that it was "the intention of the American government to conspire with Great Britain and other countries to obstruct Japan's efforts toward the establishment of peace through the creation of a new order in East Asia." It denounced the United States for "refusing to yield an inch on its impractical principles." Emperor Hirohito's rescript to the nation on the same day similarly condemned American and British obstruction of this new order, though it remained confident "that the sources of evil will be speedily eradicated and an enduring peace immutably established in East Asia." Privately, Hirohito offered unvarnished insight into Japan's desired political ends, telling his chamberlain he would "like to see the South Seas after peace was restored . . . because the area will be part of Japan's territory."[1]

In the United States, President Roosevelt also told a story of ideological rupture. In a fireside chat a day after his dramatic "infamy" address before Congress, the president said the attack at Pearl Harbor provided "the climax of a decade of international immorality." A week later Roosevelt filed a long report to Congress in which he enumerated Japan's violations of the postwar treaties since 1931. Japan, he asserted, had flouted "all principles of peace." Invoking the hallowed bywords of the liberal order, the president said his administration had endeavored to persuade Japan that its best interests lay "in maintaining and cultivating friendly relations with the United States and with all other countries that believe in *orderly and peaceful processes*."[2]

The war itself quickly unfolded in favor of Japan's regionalist ambitions. While Japanese forces attacked Pearl Harbor, they also overran Guam, Hong Kong, and Wake Island. Within a few months, colonial dominoes had fallen throughout Southeast Asia, producing unforgettable images of white overlords capitulating to their Japanese conquerors. In February 1942, more than eighty thousand British troops surrendered in Singapore, a military defeat considered, to this day, as one of Britain's worst. In March, the Dutch surrendered Indonesia; in May, the Americans did the same in the Philippines. A significant turning point, however, came just as quickly. In June 1942, Japan's gains at Pearl Harbor evaporated at the Battle of Midway. Thereafter, the conflict turned into a slow and tortuous slaughter across the vast expanse of Pacific atolls and islands. Whatever the private convictions among the young Japanese and American combatants who faced one another in unfathomable existential moments, hovering over every battlefield and landing zone were far-reaching and competing ideas of world order.

At home and abroad, Japan's campaign into the South Seas glistened with the revisionist promises of liberation and coprosperity. In January 1942, Premier Tōjō told the Diet that Japan had embarked on "truly an unprecedentedly grand undertaking . . . [to] establish everlasting peace in Greater East Asia based on a new conception, which will mark a new epoch in the annals of mankind, and proceed to construct a new world order along with our allies and friendly powers in Europe." More comprehensively, at a summer conference in Kyoto in 1942, a prominent group of Japanese intellectuals gathered under the slogan "Overcoming the Modern" and critiqued the "corrupting" influences of an Americanized modernity. As one scholar has noted, the symposium's participants believed "all the ills that had poisoned Japan were found in Americanism," which included its values, culture, and commodities.[3] The claim of liberating fellow Asians and overcoming the corrupt tenets of Anglo-Americanism was an intoxicating ideological brew carrying great moral purpose. To this end, the Japanese government reoriented the cultural programs of the Kokusai Bunka Shinkōkai toward the South Seas to help spread the Pan-Asianist scripture of Japan's alleged holy war.

Throughout occupied Southeast Asia, the KBS disseminated publications, films, and Japanese language textbooks to promote the empire's prestige and leadership. The conscious intertwining between political and cultural motives can be seen in the words of KBS Chairman Nagai Matsuzō, who asserted that the promotion of Japanese culture would make the peoples of Asia "grasp the true intention of Japanese actions" and "understand the significance of our holy war." The KBS's soft power programs thus were politically malleable—the theme of Japanese cultural importance could be tailored to American cosmopolitans or Asian nationalists. What did not change was the irrefutable message of regional primacy.[4] Tokyo's propaganda challenge also remained the same: to square its promise of liberation with coercive rule.

Japan's leaders were not unaware of a gap between theory and practice. This was made clear in November 1943 just as the empire's fortunes in the Pacific were becoming increasingly bleak. In an attempt to reinvigorate the alleged altruism of Japan's motives, the Tōjō government invited leading statesmen from around Asia to attend the so-called Greater East Asia Conference in Tokyo, under the banner of the utopian strand of Asian solidarity. The puppet heads of the Manchukuo and Nanjing regimes joined leaders from Burma, the Philippines, India, and Thailand. Although the Tokyo conference accomplished little of substance other than to issue an anti-Anglo-American "joint declaration," it nonetheless indulged the language of liberation and independence and portended postwar decolonization—even if paradoxically wedded still to Japanese autarky. As Fujitani Takashi has argued, even if we acknowledge such discourse as propaganda, "it is difficult to deny the unintended or unavoidable consequences" of officially declaring disavowals of racism and promises of greater equality.[5]

Under far more auspicious circumstances, in July 1944, seven months after the Tokyo conference, more than seven hundred delegates—including economists, financiers, politicians, and industrialists—from forty-four Allied nations trekked to northern New Hampshire to attend a virtual renaissance party for liberal internationalism. The Bretton Woods Conference, as it was called, breathed institutional life into that Wilsonian offspring, the Atlantic Charter, with the goal of stabilizing a liberal postwar economic order. It was an acknowledgment of the close and profoundly consequential relationship between national and international economies. To secure the global monetary system—the system of exchange rates and international payments that allows nations to transact with each other—the conference created the International Monetary Fund. To provide developmental financing, the World Bank was born. As in Wilson's time, the overall goal of these programs was to encourage global peace and prosperity through so-called orderly processes.[6]

One month later, at the Dumbarton Oaks Conference in Washington, DC, the Allies began laying the foundation for the United Nations, with hopes of making amends for the nearly stillborn League of Nations. Of note, according to Fujitani, similar to the effects of Japan's strategic wartime disavowals of racism, America's universalizing wartime rhetoric of freedom and self-determination not only "made it increasingly necessary to disavow racist discrimination" but to "demonstrate the sincerity of this denunciation through concrete plans." Beyond influencing the loosening of US immigration restrictions (the United States began accepting Chinese immigrants again in 1943 and Japanese immigrants in 1952), wartime rhetoric played a key role in the ensuing global era of decolonization. This is not to gloss over persistent hypocrisies and complexities. As Mark Mazower has noted, how does one square the United Nations' stated ideals with the fact that a committed segregationist, South Africa's Jan Smuts, helped draft the institution's lofty preamble? Or, more palpably, cases of violent resistance to independence movements by the colonizing powers and their allies.[7]

Self-interest, to be sure, mingled with idealism. Every institution established at Bretton Woods and Dumbarton Oaks, for better or worse, carried the ubiquitous imprint of American leadership and liberal principles. After slugging it out against fierce ideological foes in both Europe and the Pacific, the American mindset could accurately be described as *be sure not to make the same mistake twice*. Henry Luce's 1941 commentary "The American Century" represented an early and forceful expression of this evolving worldview, calling for vigorous American leadership. "In 1919," wrote Luce, "we had a golden opportunity . . . to assume the leadership of the world. . . . We did not understand that opportunity. Wilson mishandled it. We rejected it. We bungled it in the 1920s and in the confusion of the 1930s we killed it." It must not happen again, he warned Americans. "America is responsible," Luce said, "for the world-environment in which she lives." He concluded with missionary zeal, claiming "all of us are called . . . to create the first great American Century."[8] In some ways, despite different desired ends, Luce's expansive call to action mirrored Japanese rhetoric. Just as Japan viewed its struggle in Asia as holy war, Luce characterized the conflict as a holy war for a free-market, democratic order. The main ideological difference, albeit a significant one, was that of an exclusive regionalism versus a more open internationalism.

The moment of America's ideological redemption arrived in 1945. In May, Germany surrendered to Allied forces. In the Pacific, the brutal island-hopping campaign came to a halt on June 22 after the Battle of Okinawa. American commanders subsequently scheduled an invasion of the Japanese home islands to start in November. In the meantime, a methodical firebombing campaign incinerated large parts of sixty-plus Japanese cites. And then, in early August, with bewildering suddenness, came three shocks in four days. On August 6 an atomic bomb killed more than eighty thousand Japanese civilians in Hiroshima. Two days later the Soviet Union declared war on Japan. And on August 9, another A-bomb leveled the city of Nagasaki. (The sparing of Kyoto and its cultural treasures from atomic destruction on account of Secretary of War Stimson's personal intervention raises questions about the possible influence of KBS programs.)[9]

Following Nagasaki, and facing total annihilation, Emperor Hirohito finally accepted Allied terms for surrender. The forty-four-year-old emperor spoke to the nation for the first time on August 15. Filled with regret and sadness, the recorded address announced Japan's surrender and encouraged the Japanese people "to endure the unendurable." But ideology made an appearance as well. The emperor reminded his subjects of the noble Asianist goals for which they allegedly fought. "We declared war on America and Britain," asserted Hirohito, "out of our sincere desire to insure Japan's self-preservation and the stabilization of East Asia, it being far from our thought either to infringe upon the sovereignty of other nations or to embark upon territorial aggrandizement." He also extended the nation's "deepest sense of regret to our allied nations of East Asia, who have consistently cooperated with the Empire toward the emancipation of East Asia."[10] Thus, despite the deaths of an estimated twelve million Chinese from Japanese aggression, the myth of coprosperity—that Manchukuo and the Wang regime were not puppet states, but allied partners fighting side by side in a good fight for a new order in Asia—was duly perpetuated.

In the United States, President Harry S. Truman also described the end of the war in ideological terms, stating: "This is the end of the grandiose schemes of the dictators to enslave the peoples of the world, destroy their civilization, and institute a new era of darkness and degradation. This day is a new beginning in the history of freedom on this earth."[11] The uplifting words momentarily papered over aspects of the Asia-Pacific War perhaps more properly defined in moral gradations rather than absolutes. In the coming decades, Americans would be compelled to grapple morally with their government's decision to drop two nuclear bombs on civilian populations—with the second bomb coming *just three days* after the first—as well as the illegal internment of nearly 120,000 innocent Japanese Americans. But for the immediate future, the thousands of American troops and bureaucrats pouring into Japan, led by General Douglas MacArthur, seemed to affirm Truman's declaration.

The American occupation of Japan lasted nearly seven years (1945–1952).[12] Despite considerable Japanese agency, the occupation amounted to an unprecedented undertaking in nation-building and ideological overhaul. Under the banner of "demilitarization and democratization," the American authorities instituted land reform, education reform, and a free press and, of greatest significance, drafted Japan's postwar constitution. The liberal charter completely transformed Japan's polity. It turned the emperor into a depoliticized symbol of the state, abolished the House of Peers and hereditary aristocracy, mandated party cabinets, and gave women the franchise. Initially it also disbanded Japan's military. The pacifist Article 9 inserted into the constitution essentially incorporated the principles of the Kellogg Pact by prohibiting Japan from using armed forces in an offensive war.[13]

At the same time, in a move that had far-reaching effects, MacArthur chose not to prosecute Emperor Hirohito for war responsibility; instead, he used the exalted crown to drive a wedge between the nation as a whole and a culpable military clique. In other words, the occupation resurrected the 1930s "dualism" of Ambassador Grew and other so-called Japan Hands and superimposed it onto the occupation. On a practical level, this helped stabilize the occupation, but it also cut the rope to the anchor of self-reflection regarding war responsibility. In the postwar years, the Japanese people drifted in a sea of moral ambiguity, leading to the prevalence of the Grew-tinted "dark valley" thesis. According to this interpretation, a small cabal of militarists defied the emperor and civilian government and took an innocent nation down the path of militarist ruin. Grew himself publicized his convictions just before the end of the war, saying Japan's military had established a "dictatorship of terror" over the people. Such views created lasting stereotypes about Japan's polity for years to come. As KBS official Aoki Setsuichi claimed two decades after the war, "The military blatantly pressured us . . . to conduct cultural projects to camouflage military intent." As a result of this revived thesis, after the war, former officials such as Shigemitsu Mamoru, Yoshida Shigeru, and Kishi Nobusuke quietly traded in their imperialist clothes for internationalist garb. Shigemitsu subsequently became involved in the United Nations, and Yoshida served as premier for nearly seven years.[14]

The Allies' Tokyo War Crimes Tribunal (1946–1948), meanwhile, set out to make a sweeping case against Japanese militarists. In the process, it inadvertently opened up a Pandora's box to ideological sparring by charging the defendants with "crimes against peace" (conspiring to wage war)—a novel category in international law established by the Nuremberg Tribunal (1945–1946). This allowed the accused to recycle the specious claim that Japan had only sought to liberate Asian peoples from Western oppression—and that, from Manchuria to Pearl Harbor, the empire had acted in self-defense against Anglo-American encirclement. As a result, though the Allies disarmed Japan's military and effectively extirpated the militarist ethos in society, the tribunal earned the cynical moniker a "victors' justice."[15] Such a confused and conflicted legacy of the war—not unlike the sordid Lost Cause legacy of the American Civil War—has prompted a parade of postwar Japanese politicians to make controversial visits to the Yasukuni Shrine in Tokyo as well as tone-deaf remarks about Japan's wartime responsibility. The result has been repeated protests among Chinese and Koreans—not to mention protests by Japanese pacifists.[16]

In the cultural realm, the organization that had helped spread the idea of benevolent Japanese leadership in the occupied territories, the Kokusai Bunka Shinkōkai, was left in institutional limbo immediately after the war. One American scholar at the time eviscerated the KBS as an apologist for military aggression, thus challenging the society's claims of institutional autonomy and innocent dedication to the arts. Occupation officials, meanwhile, tended to associate traditional Japanese culture with feudalistic practices and thus initially suppressed it. The specter of communism in Asia, however, eventually stimulated a reappraisal and subsequent reversal of some occupation policies, the so-called reverse course, which included reconstituting the KBS. Accordingly, in 1949, many former KBS officials, including Dan Inō, Maeda Tamon, Kabayama Aisuke, and Prince Takamatsu, reprised their roles as cultural ambassadors, but this time under a mission statement that heralded "a fresh start with new ideals and goals," as part of "the rebirth of Japan as a cultural state along democratic lines."[17] And so began one aspect of Japan's postwar transformation from enemy to ally.

The first cultural projects sprouted from myriad institutions, including the KBS, Japan's Ministry of Foreign Affairs and Cultural Properties Protection Commission, the US State Department, and Japan societies. John D. Rockefeller III, a cultural advisor for Washington's 1951 Peace Mission to Japan, was a key figure. In the ensuing years Rockefeller, along with Kabayama and Matsumoto Shigeharu (a top *Dōmei* official and confidant of Premier Konoe), poured energies into establishing a nonprofit, nonpolitical center for intellectual cooperation and cross-cultural exchange in the heart of Tokyo. This was the International House of Japan (I-House), which officially opened in 1955. Rockefeller also helped organize a major touring exhibition of Japanese cultural treasures in 1953, which bore a striking resemblance to the 1936 MFA show. American critics uniformly praised the show, seen by nearly five hundred thousand people. Japan's ambassador to the United States, Araki Eikichi, meanwhile, invoked standard "soft power" assumptions, saying the exhibition "served to draw even closer the bonds of culture and friendship which exists between our countries." A 1955 publication sponsored by the Council on Foreign Relations, *Japanese and Americans: A Century of Cultural Relations*, echoed Araki's sentiments, maintaining that "cultural interchange can lay the groundwork for solution of mutual problems." It's a conviction that still resonates today.[18]

Indeed, governments around the world allocate significant monies toward cultural diplomacy, often broadly termed "public diplomacy," with the hope of advancing foreign policies and improving relations with other countries. A recent US State Department report declared outright that "culture matters," claiming—somewhat melodramatically—that "the values embedded in our artistic and intellectual traditions form a bulwark against the forces of darkness." Cultural diplomacy, it added, "helps create a 'foundation of trust' with other peoples, which policy makers can build on to reach political, economic, and military agreements . . . [and] encourages other people to give the United States the benefit of the doubt on specific policy issues." In response to such claims, one skeptic, a former UNESCO cultural official no less, warns that cultural diplomacy is being "pressed into service in the name of goods that it cannot deliver," especially when it is used to legitimize hard power tools of military action.[19] Certainly such criticism aligns with the failure of Japan's pioneering soft power campaign in the 1930s.

More reasonably, evidence suggests that genuine cultural exchange can inculcate respect for cultural diversity and that cultural diplomacy can help convey positive images of a national culture, with some potential benefit for trade and tourism. At the same time, more organically conceived cultural expressions often prove to be more credible and potent than government-sponsored programming. One need only consider the seismic impact that four long-haired lads from Liverpool had on Britain's image from one night on American television compared to three decades of cultural diplomacy by the British Council. The same can be said for more organic American and Japanese cultural exports. Japan's unofficial cultural relations in the postwar era—from Kurosawa Akira and Ozu Yasujirō's films to the widespread appeal of Studio Ghibli, Nintendo franchises, Japanese cuisine, and Hello Kitty, and more niche areas such as *manga*, cosplay, and the novels of Murakami Haruki—point to the efficacy of informal expressions of soft power.[20]

Far more weighty and problematic since World War II has been the nagging issue of world governance and the limits of liberal internationalism. The ensuing Cold War made clear that ideological antagonism among the world's most powerful nations remains the bane of Wilsonianism and collective security. The bipolar rivalry between communist Russia and the United States routinely torpedoed cooperative diplomacy. A divided United Nations epitomized the dysfunction. For the United States, the Cold War's zero-sum politics effected numerous military ventures, including covert operations in Iran, Guatemala, the Congo, Cuba, and Nicaragua and costly wars in Korea and Vietnam—and a regional security alliance with Japan backed up by the US Seventh Fleet and tens of thousands of US military personnel based in Japan and South Korea. No wonder, then, that the sudden fall of the Berlin Wall in 1989 and subsequent collapse of the Soviet Union in 1991 engendered among internationalists a burst of optimism that a cooperative liberal world order was finally possible.[21]

These hopes have proven illusory. The challenges to liberal internationalism remain formidable, particularly its reliance on a rough ideological consensus. Globally, democratic governance has struggled mightily in the face of population growth and resource scarcity, ethnic and religious strife, immigration pressures, economic inequities, and stateless terrorism. The result has been an increase in populist nationalism and autocratic tendencies around the world—and, most importantly, a renewed emphasis on power politics. The result is that one hundred years following the Great War, the issue of world governance remains highly problematic, marked by a persistent tension between liberal internationalism and power politics, and much uncertainty in relations among nations.[22]

Notes

INTRODUCTION

1. Casualty numbers for Chinese civilians vary widely. For the most comprehensive cross-listing, see "National Death Tolls for the Second World War," Necrometrics.com, http://necrometrics.com/ww2stats.htm.

2. See, for example, Michael Barnhart, *Japan Prepares for Total War: The Search for Economic Security, 1919–1941* (Ithaca, NY: Cornell University Press, 1987).

3. Terry Eagleton, *Ideology* (London: Verso, 1991), 1; Michael Howard, "Ideology and International Relations," *Review of International Studies* 15, no. 1 (January 1989): 1; John Plamenatz, *Ideology* (London: Palgrave Macmillan, 1970), 15. See also Alan Cassels, *Ideology and International Relations in the Modern World* (London: Routledge, 1996).

4. Michael Hunt, *Ideology and U.S. Foreign Policy* (New Haven, CT: Yale University Press, 1987), 137.

5. See Thomas W. Burkman, *Japan and the League of Nations: Empire and World Order, 1914–1938* (Honolulu: University of Hawai'i Press, 2008), and Frederick Dickinson, *World War I and the Triumph of the New Japan, 1919–1930* (Cambridge: Cambridge University Press, 2015).

6. Louise Young, *Japan's Total Empire: Manchuria and the Culture of Wartime Imperialism* (Berkeley: University of California Press, 1998), 156, 164.

7. See Eri Hotta, *Pan-Asianism and Japan's War 1931–1945* (New York: Palgrave, 2007); Cemil Aydin, *The Politics of Anti-Westernism in Asia: Visions of World Order in Pan-Islamic and Pan-Asian Thought* (New York: Columbia University Press, 2007); Sven Saaler and J. Victor Koschmann, eds., *Pan-Asianism in Modern Japanese History: Colonialism, Regionalism and Borders* (London: Routledge, 2006); Sven Saaler and Christopher W. A. Szpilman, eds., *Pan-Asianism: A Documentary History, 1920–Present*, 2 vols. (Lanham, MD: Rowman & Littlefield, 2011); Christopher W. A. Szpilman and Sven Saaler, "Japan and Asia," in *Routledge Handbook of Modern Japanese History*, ed. Christopher W. A. Szpilman and Sven Saaler (London: Routledge, 2017), 25–46.

8. Kakuzo Okakura, *The Book of Tea* (New York: Putnam, 1906), 3–4, 8.

9. Hotta, *Pan-Asianism*, 3, 6, 12–13, 97; Szpilman and Saaler, "Japan and Asia," 38.

10. See Jessamyn Abel, *The International Minimum: Creativity and Contradiction in Japan's Global Engagement, 1933–1964* (Honolulu: University of Hawai'i Press, 2015). To be sure, the idealistic, foundational strand of Pan-Asianism did appear to resonate with Japanese officials after 1943, though circumstances make it difficult to assess the sincerity of public declarations because the war with America had begun to turn bleak. On wartime ideological

congruences, see Akira Iriye, *Power and Culture: The Japanese-American War, 1941–1945* (Cambridge, MA: Harvard University Press, 1981).

11. Joseph S. Nye Jr., "Soft Power," *Foreign Policy*, no. 80 (Autumn 1990): 166–67.

12. Previous scholarship on the KBS has focused more on institutional formation with an emphasis on programs after 1937. See Shibasaki Atsushi, *Kindai Nihon to kokusai bunka kōryū: Kokusai Bunka Shinkōkai no sōsetsu to tenkai* [International Cultural Relations and Modern Japan: History of Kokusai Bunka Shinkōkai, 1934–1945] (Tokyo: Yūshindō Kōbunsha, 1999). Jessamyn Abel includes a chapter on the KBS in *The International Minimum*, 81–107. Jon Thares Davidann explores unofficial and often private diplomacy in *Cultural Diplomacy in U.S.-Japanese Relations, 1919–1941* (New York: Palgrave Macmillan, 2007).

13. The "cultural turn" in the study of international history covers a rich thematic field. For foundational studies, see Frank A. Ninkovich, *The Diplomacy of Ideas: U.S. Foreign Policy and Cultural Relations, 1938–1950* (New York: Cambridge University Press, 1981), and Emily S. Rosenberg, *Spreading the American Dream: American Economic and Cultural Expansion 1890–1945* (New York: Hill & Wang, 1982). For an overview of intellectual trends and a range of scholarship on cultural diplomacy, see the Explorations in Culture and International History Series, edited by Jessica C. E. Gienow-Hecht and published by Berghahn Books, especially Gienow-Hecht and Mark C. Donfried, eds., *Searching for a Cultural Diplomacy* (2010), and Gienow-Hecht and Frank Schumacher, eds., *Culture and International History* (2003). See also Akira Iriye, *Cultural Internationalism and World Order* (Baltimore: Johns Hopkins University Press, 1997), and Carolin Viktorin, Jessica C. E. Gienow-Hecht, Annika Estner, and Marcel K. Will, eds., *Nation Branding in Modern History* (New York: Berghahn Books, 2018).

14. Frank Ninkovich, *Global Dawn: The Cultural Foundation of American Internationalism, 1865–1890* (Cambridge, MA: Harvard University Press, 2009), 330.

15. David Reynolds, *From Munich to Pearl Harbor: Roosevelt's America and the Origins of the Second World War* (Chicago: Ivan R. Dee, 2002).

1. "TOO PROUD TO FIGHT"

1. On consul communication, see Barbara J. Brooks, *Japan's Imperial Diplomacy: Consuls, Treaty Ports, and War in China, 1895–1938* (Honolulu: University of Hawai'i Press, 2000), 141, and Sandra Wilson, *The Manchurian Crisis and Japanese Society, 1931–33* (New York: Routledge, 2001), 78–79. On the cabinet meeting of September 19, see Baron Harada Kumao, *Saionji-Harada Memoirs, 1931–1941*, reel 1 (Washington DC: University Publications of America, 1977), 76–79, September 23, 1931 (hereafter "Harada Diary"). Hirohito quoted by Chief Aide-de-Camp Nara Takeji, cited in Herbert Bix, *Hirohito and the Making of Modern Japan* (New York: HarperCollins, 2000), 239.

2. Stimson memo, September 22, 1931, *Foreign Relations of the United States , Japan: 1931–1941*, vol. 1 (Washington, DC: GPO, Department of State, 1943), 7–8 (hereafter *FRUS*, with specific volumes indicated; see bibliography for full details); *The Henry Lewis Stimson Diaries* (hereafter *SD*), September 28, 1931, vol. 18, 71, Manuscripts and Archives, Yale University Library, New Haven, CT; *SD*, October 9–10, 1931, vol. 18, 112–13, 118.

3. *SD*, October 9, 1931, vol. 18, 112; November 22, 1931, vol. 19, 86.

4. Thomas J. Knock, *To End All Wars: Woodrow Wilson and the Quest for a New World Order* (New York: Oxford University Press, 1992), 60–61, 71–75, 80–81; Lloyd E. Ambrosius, *Wilsonian Statecraft: Theory and Practice of Liberal Internationalism during World War I* (Wilmington, DE: SR Books, 1991), 68–92. See also Woodrow Wilson, "Peace without Victory," January 22, 1917, in Arthur S. Link, ed., *The Papers of Woodrow Wilson* (hereafter *PWW*), vol. 40 (Princeton, NJ: Princeton University Press, 1986), 533–39.

5. See "Wilson War Message," April 2, 1917, *PWW*, vol. 41, 527; John Milton Cooper Jr., *Woodrow Wilson: A Biography* (New York: Knopf, 2009), 362–89; and Knock, *To End All Wars*, 119–22. Allusion to "indispensable nation" from a comment made in 1998 by Madeleine Albright, secretary of state under President William J. Clinton.

6. Philip Gibbs, quoted in *Woodrow Wilson, Life and Letters: Armistice, March 1–November 11, 1918*, ed. Ray Stannard Baker (New York: Charles Scribner's, 1946), 584.

7. Frank Ninkovich, *The Global Republic: America's Inadvertent Rise to World Power* (Chicago: University of Chicago Press, 2014), 4. See also Iriye, *Cultural Internationalism*, 13–50; Glenda Sluga, *Internationalism in the Age of Nationalism* (Philadelphia: University of Pennsylvania Press, 2013), 11–44. Lloyd George in *Wilson, Life and Letters: Armistice*, 397; Tokyo mayor in Frederick Dickinson, "Toward a Global Perspective of the Great War: Japan and the Foundations of a Twentieth-Century World," *American Historical Review* 119, no. 4 (October 2014): 1162.

8. Wilson, September 27, 1918, *Wilson, Life and Letters: Armistice*, 428. Isiah Bowman, "Memo on Remarks by the President," December 10, 1918, *PWW*, vol. 53, 354.

9. On liberal precedent, see Ninkovich, *Global Republic*, 99–106; Mark Mazower, *Governing the World: The History of an Idea, 1815–Present* (London: Penguin, 2012), 38–48, 83–90; and Alan Sykes, *The Rise and Fall of British Liberalism* (London: Longman, 1997), 21–52, 58–68, 100–108, 133–42.

10. Erez Manela, *The Wilsonian Moment: Self-Determination and the International Origins of Anticolonial Nationalism* (Oxford: Oxford University Press, 2007), 8, and Akira Iriye, *China and Japan in a Global Setting* (Cambridge, MA: Harvard University Press, 1992), 48–49.

11. Wilson, "An Address in the City Auditorium in Pueblo, CO," September 25, 1919, *PWW*, vol. 63, 503–4.

12. Wilson to William Bullitt, December 9, 1918, *PWW*, vol. 53, 350–51; Wilson remarks, February 14, 1919, *PWW*, vol. 55, 175–77; Arthur S. Link, *The Higher Realism of Woodrow Wilson and Other Essays* (Nashville: Vanderbilt University Press, 1971); Henry Kissinger, *World Order* (New York: Penguin, 2014), 83.

13. Hugh Byas quoted in Peter Oblas, "Accessing British Empire-U.S. Diplomacy from Japan: Friendship, Discourse, Network, and the Manchurian Crisis," *Journal of American and Canadian Studies*, no. 21 (2004): 35.

14. Christopher Clark, *The Sleepwalkers: How Europe Went to War in 1914* (New York: Harper, 2012), 561.

15. Yoshino comments in *Chūō kōron* (*Central Review*), quoted in Sadao Asada, "Between the Old Diplomacy and the New, 1918–1922," *Diplomatic History* 30, no. 2 (April 2006): 212; Uchida instructions in Mizumo Hanihara Chow and Kiyofuku Chuma, *The Turning Point in US-Japan Relations* (London: Palgrave, 2016), 10, 34.

16. The system of imperialist leaseholds adopted the ninety-nine-year term from standard common law contracts, which mandated the longest possible term of a lease of real property to be ninety-nine years.

17. John J. O'Brien, "China Defies Japan: Peace Delegates Denounce Nipponese Aims as Imperialistic," *Washington Post*, March 6, 1919, 1. On the Beijing government's additional agreements with Japan, see Bruce A. Elleman, *Wilson and China: A Revised History of the Shandong Question* (Armonk, NY: M. E. Sharpe, 2002), 41–43. Wang's name was written at the time as C. T. Wang.

18. On bluffing, see Burkman, *Japan and the League*, 93–94. On the racial equality clause, see Naoko Shimazu, *Japan, Race and Equality: The Racial Equality Proposal of 1919* (New York: Routledge, 1998), 79–80, 91. On the Korean protest movement, see Manela, *Wilsonian Moment*, 119–36, 197–213.

19. On the May Fourth Movement, see Manela, *Wilsonian Moment*, 177–96. Wilson, "Pueblo Speech," September 25, 1919, *PWW*, vol. 63, 507–8. On the Wilson–Senate struggle, see John M. Cooper Jr., *Breaking the Heart of the World: Woodrow Wilson and the Fight for the League of Nations* (New York: Cambridge University Press, 2001).

20. George F. Kennan, *American Diplomacy, 1900–1950* (Chicago: University of Chicago Press, 1951), 69.

21. Ishii essay in *The New World and Japan*, March 1928, included in Kikujiro Ishii, *Diplomatic Commentaries* (Baltimore: Johns Hopkins University Press, 1936), 137–38. *Commentaries* is a translation of Ishii's 1930 memoir.

22. Emperor Taishō, "1920 Imperial Rescript on the Establishment of Peace," in Dickinson, "Toward a Global Perspective of the Great War," 1167; Burkman, *Japan and the League*, xi–xiv.

23. On the business bent in the 1920s, see Akira Iriye, *The Globalizing of America, 1913–1945* (Cambridge: Cambridge University Press, 1993), 88–102; Frank Costigliola, *Awkward Dominion: American Political, Economic, and Cultural Relations with Europe, 1919–1933* (Ithaca, NY: Cornell University Press, 1984), 31.

24. Harding address, May 14, 1920 in Warren G. Harding, "National Ideals and Policies," *Protectionist*, May 1920, 71–78. Senate address, February 10, 1922, *FRUS, 1922*, vol. 1, 303.

25. Wilson, April 15, 1919, *PWW*, vol. 57, 358; Reinsch and Koo cited in Margaret MacMillan, *Paris 1919: Six Months That Changed the World* (New York: Random House, 2002), 331, 335.

26. On domestic political pressures, see Roger Dingman, *Power in the Pacific: The Origins of Naval Arms Limitation, 1914–1922* (Chicago: University of Chicago Press, 1976), 139–59.

27. On Japan's approach to the conference, see Asada Sadao, *Ryō Taisenkan no Nichi-Bei Kankei* [American-Japanese Relations between the Wars] (Tokyo: Tokyo Daigaku Shuppankai, 1993), 51–148; and Asada, "Between the Old Diplomacy and the New." Lloyd George, *Conference of Prime Ministers and Representatives of the United Kingdom, the Dominions, and India* (London: His Majesty's Stationery Office, 1921), 14.

28. J. G. Hamilton, "Says America Has Justified Her Call," *New York Times*, November 13, 1921, 4. For a comprehensive study of the conference, see Thomas H. Buckley, *The United States and the Washington Conference, 1921–1922* (Knoxville: University of Tennessee Press, 1970).

29. The Anglo-Japanese Alliance was conceived as a bulwark against German and Russian naval power, neither of which was a concern in 1921.

30. Hamilton, "Says America Has Justified Her Call," 4. Dingman's claim that the powers were motivated mainly by "an abiding concern for domestic political power" is well supported, but it understates the impact of war trauma. Dingman, *Power in the Pacific*, 139–214.

31. On the motivations of all the naval powers, see Erik Goldstein and John Maurer, eds., *The Washington Conference, 1921–22: Naval Rivalry, East Asian Stability and the Road to Pearl Harbor* (London: Routledge, 2012).

32. Katō cited in *FRUS, 1922*, vol. 1, 69 (fn 63, 1b); Hughes statement in *SD*, vol. 27, October 30, 1934.

33. Dingman, *Power in the Pacific*, 212.

34. John Hay, Open Door Notes, *FRUS, 1899*, 129–30; and *FRUS, 1901, Affairs in China*, appendix, 12.

35. On the treaty port system and US-China relations, see Michael H. Hunt, *The Making of a Special Relationship: The United States and China to 1914* (New York: Columbia University Press, 1983).

36. See *FRUS: The Lansing Papers, 1914–1920*, vol. 2, 432–53, and Burton F. Beers, *Vain Endeavor: Robert Lansing's Attempts to End the American-Japanese Rivalry* (Durham, NC: Duke University Press, 1962), 114–16.

37. Hughes comments, November 11, 1921, *FRUS, 1922*, vol. 1, 1–2, and Akira Iriye, *After Imperialism: The Search for Order in the Far East, 1921–1931* (New York: Atheneum, 1973), 18. In the "security" clause, signatories promised "to refrain from taking advantage of conditions in China in order to seek special rights or privileges which would abridge the rights of subjects or citizens of friendly States, and from countenancing action inimical to the security of such States." See Asada, "Between the Old Diplomacy and the New," 216–26, and *SD*, September 2, 1932, 150–51.

38. Nine-Power Treaty, February 6, 1922, *FRUS, 1922*, vol. 1, 276–81.

39. Iriye, *After Imperialism*, 25–6; Katō cited in Asada, "Between the Old Diplomacy and the New," 228. See Dickinson, "Toward a Global Perspective of the Great War," 1177–78; Franklin D. Roosevelt, "Shall We Trust Japan?," *Asia*, July 1923, 478. Britain officially returned Weihai in 1930.

40. Cash figures from Payson J. Treat, *Japan and the United States, 1853–1921* (New York: Houghton Mifflin, 1921; rev. ed., 1928), 263. Shidehara quoted in Asada, "Between the Old Diplomacy and the New," 229.

41. In *Ozawa v. United States* (1922), the Supreme Court found Ozawa Takeo ineligible for citizenship under the Naturalization Act of 1906 because, contrary to his claim, he failed classification as a "white person." Immigration figures from Mae M. Ngai, "The Architecture of Race in American Immigration Law: A Reexamination of the Immigration Act of 1924," *Journal of American History* 86, no. 1 (June 1999): 74.

42. Hughes memo, March 27, 1924, *FRUS, 1924*, vol. 2, 337–38. Hanihara to Hughes, April 10, 1924; "No Veiled Threat Intended in Note," *New York Times*, April 20, 1924, 1. On Japan's view, see Chow and Chuma, *Turning Point in US-Japan Relations*, 135–67. See also Asada, *Ryō Taisenkan no Nichi-Bei Kankei*, 273–328.

43. Root comments in *SD*, Sept. 2, 1932,150-51; Hughes to Lodge, in Iriye, *After Imperialism*, 35.

44. Daniel Gorman, *The Emergence of International Society in the 1920s* (Cambridge: Cambridge University Press, 2012), 52–108, 187–93; Mazower, *Governing the World*, 141–53. See also Iriye, *Cultural Internationalism*, 51–90.

45. Tomoko Akami, *Internationalizing the Pacific: The United States, Japan and the Institute of Pacific Relations in War and Peace, 1919–45* (London: Routledge, 2002), 2, 87–97.

46. Italics mine. *FRUS, 1928*, vol. 1, 153–57. On neutrality, see Brooke L. Blower, "From Isolationism to Neutrality: A New Framework for Understanding American Political Culture, 1919–1941," *Diplomatic History* 38, no. 2 (2014): 345–76. See also Robert H. Ferrell, *Peace in Their Time: The Origins of the Kellogg-Briand Pact* (New Haven. CT: Yale University Press, 1952); and Gorman, *Emergence of International Society*, 259–308.

47. Edwin James, "15 Nations Sign Pact to Renounce War in Paris Room Where League Was Born; Briand Dedicates It to Nations' Dead," *New York Times*, August 28, 1928, 1; "Briand Calls Pact Direct Blow to War," *New York Times*, August 28, 1928, 5; *Springfield Republican*, August 28, 1928.

48. "Briand Dedicates It to Nations' Dead," *New York Times*; Coolidge quoted in Henry Cabot Lodge Jr., "The Meaning of the Kellogg Treaty," *Harper's*, December 1928, 38. Stanley Hoffman, "The Crisis of Liberal Internationalism," *Foreign Policy*, no. 98 (Spring 1995): 161.

49. Ishii, *Diplomatic Commentaries*, 243–44; Lodge, "Meaning of the Kellogg Treaty," 41. "Involvement without commitment" in George C. Herring, *The American Century and Beyond: U.S. Foreign Relations, 1893–2014* (Oxford: Oxford University Press, 2017), 137. See also Warren I. Cohen, *Empire without Tears: America's Foreign Relations, 1921–1933* (New York: Knopf, 1987).

50. France and Italy also participated but became disaffected early and declined to sign the ensuing treaty.

51. *SD*, January 7, 1930, vol. 11, 45; January 20, 1930, vol. 12, 47–49; February 3, 1930, vol. 12, 113. James B. Crowley, *Japan's Quest for Autonomy: National Security and Foreign Policy, 1930–1938* (Princeton, NJ: Princeton University Press, 1966), 38–48.

52. Ishii, *Diplomatic Commentaries*, 320–24. Crowley, *Japan's Quest for Autonomy*, 48–66.

53. Michiko Ito, "The Japanese Institute of Pacific Relations and the Kellogg Pact," in *Hawai'i at the Crossroads of the U.S. and Japan before the Pacific War*, ed. Jon Thares Davidann (Honolulu: University of Hawai'i Press, 2008), 78–82, 89. Another criticism was the pact being signed "in the name of the peoples" instead of the emperor. On the 1929 IPR conference, see Akami, *Internationalizing the Pacific*, 139–65, and Burkman, *Japan and the League*, 162–64.

54. Wakatsuki quoted in Dickinson, *World War I*, 180. Stimson address, April 22, 1930, *SD*, vol. 11, 63–65; "Three Nations Join in World Broadcast Lauding Navy Pact," *New York Times*, October 28, 1930, 1.

55. Iriye, *Globalizing America*, 103.

56. Henry L. Stimson, *The Far Eastern Crisis* (New York: Harper and Bros., 1936), 3.

2. TOWARD TWO WORLDS

1. *SD*, January 5, 1933, vol. 24, 77–78.

2. Sandra Wilson, "Containing the Crisis: Japan's Diplomatic Offensive in the West, 1931–1933," *Modern Asian Studies* 29 (May 1995): 340. See also Burkman, *Japan and the League*, 165–93.

3. See Ian Nish, *Japanese Foreign Policy in the Interwar Period* (Westport, CT: Praeger, 2002), 76–77. On domestic popular support for the military, see Young, *Japan's Total Empire*, 55–114, 130–40.

4. *SD*, November 19, 1931, vol. 19, 73–74; November 5, 1931, vol. 19, 6. Hoover memo to cabinet, October 19, 1931, *The Memoirs of Herbert Hoover: The Cabinet and Presidency, 1920–1933* (New York: Macmillan, 1952), 368–69.

5. William E. Leuchtenburg, *Herbert Hoover* (New York: Times Books, 2009), 6–14.

6. *SD*, October 9, 1931, vol. 18, 111; Hoover remarks, *Memoirs*, 366; *SD*, October 6, 1931, vol. 18, 105.

7. *SD*, November 16, 1931, vol. 19, 49.

8. "League Seeks Five for Inquiry," *New York Times*, December 12, 1931, 10.

9. "Premier Insists Japan Does Not Want Manchuria," *Chicago Tribune*, December 28, 1931, 8.

10. Hallet Abend, "Japanese Admit Aim to Hold Manchuria," *New York Times*, January 1, 1932, 19; Ki Inukai, "World's 1932 Hopes Voiced by Leaders," *New York Times*, January 1, 1932, 2. On emperor's reaction, see Bix, *Hirohito*, 246.

11. *SD*, January 3, 1932, vol. 20, 4.

12. James Crowley has noted that the distinction between Tanaka versus Shidehara continental policy in the late 1920s was not *whether* to defend Japan's interests in Manchuria but rather *how* to go about protecting those interests. See Crowley, *Japan's Quest for Autonomy*, 31–34. On press reaction, see Young, *Japan's Total Empire*, 80.

13. *SD*, September 30, 1931, vol. 18, 77.

14. Hallet Abend, "China Threatens U.S. with Ending Parley," *New York Times*, April 11, 1931, 6; Hallet Abend, "Nanking Votes End of Foreign Rights," *New York Times*, May 5, 1931, 10.

15. See Mark R. Peattie, *Ishiwara Kanji and Japan's Confrontation with the West* (Princeton, NJ: Princeton University Press, 1975), esp. 27–83.

16. *Documents on the Tokyo International Military Tribunal: Charter, Indictment and Judgments*, Robert Cryer and Neil Boister, eds. (Oxford: Oxford University Press, 2008), 314; Crowley, *Japan's Quest for Autonomy*, 114–21; Wakatsuki remarks cited by Baron Harada, Harada Diary, September 14, 1931, reel 1, 55. Shidehara cable in Takehiko Yoshihashi, *Conspiracy at Mukden: The Rise of the Japanese Military* (New Haven, CT: Yale University Press, 1963), 154.

17. See Harada Diary, August 21, 1931, 39, and October 2, 1931, 103–4. On reformists, see Sharon Minichiello, *Retreat from Reform: Patterns of Political Behavior in Interwar Japan* (Honolulu: University of Hawai'i Press, 1984).

18. Wilson, "Containing the Crisis," 519–33. Japanese regionalism began to complicate IPR ideals by the late 1920s. See Jon Thares Davidann, "'Colossal Illusions,'" in *Hawai'i at the Crossroads of the U.S. and Japan before the Pacific War*, ed. Jon Thares Davidann (Honolulu: University of Hawai'i Press, 2008), 42–67; and Akami, *Internationalizing the Pacific*, 114–17, 139–66.

19. "Japan's Foreign Minister Explains Nation's Stand," *Spartanburg Herald*, November 23, 1931, 2; Baron Dan Takuma, "Japan's Interests in Manchuria," *Times*, December 10, 1931, 8; Bix, *Hirohito*, 239.

20. On remembrance, see Naoko Shimazu, *Japanese Society at War: Death, Memory and the Russo-Japanese War* (Cambridge: Cambridge University Press, 2009). On the development of the SMR zone before the 1931 crisis, see Yoshihisa Tak Matsusaka, *The Making of Japanese Manchuria, 1904–1932* (Cambridge, MA: Harvard University Press, 2003), and Ramon H. Myers, "Japanese Imperialism in Manchuria: The South Manchurian Railway Company,

1906–1933," in *The Japanese Informal Empire in China, 1895–1937*, ed. Peter Duus, Ramon H. Myers, Mark R. Peattie, 101–32 (Princeton, NJ: Princeton University Press, 1989).

21. K. K. Kawakami, *Manchukuo: Child of Conflict* (New York: Macmillan, 1933), v–vi.

22. See Kevin Doak, *Dreams of Difference : The Japan Romantic School and the Crisis of Modernity* (Berkeley: University of California Press, 1994); Tetsuo Najita and Harry Harootunian, "Japanese Revolt against the West: Political and Cultural Criticism in the Twentieth Century," in *The Cambridge History of Japan*, vol. 6, ed. Peter Duus, 711–74 (Cambridge: Cambridge University Press, 1989); James Heiseg and John Maraldo, eds., *Rude Awakenings: Zen, the Kyoto School, and the Question of Nationalism* (Honolulu: University of Hawai'i Press, 1995); Aydin, *Politics of Anti-Westernism*, esp. 111–21, 141–88; Jacqueline Stone, "Japanese Lotus Millennialism," in *Millennialism, Persecution, and Violence*, ed. Catherine Wessinger, 261–74 (Syracuse, NY: Syracuse University Press, 2000); W. Miles Fletcher, *The Search for a New Order: Intellectuals and Fascism in Prewar Japan* (Chapel Hill: University of North Carolina Press, 1982).

23. K. K. Kawakami, *Japan's Pacific Policy* (New York: E. P. Dutton & Co., 1922), 151.

24. Baron Wakatsuki, "The Aims of Japan," *Foreign Affairs* 13, no. 4 (July 1935): 585–56; Viscount Kikujiro Ishii, "The Permanent Bases of Japanese Foreign Policy," *Foreign Affairs* 11, no. 2 (January 1933): 220–29.

25. Stimson note, January 7, 1932, *FRUS, Japan*, vol. 1, 76.

26. Stimson to Hymans, *SD*, April 22, 1932, vol. 21, 142.

27. Hornbeck in *SD*, January 6, 1932, vol. 20, 10, and *SD*, January 9, 1932, vol. 20, 29. On critics, see Armin Rappaport, *Henry L. Stimson and Japan, 1931–33* (Chicago: University of Chicago Press, 1963), 97–98. Inukai in Katsumi Usui, "Japanese Approaches to China in the 1930s," in *American, Chinese and Japanese Perspectives*, ed Akira Iriye and Warren Cohen (Lanham, MD: Rowman & Littlefield, 1990), 95. Bix, *Hirohito*, 247. Yoshizawa in Christopher Thorne, *The Limits of Foreign Policy: The West, the League and the Far Eastern Crisis of 1931–1933* (New York: G. P. Putnam's, 1972), 204.

28. Wilfrid Fleisher, *Volcanic Isle* (New York: Doubleday, 1941), 195. Shiratori in Hornbeck memo, September 20, 1933, Central Files, Record Group 59, 033.9411, National Archives, College Park, MD (hereafter NACP).

29. See Bix, *Hirohito*, 250–51; and Alvin Coox, *Nomonhan: Japan against Russia, 1939* (Stanford, CA: Stanford University Press, 1985), 44–45.

30. Figures from *New York Times*, February 3, 1932, 14.

31. Despite public outrage, observers mostly recommended restraint. See Thorne, *Limits of Foreign Policy*, 210–25, 233–46. Hoover to Lamont, cited in Harada Diary, February 16, 1932, reel 1, 245–46. *SD*, January 29, 1932, vol. 20, 111, and *SD*, February 15, 1932, 175.

32. *SD*, February 5, 1932, vol. 20, 141; "League Association Fears Our Isolation," *New York Times*, February 12, 1932, 3; "Our Stand on League Blamed in War Crisis," *New York Times*, February 2, 1932, 19.

33. *SD*, February 15, 1932, vol. 20, 174, and *SD*, February 21, 1932, vol. 20, 197, 200. On US-British discord, see Thorne, *Limits of Foreign Policy*, 247–72; Baldwin quoted at 247, 262.

34. Stimson to Borah, February 23, 1932, *FRUS, Japan*, vol. 1, 83–87.

35. "Coupling of Pacts Denied," *New York Times*, February 26, 1932, 1; "Says Stimson View May Prolong Clash," *New York Times*, February 26, 1932, 13.

36. "Three Nations Join in World Broadcast Lauding Navy Pact," *New York Times*, October 28, 1930, 1.

37. Hugh Byas, "Japan Plans to Quit Shanghai Zone Soon," *New York Times*, March 4, 1932, 4.

38. Matsudaira quoted in *SD*, April 25, 1932, vol. 21, 156–57.

39. *SD*, March 9, 1932, vol. 21, 51.

40. See, for example, "Japan's Premier Is Fifth Leader Slain in 12 Years," *Chicago Tribune*, May 16, 1932, 2.

41. For a discussion of one extremist group, see Stephen S. Large, "Nationalist Extremism in Early Shōwa Japan: Inoue Nisshō and the 'Blood-Pledge Corps Incident', 1932," *Modern Asian Studies* 35, no. 3 (July 2001): 533–64.

42. On Uchida's Kwantung sympathies, see Harada Diary, October 24, 1931, and April 24, 1932, reel 1, 119–24, 315.
43. Lytton address, October 19, 1932, "The Problem in Manchuria," published in *International Affairs* 11, no. 6 (November 1932): 745–46. Lytton's disappointment recorded by Hugh Byas in Oblas, "Accessing British Empire-U.S. Diplomacy," 49.
44. *SD*, July 27, 1932, vol. 23, 105–6. Hoover's mistaken references to Konoe is in Hoover, *Memoirs*, 365, 372.
45. Henry L. Stimson, "The Pact of Paris: Three Years of Development," address at the New York Council on Foreign Relations, August 8, 1932, reprinted in *Foreign Affairs* 2, no. 1, special supplement (1932): iii–viii.
46. *SD*, August 10, 1932, vol. 23, 134–35.
47. "Olympic Sale Goes over 1,300,000 Mark," *New York Times*, July 21, 1932, 1; *Chicago Tribune* essay was reprinted in *Los Angeles Times*, August 14, 1932, 3. Lothrop Stoddard, *The Rising Tide of Color: The Threat against White World-Supremacy* (New York: Scribner, 1920). On the impact of the Olympics and sport on international relations in the 1930s, see Barbara J. Keys, *Globalizing Sport: National Rivalry and International Community in the 1930s* (Cambridge, MA: Harvard University Press, 2006).
48. Burkman, *Japan and the League*, 146–47.
49. Nitobe address, "Japan, the League of Nations, and the Peace Pact," in *Lectures on Japan* (Tokyo: Kenkyusha, 1936); republished in Antony Best, ed., *Imperial Japan and the World, 1931–1945* (London: Routledge, 2010), 18–22. On American reception, see Burkman, *Japan and the League*, 183.
50. Uchida speech, *New York Times*, August 25, 1932, 1; "Scorched earth" quoted in Nish, *Japanese Foreign Policy*, 86. On Uchida and ideology, see Rustin Gates, "Pan-Asianism in Prewar Japanese Foreign Affairs: The Curious Case of Uchida Yasuya," *Journal of Japanese Studies* 37, no. 1 (Winter 2011): 1–27.
51. Protocol, *New York Times*, September 16, 1932, 8; Xie quoted in "Manchukuo Asks World Recognition," *New York Times*, September 16, 1932, 8.
52. *Report of the Commission of Enquiry* (Geneva: League of Nations Publications, 1932); letters to the commission, 105. *Economist*, November 26, 1932, reprinted in *Pacific Affairs* 6, no. 1 (January 1933): 44.
53. See David J. Lu, *Agony of Choice: Matsuoka Yosuke and the Rise and Fall of the Japanese Empire, 1880–1946* (Lanham, MD: Lexington Books, 2003), 81–85.
54. Radio comments cited in *New York Times*, December 5, 1932, 8. Yen's name in pinyin is Yan Huiqing.
55. Matsuoka address reprinted in *Japan's Case in the Sino-Japanese Dispute as Presented before the Special Session of the Assembly of the League of Nations* (Geneva: Japanese Delegation, 1933), 10–22.
56. Ibid., 27–33; "Japan & Nazarene," *Time*, December 19, 1932, 14–15.
57. Lady Drummond-Hay, "Matsuoka Claims for Japan 'a World Spiritual Mission,'" *New York Times*, January 8, 1933, XX4.
58. League of Nations, *Official Journal*, special supplement, no. 112 (February 1933): 14–16.
59. Ibid., 16–20.
60. Ibid.; Stuart Brown, "Japan Stuns World, Withdraws from League," February 24, 1933, UPI Archives, http://100years.upi.com/sta_1933-02-24.html.
61. Grew remarks, March 27, 1933, *Ten Years in Japan* (New York: Simon & Schuster, 1944), 84.
62. Elihu Root, "A Requisite for the Success of Popular Democracy," *Foreign Affairs* 1, no. 1 (September 15, 1922): 8. Byas in Oblas, "Accessing British Empire-U.S. Diplomacy," 36.
63. John V. A. MacMurray, cited in Arthur Waldron, ed., *How the Peace Was Lost* (Stanford, CA: Hoover Institution Press, 1992), 130. "Japan Alone," *New York Times*, February 26, 1933, E4.
64. The phrase is Louise Young's from *Japan's Total Empire*, 15.

3. JAPAN'S CHARM OFFENSIVE (1933–1934)

1. League of Nations, *Official Journal*, 14; "Japan Alone," *New York Times*, February 26, 1933, E4.
2. Hornbeck memo of Debuchi–Hornbeck discussion, January 10, 1933, *FRUS, 1933*, vol. 3, 47.
3. Fleisher, *Volcanic Isle*, 196. Fleisher was editor of the English-language daily *Japan Advertiser*, 1929–1940.
4. Matsuoka cited in *Japan's Case*, 64.
5. On US-Japan trade statistics in the 1930s, see Mira Wilkins, "The Role of U.S. Business," in *Pearl Harbor as History*, ed. by Dorothy Borg and Shumpei Okamoto, 341–76 (New York: Columbia University Press, 1973).
6. On the Foreign Ministry's conceptualization of a cultural strategy, see Shibasaki, *Kindai Nihon*, 63–119. Nitobe, "On American Attitudes toward Japan," cited in Ota Yuzo, "Difficulties Faced by Native Japan Interpreters," in *Searching for a Cultural Diplomacy*, ed. Jessica C. E. Gienow-Hecht and Mark C. Donfried (New York: Berghahn Books, 2010), 201.
7. Reynolds, *From Munich to Pearl Harbor*, 35–36.
8. *Time*, March 6, 1933, 12–13. Quotation from Richard D. Burns, "Cordell Hull: A Study in Diplomacy, 1933–1941" (Ph.D. diss., University of Illinois, 1960), 2; Grace Tully, *FDR: My Boss* (New York: Scribner's, 1949), 184; Irwin Gellman, *Secret Affairs: Franklin Roosevelt, Cordell Hull, and Sumner Welles* (Baltimore: Johns Hopkins University Press, 1995), 31, 93–94.
9. On Grew's dualism, see also Waldo Heinrichs, *American Ambassador: Joseph C. Grew and the Development of the United States Diplomatic Tradition* (Boston: Little, Brown, 1966).
10. Upton Close, "The Pacific Picture," *Saturday Evening Post*, March 24, 1934, 17; *Fortune*, September 1936, 50.
11. Hotta, *Pan-Asianism*, 1, 6, 12–13, 49, 82–83. See also Wilson, *Manchurian Crisis*, 20, 55, 88.
12. See Shizhang Hu, *Stanley K. Hornbeck and the Open Door Policy, 1919–1937* (Westport, CT: Greenwood Press, 1995), 2–8, 116–20, 129–39, 231–33.
13. Hull memo, March 31, 1933, General Records, 1930–1939, RG 59, 033.9411, NACP; "Foreword," *Japan's Case*.
14. "Matsuoka Finds Us Inconsistent," *New York Times*, April 2, 1933, E1; "Greeting to Mr. Matsuoka," *Morning Oregonian*, April 7, 1933, 6.
15. "Roosevelt Candor Is Praised by Ishii," *New York Times*, May 30, 1933, 3; joint statement in "Ishii Talks Ended on a Friendly Note," *New York Times*, May 28, 1933, 3; "Japan Envoy Heads for Parley," *New York Times*, May 18, 1933, 1933, 8; "The New Deal in Japanese-American Relations," *Literary Digest*, June 17, 1933, 12.
16. Office File (hereafter "OF") 197, Box 1, Japan, '33–34, FDR Library; "Japan's Emperor, Receiving First U.S. Newspaper Man, Calls Amity with America Essential to Peace of World," *World-Telegram*, June 23, 1933, 1.
17. Wilson, "Containing the Crisis," 347; Horiounichi to Uchida, May 8, 1933, Archives of the Japanese Ministry of Foreign Affairs, Tokyo, Japan (hereafter MOFA) (Honpō ni okeru kyōkai oyobi bunkadantaikankei zakken: kokusaibunka –shinkōkaikankei, no. 1 and 2).
18. *Official Guide Book of the Fair, 1933* (Chicago: Century of Progress, 1933), 95, rare books archive, State Historical Society, Madison, Wisconsin. Robert Randolph quoted in *Japan Advertiser*, March 24, 1934, 1.
19. Sterling Fisher Jr., "Japan Feels the Hand of a New Guide," *New York Times*, January 7, 1934, SM5; *Time*, May 21, 1934, 21.
20. AP article from "Japan's New Envoy Hopeful of Peace," *New York Times*, February 10, 1934, 5; "Japan's New Ambassador," *New York Herald Tribune*, December 18, 1933, 14. See Saitō's addresses to American audiences in Hirosi [Hiroshi] Saito, *Japan's Policies and Purposes* (Boston: Marshall Jones, 1935), and his essays in Japanese publications in Hotta, *Pan-Asianism*, 99.

21. Grew diary, January 23, 1934, *Ten Years*, 115; see also *FRUS, 1934*, vol. 3, 15–16, and Harada Diary, February 1934, reel 1, 800; *Christian Century*, January 31, 1934, 139–40.

22. Hamilton diary, October 2, 1933, Central Files, 1930–1939, RG 59, Box 223, 111.22/77, NACP; Grew cable to Hull, October 3, 1933, *FRUS, Japan*, vol. 1, 123–26.

23. Hamilton diary, October 10, 1933.

24. Ibid. Fleisher, *Volcanic Isle*, 197.

25. Cited in Shimada Toshihiko, "Designs on North China, 1933–1937," trans. J. B. Crowley, in James W. Morley, ed., *The China Quagmire: Japan's Expansion on the Asian Continent, 1933–1941* (New York: Columbia University Press, 1983), 77. Matsui Iwane, "Dai Ajia Kyokai Soritsu Shushi" ("The Reasons for the Founding of the Greater Asia Association," 1933), trans. by Torsten Weber, in Saaler and Szpilman, *Pan-Asianism*, 143.

26. Roy Mathew Frisen, "Japanophobia," *Forum*, October 1933, 241; Eileen Tupper and George McReynolds, *Japan in American Public Opinion* (New York: Macmillan, 1937), 363.

27. Hirota address in *New York Times*, January 23, 1934, 5. Italics mine.

28. Grew, January 23 and February 8, 1934, *Ten Years*, 115, 118–19; "I can often plant" in John Dower, *Empire and Aftermath: Yoshida Shigeru and the Japanese Experience, 1878–1954* (Cambridge, MA: Harvard University Press, 1979), 108.

29. Exchange of notes, February 21 and March 3, 1934, *FRUS, Japan*, vol. 1, 127–29.

30. Editorials cited in Tupper and McReynolds, *Japan in American Public Opinion*, 375; T. A. Bisson, "American-Japanese Problems Attacked in Friendlier Vein," *New York Times*, April 1, 1934, XX3.

31. See Masayoshi Matsumura, *Baron Kaneko and the Russo-Japanese War (1904–05): A Study in the Public Diplomacy of Japan*, trans. Ian Ruxton (Morrisville, NC: Lulu Press, 2009). For other examples in the early twentieth century, see Michael Auslin, *Pacific Cosmopolitans: A Cultural History of U.S.-Japan Relations* (Cambridge, MA: Harvard University Press, 2011); and Davidann, *Cultural Diplomacy*.

32. *Literary Digest*, March 10, 1934, 15; Iyesato [Iesato] Tokugawa, "Prince Says Japan Needs Our Amity," *New York Times*, February 26, 1934, 11. Taft and DeWolf Perry speeches cited in *New York Times*, "Japan Shuns War, Says Tokugawa," February 28, 1934, 7. Henry Taft was the brother of former president William Howard Taft (1857–1930).

33. Hornbeck memo, December 1933, Central Files, 1930–39, RG59, 033.9411, Tokugawa, Iyesato [Iesato], NACP.

34. On the origins and growth of international cultural relations, see Iriye, *Cultural Internationalism*, 13–90. On the origins of cultural policy in Japan, see Shibasaki, *Kindai Nihon*, 33–89.

35. In 1925, the USSR established the All-Union Society for Cultural Relations with Foreign Countries (VOKS); in 1934, Great Britain established the British Council.

36. Amō memo in Tomoko Akami, *Soft Power of Japan's War State: The Board of Information and D ōmei News Agency in Foreign Policy, 1934–45* (Dordrecht: Republic of Letters, 2014), 70.

37. *Kokusai Bunka Shinkokai: Prospectus and Scheme* (Tokyo: Kokusai Bunka Shinkokai, 1934), 1–3.

38. Prince Fumimaro Konoye [Konoe], "Foreword," *K.B.S. Quarterly* 1 (April–June 1935): 1.

39. Unofficial translation by Japan's Foreign Office, *FRUS, Japan*, vol. 1, 224–25; "Japan Resents World Powers' Aid to China," *Washington Post*, April 18, 1934, 1.

40. Grew to Hull, April 20, 1934, *FRUS, Japan*, vol. 1, 223-25.

41. Grew cable to Hull, April 26, 1934, *FRUS, 1934*, vol. 3, 140; Grew letter to Hull, May 4, 1934, ibid., 162.

42. Shimada, "Designs on North China," 81–82.

43. Hugh Byas, "Japan Assures U.S. on Rights in China," *New York Times*, April 28, 1934; Saitō comment, April 23, 1934, reported in *New York Times*, April 24, 1934, 10.

44. Hirota cited in Harada Diary, October 25, 1933, reel 1, 722.

45. Ishii, *Diplomatic Commentaries*, 123.

46. Stimson, *Far Eastern Crisis*, 236, and *SD*, March 3, 1932, vol. 21, 32. Roosevelt, "Annual Message," December 6, 1904, *FRUS, 1904*, xli. On US hegemony, see Lars Schoultz,

Beneath the United States: A History of U.S. Policy Toward Latin America (Cambridge, MA: Harvard University Press, 1998), 154–271.

47. *SD*, March 3, 1932, vol. 21, 32; *Japan Advertiser*, September 3, 1932. On the origins of the Good Neighbor Policy, see Schoultz, *Beneath the United States*, 272–315.

48. Hull official reply to Japan, April 30, 1934, *FRUS, Japan*, vol. 1, 231; Hull, May 1, 1934, *FRUS, 1934*, vol. 3, 153.

49. C. T. [Zhengting] Wang, "The Pan-Asiatic Doctrine of Japan," *Foreign Affairs* 13, no. 1 (October 1934): 59–67.

50. Fleisher, *Volcanic Isle*, 44.

51. Comments quoted in *FRUS, 1934*, vol. 3, 654–61; *FRUS, Japan*, vol. 1, 232–36. The Carlton is now the St. Regis Hotel.

52. Ibid.

53. Grew to Hull, Telegram No. 798, May 22, 1934, State Department Central Files, 1930-39, RG 59, 894.43-International Cultural Relations/I, NACP.

54. "Noted Tokyo Prince to Pay Visit Here," *New York Times*, March 2, 1934, 24; "Prince Says Japan Wants China's Aid," *New York Times*, June 7, 1934, 10; FDR Library, OF 197, Box 1, Japan, '33–34; "Congress 'Amazes' Japanese Prince," *New York Times*, June 15, 1934, 12. On perception as liberal, see also Hoover, *Memoirs*, 365, 372.

55. Grew memo, July 5, 1934, Telegram No. 879, 033.9411, Konoe, Fumimaro/32, State Dept Central Files, 1930–39, RG 59, Box 64, NACP.

56. "Japan Appears to Most Americans Like Germany before War—Konoe," *Osaka Mainichi*, August 8, 1934, 1. The Tydings–McDuffie Act (March 1934) guaranteed full Philippine independence by 1946.

57. See Yoshitake Oka, *Konoe Fumimaro: A Political Biography*, trans. Shumpei Okamoto and Patricia Murray (Tokyo: University of Tokyo Press, 1983), 10–15; and Brooks, *Japan's Imperial Diplomacy*, 31–32, 40–41.

58. Konoe Fumimaro, "General Report," *Japan Times and Mail*, August 8, 1934, 1.

59. "Japan Appears to Most Americans," 1; "U.S. Public Has Little Knowledge of Japan; Parity, Equality Mixed: Prince Konoe Concludes Observation of American Trip by Urging Creation of Adequate Institutions for Correct Representation of Japan in U.S.," *Osaka Mainichi*, August 9, 1934, 1; "House, Dawes Hold Opposite Views on Japan," *Japan Times and Mail*, August 8, 1934, 1; Prince Fumimaro Konoe, "Japan Should Expound Her China Policy to World to Dispel Suspicion Regarding Her Motives," *Japan Advertiser*, September 5, 1934, 1.

60. Annual report quoted in Edwin O. Reischauer, *Japan Society 1907–1982* (New York: Japan Society Gallery, 1982), 36. The KBS eventually opened other branch offices in Paris, Berlin, Buenos Aires, Rome, Geneva, and Melbourne.

61. Masaharu Anesaki, *Art, Life, and Nature in Japan* (Boston: Marshall Jones, 1933), 5.

62. Edward Price Bell, "Japan Is for Peace, Says Okada," *Literary Digest*, September 1, 1934, 3, 29–31.

63. Shibasaki, *Kindai Nihon*, 92.

64. *NIPPON* technically was published by Natori's Nippon Kōbō Company. For an analysis of Natori's propaganda work, see Andrea Germer, "Visual Propaganda in Wartime East Asia: The Case of Natori Yōnosuke," *Asia-Pacific Journal* 9, no. 20 (May 2011), http://www.japanfocus.org/-Andrea-Germer/3530/article.html. See also Gennifer Weisenfeld, "Touring Japan-as-Museum: *NIPPON* and Other Japanese Imperialist Travelogues," *Positions* 8, no. 3 (Winter 2000): 747–93.

65. Konoe Fumimaro, "Movement in Japan for Promotion of Cultural Relations with Foreign Countries," *NIPPON* 1 (October 1934): 50; Ayské [Aisuke] Kabayama, "What Has Japan in Store?," *NIPPON* 3 (1935): 7; Hirota Kōki, "Study Japan," *NIPPON* 4 (1935): 9.

66. For Japanese naval perspectives in the 1930s, see Asada, *Ryō Taisenkan no Nichi-Bei Kankei*, 205–71, and *From Mahan to Pearl Harbor: The Imperial Japanese Navy and the United States* (Annapolis, MD: Naval Institute Press, 2006). See also Stephen Pelz, *Race to Pearl Harbor: The Failure of the Second London Naval Conference and the Onset of World War II* (Cambridge, MA: Harvard University Press, 1974).

67. Pelz, *Race to Pearl Harbor*, 25, 74–82.

68. Saitō and Hull statements, *New York Times*, December 30, 1934, 14.

4. THE HIGH TIDE OF CULTURAL DIPLOMACY (1935–1936)

1. Hornbeck memo, January 3, 1935, President's Secretary's File: Diplomatic Correspondence, 1935–36, Box 42, FDR Library (hereafter cited as PSF); Grew letter to Hull, December 27, 1934, ibid., 825–26; Grew to Hull, March 22, 1935, ibid., 88–89.

2. A similar tour occurred in 1931, before Japan's government defended the actions of the Kwantung Army. See John Gripentrog, "The Transnational Pastime: Baseball and American Perceptions in the 1930s," *Diplomatic History* 34, no. 2 (April 2010): 254–58, and Sayuri Guthrie-Shimizu, *Transpacific Field of Dreams: How Baseball Linked the United States and Japan in Peace and War* (Chapel Hill: University of North Carolina Press, 2012), 133–39.

3. "100,000 Acclaim Ruth at Tokio, Halting Traffic to Pay Tribute," *New York Herald Tribune*, November 3, 1934, 15; "Ruth Conquers Japan," *Sporting News*, November 8, 1934, 1.

4. "65,000 Japanese See Babe Ruth Make Debut on Foreign Diamond," *New York Herald Tribune*, November 5, 1934, 12; Jimmy Powers, "Ruth, an Idol and Diplomat, Wins Japan as He Won U.S.," *Washington Post*, November 13, 1934, 17; Gordon Mackay, "Mack, Back from Orient, Says Game Must Not Lose Ruth," *Sporting News*, January 17, 1935, 3.

5. Berry quoted in Allen Guttmann, *From Ritual to Record: The Nature of Modern Sports* (New York: Columbia University Press, 1978), 95–96; Henry Chauncey, "Japan Plays the American National Game," *Literary Digest*, November 24, 1934, 39.

6. *Baseball Magazine*, January 1935, 338. Italics mine. Powers, "Ruth, an Idol and Diplomat." Mack cited in *Sporting News*, February 14, 1935, 4.

7. Tokugawa quoted in "Calls Baseball Bond between U.S., Japan," *New York Times*, November 16, 1934, 29.

8. KBS roundtable-style proceedings, March 29, 1935, MOFA, I.1.10. Associations (KBS) (Honpō ni okeru kyōkai oyobi bunkadantaikankei zakken: kokusaibunka –shinkōkaikankei, no. 1 and 2), 239.

9. Anesaki speeches cited in ibid.

10. Edward A. Jewell, "Art of Japanese at Metropolitan," *New York Times*, February 19, 1935, 19; *Bulletin of the Metropolitan Museum of Art* 30 (February 1935): 27–32; Dan Inō, "Broadening Cultural Contacts," *K.B.S. Quarterly* 1 (January–March 1936): 3; Aoki to Shigemitsu, March 22, 1935, MOFA, I.1.10. Associations (KBS) (Honpō ni okeru kyōkai oyobi bunkadantaikankei zakken: kokusaibunka–shinkōkaikankei, no. 1 and 2).

11. Hugh Byas, "Americans Seeing Gardens of Japan," *New York Times*, May 14, 1935, 7.

12. Mrs. [Romayne] Benjamin S. Warren, "The Garden Club of America in Japan," *Bulletin of the Garden Club of America*, no. 17 (September 1935): 19, 30.

13. KBS, "Directors Proceedings: Garden Club," July 30, 1935, Kokusai bunka shinkoukai rijikai narabini hyougikai gijiroku, Japan Foundation Archives, Tokyo, Japan.

14. Warren, "Garden Club of America in Japan," 25–27, 34–35, 56.

15. *K.B.S. Quarterly* 1 (April–June 1935): 29; KBS, "Directors Proceedings: Garden Club," July 30, 1935. Grew, April 17, 1935, 894.43-international cultural relations/2, State Dept Central Files, 1930-39, RG 59, Box 64, NACP.

16. "Dolls Will Tour Japan," *New York Times*, May 29, 1935, 23; "La Guardia's Dolls Bow to Emperor," *New York Times*, June 21, 1935, 21.

17. Grew diary, June 20, 1935, *Ten Years*, 156–57. Tourism figures in *The Japan Yearbook, 1937* (Tokyo: Foreign Affairs Association of Japan, 1937), 663–65.

18. *Sporting News*, November 1, 1934, 4.

19. Prescott Sullivan, "O'Doul Fears Politeness of Japanese Ballplayers," *San Francisco Chronicle*, March 7, 1935, 17; Ed Hughes, "Japanese Nine Pounds Sheehan for 8–1 Victory," *San Francisco Chronicle*, March 26, 1935, A13.

20. "No Wonder the Umpire Looks Surprised," *Salt Lake Tribune*, May 29, 1935, 16; "Tokyo Giants Battle Royal Community," *Salt Lake Tribune*, May 30, 1935, 13; "Tokyo Giants Triumph over Local Clubs," *Salt Lake Tribune*, June 2, 1935, B8; Ronald McIntyre, "Between You and Me," *Milwaukee Sentinel*, June 13, 1935, S2; Hank Casserly, "Record Crowd Sees Blues Beat Jap Stars, 9–3," *Capital Times*, June 13, 1935, S1.

21. "Goodwill Helps," *Los Angeles Times*, June 24, 1935, A4.

22. Claudia Cranston, "Out Where the East Begins," *Good Housekeeping*, January 1937, 159; J. P. McEvoy, "Meet the Moga," *Saturday Evening Post*, September 21, 1935, 38; George Brandt, "East-to-West: Japan," *Scribner's Magazine*, April 1937, 65–66; Edward Price Bell, "Japan Has Become Occidentalized," *Literary Digest*, August 4, 1934, 16.

23. *Fortune*, September 1936, 142; S. I. Hayakawa, "Japanese Sensibility," *Harper's*, December 1936, 98–103; "U.S. Movies Changing Japan's Mode of Living," *Washington Post*, January 17, 1937, 5.

24. McEvoy, "Meet the Moga," 20, 38; Hugh Byas, "Film Notes from Tokyo," *New York Times*, October 8, 1933, X4; *Time*, April 26, 1937, 43; *New York Herald Tribune*, April 11, 1937, VII, 3; "U.S. Movies," *Washington Post*, 5.

25. *Fortune*, September 1936, 85; Robert K. Reischauer, "Conflicts Inside Japan," *Harper's*, July 1936, 159. Reischauer's younger brother, Edwin, became a professor of Japanese history at Harvard University; in 1961, President John F. Kennedy appointed him as ambassador to Japan. Bell, "Japan Has Become Occidentalized," 16.

26. Wallace Donham, "Japan Advances," *Saturday Evening Post*, July 6, 1935, 10–11; A. J. Billingham, "Hsinking [Changchun] Is Transformed," *New York Times*, August 4, 1935, XX4.

27. Eugene J. Young, "Japanese Leaders Hit Militarists," *San Francisco Chronicle*, February 3, 1935, 1.

28. For memo and contextual analysis, see Waldron, *How the Peace Was Lost*, 131. Hornbeck cited in Barnhart, *Japan Prepares*, 116–17.

29. On Japan-China negotiations, see Crowley, *Japan's Quest for Autonomy*, 214–24, and Marjorie Dryburgh, *North China and Japanese Expansion, 1933–1937* (Richmond, UK: Curzon, 2000), 24–59.

30. Hugh Byas, "Japan Prepares 4-Province Regime in North China," *New York Times*, June 12, 1935, 1; "Japan's Army Reasserts Its Importance," *Christian Century*, June 12, 1935, 780; Grew to Hull, June 24, 1935, *FRUS, 1935*, vol. 3, 274, and June 29, 1935, ibid., 283–84.

31. Grew diary, April 4, 1933, *Ten Years*, 545. For Hornbeck, see Doenecke, *The Diplomacy of Frustration* (Stanford, CA: Hoover Institution Press, 1981), 13, 79. For Grew's references to the *New York Times*, see *FRUS, 1934*, vol. 3, 51, 677; ibid., 41.

32. Hull speeches, June 17 and June 24, 1935, Central Files, 1930-39, RG 59, Box 209, NACP.

33. Neutrality Act, August 31, 1935, US Department of State, Publication 1983, *Peace and War: United States Foreign Policy, 1931–1941* (Washington, DC: US Government Printing Office, 1943), 265–71; Blower, "From Isolationism to Neutrality," 369. Italics mine.

34. Roosevelt to House, September 17, 1935, in *F.D.R., His Personal Letters, 1928–1945* [hereafter *Letters*] (New York: Duell, Sloan and Pearce, 1950), 506–7. On isolationism, consult Wayne Cole, *Roosevelt and the Isolationists, 1932–1945* (Lincoln: University of Nebraska Press, 1983).

35. Col. Edward M. House, "Wanted: A New Deal among Nations," *Liberty*, September 14, 1935, 44–47; Konoe Fumimaro, "How to Secure Lasting Peace," *Liberty*, December 7, 1935, 31.

36. On the history of Japan's news agencies, see Tomoko Akami, *Japan's News Propaganda and Reuters' News Empire in Northeast Asia, 1870–1934* (Dordrecht: Republic of Letters, 2012), and *Soft Power of Japan's War State*. Hirota statement, *New York Times*, May 5, 1935, S12.

37. On newspapers, see Peter O'Connor, *The English-Language Press Networks of East Asia, 1918–1945* (Folkestone, UK: Global Oriental, 2010). On paid writers and tours, see Barak Kushner, *The Thought War: Japanese Imperial Propaganda* (Honolulu: University of Hawai'i Press, 2006), 40–43, and O'Connor, *English-Language Press Networks*, 145, 190–91, 208–9, 216–17, 222. On the Japanese American community, see Eiichiro Azuma, *Between Two Empires: Race, History, and Transnationalism in Japanese America* (New York: Oxford University Press, 2005), 171–83. NHK broadcast from http://www3.nhk.or.jp/nhkworld/en/chronology/chrono/1935-1939.html. NHK programming in Jane M. J. Robbins, "Tokyo Calling: Japanese Overseas Radio Broadcasting 1937–1945" (Ph.D. diss., Sheffield University, 1997), 37–43.

38. See June Grasso, *Japan's "New Deal" for China: Propaganda Aimed at Americans before Pearl Harbor* (London: Routledge, 2019).

39. Konoe on Hornbeck, "Some Impressions of America Brought by Prince Konoe," *Japan Advertiser*, September 5, 1934; Kabayama to Hornbeck, January 10 and January 20, 1936, State Department Central Files, 1930–39, RG 59, 894.43-International Cultural Relations/2, NACP.

40. Sterling Fisher Jr., "Garner and Party Land in Yokohama," *New York Times*, October 28, 1935, 1. "Japan's Welcome Thrills Americans," *New York Times*, October 30, 1935, 9.

41. Hugh Byas, "Japan Is Seeking a North-China Showdown," *New York Times*, October 31, 1935, 9.

42. See Crowley, *Japan's Quest for Autonomy*, 224–243, and Dryburgh, *North China*, 60–98. Nathaniel Peffer, "Japan Ready to Act against China Again," *New York Times*, November 3, 1935, E6.

43. Hornbeck memo, December 2, 1935, *FRUS, 1935*, vol. 3, 463–67. Hull text, *New York Times*, December 6, 1935, 16.

44. Amō reported in Byas, "Japan Rules out Nine-Power Pact," *New York Times*, December 7, 1935, 1.

45. FDR speech, January 3, 1936, *FRUS, 1936*, vol. 3, 122–23; FDR to Dodd, January 6, 1936, *Letters*, 543.

46. See Richard Slotkin, *Gunfighter Nation: The Myth of the Frontier in Twentieth-Century America* (Norman: University of Oklahoma Press, 1998), and Walter McDougall, *Promised Land, Crusader State: The American Encounter with the World since 1776* (Boston: Mariner Books, 1997), 15–100.

47. Grew diary, January 5, 1936, in *Ten Years*, 162–63; Hirota text, *New York Times*, January 21, 1936, 19.

48. Hugh Byas, "Japan's Aim in Orient Voiced," *New York Times*, January 22, 1936, 1, 9; Nathaniel Peffer, "China's Students Spur Resistance to Japan," *New York Times*, January 26, 1936, E6.

49. Saitō speech, "Saito Defends Japan's Aims in Speech Here," *New York Herald Tribune*, February 1, 1936, 6.

50. Pittman speech, February 10, 1936, *Congressional Record*, 74th Congress, 2nd session, vol. 8, pt. 2, 1703.

51. Sterling Fisher Jr., "Japan Viewed as Paying Penalty for Glorification of Assassins," *New York Times*, February 27, 1936, 13.

52. "Machida Is Viewed as an Anti-Fascist," *New York Times*, February 29, 1936, 4; "Genro, Godling, and Ginger," *Time*, March 16, 1936, 24; Hugh Byas, "Hirota Is Creating a Strong Cabinet," *New York Times*, March 6, 1936, 1; Grew to Hull, March 9, 1936, *FRUS, 1936*, vol. 4, 759; Sterling Fisher Jr., "Militarists Lose Control at Tokyo," *New York Times*, March 6, 1936, 14; "Japan's Crisis," *Christian Century*, March 11, 1936, 392, 394.

53. Walter LaFeber, *The Clash: A History of U.S.-Japan Relations* (New York: W. W. Norton, 1997), 181; Charles Neu, *The Troubled Encounter: The U.S. and Japan* (New York: Wiley, 1975), 151.

54. Hirota quoted in Mark C. Michelson, "A Place in the Sun: The Foreign Ministry and Perceptions and Policies in Japan's International Relations, 1931–1941" (Ph.D. diss., University of Illinois, 1979), 140. Text of Saitō speech, *New York Times*, March 1, 1936, 31.

55. Cited in John P. Marquand, *Mr. Moto's Three Aces* (Boston: Little, Brown, 1938), 102, 378–79.

56. Jerome D. Greene, review of Saito's *Japan's Policies and Purposes*, *Pacific Affairs* 9, no. 2 (June 1936): 281–84; Yoshida-Hull discussion, *FRUS, Japan*, vol. 1, 241–44.

57. James R. Young, *Behind the Rising Sun* (New York: Doubleday, Doran, and Co., 1942), 62; Bix, *Hirohito*, 311.

58. Kabayama in Jessamyn R. Abel, "Cultural Internationalism and Japan's Wartime Empire: The Turns of the *Kokusai Bunka Shinkōkai*," in *Tumultuous Decade: Empire, Society, and Diplomacy in 1930s Japan*, ed. Masato Kimura and Tosh Minohara (Toronto: University of Toronto Press, 2013), 24, and Shibasaki, *Kindai Nihon*, 106. Dan, "Broadening Cultural Contacts," 2–3.

59. "'Fair Harvard,' America's First College, Celebrates its 300th Birthday," *Washington Post*, September 13, 1936, 5.
60. Louis M. Lyons, "Harvard Hails Great Scholars," *Boston Globe*, September 17, 1936, morning edition, 1; "10,000 at Harvard Exercises," *Boston Globe*, September 17, 1936, evening edition, 1.
61. Cited in A. J. Philpott, "Exhibition of Japan's Art Opens at Museum," *Daily Boston Globe*, September 11, 1936, 19; also in Edward Jewell, "Japanese Exhibit at Boston Museum," *New York Times*, September 11, 1936, 29.
62. Sibilla Skidelsky, "Treasures of Art from Japanese Galleries Lent to Boston Museum for Harvard Tercentenary," *Washington Post*, October 4, 1936, 6; Royal Cortissoz, "The Painting and Sculpture of Japan," *New York Herald Tribune*, September 27, 1936, 10; Jewell, "Japanese Exhibit at Boston Museum," 29; Louis Ledoux, "Japanese Painting and Sculpture: The Important Loan Exhibition in Boston," *American Magazine of Art*, September 1936, 561; Edward Jewell, "Boston Savors Ageless Japanese Art," *New York Times*, September 20, 1936, X8.
63. Skidelsky, "Treasures of Art," 6; Eugene J. Young, *Powerful America: Our Place in a Re-arming World* (New York: Frederick A. Stokes, 1936), 271–72.
64. Skidelsky, "Treasures of Art," 6; Ledoux, "Japanese Painting and Sculpture," 572; Irma Whitney, "Emperor's Own Treasures in Japanese Loan Exhibition," *Boston Herald*, September 12, 1936, 12; Langdon Warner, "Japanese Art Seen in Its Full Glory," *Boston Evening Transcript*, September 12, 1936, 4; Cortissoz, "Painting and Sculpture of Japan," 10.
65. Philpott, "Exhibition of Japan's Art," 19. Grew to Edgell, October 16, 1936, Grew Letters, A–J, 2, Houghton Library, Harvard University; conversation with Hirota, November 30, 1936, Grew, *Ten Years*, 190; with Emperor Hirohito, February 1, 1937, Grew, *Ten Years*, 204.
66. Lin Yutang, "Philosophic China Faces Militaristic Japan," *New York Times*, December 27, 1936, SM4.
67. "Nature's Smile," *Atlantic Monthly*, April 1937, 502; Ishimoto (Katō) Shidzue [Shizue], *Facing Two Ways: The Story of My Life* (New York: Farrar & Rinehart, 1935), 261.
68. Nathaniel Peffer, "Japan and Germany: Fateful Parallels," *New York Times*, September 13, 1936, SM6.

5. A NEW ORDER IN EAST ASIA (1937–1938)

1. *Kokusai Bunka Shinkokai*, 2.
2. Roosevelt speech, October 5, 1937, *FRUS, Japan*, vol. 1, 381.
3. Grew, January 1, 1937, *Ten Years*, 192; "The Japanese-German Pact," *New York Times*, November 26, 1936, 30.
4. Watsuji Tetsurō, cited in *Sourcebook for Modern Japanese Philosophy: Selected Documents*, ed. David A. Dilworth and Valdo H. Viglielmo (Westport, CT: Greenwood Press, 1998), 259; *Kokutai no hongi: Cardinal Principles of the National Entity of Japan*, trans. John Gauntlett, ed. Robert Hall (Cambridge, MA: Harvard University Press, 1949); Masao Maruyama, *Thought and Behaviour in Modern Japanese Politics* (Oxford: Oxford University Press, 1963), 7. See also Alan Tansman, *The Aesthetics of Japanese Fascism* (Berkeley: University of California Press, 2009), 150–68.
5. Satō address, March 12, 1937, cited in Hugh Byas, "Sato Denies Japan Is Facing a Crisis," *New York Times*, March 12, 1937, 15; Nish, *Japanese Foreign Policy*, 115; and Grew cable to Hull, PSF: Confidential, Telegram #86, FDR Library.
6. See *New York Times* pieces on March 10, 12, 13, 14, 16, 21, and 28, 1937. Grew to Hull, March 13, 1937, PSF: Confidential, Telegram #90, FDR Library.
7. *Philadelphia Inquirer*, January 23, 1937, 14; *Washington Post*, January 31, 1937, 6; February 3, 1937, 11. "No. 1 Japanese," *Time*, February 15, 1937, 61–62.
8. Grew, *Ten Years*, 207; "Helen Keller Hailed as Miracle in Japan," *New York Times*, April 16, 1937, 25. Keller quoted in the *Japan Advertiser*, July 6, 1937, and attached to a letter from Keller's personal secretary to FDR on July 28, 1937, FDR Library, PPF 2169: Helen

Keller. KBS directors' meeting, May 14, 1937, Kokusai bunka shinkoukai rijikai narabini hyougikai gijiroku, Japan Foundation Archives.

9. "Japan Turns toward Peace," *Christian Century*, May 19, 1937, 640; "Japanese Shift Their Foreign Policy," *Business Week*, May 29, 1937, 53; Grew cable to Hull, May 17, 1937, PSF: Confidential, Dispatches, Japan, 3/11/37-3/18/38, FDR Library.

10. *New York Times*, December 13, 1936, XX10; Brandt, "East-to-West," 74. Trade data, FDR Library, OF 197, Japan 1935–1937, and letter, 9/11/37, OF150c, Chinese-Japanese War, January–September 1937.

11. Hugh Byas, "Konoye Urges Unity in Japanese Spirit" and "Konoye Seeks to Unify Japan," *New York Times*, June 5, 1937, 9, and July 11, 1937, 102. Ballantine, June 2, 1937, *FRUS, 1937*, vol. 4, 717; Grew to Hull, May 17, 1937, PSF: Confidential, Japan, 3/11/37-3/18/38, FDR Library.

12. "Konoye Seeks to Unify Japan," 102. Saionji comment cited in Harada Diary, August 13, 1936, reel 1, 1565.

13. Konoe quoted in "Konoye Urges Unity in Japanese Spirit"; Oka, *Konoe*, 53.

14. On Japan-Chinese relations in 1935–1937, see Dryburgh, *North China*, 99–133. Tōjō cited in John Hunter Boyle, *China and Japan at War, 1937–1945: The Politics of Collaboration* (Stanford, CA: Stanford University Press, 1972), 49.

15. James B. Crowley, "A Reconsideration of the Marco Polo Bridge Incident," *Journal of Asian Studies* 22, no. 3 (May 1963): 278; Masamichi Rōyama, *Foreign Policy of Japan: 1914–1939* (Tokyo: JCIPR, 1941), 111. See also Dryburgh, *North China*, 134–67, and Rana Mitter, *Forgotten Ally: China's World War II, 1937–1945* (New York: Houghton Mifflin Harcourt, 2013), 79–97.

16. Hugh Byas, "Accord Is Reached in Peiping Conflict," *New York Times*, July 9, 1937, 1; Hull, *FRUS, Japan*, vol. 1, 321; Hull, *FRUS, 1937*, vol. 3, 148.

17. Hallett Abend, *Chaos in Asia* (New York: Ives Washburn, 1939), 14.

18. Oka, *Konoe*, 54; Crowley, "Reconsideration," 283–85; Eri Hotta, *Japan 1941: Countdown to Infamy* (New York: Knopf, 2013), 31; Grew cable, July 13, 1937, *Ten Years*, 211.

19. Hull statement, OF 150-C, Chinese-Japanese War, 1937, FDR Library. Italics mine.

20. Chiang quoted in *New York Times*, July 20, 1937, 16.

21. Bix, *Hirohito*, 322.

22. "Japanese Occupy Peiping," *New York Times*, August 9, 1937, 1; Konoe statement, *FRUS, Japan*, vol. 1, 336; *New York Times*, August 12, 1937, 18.

23. Abend, *Chaos in Asia*, 265.

24. Barnhart, *Japan Prepares*, 91; Fleisher, *Volcanic Isle*, 139; "Japan and China at War," *Bulletin of International News* 14, no. 5 (September 4, 1937): 3–11; Grew to Hull, August 27, 1937, PSF: Confidential, Telegram #321, FDR Library.

25. Fleisher, *Volcanic Isle*, 137–46; Bix, *Hirohito*, 325; Hirota in *New York Times*, September 5, 1937, 21.

26. Stimson to Hull, August 30, 1937, Papers of Cordell Hull, Library of Congress, Box 41; Hull to Grew, September 2, 1937, *FRUS, 1937*, vol. 3, 508; Grew, September 20, 1937, *Ten Years*, 217–18.

27. *Life*, October 4, 1937; Bruce Bliven, "On Hating the Japanese," *New Republic*, September 22, 1937, 177; *Time*, January 3, 1938.

28. Robert Dallek, *Franklin D. Roosevelt and American Foreign Policy, 1932–45* (Oxford: Oxford University Press, 1979), 148.

29. Text of speech, October 5, 1937, *FRUS, Japan*, vol. 1, 379–83.

30. *New York Herald Tribune*, October 6, 1937. Press conference, October 6, 1937, *The American Presidency Project*, ed. Gerhard Peters and John T. Woolley, http://www.presidency.ucsb.edu/ws/index.php?pid=15478.

31. FDR to Peabody, October 16, 1937, and Col. House, October 19, 1937, *Letters*, 716–19.

32. Grew remarks in John K. Emmerson, "Principles versus Realities," in *Pearl Harbor Reexamined: Prologue to the Pacific*, ed. Hilary Conroy and Harry Wray (Honolulu: University of Hawai'i Press, 1990), 37; Hull to Grew, October 16, 1937, *FRUS, 1937*, vol. 3, 116; Grew diary, October 30, 1937, Harvard Houghton Library; Hornbeck memo, October 7, 1937, *FRUS, 1937*, vol. 3, 596.

33. Dan's comments in Shibasaki, *Kindai Nihon*, 135; Villard to Ishii, *New York Herald Tribune*, October 9, 1937, 14.

34. Hidemaro's comments in "Finds 'Propaganda' for China in America," *New York Times*, October 17, 1937, 39. Konoe penned his letter in September; FDR received it on November 9, 1937; Central Files, 1930–39, RG59, Box 64, NACP. On pamphlet, see Grasso, *Japan's "New Deal,"* 95–98.

35. Nagai Ryūtarō, "Holy War for the Reconstruction of Asia," reprinted in *Nihon Bunka* 10 (November 1937), cited in Saaler and Szpilman, *Pan-Asianism*, 156; text of Saitō radio address, *New York Times*, October 27, 1937, 3; Saitō Chicago address, February 9, 1935, cited in Saito, *Japan's Policies*, 24.

36. Roosevelt's instructions to his envoy, Norman Davis, in Dallek, *Franklin D. Roosevelt and American Foreign Policy*, 152. Edwin L. James, *New York Times*, November 21, 1937, 65. See also Cordell Hull, *The Memoirs of Cordell Hull*, vol. 1 (New York: Macmillan, 1948), 550–55. Conference statement in *Peace and War*, 392–94; Konoe statement in Usui, "Japanese Approaches," 111.

37. Hull memo, November 1937, Hull Papers, Library of Congress, Box 74-75.

38. Hull, December 17, 1937, *FRUS, Japan*, vol. 1, 530; FDR, December 13, 1937, ibid., 523; Fleisher, *Volcanic Isle*, 201. Sanctions in Dallek, *Franklin D. Roosevelt and American Foreign Policy*, 154; Ickes, December 18, 1937, *The Secret Diary of Harold L. Ickes* (New York: Simon & Schuster, 1953), 279.

39. Konoe message and pamphlet (by "Fuko-An"), December 17, 1937, Central Files, 1930–39, RG 59, Box 64, NACP.

40. "President Opposes War Referendum," *New York Times*, December 18, 1937, 3.

41. F. Tillman Durdin, "All Captives Slain," *New York Times*, December 18, 1937, 1; Durdin, "Japanese Atrocities Marked Fall of Nanking [Nanjing] after Chinese Command Fled," *New York Times*, January 9, 1938, 38; C. Yates McDaniel, "Nanking Horror Described in Diary of War Reporter," *Chicago Tribune*, December 18, 1937, 8.

42. *Reader's Digest*, "The Sack of Nanking," July 1938, and "We Were in Nanking," October 1938; H. J. Timperley, ed., *Japanese Terror in China* (New York: Modern Age Books, 1938). The massacre remains a contested topic regarding numbers killed with estimates ranging from forty thousand to two hundred thousand. See Joshua A. Fogel, ed., *The Nanjing Massacre in History and Historiography* (Berkeley: University of California Press, 2000).

43. Boyle, *China and Japan at War*, 55. Suetsugu interview originally published in *Kaizō*, December 11, 1937, and reprinted in *Japan Advertiser*, January 6, 1938.

44. Frederick Moore, *With Japan's Leaders* (New York: C. Scribner's Sons, 1942), 305–7. See also Edward Said, *Orientalism* (New York: Vintage Books, 1979).

45. "Chiang Calls Nation to Fight to Victory," *New York Times*, December 17, 1937, 4. The Nazi Party was drawn to Japan's "dynamism," the German Army had close ties to China, and the Foreign Office sought a balance, recognizing Japanese power while seeking to protect trade with China. See John P. Fox, *Germany and the Far Eastern Crisis, 1931–1938: A Study of Diplomacy and Ideology* (Oxford: Clarendon Press, 1982), 79–290.

46. See Crowley's discussion in *Japan's Quest for Autonomy*, 359–78.

47. Bix, *Hirohito*, 326–31; Robert J. C. Butow, *Japan's Decision to Surrender* (Stanford, CA: Stanford University Press, 1954), 170–75; Hotta, *Japan 1941*, 130.

48. Hugh Byas, "Imperial Council Meets," January 12, 1938, 1. Hotta, *Pan-Asianism*, 161–62; text of statement, *New York Times*, January 16, 1938, 33.

49. Nathaneil Peffer, "Course of War in China Forces Japan to Pause," *New York Times*, January 16, 1938, 65; Bix, *Hirohito*, 343–44; Rōyama cited in Han Jung-Sun, "Rationalizing the Orient: The 'East Asia Cooperative Community' in Prewar Japan," *Monumenta Nipponica* 60, no. 4 (Winter 2005): 505; Grew, February 12, 1938, *FRUS, 1938*, vol. 3, 82.

50. See Fox, *Germany and the Far Eastern Crisis*, 290–331.

51. "Japan Will Set up New Puppet State," *New York Times*, March 23, 1938; Grew to Hull, March 19, 1938, and April 11, 1938, *FRUS, 1938*, vol. 3, 127, 138–39.

52. Hull to Grew, February 3, 1938, *FRUS, 1938*, vol. 3, 65–66; Grew diary, February 10, 1938, *Ten Years*, 243; FDR to Hull, January 28, 1938, *FRUS, 1938*, vol. 4, 250; "Anti-Japanese Boycott Spreads," *Business Week*, January 8, 1938, 24–27.

53. AP story reprinted in "Canton Is Ablaze under New Raids," *New York Times*, June 9, 1938, 1. *Nation*, June 18, 1938, 686. Grew diary, July 1, 1938, *Ten Years*, 249.
54. Poll, June 1938, from Hadley Cantril, ed., *Public Opinion, 1935–1946* (Princeton, NJ: Princeton University Press, 1951), 1186; "A Way of Life," *New York Times*, June 15, 1938, 22; Barzun quoted in Harold E. Stearns, ed., *America Now* (New York: C. Scribner's Sons, 1938), 471. Hull to Grew, February 3, 1938, *FRUS, 1938*, vol. 3, 65–66.
55. On the Price Committee, see Donad J. Friedman, *The Road from Isolation: The Campaign of the American Committee for Non-Participation in Japanese Aggression, 1938–1941* (Cambridge, MA: Harvard University Press, 1970).
56. "Bad feelings" in "Good-Will Institute Set up Here by Japan," *New York Times*, March 29, 1939, 17; Kabayama memo, May 26, 1938, Japan Foundation Archives, Box C (1)-5; *K.B.S. Quarterly*, April 1937–March 1938, 2; and Shibasaki, *Kindai Nihon*, 143–44. *NIPPON* reference in *K.B.S. Quarterly*, April 1937–March 1938, 6; Weisenfeld, "Touring Japan-as-Museum," 770. Figures in Akami, *Internationalizing the Pacific*, 228.
57. Kōsaku Hamada, "Eastern Civilization and Japan," *NIPPON* 14 (1938): 3; Hotumi Ozaki, "China Whither?," *NIPPON* 15 (1938): 35–40; *Almanac* cited in *New York Times*, June 1, 1938, 10.
58. KBS request, April 12, 1938, and State Department reply, April 15, State Department Central Files, 1930–39, RG 59, 811.4279/58, Box 5066, NACP. "Artists Congress Denounces Japan," *New York Times*, December 18, 1937, 22.
59. Konoe statement, "The First Anniversary," *Japan Times*, July 7, 1938.
60. Morgenthau to FDR, October 17, 1938, in *The Presidential Diaries of Henry Morgenthau, Jr., 1938–1945*, FDR Library, reel 1, 44.
61. *FRUS, Japan*, vol. 1, 785–90.
62. Ibid, 477–81.
63. Fletcher, *Search for a New Order*, 115. See also James B. Crowley, "Intellectuals as Visionaries of the New Asian Order," in *Dilemmas of Growth in Prewar Japan*, ed. James W. Morley, 319–73 (Princeton, NJ: Princeton University Press, 1971). "9-Power Pact Held Obsolete by Japan," *New York Times*, November 4, 1938, 1; Arita to Hull, *New York Times*, November 19, 1938, 2.
64. All newspaper accounts from November 3, 1938. On editorial analysis, see Earl Leaf, "Strong and United Support," *Amerasia*, December 1938, 496–501, 512. W. B. Courtney, "Japan's Dictator," *Collier's*, October 1, 1938, 1.
65. Konoe statement in *New York Times*, December 23, 1938, 8. Hugh Byas, "Tokyo Press Calls U.S. Tool of Britain," *New York Times*, December 22, 1938, 1. *Japan's Diplomacy: Its Aims and Principles* (Tokyo: Japan Times and Mail, 1939), foreword.
66. Robbins, "Tokyo Calling," 56–57. Kabayama in Grasso, *Japan's "New Deal,"* 59. Minowa quoted in Shibasaki, *Kindai Nihon*, 152. Cultural agreements in *Japan Advertiser*, November 26, 1938. Tim Cross, *The Ideologies of Japanese Tea* (Leiden: Brill, 2009), 93–94.
67. Morgenthau, *Presidential Diaries*, October 17, 1938, 44.

6. "THIS MAD WORLD OF OURS" (1939–1940)

1. Hotta, *Pan-Asianism*, 173; Bix, *Hirohito*, 350; Akira Iriye, *The Origins of the Second World War in Asia and the Pacific* (New York: Longman, 1987), 73.
2. Carol Gluck, *Japan's Modern Myths: Ideology in the Late Meiji Period* (Princeton, NJ: Princeton University Press, 1985), 4; Reto Hofmann, *The Fascist Effect: Japan and Italy, 1915–1952* (Ithaca, NY: Cornell University Press, 2015), 75, 136; Louise Young, "When Fascism Met Empire in Japanese-Occupied Manchuria," *Journal of Global History* 12, no. 2 (2017): 274–96; and Ethan Mark, "Japan's 1930s: Crisis, Fascism, and Social Imperialism," in *Routledge Handbook of Modern Japanese History*, ed. Christopher W. A. Szpilman and Sven Saaler, 237–50 (London: Routledge, 2017). See also Maruyama, *Thought and Behaviour*, and E. Bruce Reynolds, ed., *Japan in the Fascist Era* (New York: Palgrave Macmillan, 2004).

3. Harada Diary, September 23, 1931, reel 1, 68; Hiranuma speeches in Hugh Byas, "Japan's Leaders Warn World," *New York Times*, January 21, 1939, and in Saaler and Spzilman, *Pan-Asianism*, 196–99.

4. Yonai cited in Abend, *Chaos in Asia*, 214.

5. Pollard's address (December 1938) published as "Dynamics of Japanese Imperialism," *Pacific Historical Review* 8, no. 1 (March 1939): 5–34; Nathaniel Peffer, "Japan Counts the Cost," *Harper's*, September 1937, 356. See also John Dower, *War without Mercy: Race and Power in the Pacific War* (New York: Pantheon Books, 1986), 262–90.

6. Economic data from Morgenthau, *Presidential Diaries*, 66, and A. J. B., "World Sources of Petroleum," *Bulletin of International News* 17, no. 13 (June 29, 1940): 769–76; Hull speech, April 25, 1939, *Peace and War*, 458–60.

7. John Gunther, "This Peace Is a Cheat," *Saturday Evening Post*, November 27, 1937, esp. 65–68.

8. Peter Duus, "Introduction: Japan's Wartime Empire: Problems and Issues," in *The Japanese Wartime Empire, 1931–1945*, ed. Peter Duus, Ramon H. Myers, and Mark R. Peattie (Princeton, NJ: Princeton University Press, 1996), xxiv. See also Yasuba Yasukichi, "Did Japan Ever Suffer from a Shortage of Natural Resources before World War II?," *Journal of Economic History* 56, no. 3 (September 1996): 543–60. Kawakami, *Japan Speaks*, 106–7; Ishii, *Diplomatic Commentaries*, 114.

9. Peffer, "Japan Counts the Cost," 356. Business complaints, FDR Library, OF197, Japan 1935–1937.

10. Morgenthau memo, *Presidential Diaries*, October 17, 1938, 45–46; Hornbeck memo, "predatory advance," quoted in Michael Schaller, *The U.S. Crusade in China, 1938–1945* (New York: Columbia University Press, 1979), 25–26; Hornbeck's memo, December 22, 1938, *FRUS, 1938*, vol. 3, 425–26.

11. Max Hamilton, "The Situation in the Far East," Army War College, Washington, DC, January 6, 1939, RG 59, Box 194, NACP; Michael A. Barnhart, "The Origins of the Second World War in Asia and the Pacific: Synthesis Possible?," *Diplomatic History* 20, no. 2 (Spring 1996): 243.

12. Hamilton, "Situation in the Far East."

13. Text of speech reprinted in *New York Times*, January 5, 1939, 12.

14. Vandenberg, February 1939, quoted in Henry Kissinger, *Diplomacy* (New York: Simon & Schuster, 1994), 385.

15. The Czech rump state became known as the Protectorate of Bohemia and Moravia. The eastern half became a Nazi client state, the Slovak Republic, some of which was ceded to fascist Hungary.

16. *New York Times*, March 17, 1939, 1; ibid., April 1, 1939, 1; Hugh Byas, "Japan Plans Steps to Profit by Crisis," *New York Times*, March 23, 1939, 8.

17. FDR, April 14, 1939, in Morgenthau, *Presidential Diaries*.

18. *New York Times*, April 16, 1939, 1, and April 29, 1939, 1.

19. Roosevelt cited in *New York Times*, May 1, 1939, 1. Wallace comments in *New York Times*, May 3, 1939, 1, 16, and David Allen, "The League of Nations at the New York World's Fair, 1939–40," in *International Organizations and the Media in the Nineteenth and Twentieth Centuries*, ed. Jonas Brendebach, Martin Herzer, and Heidi Tworek, 91–116 (London: Routledge, 2018).

20. *The Japanese Pavilion* by the Japanese Commission to the New York World's Fair (1939), and *Far Eastern Trade* 1 (Spring 1939): 15–17.

21. Russell Porter, "Japan Dedicates Pavilion," *New York Times*, June 3, 1939, 6. Young comment cited in Earl H. Leaf, "Report on Japanese Propaganda in the United States," November 1939, Stanley K. Hornbeck Papers, Box 355, Hoover Institution Archives.

22. "Japan Accepts Bid for Fair Display," *New York Times*, August 22, 1937, N1, 4.

23. See Coox, *Nomonhan*.

24. *New York Times*, June 14, 1939, 1. Shigemitsu cited in Malcolm Kennedy, *The Estrangement of Great Britain and Japan, 1917–35* (Berkeley: University of California Press, 1969), 340.

25. "Japanese Claim a 'Great Victory' in British Talks," *Atlanta Constitution*, July 23, 1939, 1–2. See also *New York Times*, June 15, 1939, 12; June 16, 1939, 1; June 23, 1939, 11; and July 22, 1939, 1. "Women Insulted at Tientsin," *Argus* (Melbourne), June 27, 1939, 1.

26. Johnson to Hull, July 13, 1939, *FRUS, Japan*, vol. 1, 661; Hull and Horinouchi, July 10, 1939, ibid., 656–57.

27. K. K. Kawakami, North American Newspaper Alliance, reprinted in the *New York Times*, October 1, 1940, 5.

28. Hugh Byas, "Treaty Stuns Japan," *New York Times*, July 28, 1939, 1; *FRUS, Japan*, vol. 2, 189–90; Trade statistics from *Time*, August 7, 1939, 50.

29. Morgenthau memo, July 31, 1939, *Presidential Diaries*, 206–7; Abend, *Chaos in Asia*, 26–27.

30. Gallup Poll, July 23, 1939, from George Gallup, *The Gallup Poll* (New York: Random House, 1972), 168.

31. Hearst newspapers, reported by the British embassy, August 8, 1939, "Atlantic Archive," http://archive.atlantic-archive.org/745/. A. Whitney Griswold, "Facing Facts about a New Japanese-American Treaty," *Asia*, November 1939, 615; Nathaniel Peffer, "In an Era of Unreason," *Harper's*, March 1939, 337–43.

32. On Anti-Comintern Pact, see Nish, *Japanese Foreign Policy*, 133–34; and Iriye, *Origins of the Second World War*, 79–81.

33. Roosevelt, *Letters*, 915–16.

34. On anti-interventionism, see Justus D. Doenecke, *Storm on the Horizon: The Challenge to American Intervention, 1939–1941* (Lanham, MD: Rowman & Littlefield, 2003). Lindbergh and Thompson quoted in Lynne Olson, *Those Angry Days: Roosevelt, Lindbergh, and America's Fight over World War II, 1939–1941* (New York: Random House, 2014), 71–72, 79; FDR to Morgenthau, May 20, 1940, *Presidential Diaries*, 563.

35. FDR to Morgenthau, June 30, 1939, *Presidential Diaries*, 157. The four senators had kept neutrality revision bottled up.

36. Gallup Polls cited in *New York Times*, October 14, 1939, 14.

37. Vandenberg quoted in Reynolds, *From Munich to Pearl Harbor*, 66; *New York Times*, November 4, 1939, 1.

38. Memo cited in Grew, *Ten Years*, 294–97.

39. Text of speech, ibid., 289–94.

40. On Japanese perceptions of Grew's dualism, see Harada Diary, November 4, 1938, reel 2, 2324. *Time*, October 30, 1939, 21; Shakespeare, *Hamlet*, Act 2, Scene 2.

41. Grew to Hull, November 4, 1939, PSF: Confidential, Telegram #574, FDR Library; Abend, *Chaos in Asia*, 301–2.

42. *Nichi Nichi*, September 7, 1938, 1, with Grew memo, November 21, 1939, Central Files, 1930–39, RG 59, Box 64, 111.46/39 and 111.46/22, NACP. The State Department created a Division of Cultural Relations in 1938. See Ninkovich, *Diplomacy of Ideas*, 24–60.

43. Leaf, letter to Hornbeck, November 30, 1939, and attachment, "Report," Hornbeck Papers, Box 355, Hoover Institution Archives.

44. Grew to Hull, December 1, 1939, PSF: Confidential, #4359, FDR Library; Grew cable, December 18, 1939, *FRUS, 1939*, vol. 3, 620–22.

45. Hornbeck memo, December 19, 1939, quoted in Chihiro Hosoya, "Miscalculations in Deterrent Policy: U.S.-Japanese Relations, 1938–1941," in Conroy and Wray, *Pearl Harbor Reexamined*, 55–56; Emmerson, "Principles versus Realities," 38.

46. Poll, February 1940, from Cantril, *Public Opinion*, 775, 942. Grew memo, January 15, 1940, *FRUS, 1940*, vol. 4, 958; Hornbeck reply, January 16, 1940, ibid., 961; Hornbeck memo to Hull, May 24, 1940, ibid., 334.

47. Abend, *Chaos in Asia*, 23; Kenneth J. Ruoff, *Imperial Japan at Its Zenith: The Wartime Celebration of the Empire's 2,600th Anniversary* (Ithaca, NY: Cornell University Press, 2010), 17.

48. "Stimson Asks Curb on Arms to Japan," *New York Times*, January 11, 1940 1, 4. "Peril in Embargo Stressed," UP wire published in *New York Times*, March 24, 1940, 21; Hugh Byas, "U.S. Help to China Angers Japanese," *New York Times*, March 9, 1940, 5; Arita statements, February 29, 1940, *FRUS, Japan*, vol. 1, 55.

49. Hull meetings with Horinouchi, January 31 and April 20, 1940, *FRUS, Japan*, vol. 1, 54, 284. On Japan's trade in Latin America, "Japan Invades Latin America," *American Mercury*, March 1935, 299–306. On informal imperialism, see Wolfgang J. Mommsen, *Theories of Imperialism*, trans. P. S. Falla (Chicago: University of Chicago Press, 1977), 86–99. See also William Appleman Williams, *The Tragedy of American Diplomacy* (Cleveland: World Publishing Company, 1959).

50. Hugh Byas, "Japan Looks to Wang to Launch 'New Order,'" *New York Times*, March 31, 1940, 71; Douglas Robertson, "Wang in Inaugural Defers to Japan," *New York Times*, March 31, 1940, 38.

51. "Wang Recognition Is Refused by Hull," *New York Times*, March 31, 1940, 1; "U.S.A.—World's Policeman," *East Asian Review* 3, no. 12 (April 25, 1940): 3–6; "Why Did Japan Intervene in China?," *East Asia Review* 4, no. 2 (May 25, 1940): 3.

52. "Business Plan for KBS' New York Institute," 1940, Box C (1)-5; and "Conclusion," in *Kokusai bunka jigyou no nanakanen (International Cultural Projects in the Past 7 Years)* (Tokyo: KBS, 1940), 3, 61, Japan Foundation Archives. Robbins, "Tokyo Calling," 61–64.

53. *New York Times*, April 9, 1940, 1. See Nagaoka Shinjirō, "Economic Demands on the Dutch East Indies," in *Fateful Choice: Japan's Advance into Southeast Asia, 1941*, ed. James W. Morley, trans. Robert A. Scalapino (New York: Columbia University Press, 1980), 128–29.

54. Fleisher, *Volcanic Isle*, 326.

55. See Ikuhiko Hata, "The Army's Move into Northern Indochina," in Morley, *Fateful Choice*, 158–59, and Nish, *Japanese Foreign Policy*, 144.

56. Hugh Byas, "Japan Demands Vast Sphere," *New York Times*, June 30, 1940, 1.

57. FDR, May 26, 1940, *American Presidency Project*, http://www.presidency.ucsb.edu/ws/?pid=15959.

58. Ibid.

59. See *New York Times*, May 17, 1940, 1, 10.

60. *United States Statutes at Large, 1939–41*, vol. 54, pt. 1 (Washington, DC: US Government Printing Office, 1941), 779–80. David Kaiser, *No End Save Victory: How FDR Led the Nation into War* (New York: Basic Books, 2014), 115–16. *FRUS, Japan*, vol. 2, 211–13.

61. See Kaiser, *No End Save Victory*, 78–80.

7. "SO MANY UNEXPLAINABLE THINGS ARE HAPPENING" (1940–1941)

1. Grew cable to Hull, September 12, 1940, in Joseph C. Grew *Turbulent Era : A Diplomatic Record of Forty Years, 1904–1945* (Boston: Houghton Mifflin, 1952), 1225. On "Don't Miss the Bus!" mindset, see Tōgō Shigenori, *The Cause of Japan* (New York: Simon & Schuster, 1956), 46.

2. Moore, *With Japan's Leaders*, 131; Lu, *Agony of Choice*, 138–45; Hotta, *Japan 1941*, 59; Hull, *Memoirs*, vol. 1, 902.

3. Wilfred Fleisher interview of Matsuoka, *New York Herald Tribune*, July 22, 1940, 1.

4. "Konoye Asserts Japan Will Lead in 'World Order,'" *New York Herald Tribune*, July 24, 1940, 1.

5. John Blum, *Years of Urgency: 1938–1941* (New York: Houghton Mifflin, 1965), 350–53; *FRUS, Japan*, vo. 2, 216–18.

6. Hugh Byas, "Warning to U.S. Is Seen in Tokyo," *New York Times*, September 28, 1940, 1; State Department statement, August 9, 1940, *FRUS, Japan*, vol. 2, 218–20.

7. Lu, *Agony of Choice*, 145–48, 156–57.

8. "Japan's New Order Expanded to Cover Greater East Asia," *New York Times*, August 2, 1940, 1, 7. Ethan Mark, "The Perils of Co-Prosperity: Takeda Rintarō, Occupied Southeast Asia, and the Seductions of Postcolonial Empire," *American Historical Review* 119, no. 4 (October 2014): 1198–99.

9. "Japan's New Order Expanded," 1. Hata, "Army's Move into Northern Indochina," 172–73. Michelson, "Place in the Sun," 247.
10. Lu, *Agony of Choice*, 154–62; Asada, *From Mahan to Pearl Harbor*, 220–21.
11. Tripartite Pact text, Avalon Project, http://avalon.law.yale.edu/wwii/triparti.asp.
12. Ibid. Asada, *From Mahan to Pearl Harbor*, 229; Kawakami, North American Newspaper Alliance, reprinted in *New York Times*, October 1, 1940, 5.
13. Ishii quoted in Michelson, "Place in the Sun," 250; Konoe in Fleisher, *Volcanic Isle*, 45; and Oka, *Konoe*, 105–6. Konoe press conference in Byas, "Warning to U.S.," 1.
14. Hugh Byas, "Japan Warns U.S. to Bow to Axis," *New York Times*, October 5, 1940, 1. Matsuoka, October 13, 1940, quoted in *New York Journal of Commerce*, October 14, 1940. Grew diary, October 22, 1940, *Ten Years*, 347.
15. *NIPPON*, special issue, 24 (1940): 11, 13–14. James J. Halsema, *1940 Japan-America Student Conference Diary*, Center for East Asian Studies, University of Kansas, Electronic Series, no. 1. Leaf to Hornbeck, November 1940, Hornbeck Papers, Box 274, Hoover Institution Archives.
16. Alfred A. Berle, memo, October 17, 1940, *FRUS, Japan*, vol. 2, 115–16; Poll, September 30, 1940, from Cantril, *Public Opinion*, 775; Gallup Poll printed in *New York Times*, October 20, 1940, 41; Warren Cohen, *America's Response to China: An Interpretive History of Sino-American Relations* (New York: Wiley, 1971), 150–51.
17. Knox quoted in Asada, *From Mahan to Pearl Harbor*, 227; FDR speech, *American Presidency Project*, http://www.presidency.ucsb.edu/ws/?pid=15869; Hull speech, October 26, 1940, Department of State, *Peace and War*, 581–91.
18. See Ben-Ami Shillony, *Politics and Culture in Wartime Japan* (Oxford: Clarendon Press, 1991), 3–4; Fletcher, *Search for a New Order*, 57–59; "Japan Is Sad," *Current History*, November 7, 1940, 27; Grew letter to FDR, December 14, 1940, *Ten Years*, 361.
19. See, for example, Hugh Byas in *New York Times*, November 10 and November 12, 1940. Konoe in Ruoff, *Imperial Japan*, 15–17. Kenneth Colegrove, "The New Order in East Asia," *Far Eastern Quarterly* 1, no. 1 (November 1941): 19, 22.
20. "Treaty Concerning Basic Relations between Japan and China, 1940," in *Japan: A Documentary History*, ed. David J. Lu, vol. 2, 420–21 (London: Routledge, 1996).
21. Frank L. Kluckhohn, "U.S. lending China $100,000,000 More," *New York Times*, December 1, 1940, 1. The administration also financed an all-volunteer air force in China. See Schaller, *U.S. Crusade in China*, 65–85.
22. Matsuoka speech, December 19, 1940, *FRUS, Japan*, vol. 2, 123–28; Grew to FDR, December 14, 1940, *Ten Years*, 359–61.
23. FDR, December 29, 1940, *FRUS, Japan*, vol. 2, 173–81; Roosevelt to Grew, January 21, 1941, *Ten Years*, 361.
24. FDR, January 6, 1941, *American Presidency Project*, http://www.presidency.ucsb.edu/ws/index.php?pid=16092.
25. Matsuoka speech, January 21, 1941, reprinted in *Contemporary Japan*, February 1941, 1–6; Konoe comments, January 21, 1941, quoted in *New York Times*, January 22, 1941, 8; Hugh Byas, "Konoe Takes Onus of War with China," *New York Times*, January 28, 1941, 9.
26. *Los Angeles Times*, January 27, 1941, 1; Grew on Matsuoka, January 18, 1941, *Ten Years*, 366; Matsuoka, "Empty Dreams," February 17, 1941, Hull Papers, Library of Congress, Box 74; Grew to Hull, January 22, 1941, PSF: Confidential, Tel. #102, FDR Library; Grew to Hull, January 27, 1941, PSF: Confidential, Tel. #125, FDR Library. Gallup Poll, *New York Times*, February 23, 1941.
27. Henry Luce, "The American Century," *Life*, February 17, 1941, 61–62.
28. FDR address, March 15, 1941, *American Presidency Project*, http://www.presidency.ucsb.edu/ws/?pid=16089. Hugh Byas, "Roosevelt Speech Causes Stir in Tokyo," *New York Times*, March 17, 1941, 5. Stark to Kimmel, April 4, 1941, *Pearl Harbor Attack Hearings*, 79th Congress (1946), Part 16, 2161.
29. Matsuoka quoted in *Contemporary Japan*, May 1941.
30. See Lu, *Agony of Choice*, 197–99.
31. C. Brooks Peters, "Matsuoka Greeted Royally in Berlin, *New York Times*, March 27, 1941, 1; Ribbentrop and Matsuoka, March 27, 1941, BBC Monitoring Service, New School for

Social Research, http://www.ibiblio.org/pha/policy/1941/410327a.html . See also Lu, *Agony of Choice*, 200–203.

32. Konoe quoted in *New York Times*, April 14, 1941, 10.

33. Matsuoka cited in Tōgō, *Cause of Japan*, 78, and Lu, *Agony of Choice*, 219. FDR in *Letters*, 1126.

34. Moore, *With Japan's Leaders*, 178. Nomura quoted in Robert Aura Smith, "The Japanese Don't Understand Us," *American Mercury*, May 1941, 542.

35. *FRUS, Japan*, vol. 2, 398–406. See also Robert J. C. Butow, *The John Doe Associates: Backdoor Diplomacy for Peace, 1941* (Stanford, CA: Stanford University Press, 1974).

36. April 16, 1941, *FRUS, Japan*, vol. 2, 406–10.

37. Konoye Fumimaro, *The Memoirs of Prince Fumimaro Konoye* [Konoe], trans. from the *Asahi Shimbun* (Tokyo: Okuyama Service, 1945). See also Tōgō, *Cause of Japan*, 64–70, and *FRUS, Japan*, vol. 2, 398–402. Hull's nonrecognition statement in "Hull Takes Guarded View of Moscow-Tokyo Accord," *Milwaukee Journal*, April 14, 1941, 4.

38. Konoye, *Memoirs*, 7–13. Hirohito cited, April 21, 1941, in Kido Koichi, *The Diary of Marquis Kido, 1931–45* (Frederick, MD: University Publications of America, 1984), 272 (trans. in Hotta, *Japan 1941*, 56).

39. Waldo Heinrichs, *Threshold of War: Franklin D. Roosevelt and American Entry into World War II* (New York: Oxford University Press, 1988), 50; see also 49–54, 70–78, 96–99. Matsuoka in Hotta, *Japan 1941*, 67–68, 71.

40. Matsuoka "five birds" comment in Otto D. Tolischus, "Matsuoka Rejects Idea of Trip to U.S.," *New York Times*, May 5, 1941, 8. Otto D. Tolischus, "Matsuoka Visions Axis 'Millenium,'" *New York Times*, April 27, 1941, 17. George Sansom, "Liberalism in Japan," *Foreign Affairs*, April 1941, 553.

41. Liaison meetings in Hotta, *Japan 1941*, 111–12. May 12 document, *FRUS, Japan*, vol. 2, 420–37; Hull and Hitlerism, ibid., 411–15; Matsuoka-Grew conversation, May 14, 1941, ibid., 145–48. Hitler's "patience" at this time, in the face of Lend-Lease, stemmed from larger strategic concerns.

42. Hull reply and oral statement, *FRUS, Japan*, vol. 2, 483–94. For an extensive look at the Roosevelt administration's global security concerns in 1941, see Heinrichs, *Threshold of War*. For a revisionist view of the Hull-Nomura talks, see Jonathan G. Utley, *Going to War with Japan, 1937–1941* (Knoxville: University of Tennessee Press, 1985).

43. See FDR campaign speeches on September 11 and October 30, 1940, *American Presidency Project*, http://www.presidency.ucsb.edu/ws/?pid=16005 and http://www.presidency.ucsb.edu/ws/?pid=15887.

44. FDR, May 27, 1941, ibid., http://www.presidency.ucsb.edu/ws/?pid=16120.

45. *New York Times*, June 23, 1941, 16; Hosoya Chihiro, "The Japanese-Soviet Neutrality Pact," in Morley, *Fateful Choice*, trans. Peter A. Berton, 91–94.

46. Matsuoka quoted in *New York Times*, June 24, 1941, 3.

47. Moore, *With Japan's Leaders*, 188; *FRUS, Japan*, vol. 2, 493. Transcripts of Liaison Conferences, June 25, 26, 27, 28, and 30, in *Japan's Decision for War: Records of the 1941 Policy Conferences*, trans. and ed. by Nobutaka Ike (Stanford, CA: Stanford University Press, 1967), 56–77; Matsuoka "great men" comment, June 30, 1941, in ibid., 72.

48. *Japan's Decision for War*, 70–77.

49. Imperial Conference, document and official statements, July 2, 1941, in ibid., 77–92.

50. Tomita Aijiro, governor of Hiroshima prefecture, cited in Harada Diary, May 12, 1938, reel 2, 2113; Konoe, interview, June 29, 1941, by United Press in *New York Times*, June 30, 1941, 7; July 2, 1941, 5; and July 7, 1941, 1.

51. Konoe could not force Matsuoka to resign, so the only way to remove him was for the cabinet to resign. Matsuoka and Tōjō statements, 38th and 39th Liaison Conferences, July 10 and 12, 1941, in *Japan's Decision for War*, 93–102.

52. Lu, *Agony of Choice*, 238–39; Nish, *Japanese Foreign Policy*, 188. On Matusoka's viewpoint, see Tōgō, *Cause of Japan*, 81.

53. US Department of Defense, *The "Magic" Background of Pearl Harbor*, vol. 2, *May 12, 1941–August 6 1941* (Washington, DC: US Government Printing Office, 1977); *New York Times*, July 24, 1941, 6; Welles to Nomura, July 23, 1941, *FRUS, Japan*, vol. 2, 525.

54. FDR to Nomura, July 24, 1941, *FRUS, Japan*, vol. 2, 529; see also FDR, *Letters*, 1189–90.
55. FDR, July 25, 1941, in *Vital Speeches of the Day* 7, no. 21 (August 15, 1941): 664. Moore, *With Japan's Leaders*, 218–19.
56. Japanese troops cited in *New York Times*, July 30, 1941, 4. Konoe referred to increased talk of "encirclement" in Konoye, *Memoirs*; Japanese official quoted in *New York Times*, August 3, 1941, 1, E1.
57. The Atlantic Charter was announced on August 14, 1941. Text, Avalon Project, Yale Law School, http://avalon.law.yale.edu/wwii/atlantic.asp. On the charter, see Elizabeth Borgwardt, *A New Deal for the World: America's Vision for Human Rights* (Cambridge, MA: Harvard University Press, 2005), esp. 14–45. On FDR's consistent condemnation of the colonial system, see Warren Kimball, *The Juggler: Franklin Roosevelt as Wartime Statesman* (Princeton, NJ: Princeton University Press, 1991), 127–57. Nagai commentary in *Japan Times and Advertiser*, September 11, 1941.
58. Konoye, *Memoirs*; Konoe comments recorded by Matsumoto Shigeharu, cited in Marius Jansen, review of *Shōwashi e no ichishōgen*, *Journal of Japanese Studies* 14, no. 2 (Summer 1988): 462–63.
59. *FRUS, Japan*, vol. 2, 550–59; Herbert Feis, *Road to Pearl Harbor: The Coming of the War between the United States and Japan* (Princeton, NJ: Princeton University Press, 1950), 259.
60. Imperial Conference minutes, September 6, 1941, in *Japan's Decision for War*, 133–64.
61. *FRUS, Japan*, vol. 2, September 25, 1941, 637–40, and October 2, 1941, 656–61. Racist references to the Japanese as "vigorous little men" or similar expressions were not uncommon in the American press in the 1930s.
62. Butow, *Japan's Decision*, 267.
63. Tōgō presentation, Imperial Conference, November 5, 1941, in *Japan's Decision for War*, 212. MAGIC intercept #726, Tōgō to telegram to Nomura, November 4, 1941, "Proposal A," Documents Related to World War II, http://ibiblio.org/pha/timeline/411104b.html.
64. *FRUS, Japan*, vol. 2, 740–43.
65. Plan B, November 20, 1941, ibid., 755–56; Tōgō to Nomura, November 22, 1941, *"Magic" Background of Pearl Harbor*, vol. 4, no. 162; FDR statement, paraphrased by Stimson, *SD*, November 25, 1941, vol. 36, 48–49.
66. Welles, October 13, 1941, *FRUS, Japan*, vol. 2, 685; Hull reply, November 26, 1941, ibid., 768–70.
67. Tōgō in *New York Times*, December 1, 1941, 1; Tosh Minohara, "'No Choice but to Rise': Tōgō Shigenori and Japan's Decision for War," in Kimura and Minohara, *Tumultuous Decade*, 258; Tōgō, *Cause of Japan*, 188.
68. Tyler Dennett, "Japan's 'Monroe Doctrine' Appraised," *Annals of the American Academy of Political and Social Science* 215 (May 1941): 62.
69. December 7, 1941, *FRUS, Japan*, vol. 2, 770–92.
70. Shimada, October 30, 1941, cited in Asada, *From Mahan to Pearl Harbor*, 273.

EPILOGUE

1. *FRUS, Japan*, vol. 2, 790, 792. Hirohito comments from the diary of his chamberlain, Ogura Kuraji, December 25, 1941, published by *Bungei shunjū* magazine in 2007.
2. Roosevelt, December 8 and December 15, 1941, *American Presidency Project*. Italics mine.
3. Tōjō quoted in Peter Duus, "Introduction," xxiii; Harry Harootunian, *Overcome by Modernity: History, Culture and Community in Interwar Japan* (Princeton, NJ: Princeton University Press, 2000), ch. 2.
4. Nagai quoted in Abel, "Cultural Internationalism," 37–38.
5. On comparisons between Tokyo's declarations and liberal internationalism, especially the Atlantic Charter, see Iriye, *Power and Culture*, esp. 112–21, and Abel, *International Mini-*

mum, 194–217. Takashi Fujitani, *Race for Empire: Koreans as Japanese and Japanese as Americans during World War II* (Berkeley: University of California Press, 2011), 23.

6. See Borgwardt, *New Deal for the World*, 88–193, and Mazower, *Governing the World*, 191–213.

7. Fujitani, *Race for Empire*, 17. Mark Mazower, *No Enchanted Palace: The End of Empire and the Ideological Origins of the United Nations* (Princeton, NJ: Princeton University Press, 2009), 19.

8. On FDR's pragmatic liberalism, see Kimball, *Juggler*, 185–200. Luce, "American Century," 61–65.

9. On the war's final months, see Richard Frank, *Downfall: The End of the Imperial Japanese Empire* (New York: Random House, 1999), and Tsuyoshi Hasegawa, *Racing the Enemy: Stalin, Truman, and the Surrender of Japan* (Cambridge, MA: Belknap Press, 2006). Stimson knew about Kyoto's cultural treasures since at least the 1920s, when he visited the city. This study suggests that, given the extent of KBS activities in the 1930s, a reasonable inference is that its programs reinforced Stimson's awareness of Kyoto's cultural importance. Still, why did Stimson, after approving the strategic bombing of more than sixty Japanese cities, choose to spare a cultural center? See Jason M. Kelly, "Why Did Henry Stimson Spare Kyoto from the Bomb? Confusion in Postwar Historiography," *Journal of American-East Asian Relations* 19, no. 2 (2012): 183–203.

10. Hirohito surrender speech, https://www.mtholyoke.edu/acad/intrel/hirohito.htm.

11. Truman statement, August 16, 1945, https://www.trumanlibrary.gov/library/public-papers/105/proclamation-2660-victory-east-day-prayer.

12. Officially it was called the "Allied" occupation of Japan, but Gen. MacArthur was the supreme decision maker.

13. The occupation historiography is voluminous. See especially John Dower, *Embracing Defeat: Japan in the Wake of World War II* (New York: W. W. Norton, 1999), and Eiji Takemae, *Inside GHQ: The Allied Occupation of Japan and Its Legacy*, trans. Robert Ricketts and Sebastian Swann (New York: Continuum, 2002). See also Hiroshi Kitamura, *Screening Enlightenment: Hollywood and the Cultural Reconstruction of Defeated Japan* (Ithaca, NY: Cornell University Press, 2010). On race relations, see Yukiko Koshiro, *Trans-Pacific Racisms and the U.S. Occupation of Japan* (New York: Columbia University Press, 1999).

14. See Dower, *Embracing Defeat*, 277–301, and Bix, *Hirohito*, 541–618. Grew, *Ten Years*, 217. See also Masanori Nakamura, *The Japanese Monarchy: Ambassador Grew and the Making of the "Symbol Emperor System "* (Armonk, NY: M. E. Sharpe, 1992). Aoki cited in Shibasaki, *Kindai Nihon*, 128. To this day the Japan Society of Boston bestows an internationalist award in Shigemitsu's name. On Yoshida, see Dower, *Empire and Aftermath*. On the politics of surrender, see Marc Gallicchio, *The Scramble for Asia: U.S. Military Power in the Aftermath of the Pacific War* (Lanham, MD: Rowman & Littlefield, 2008).

15. See Richard Minear, *Victors' Justice: Tokyo War Crimes Trial* (Princeton, NJ: Princeton University Press, 1972), and Yuma Totani, *The Tokyo War Crimes Trial: The Pursuit of Justice in the Wake of World War II* (Cambridge, MA: Harvard University Asia Center, 2009). Hirota was the lone civilian leader to be hanged. Matsuoka died in prison in 1946 from tuberculosis. Konoe committed suicide in December 1945.

16. Yasukuni shrine was founded in 1869 to memorialize Japan's war dead. See especially Akiko Takenaka, *Yasukuni Shrine: History, Memory, and Japan's Unending Postwar* (Honolulu: University of Hawai'i Press, 2015), 131–89.

17. Harley F. MacNair, "Japan and the Pacific," *Review of Politics* 4, no. 3 (July 1942): 353. *Kokusai Bunka Shinkokai: Organization and Program* (Tokyo: Kokusai Bunka Shinkokai, 1949), 1.

18. "The Best from Japan," *New York Times*, January 25, 1953, SM18. Statement by Ambassador Araki Eikichi at the closing of the exhibition, December 11, 1953, "Japanese Art-MISC," Office of the Secretary Records, Metropolitan Museum of Art Archives. Robert S. Schwantes, *Japanese and Americans: A Century of Cultural Relations* (New York: Harper & Brothers, 1955), vii.

19. "Cultural Diplomacy: The Lynchpin of Public Diplomacy," Report of the Advisory Committee on Cultural Diplomacy, US Department of State, Washington, DC (September

2005), https://2009-2017.state.gov/pdcommission/reports/54256.htm. Yudhishthir Raj Isar, "Cultural Diplomacy: An Overplayed Hand?," *Cultural Diplomacy Magazine*, Winter 2010, 29–44.

20. See Douglas McGray, "Japan's Gross National Cool," *Foreign Policy*, May/June 2002, 45–54.

21. See especially Francis Fukuyama, "The End of History?," *National Interest* 16 (Summer 1989): 3–18.

22. See G. Ikenberry, Thomas Knock, Anne-Marie Slaughter, and Tony Smith, *The Crisis of American Foreign Policy: Wilsonianism in the Twenty-First Century* (Princeton, NJ: Princeton University Press, 2011); and Tony Smith, *Why Wilson Matters: The Origins of American Liberal Internationalism and Its Crisis Today* (Princeton, NJ: Princeton University Press, 2017).

Bibliography

PRIMARY SOURCES

Archives

Franklin D. Roosevelt Presidential Library, Hyde Park, New York.
  President Franklin D. Roosevelt Papers.

Houghton Library, Harvard University, Cambridge, Massachusetts.
  Joseph C. Grew Papers.

Japan Foundation, Tokyo, Japan.
  Records of the Kokusai Bunka Shinkōkai (Society for International Cultural Relations).

Japanese Ministry of Foreign Affairs, Tokyo, Japan.
  I.1.10. Associations (KBS).

Library of Congress, Washington, DC.
  Cordell Hull Papers.

Metropolitan Museum of Art Archives, New York.
  Office of the Secretary Records, Japanese Art-MISC.

National Archives and Records Administration, College Park, Maryland.
  Record Group (RG) 59, General Records of the United States Department of State.
  Records of the Department of State Relating to the Internal Affairs of Japan, 1930–39.
  Records of the Department of State, International Cultural Relations/I.
  Records of the Department of State, International Cultural Relations/II.

Yale University Library, New Haven, Connecticut.
Henry Lewis Stimson Diaries.

Published Documents

Appeal of the Chinese Government: Report of the Commission of Enquiry. Geneva: League of Nations Publications, 1932.
Congressional Record. Washington, DC: US Government Printing Office, 1873–.
Department of State. *Papers Relating to the Foreign Relations of the United States* and *Foreign Relations of the United States: Diplomatic Papers* (*FRUS*).
———. *1899*. Vol. 2. Washington, DC: US Government Printing Office, 1899.
———. *1901, Affairs in China*. Washington, DC: US Government Printing Office, 1901.
———. *1904*. Washington, DC: US Government Printing Office, 1904.
———. *The Lansing Papers, 1914–1920*. Vol. 2. Washington, DC: US Government Printing Office, 1914–1920.
———. *1922*. Vol. 1. Washington, DC: US Government Printing Office, 1922.
———. *1924*. Vol. 2. Washington, DC: US Government Printing Office, 1924.
———. *1928*. Vol. 2. Washington, DC: US Government Printing Office, 1942–1943.
———. *1932*. Vols. 3 and 4. Washington, DC: US Government Printing Office, 1947–1948.
———. *1933*. Vol. 3. Washington, DC: US Government Printing Office, 1949.
———. *1934*. Vol. 3. Washington, DC: US Government Printing Office, 1950.
———. *1935*. Vol. 3. Washington, DC: US Government Printing Office, 1953.
———. *1936*. Vol. 4. Washington, DC: US Government Printing Office, 1954.
———. *1937*. Vols. 1 and 4. Washington, DC: US Government Printing Office, 1954.
———. *1938*. Vols. 3 and 4. Washington, DC: US Government Printing Office, 1954–1955.
———. *1939*. Vol. 3. Washington, DC: US Government Printing Office, 1955.
———. *1940*. Vol. 4. Washington, DC: US Government Printing Office, 1955.
———. *1941*. Vols. 4 and 5. Washington, DC: US Government Printing Office, 1956.
———. *Japan: 1931–1941*. Vols. 1 and 2. Washington, DC: US Government Printing Office, 1943.
———. *Peace and War: United States Foreign Policy, 1931–1941*. Washington, DC: US Government Printing Office, 1983.
Documents on the Tokyo International Military Tribunal: Charter, Indictment and Judgments. Edited by Robert Cryer and Neil Boister. Oxford: Oxford University Press, 2008.
F.D.R., His Personal Letters, 1928–1945. New York: Duell, Sloan and Pearce, 1950.
Japan's Decision for War: Records of the 1941 Policy Conferences. Translated and edited by Nobutaka Ike. Stanford, CA: Stanford University Press, 1967.
The Japan Yearbook. Tokyo: Foreign Affairs Association of Japan, 1931–1952.
Kokutai no hongi: Cardinal Principles of the National Entity of Japan. Translated by John Gauntlett. Edited by Robert Hall. Cambridge, MA: Harvard University Press, 1949.
The "Magic" Background of Pearl Harbor. 5 vols. Washington, DC: US Government Printing Office, 1977.
The Papers of Woodrow Wilson. 69 vols. Edited by Arthur S. Link et al. Princeton, NJ: Princeton University Press, 1966–1994.
The Public Papers and Addresses of Franklin D. Roosevelt, 1937. New York: Macmillan, 1941.
United States Statutes at Large, 1939–41. Vol. 54, part 1. Washington, DC: US Government Printing Office, 1941.

Newspapers and Periodicals

Amerasia
American Magazine of Art
American Mercury
Asia

Atlanta Constitution
Atlantic Monthly
Baseball Magazine
Boston Evening Transcript
Boston Globe
Boston Herald
Business Week
Capital Times
Cincinnati Times-Star
Chicago Daily News
Chicago Tribune
Christian Century
Christian Science Monitor
Cleveland Plain Dealer
Collier's
Contemporary Japan
Current History
Detroit Free Press
East Asia Review
Economist
Far Eastern Trade
Fargo Forum
Foreign Affairs
Fortune
Forum
Good Housekeeping
Harper's
Japan Advertiser
Japan Times and Mail
Kalamazoo Gazette
Kansas City Star
K.B.S. Quarterly
Lewistown Morning Tribune
Liberty
Life
Literary Digest
Los Angeles Times
Louisville Courier-Journal
Milwaukee Journal
Milwaukee Sentinel
Nation
National Geographic
New Republic
Newsweek
New York Herald Tribune
New York Sun
New York Times
New York World-Telegram
Nichi Nichi
NIPPON
Oregonian
Osaka Mainichi
Pacific Affairs
Philadelphia Inquirer
Philadelphia Record
Pocatello Tribune

Political Science Quarterly
Reader's Digest
Salt Lake Tribune
San Francisco Chronicle
San Francisco Examiner
Saturday Evening Post
Scribner's Magazine
Seattle Daily Times
Seattle Post-Intelligencer
Spartanburg Herald
Spokane Spokesman Review
Sporting News
Springfield Republican
St. Louis Post-Dispatch
Time
Washington Evening-Star
Washington Post
Wisconsin State Journal

Contemporaneous Publications and Accounts, Including Diaries and Memoirs

Abend, Hallett. *Chaos in Asia.* New York: Ives Washburn, 1939.
Anesaki, Masaharu. *Art, Life, and Nature in Japan.* Boston: Marshall Jones, 1933.
Buck, Pearl. *The Good Earth.* New York: John Day, 1931.
Byas, Hugh. *Government by Assassination.* New York: Knopf, 1942.
Carr, E. H. *The Twenty Years' Crisis, 1919–1939: An Introduction to the Study of International Relations.* New York: Harper & Row, 1964. First published 1939.
Close, Upton. *Behind the Face of Japan.* New York: Farrar & Rinehart, 1934.
Colegrave, Kenneth W. *Militarism in Japan.* New York: World Peace Foundation, 1936.
———. "The New Order in East Asia." *Far Eastern Quarterly* 1, no. 1 (November 1941): 5–24.
Dennett, Tyler. "Japan's 'Monroe Doctrine' Appraised." *Annals of the American Academy of Political and Social Science* 215 (May 1941): 61–65.
Fleisher, Wilfried. *Volcanic Isle.* New York: Doubleday, 1941.
Grew, Joseph C. *Ten Years in Japan: A Contemporary Record Drawn from the Diaries and Private Official Papers of Joseph C. Grew, United States Ambassador to Japan, 1932–1942.* New York: Simon & Schuster, 1944.
———. *Turbulent Era: A Diplomatic Record of Forty Years, 1904–1945.* Boston: Houghton Mifflin, 1952.
Griswold, A. Whitney. *The Far Eastern Policy of the United States.* New Haven, CT: Yale University Press, 1938.
Gunther, John. *Inside Asia.* New York: Harper & Bros., 1939.
Halsema, James J. *1940 Japan-America Student Conference Diary.* Center for East Asian Studies, University of Kansas, Electronic Series, no. 1.
Harada, Baron Kumao. *Saionji-Harada Memoirs, 1931–1941.* Washington, DC: University Publications of America, 1977.
Harada, Jiro. *The Lesson of Japanese Architecture.* New York: Studio Publications, 1936.
Hoover, Herbert C. *The Memoirs of Herbert Hoover: The Cabinet and Presidency, 1920–1933.* New York: Macmillan, 1952.
Hull, Cordell. *The Memoirs of Cordell Hull.* New York: Macmillan, 1948.
Ickes, Harold L. *The Secret Diary of Harold L. Ickes.* New York: Simon & Schuster, 1953.
Ireland, Tom. *War Clouds in the Skies of the Far East.* New York: G. P. Putnam's Sons, 1935.
Ishii, Kikujiro. *Diplomatic Commentaries.* Translated and edited by William R. Langdon. Baltimore: Johns Hopkins University Press, 1936.

Ishimoto, Shidzue. *Facing Two Ways*. New York: Farrar & Rinehart, 1935.
Kawakami, K. K. *Japan's Pacific Policy*. New York: E. P. Dutton, 1922.
———. *Manchukuo: Child of Conflict*. New York: Macmillan, 1933.
Kido, Koichi. *The Diary of Marquis Kido, 1931–45*. Frederick, MD: University Publications of America, 1984.
Konoye [Konoe], Fumimaro. *The Memoirs of Prince Fumimaro Konoye*. Translated from the *Asahi Shimbun*. Tokyo: Okuyama Service, 1945.
Ledoux, Louis. *The Art of Japan*. New York: Japan Society, 1927.
Marquand, John. *Mr. Moto's Three Aces*. Boston: Little, Brown, 1938.
Moore, Frederick. *With Japan's Leaders: An Intimate Record of Fourteen Years as Counsellor to the Japanese Government, Ending Dec. 7, 1941*. New York: C. Scribner's Sons, 1942.
Morgenthau, Henry, Jr. *The Presidential Diaries of Henry Morgenthau, Jr., 1938–1945*. Frederick, MD: University Publications of America, 1981.
Official Guide Book of the Fair, 1933. Chicago: Century of Progress, 1933.
Okakura, Kakuzo. *The Book of Tea*. New York: Putnam, 1906.
Phillips, Henry Albert. *Meet the Japanese*. Philadelphia: J. B. Lippincott, 1932.
Pollard, Robert T. "Dynamics of Japanese Imperialism." *Pacific Historical Review* 8, no. 1 (March 1939): 5–34.
Preininger, Margaret. *Japanese Flower Arrangement for Modern Homes*. Boston: Little, Brown, 1936.
Price, Willard. *Children of the Rising Sun*. New York: Reynal & Hitchcock, 1938.
Rōyama, Masamichi. *Foreign Policy of Japan: 1914–1939*. Tokyo: JCIPR, 1941.
Saito, Hirosi [Hiroshi]. *Japan's Policies and Purposes*. Boston: Marshall Jones, 1935.
Scherer, James A. B. *Japan Defies the World*. New York: Bobbs-Merrill, 1938.
Shotwell, James T. *War as an Instrument of National Policy and Its Renunciation in the Pact of Paris*. New York: Harcourt Brace and Co., 1929.
Snow, Edgar. *Red Star over China*. New York: Random House, 1938.
Stearns, Harold E., ed. *America Now*. New York: C. Scribner's Sons, 1938.
Stimson, Henry L. *The Far Eastern Crisis: Recollections and Observations*. New York: Harper & Bros., 1936.
Stimson, Henry L., and McGeorge Bundy. *On Active Service in Peace and War*. New York: Harper, 1947.
Stoddard, Lothrop. *The Rising Tide of Color against White World-Supremacy*. New York: Scribner, 1920.
Timperley, H. J., ed. *The Japanese Terror in China*. New York: Modern Age Books, 1938.
Tōgō, Shigenori. *The Cause of Japan*. Translated and edited by Togo Fumihiko and Ben Bruce Blakeney. New York: Simon & Schuster, 1956.
Treat, Payson. *Japan and the United States, 1853–1921*. New York: Houghton Mifflin, 1928.
Tupper, Eileen, and George McReynolds. *Japan in American Public Opinion*. New York: Macmillan, 1937.
Utley, Freda. *Japan's Feet of Clay*. London: Faber & Faber, 1936.
Warren, Mrs. [Romayne] Benjamin S. "The Garden Club of America in Japan." *Bulletin of the Garden Club of America*, no. 17 (September 1935): 16–59.
Wright, Frank Lloyd. *An Autobiography*. New York: Longman's, Green, 1932.
Wright, Quincy, and Carl J. Nelson. "American Attitudes toward Japan and China, 1937–38." *Public Opinion Quarterly* 3, no. 1 (January 1939): 46–62.
Young, Eugene J. *Powerful America: Our Place in a Re-arming World*. New York: Frederick A. Stokes, 1936.
Young, James. *Behind the Rising Sun*. New York: Doubleday, 1941.

SECONDARY SOURCES: ARTICLES, BOOKS, DISSERTATIONS

Abel, Jessamyn. "Cultural Internationalism and Japan's Wartime Empire: The Turns of the Kokusai Bunka Shinkōkai." In Kimura and Minohara, *Tumultuous Decade*, 17–43.

———. *The International Minimum: Creativity and Contradiction in Japan's Global Engagement, 1933–1964*. Honolulu: University of Hawai'i Press, 2015.
Akami, Tomoko. *Internationalizing the Pacific: The United States, Japan and the Institute of Pacific Relations in War and Peace, 1919–45*. London: Routledge, 2002.
———. *Japan's News Propaganda and Reuters' News Empire in Northeast Asia, 1870–1934*. Dordrecht: Republic of Letters, 2012.
———. *Soft Power of Japan's War State: The Board of Information and Dōmei News Agency in Foreign Policy, 1934–45*. Dordrecht: Republic of Letters, 2014.
Allen, David. "The League of Nations at the New York World's Fair, 1939–40." In *International Organizations and the Media in the Nineteenth and Twentieth Centuries*, edited by Jonas Rendebach, Martin Herzer, and Heidi Tworek, 91–116. London: Routledge, 2018.
Ambrosius, Lloyd. *Wilsonian Statecraft: Theory and Practice of Liberal Internationalism during World War I*. Wilmington, DE: Scholarly Resources, 1991.
Asada, Sadao. "Between the Old Diplomacy and the New, 1918–1922: The Washington System and the Origins of Japanese-American Rapprochement." *Diplomatic History* 30, no. 2 (April 2006): 211–30.
———. *From Mahan to Pearl Harbor: The Imperial Japanese Navy and the United States*. Annapolis, MD: Naval Institute Press, 2006.
———. *Ryō Taisenkan no Nichi-Bei Kankei* [American-Japanese Relations between the Wars]. Tokyo: Tokyo Daigaku Shuppankai, 1993.
Auslin, Michael. *Pacific Cosmopolitans: A Cultural History of U.S.-Japan Relations*. Cambridge, MA: Harvard University Press, 2011.
Aydin, Cemil. *The Politics of Anti-Westernism in Asia: Visions of World Order in Pan-Islamic and Pan-Asian Thought*. New York: Columbia University Press, 2007.
Azuma, Eiichiro. *Between Two Empires: Race, History, and Transnationalism in Japanese America*. New York: Oxford University Press, 2005.
Baker, Ray Stannard, ed. *Woodrow Wilson, Life and Letters*. New York: Charles Scribner's, 1946.
Barnhart, Michael A. "Hornbeck Was Right: The Realist Approach to American Policy to Japan." In Conroy and Wray, *Pearl Harbor Reexamined*, 65–72.
———. *Japan Prepares for Total War: The Search for Economic Security, 1919–1941*. Ithaca, NY: Cornell University Press, 1987.
———. "The Origin of the Second World War in Asia and the Pacific: Synthesis Possible?" *Diplomatic History* 20, no. 2 (Spring 1996): 241–60.
Baughman, James L. *Henry R. Luce and the Rise of the American News Media*. Boston: Twayne, 1987.
Beers, Burton F. *Vain Endeavor: Robert Lansing's Attempts to End the American-Japanese Rivalry*. Durham, NC: Duke University Press, 1962.
Ben-Zvi, Abraham. *Prelude to Pearl Harbor: A Study of American Images toward Japan, 1940–41*. New York: Vantage Press, 1979.
Best, Antony. *Britain, Japan and Pearl Harbor: Avoiding War in East Asia, 1936–1941*. London: Routledge, 1995.
———, ed. *Imperial Japan and the World, 1931–1945*. London: Routledge, 2010.
Bix, Herbert P. *Hirohito and the Making of Modern Japan*. New York: HarperCollins, 2000.
Blower, Brooke L. "From Isolationism to Neutrality: A New Framework for Understanding American Political Culture, 1919–1941." *Diplomatic History* 38 (2014): 345–46.
Blum, John. *Years of Urgency: 1938–1941*. New York: Houghton Mifflin, 1965.
Borg, Dorothy. *The United States and the Far Eastern Crisis of 1933–1938: From the Manchurian Incident through the Initial Stage of the Undeclared Sino-Japanese War*. Cambridge, MA: Harvard University Press, 1964.
Borg, Dorothy, and Shumpei Okamoto, eds. *Pearl Harbor as History: Japanese-American Relations, 1931–1941*. New York: Columbia University Press, 1973.
Borgwardt, Elizabeth. *A New Deal for the World: America's Vision for Human Rights*. Cambridge, MA: Harvard University Press, 2005.
Boyle, John Hunter. *China and Japan at War, 1937–1945: The Politics of Collaboration*. Stanford, CA: Stanford University Press, 1972.

Brendon, Piers. *The Dark Valley: A Panorama of the 1930s*. New York: Knopf, 2000.
Brinkley, Douglas, and David R. Facey-Crowther, eds. *The Atlantic Charter*. London: Macmillan, 1994.
Brooks, Barbara J. *Japan's Imperial Diplomacy: Consuls, Treaty Ports, and War in China, 1895–1938*. Honolulu: University of Hawai'i Press, 2000.
Buckley, Thomas. *The United States and the Washington Conference, 1921–1922*. Knoxville: University of Tennessee, 1970.
Burkman, Thomas W. *Japan and the League of Nations: Empire and World Order, 1914–1938*. Honolulu: University of Hawai'i Press, 2008.
Burns, James MacGregor. *Roosevelt: The Lion and the Fox*. New York: Harcourt Brace, 1954.
Burns, Richard D. "Cordell Hull: A Study in Diplomacy, 1933–1941." Ph.D. diss., University of Illinois, 1960.
Butow, Robert J. C. *Japan's Decision to Surrender*. Stanford, CA: Stanford University Press, 1954.
———. *The John Doe Associates: Backdoor Diplomacy for Peace, 1941*. Stanford, CA: Stanford University Press, 1974.
———. *Tojo and the Coming of the War*. Stanford, CA: Stanford University Press, 1961.
Cantril, Hadley, ed. *Public Opinion, 1935–1946*. Princeton, NJ: Princeton University Press, 1951.
Cassels, Alan. *Ideology and International Relations in the Modern World*. London: Routledge, 1996.
Chow, Mizumo Hanihara, and Kiyofuku Chuma. *The Turning Point in US-Japan Relations*. London: Palgrave, 2016.
Clark, Christopher. *The Sleepwalkers: How Europe Went to War in 1914*. New York: Harper, 2012.
Cohen, Warren I. *America's Response to China: An Interpretive History of Sino-American Relations*. New York: Wiley, 1971.
———. *The Chinese Connection: Roger S. Greene, Thomas W. Lamont, George E. Sokolsky and American-East Asian Relations*. New York: Columbia University Press, 1978.
———. *Empire without Tears: America's Foreign Relations, 1921–1933*. New York: Knopf, 1987.
Cole, Wayne. *Roosevelt and the Isolationists, 1932–1945*. Lincoln: University of Nebraska Press, 1983.
Conroy, Hilary, and Harry Wray, eds. *Pearl Harbor Reexamined: Prologue to the Pacific War*. Honolulu: University of Hawai'i Press, 1990.
Cooper, John M., Jr. *Breaking the Heart of the World: Woodrow Wilson and the Fight for the League of Nations*. New York: Cambridge University Press, 2001.
———. *Woodrow Wilson: A Biography*. New York: Knopf, 2009.
Coox, Alvin. *Nomonhan: Japan against Russia, 1939*. 2 vols. Stanford, CA: Stanford University Press, 1985.
Costigliola, Frank. *Awkward Dominion: American Political, Economic, and Cultural Relations with Europe, 1919–1933*. Ithaca, NY: Cornell University Press, 1984.
Craft, Stephen G. *V.K. Wellington Koo and the Emergence of Modern China*. Lexington: University Press of Kentucky, 2004.
Cross, Tim. *The Ideologies of Japanese Tea*. Leiden: Brill, 2009.
Crowley, James B. "Intellectuals as Visionaries of the New East Asian Order." In Morley, *Dilemmas of Growth*, 319–73.
———. *Japan's Quest for Autonomy: National Security and Foreign Policy, 1930–1938*. Princeton, NJ: Princeton University Press, 1966.
———. "A Reconsideration of the Marco Polo Bridge Incident." *Journal of Asian Studies* 22, no. 3 (May 1963): 277–91.
Current, Richard N. *Secretary Stimson: A Study in Statecraft*. New Brunswick, NJ: Rutgers University Press, 1954.
Dallek, Robert. *Franklin D. Roosevelt and American Foreign Policy, 1932–1945*. Oxford: Oxford University Press, 1979.

Davidann, Jon Thares. "'Colossal Illusions.'" In *Hawai'i at the Crossroads of the U.S. and Japan before the Pacific War*, edited by Jon Thares Davidann, 42–67. Honolulu: Hawai'i University Press, 2008.

———. *Cultural Diplomacy in U.S.-Japanese Relations, 1919–1941*. Basingstoke, UK: Palgrave Macmillan, 2007.

Dawidof, Nicholas. *The Catcher Was a Spy: The Mysterious Life of Moe Berg*. New York: Pantheon, 1994.

Dickinson, Emily. "XLVII" in *Poems*, Second Series, edited by Thomas W. Higginson and Mabel Loomis Todd. Boston: Roberts Brothers, 1892, 73.

Dickinson, Frederick. "Toward a Global Perspective of the Great War: Japan and the Foundations of a Twentieth-Century World." *American Historical Review* 119, no. 4 (October 2014): 1154–83.

———. *World War I and the Triumph of the New Japan, 1919–1930*. Cambridge: Cambridge University Press, 2015.

Dilworth, David A., and Valdo H. Viglielmo, eds. *Sourcebook for Modern Japanese Philosophy: Selected Documents*. Westport, CT: Greenwood Press, 1998.

Dingman, Roger. *Power in the Pacific: The Origins of Naval Arms Limitation, 1914–1922*. Chicago: University of Chicago Press, 1976.

Divine, Robert. *The Reluctant Belligerent: American Entry into World War II*. New York: Wiley, 1979.

Doak, Kevin. *Dreams of Difference: The Japan Romantic School and the Crisis of Modernity*. Berkeley: University of California Press, 1994.

Doenecke, Justus D. *The Diplomacy of Frustration: The Manchurian Crisis of 1931–1933 as Revealed in the Papers of Stanley K. Hornbeck*. Stanford, CA: Hoover Institution Press, 1981.

———. *When the Wicked Rise: American Opinion-Makers and the Manchurian Crisis of 1931–1933*. Lewisburg, PA: Bucknell University Press, 1983.

Doenecke, Justus D., and Mark A. Stoler. *Debating Franklin D. Roosevelt's Foreign Policies, 1933–45*. Lanham, MD: Rowman & Littlefield, 2005.

Dower, John. *Embracing Defeat: Japan in the Wake of World War II*. New York: W. W. Norton, 1999.

———. *Empire and Aftermath: Yoshida Shigeru and the Japanese Experience, 1878*–Cambridge, MA: Harvard University Press, 1979.

———. *War without Mercy: Race and Power in the Pacific War*. New York: Pantheon Books, 1986.

Drea, Edward J. *Japan's Imperial Army: Its Rise and Fall, 1853–1945*. Lawrence: University Press of Kansas, 2009.

Dryburgh, Marjorie. *North China and Japanese Expansion, 1933–1937: Regional Power and the National Interest*. Richmond, UK: Curzon, 2000.

Duara, Prasenjit. *Sovereignty and Authenticity: Manchukuo and the East Asian Modern*. Lanham, MD: Rowman & Littlefield, 2003.

Duus, Peter. "Introduction: Japan's Wartime Empire: Problems and Issues." In Duus, Myers, and Peattie, *Japanese Informal Empire*, xi–xxix.

Duus, Peter, Ramon H. Myers, Mark R. Peattie, eds. *The Japanese Informal Empire in China, 1895–1937*. Princeton, NJ: Princeton University Press, 1989.

———. eds. *The Japanese Wartime Empire, 1931–1945*. Princeton, NJ: Princeton University Press, 1996.

Eagleton, Terry. *Ideology*. London: Verso, 1991.

Eastman, Lloyd. *The Abortive Revolution: China under Nationalist Rule, 1927–1937*. Cambridge, MA: Harvard University Press, 1974.

Elleman, Bruce A. *Wilson and China: A Revised History of the Shandong Question*. Armonk, NY: M. E. Sharpe, 2002.

Ellis, L. Ethan. *Republican Foreign Policy, 1921–1933*. New Brunswick, NJ: Rutgers University Press, 1968.

Emmerson, John K. "Principles versus Realities." In Conroy and Wray, *Pearl Harbor Reexamined*, 37–46.

Fairbank, John K. *Trade and Diplomacy on the China Coast: The Opening of the Treaty Ports, 1842–1854.* Cambridge, MA: Harvard University Press, 1953.
Feis, Herbert. *The Road to Pearl Harbor: The Coming of the War between the United States and Japan.* Princeton, NJ: Princeton University Press, 1950.
Ferrell, Robert H. *American Diplomacy in the Great Depression.* New Haven, CT: Yale University Press, 1957.
———. *Peace in Their Time: The Origins of the Kellogg-Briand Pact.* New Haven, CT: Yale University Press, 1952.
Finn, Richard. *Winners in Peace: MacArthur, Yoshida, and Postwar Japan.* Berkeley: University of California Press, 1992.
Fletcher, W. Milo. *The Search for a New Order: Intellectuals and Fascism in Prewar Japan.* Chapel Hill: University of North Carolina Press, 1982.
Fogel, Joshua A., ed. *The Nanjing Massacre in History and Historiography.* Berkeley: University of California Press, 2000.
Fox, John P. *Germany and the Far Eastern Crisis, 1931–1938: A Study of Diplomacy and Ideology.* Oxford: Clarendon Press, 1982.
Frank, Richard. *Downfall: The End of the Imperial Japanese Empire.* New York: Random House, 1999.
Friedman, Donald J. *The Road from Isolation: The Campaign of the American Committee for Non-Participation in Japanese Aggression, 1938–1941.* Cambridge, MA: Harvard University Press, 1970.
Fujitani, Takashi. *Race for Empire: Koreans as Japanese and Japanese as Americans during World War II.* Berkeley: University of California Press, 2011.
Fukuyama, Francis. "The End of History?" *National Interest* 16 (Summer 1989): 3–18.
Gallicchio, Marc S. *The African-American Encounter with Japan and China, 1895–1945: Black Internationalism in Asia.* Chapel Hill: University of North Carolina Press, 2000.
———. *The Scramble for Asia: U.S. Military Power in the Aftermath of the Pacific War.* Lanham, MD: Rowman & Littlefield, 2008.
Gates, Rustin. "Pan-Asianism in Prewar Japanese Foreign Affairs: The Curious Case of Uchida Yasuya." *Journal of Japanese Studies* 37, no. 1 (Winter 2011): 1–27.
Gellman, Irwin F. *Good Neighbor Diplomacy: United States Policies in Latin America, 1933–1945.* Baltimore: Johns Hopkins University Press, 1979.
———. *Secret Affairs: Franklin Roosevelt, Cordell Hull, and Sumner Welles.* Baltimore: Johns Hopkins University Press, 1995.
Germer, Andrea. "Visual Propaganda in Wartime East Asia: The Case of Natori Yōnosuke." *Asia-Pacific Journal* 9, no. 20 (May 9, 2011).http://www.japanfocus.org/-Andrea-Germer/3530/article.html.
Gienow-Hecht, Jessica, and Frank Schumacher, eds. *Culture and International History.* New York: Berghahn Books, 2003.
Gienow-Hecht, Jessica C. E., and Mark C. Donfried, eds. *Searching for a Cultural Diplomacy.* New York: Berghahn Books, 2010.
Gluck, Carol. *Japan's Modern Myths: Ideology in the Late Meiji Period.* Princeton, NJ: Princeton University Press, 1985.
Goldstein, Erik, and John Maurer, eds. *The Washington Conference, 1921–22: Naval Rivalry, East Asian Stability and the Road to Pearl Harbor.* London: Routledge, 2012.
Gordon, Andrew. *A Modern History of Japan: From Tokugawa Times to the Present.* New York: Oxford University Press, 2003.
Gorman, Daniel. *The Emergence of International Society in the 1920s.* Cambridge: Cambridge University Press, 2012.
Graebner, Norman A., ed. *Ideas and Diplomacy: Readings in the Intellectual Traditions of American Foreign Policy.* New York: Oxford University Press, 1964.
Grasso, June. *Japan's "New Deal" for China: Propaganda Aimed at Americans before Pearl Harbor.* London: Routledge, 2019.
Gripentrog, John. "High Culture to the Rescue: Japan's Nation Branding in the United States, 1934–1940." In Viktorin, Gienow-Hecht, Estner, and Will, *Nation Branding in Modern History*, 101–23.

———. "Power and Culture: Japan's Cultural Diplomacy in the United States, 1934–1940." *Pacific Historical Review* 84, no. 4 (Pacific Coast Branch, American Historical Association, and University of California Press, 2015): 478–516.

———. "The Transnational Pastime: Baseball and American Perceptions in the 1930s." *Diplomatic History* 34, no. 2 (April 2010): 247–73.

Guthrie-Shimizu, Sayuri. *Transpacific Field of Dreams: How Baseball Linked the United States and Japan in Peace and War*. Chapel Hill: University of North Carolina Press, 2012.

Guttmann, Allen. *From Ritual to Record: The Nature of Modern Sports*. New York: Columbia University Press, 1978.

Han, Jung-Sun. "Rationalizing the Orient: The 'East Asia Cooperative Community' in Prewar Japan." *Monumenta Nipponica* 60, no. 4 (Winter 2005): 481–514.

Harootunian, Harry. *Overcome by Modernity: History, Culture and Community in Interwar Japan*. Princeton, NJ: Princeton University Press, 2000.

Hasegawa, Tsuyoshi. *Racing the Enemy: Stalin, Truman, and the Surrender of Japan*. Cambridge, MA: Belknap Press, 2006.

Hata, Ikuhiko. "The Army's Move into Northern Indochina." Translated by Robert A. Scalapino. In Morley, *Fateful Choice*, 155–63.

Hearden, Patrick J. *Architects of Globalism: Building a New World Order during WWII*. Fayetteville: University of Arkansas Press, 2002.

Heinrichs, Waldo. *American Ambassador: Joseph C. Grew and the Development of the United States Diplomatic Tradition*. Boston: Little, Brown, 1966.

———. *Threshold of War: Franklin D. Roosevelt and American Entry into World War II*. New York: Oxford University Press, 1988.

Heiseg, James W., and John C. Maraldo, eds. *Rude Awakenings: Zen, the Kyoto School, and the Question of Nationalism*. Honolulu: University of Hawai'i Press, 1995.

Herring, George C. *The American Century and Beyond: U.S. Foreign Relations, 1893–2014*. Oxford: Oxford University Press, 2017.

Herzstein, Robert E. *Henry R. Luce, Time, and the American Crusade in Asia*. Cambridge: Cambridge University Press, 2005.

Hirobe, Izumi. *Japanese Pride, American Prejudice: Modifying the Exclusion Clause of the 1924 Immigration Act*. Stanford, CA: Stanford University Press, 2001.

Hoffman, Stanley. "The Crisis of Liberal Internationalism." *Foreign Policy*, no. 98 (Spring 1995): 159–77.

Hofmann, Reto. *The Fascist Effect: Japan and Italy, 1915–1952*. Ithaca, NY: Cornell University Press, 2015.

Hollingsworth, James. "William R. Castle and Japanese-American Relations, 1929–1933." Ph.D. diss., Texas Christian University, 1971.

Hosoya, Chihiro. "The Japanese-Soviet Neutrality Pact." Translated by Peter A. Berton. In Morley, *Fateful Choice*, 44–85.

———. "Miscalculations in Deterrent Policy: U.S.-Japanese Relations, 1938–1941." In Conroy and Wray, *Pearl Harbor Reexamined*, 51–64.

Hotta, Eri. *Japan 1941: Countdown to Infamy*. New York: Knopf, 2013.

———. *Pan-Asianism and Japan's War, 1931–1945*. New York: Palgrave, 2007.

Howard, Michael. "Ideology and International Relations," *Review of International Studies* 15, no. 1 (January 1989): 1–10.

Hu, Shizhang. *Stanley K. Hornbeck and the Open Door Policy, 1919–1937*. Westport, CT: Greenwood Press, 1995.

Hunt, Michael H. *Ideology and U.S. Foreign Policy*. New Haven, CT: Yale University Press, 1987.

———. *The Making of a Special Relationship: The United States and China to 1914*. New York: Columbia University Press, 1983.

Ienaga, Saburo. *The Pacific War: World War II and the Japanese, 1931–1945*. New York: Pantheon Books, 1978.

Ikenberry, G., Thomas, Knock, Anne-Marie Slaughter, and Tony Smith. *The Crisis of American Foreign Policy: Wilsonianism in the Twenty-First Century*. Princeton, NJ: Princeton University Press, 2011.

Iriye, Akira. *Across the Pacific: An Inner History of American-East Asian Relations*. New York: Harcourt, Brace, and World, 1967.
———. *After Imperialism: The Search for Order in the Far East, 1921–1931*. New York: Atheneum, 1973.
———. *China and Japan in a Global Setting*. Cambridge, MA: Harvard University Press, 1992.
———. *Cultural Internationalism and World Order*. Baltimore: Johns Hopkins University Press, 1997.
———. *The Globalizing of America, 1913–1945*. Vol. 3 of *The Cambridge History of American Foreign Relations*, edited by Warren I. Cohen. New York: Cambridge University Press, 1993.
———. *The Origins of the Second World War in Asia and the Pacific*. New York: Longman, 1987.
———. *Power and Culture: The Japanese-American War, 1941–1945*. Cambridge, MA: Harvard University Press, 1981.
Iriye, Akira, and Warren I. Cohen, eds. *American, Chinese and Japanese Perspectives on Wartime Asia, 1931–1949*. Lanham, MD: Rowman & Littlefield, 1990.
Irokawa, Daikichi. *The Age of Hirohito*. New York: Free Press, 1995.
Ito, Michiko. "The Japanese Institute of Pacific Relations and the Kellogg Pact." In *Hawai'i at the Crossroads of the U.S. and Japan before the Pacific War*, edited by Jon Thares Davidann, 68–95. Honolulu: University of Hawai'i Press, 2008.
Jansen, Marius. *The Making of Modern Japan*. Cambridge, MA: Belknap Press, 2002.
Jonas, Manfred. *Isolationism in America*. Ithaca, NY: Cornell University Press, 1966.
Kaiser, David. *No End Save Victory: How FDR Led the Nation into War*. New York: Basic Books, 2014.
Kasza, Gregory J. *The State and the Mass Media in Japan, 1918–1945*. Berkeley: University of California Press, 1988.
Kawamura, Noriko. "Emperor Hirohito and Japan's Decision to Go to War with the United States Reexamined." *Diplomatic History* 31, no. 1 (2007): 51–79.
———. "Wilsonian Idealism and Japanese Claims at the Paris Peace Conference." *Pacific Historical Review* 66, no. 4 (1997): 503–26.
Kelly, Jason M. "Why Did Henry Stimson Spare Kyoto from the Bomb? Confusion in Postwar Historiography." *Journal of American-East Asian Relations* 19, no. 2 (2012): 183–203.
Kennan, George F. *American Diplomacy, 1900–1950*. Chicago: University of Chicago Press, 1951.
Kennedy, David. *Freedom from Fear: The American People in Depression and War, 1929–1945*. New York: Oxford University Press, 1999.
Kennedy, Malcolm. *The Estrangement of Great Britain and Japan, 1917–35*. Berkeley: University of California Press, 1969.
Keys, Barbara J. *Globalizing Sport: National Rivalry and International Community in the 1930s*. Cambridge, MA: Harvard University Press, 2006.
———. "Spreading Peace, Democracy, and Coca-Cola." *Diplomatic History* 28, no. 2 (April 2004): 165–96.
Kimball, Warren F. *The Juggler: Franklin Roosevelt as Wartime Statesman*. Princeton, NJ: Princeton University Press, 1991.
Kimura, Masato, and Tosh Minohara, eds. *Tumultuous Decade: Empire, Society, and Diplomacy in 1930s Japan*. Toronto: University of Toronto Press, 2013.
Kissinger, Henry. *Diplomacy*. New York: Simon & Schuster, 1994.
———. *World Order*. New York: Penguin, 2014.
Kitamura, Hiroshi. *Screening Enlightenment: Hollywood and the Cultural Reconstruction of Defeated Japan*. Ithaca, NY: Cornell University Press, 2010.
Knock, Thomas. *To End All Wars: Woodrow Wilson and the Quest for a New World Order*. New York: Oxford University Press, 1992.
Koshiro, Yukiko. *Trans-Pacific Racisms and the U.S. Occupation of Japan*. New York: Columbia University Press, 1999.

Kushner, Barak. *The Thought War: Japanese Imperial Propaganda*. Honolulu: University of Hawaiʻi Press, 2006.
LaFeber, Walter. *The Clash: A History of U.S.-Japan Relations*. New York: W. W. Norton, 1997.
———. *The New Empire, 1860–1898*. Ithaca, NY: Cornell University Press, 1998.
Lamb, Margaret, and Nicholas Tarling, eds. *From Versailles to Pearl Harbor*. New York: Palgrave, 2001.
Langer, William L., and S. Everett Gleason. *The Undeclared War, 1940–1941*. New York: Harper & Bros., 1953.
Large, Stephen S. "Nationalist Extremism in Early Shōwa Japan: Inoue Nisshō and the 'Blood-Pledge Corps Incident', 1932." *Modern Asian Studies* 35, no. 3 (July 2001): 533–64.
Leuchtenburg, William E. *Herbert Hoover*. New York: Times Books, 2009.
———. *Perils of Prosperity, 1914–1932*. Chicago: University of Chicago Press, 1993.
Levin, N. Gordon. *Woodrow Wilson and World Politics: America's Response to War and Revolution*. New York: Oxford University Press, 1968.
Link, Arthur S. *The Higher Realism of Woodrow Wilson and Other Essays*. Nashville: Vanderbilt University Press, 1971.
———. *Woodrow Wilson: Revolution, War, and Peace*. Wheeling, IL: Harlan Davidson, 1979.
Lu, David J. *Agony of Choice: Matsuoka Yosuke and the Rise and Fall of the Japanese Empire, 1880–1946*. Lanham, MD: Lexington Books, 2003.
Macmillan, Margaret. *Paris 1919: Six Months That Changed the World*. New York: Random House, 2003.
Manela, Erez. *The Wilsonian Moment: Self-Determination and the International Origins of Anticolonial Nationalism*. Oxford: Oxford University Press, 2007.
Mark, Ethan. "Japan's 1930s: Crisis, Fascism, and Social Imperialism." In Szpilman and Saaler, *Routledge Handbook of Modern Japanese History*, 237–50.
———. "The Perils of Co-Prosperity: Takeda Rintarō, Occupied Southeast Asia, and the Seductions of Postcolonial Empire." *American Historical Review* 119, no. 4 (October 2014): 1184–1206.
Maruyama, Masao. *Thought and Behaviour in Modern Japanese Politics*. Oxford: Oxford University Press, 1963.
Matsuda, Takeshi. *Soft Power and Its Perils: U.S. Cultural Policy in Early Postwar Japan and Permanent Dependency*. Stanford, CA: Stanford University Press, 2007.
Matsumura, Masayoshi. *Baron Kaneko and the Russo-Japanese War (1904–05): A Study in the Public Diplomacy of Japan*. Translated by Ian Ruxton. Morrisville, NC: Lulu Press, 2009.
Matsusaka, Yoshihisa Tak. *The Making of Japanese Manchuria, 1904–1932*. Cambridge, MA: Harvard University Press, 2003.
Mauch, Peter. "Revisiting Nomura's Diplomacy: Ambassador Nomura's Role in the Japanese-American Negotiations, 1941." *Diplomatic History* 28, no. 3 (2004): 353–83.
Mazower, Mark. *Governing the World: The History of an Idea, 1815–Present*. London: Penguin, 2012.
———. *No Enchanted Palace: The End of Empire and the Ideological Origins of the United Nations*. Princeton, NJ: Princeton University Press, 2009.
McDougall, Walter. *Promised Land, Crusader State: The American Encounter with the World since 1776*. Boston: Mariner Books, 1997.
Michelson, Mark C. "A Place in the Sun: The Foreign Ministry and Perceptions and Policies in Japan's International Relations, 1931–1941." Ph.D. diss., University of Illinois, 1979.
Minear, Richard. *Victors' Justice: Tokyo War Crimes Trial*. Princeton, NJ: Princeton University Press, 1972.
Minichiello, Sharon. *Retreat from Reform: Patterns of Political Behavior in Interwar Japan*. Honolulu: University of Hawaiʻi Press, 1984.
Minohara, Tosh. "'No Choice but to Rise': Tōgō Shigenori and Japan's Decision for War." In Kimura and Minohara, *Tumultuous Decade*, 258–76.
Mitter, Rana. *Forgotten Ally: China's World War II, 1937–1945*. New York: Houghton Mifflin Harcourt, 2013.

Mommsen, Wolfgang J. *Theories of Imperialism.* Translated by P. S. Falla. Chicago: University of Chicago Press, 1977.
Morison, Elting E. *Turmoil and Tradition: A Study of the Life and Times of Henry L. Stimson.* Boston: Houghton Mifflin, 1960.
Morley, James W., ed. *The China Quagmire: Japan's Expansion on the Asian Continent, 1933–1941.* New York: Columbia University Press, 1983.
———, ed. *Dilemmas of Growth in Prewar Japan.* Princeton, NJ: Princeton University Press, 1971.
———, ed. *Fateful Choice: Japan's Advance into Southeast Asia, 1941.* New York: Columbia University Press, 1980.
Myers, Ramon H. "Japanese Imperialism in Manchuria: The South Manchurian Railway Company, 1906–1933." In Duus, Myers, and Peattie, *Japanese Informal Empire,* 101–32.
Nagaoka, Shinjirō. "Economic Demands on the Dutch East Indies." Translated by Robert A. Scalapino. In Morley, *Fateful Choice,* 125–53.
Najita, Tetsuo, and Harry Harootunian. "Japanese Revolt against the West: Political and Cultural Criticism in the Twentieth Century." In *The Cambridge History of Japan,* vol. 6, edited by Peter Duus, 711–74. Cambridge: Cambridge University Press, 1989.
Nakamura, Masanori. *The Japanese Monarchy: Ambassador Grew and the Making of the "Symbol Emperor System."* Armonk, NY: M. E. Sharpe, 1992.
Neu, Charles. *The Troubled Encounter: The U.S. and Japan.* New York: Wiley, 1975.
Neumann, William L. *America Encounters Japan: From Perry to MacArthur.* Baltimore: Johns Hopkins University Press, 1963.
Ngai, Mae M. "The Architecture of Race in American Immigration Law: A Reexamination of the Immigration Act of 1924." *Journal of American History* 86, no. 1 (June 1999): 67–92.
Ninkovich, Frank A. *The Diplomacy of Ideas: U.S. Foreign Policy and Cultural Relations, 1938–1950.* New York: Cambridge University Press, 1981.
———. *Global Dawn: The Cultural Foundation of American Internationalism, 1865–1890.* Cambridge, MA: Harvard University Press, 2009.
———. *The Global Republic: America's Inadvertent Rise to World Power.* Chicago: University of Chicago Press, 2014.
———. *The Wilsonian Century: U.S. Foreign Policy since 1900.* Chicago: University of Chicago Press, 1999.
Nish, Ian. *Japanese Foreign Policy, 1869–1942: Kasumigaseki to Miyakezaka.* London: Routledge & Kegan Paul, 1977.
———. *Japanese Foreign Policy in the Interwar Period.* Westport, CT: Praeger, 2002.
———. *Japan's Struggle with Internationalism: Japan, China, and the League of Nations, 1931–3.* London: Routledge & Kegan Paul, 1993.
Nye, Joseph S., Jr. "Soft Power." *Foreign Policy,* no. 80 (Autumn 1990): 153–71.
Oblas, Peter B. "Accessing British Empire-US Diplomacy from Japan: Friendship, Discourse, Network, and the Manchurian Crisis." *Journal of American and Canadian Studies,* no. 21 (2004): 27–64.
O'Connor, Peter. *The English-Language Press Networks of East Asia, 1918–1945.* Folkestone, UK: Global Oriental, 2010.
Ogata, Sadako N. *Defiance in Manchuria: The Making of Japanese Foreign Policy, 1931–1932.* Westport, CT: Greenwood Press, 1984. First published 1964.
Oka, Yoshitake. *Konoe Fumimaro: A Political Biography.* Translated by Shumpei Okamoto and Patricia Murray. Tokyo: University of Tokyo Press, 1983.
Olson, Lynne. *Those Angry Days: Roosevelt, Lindbergh, and America's Fight over World War II, 1939–1941.* New York: Random House, 2014.
Osgood, Robert. *Ideals and Self-Interest in American Foreign Relations: The Great Transformation of the Twentieth Century.* Chicago: University of Chicago Press, 1953.
Ota, Yuzo. "Difficulties Faced by Native Japan Interpreters." In Gienow-Hecht and Donfried, *Searching for a Cultural Diplomacy,* 189–211.
Paine, S. C. M. *The Japanese Empire: Grand Strategy from the Meiji Restoration to the Pacific War.* Cambridge: Cambridge University Press, 2017.

Pash, Sidney L. *The Currents of War: A New History of American-Japanese Relations, 1899–1941*. Lexington: University Press of Kentucky, 2014.
Payne, Stanley. *A History of Fascism, 1914–1945*. Madison: University of Wisconsin Press, 1996.
Peattie, Mark R. *Ishiwara Kanji and Japan's Confrontation with the West*. Princeton, NJ: Princeton University Press, 1975.
Pelz, Stephen. *Race to Pearl Harbor: The Failure of the Second London Naval Conference and the Onset of World War II*. Cambridge, MA: Harvard University Press, 1974.
Plamenatz, John. *Ideology*. London: Palgrave Macmillan, 1970.
Rappaport, Armin. *Henry L. Stimson and Japan, 1931–33*. Chicago: University of Chicago Press, 1963.
Reischauer, Edwin O. *Japan Society, 1907–1982*. New York: Japan Society, 1982.
———. "What Went Wrong?" In Morley, *Dilemmas of Growth*, 489–510.
Reynolds, David. *From Munich to Pearl Harbor: Roosevelt's America and the Origins of the Second World War*. Chicago: Ivan R. Dee, 2002.
Reynolds, E. Bruce, ed. *Japan in the Fascist Era*. New York: Palgrave Macmillan, 2004.
Rickman, Barney Jordan. "The Japan Connection: The Ideology of American Co-operation with Japan, 1922–1952." Ph.D. diss., University of Connecticut, 1990.
Rimer, J. Thomas, ed. *Culture and Identity: Japanese Intellectuals during the Interwar Years*. Princeton, NJ: Princeton University Press, 1990.
Robbins, Jane. *Tokyo Calling: Japanese Overseas Radio Broadcasting 1937–1945*. Florence: European Press, 2001.
Rosenberg, Emily. *Financial Missionaries to the World: The Politics and Culture of Dollar Diplomacy, 1900–1930*. Cambridge, MA: Harvard University Press, 1999.
———. *Spreading the American Dream: American Economic and Cultural Expansion, 1890–1945*. New York: Hill & Wang, 1982.
Ruoff, Kenneth J. *Imperial Japan at Its Zenith: The Wartime Celebration of the Empire's 2,600th Anniversary*. Ithaca, NY: Cornell University Press, 2010.
Rydell, Robert. *World of Fairs*. Chicago: University of Chicago Press, 1993.
Saaler, Sven, and J. Victor Koschmann, eds. *Pan-Asianism in Modern Japanese History: Colonialism, Regionalism and Borders*. London: Routledge, 2006.
Saaler, Sven, and Christopher W. A. Szpilman, eds., *Pan-Asianism: A Documentary History, 1920–Present*. 2 vols. Lanham, MD: Rowman & Littlefield, 2011.
Said, Edward. *Orientalism*. New York: Vintage Books, 1979.
Schaller, Michael. *American Occupation of Japan: Origins of the Cold War in Asia*. New York: Oxford University Press, 1985.
———. *The U.S. Crusade in China, 1938–1945*. New York: Columbia University Press, 1979.
Schoultz, Lars. *Beneath the United States: A History of U.S. Policy toward Latin America*. Cambridge, MA: Harvard University Press, 1998.
Schroeder, Paul W. *The Axis Alliance and Japanese-American Relations, 1941*. Ithaca, NY: Cornell University Press, 1958.
Schwantes, Robert S. *Japanese and Americans: A Century of Cultural Relations*. New York: Harper, 1955.
Scully, Eileen. *Bargaining with the State from Afar: American Citizenship in Treaty Port China, 1844–1942*. New York: Columbia University Press, 2001.
Shibasaki, Atsushi. *Kindai Nihon to kokusai bunka kōryū: Kokusai Bunka Shinkōkai no sōsetsu to tenkai* [International Cultural Relations and Modern Japan: History of Kokusai Bunka Shinkōkai, 1934–1945]. Tokyo: Yūshindō Kōbunsha, 1999.
Shibusawa, Naoko. *America's Geisha Ally: Reimagining the Japanese Enemy*. Cambridge, MA: Harvard University Press, 2010.
Shillony, Ben-Ami. *Politics and Culture in Wartime Japan*. Oxford: Clarendon Press, 1991.
Shimada, Toshihiko. "Designs on North China, 1933–1937." Translated by J. B. Crowley. In Morley, *China Quagmire*, 11–232.
Shimazu, Naoko. *Japan, Race and Equality: The Racial Equality Proposal of 1919*. New York: Routledge, 1998.

———. *Japanese Society at War: Death, Memory and the Russo-Japanese War*. Cambridge: Cambridge University Press, 2009.
Slotkin, Richard. *Gunfighter Nation: The Myth of the Frontier in Twentieth-Century America*. Norman: University of Oklahoma Press, 1998.
Sluga, Glenda. *Internationalism in the Age of Nationalism*. Philadelphia: University of Pennsylvania Press, 2013.
Smith, Tony. *Why Wilson Matters: The Origins of American Internationalism and Its Crisis Today*. Princeton, NJ: Princeton University Press, 2017.
Stoler, Mark A. *Allies in War: Britain and America against the Axis Powers, 1940–1945*. London: Hodder Arnold, 2005.
Stone, Jacqueline. "Japanese Lotus Millennialism." In *Millennialism, Persecution, and Violence*, edited by Catherine Wessinger, 261–74. Syracuse, NY: Syracuse University Press, 2000.
Susman, Warren. *Culture as History*. New York: Pantheon, 1984.
Sykes, Alan. *The Rise and Fall of British Liberalism*. London: Longman, 1997.
Szpilman, Christopher W. A., and Sven Saaler, eds. *Handbook of Modern Japanese History*. London: Routledge, 2017.
Takemae, Eiji. *Inside GHQ: The Allied Occupation of Japan and Its Legacy*. Translated by Robert Ricketts and Sebastian Swann. New York: Continuum, 2002.
Takenaka, Akiko. *Yasukuni Shrine: History, Memory, and Japan's Unending Postwar*. Honolulu: University of Hawai'i Press, 2015.
Tanaka, Stefan. *Japan's Orient: Rendering Pasts into History*. Berkeley: University of California Press, 1993.
Tansman, Alan. *The Aesthetics of Japanese Fascism*. Berkeley: University of California Press, 2009.
Thorne, Christopher. *The Limits of Foreign Policy: The West, the League and the Far Eastern Crisis of 1931–1933*. London: Hamilton, 1972.
Tipton, Elise K., and Clark, John, eds. *Being Modern in Japan: Culture and Society from the 1910s to the 1930s*. Honolulu: University of Hawai'i Press, 2000.
Toland, John. *The Decline and Fall of the Japanese Empire, 1936–1945*. New York: Random House, 1970.
Tooze, Adam. *The Deluge: The Great War, America and the Remaking of the Global Order, 1916–1931*. London: Penguin, 2014.
Totani, Yuma. *The Tokyo War Crimes Trial: The Pursuit of Justice in the Wake of World War II*. Cambridge, MA: Harvard University Asia Center, 2009.
Tsuchida, Akio. "China's 'Public Diplomacy' toward the United States before Pearl Harbor." *Journal of American-East Asian Relations* 17 (2010): 35–55.
Tuchman, Barbara. *Stilwell and the American Experience in China, 1911–1945*. New York: Macmillan, 1970.
Usui, Katsumi. "Japanese Approaches to China in the 1930s: Two Alternatives." In Iriye and Cohen, *American, Chinese, and Japanese Perspectives*, 93–116.
Utley, Jonathan G. *Going to War with Japan, 1937–1941*. Knoxville: University of Tennessee Press, 1985.
Viktorin, Carolin, Jessica C. E. Gienow-Hecht, Annika Estner, and Marcel K. Will, eds. *Nation Branding in Modern History*. New York: Berghahn Books, 2018.
Waldron, Arthur, ed. *How the Peace Was Lost: The 1935 Memorandum Developments Affecting American Policy in the Far East, Prepared for the State Department by John Van Antwerp MacMurray*. Stanford, CA: Hoover Institution Press, 1992.
Weinberg, Albert. *Manifest Destiny*. Baltimore: Johns Hopkins Press, 1935.
Weisenfeld, Gennifer. "Touring Japan-as-Museum: *NIPPON* and Other Japanese Imperialist Travelogues." *Positions* 8, no. 3 (Winter 2000): 747–93.
Wilkins, Mira. "The Role of Business." In Borg and Okamoto, *Pearl Harbor as History*, 341–76.
Williams, William Appleman. *The Tragedy of American Diplomacy*. Cleveland: World, 1959.
Wilson, Sandra. "Containing the Crisis: Japan's Diplomatic Offensive in the West, 1931–1933." *Modern Asian Studies* 29, no. 2 (May 1995): 337–72.

———. *The Manchurian Crisis and Japanese Society, 1931–33*. New York: Routledge, 2001.
Woolley, John T., and Gerhard Peters, eds. *The American Presidency Project*. https://www.presidency.ucsb.edu/.
Yamamoto, Eriko. "Cheers for Japanese Athletes: The 1932 Los Angeles Olympics and the Japanese American Community." *Pacific Historical Review* 69, no. 3 (August 2000): 399–430.
Yasuba, Yasukichi. "Did Japan Ever Suffer from a Shortage of Natural Resources before World War II?" *Journal of Economic History* 56, no. 3 (September 1996): 543–60.
Yoshihashi, Takehiko. *Conspiracy at Mukden: The Rise of the Japanese Military*. New Haven, CT: Yale University Press, 1963.
Young, Louise. *Japan's Total Empire: Manchuria and the Culture of Wartime Imperialism*. Berkeley: University of California Press, 1998.
———. "When Fascism Met Empire in Japanese-Occupied Manchuria." *Journal of Global History* 12, no. 2 (2017): 274–96.
Zeiler, Thomas W. *Unconditional Defeat: Japan, America, and the End of World War II*. Lanham, MD: Rowman & Littlefield, 2003.

Index

Abe Nobuyuki, 167, 169, 170, 172
Abend, Hallett, 41, 156, 166, 169, 172
Alliance Française, 82
America-Japan Society, 81, 151, 169, 188
American Artists Congress, 147
American Committee for Non-Participation in Japanese Aggression, 145–146, 170
Amō Doctrine, 85, 118
Amō Eiji, 77, 86, 87, 89, 112, 114; "bombshell" press conference and, 84–85; Hirota's Three Principles clarified by, 112; on Nine-Power Treaty, 113; on propaganda, 83
Anglo-Japanese alliance, 23, 220n29
Anesaki Masaharu, 83, 90, 99–100, 119
Anti-Comintern Pact (1936), 123, 126, 166
Aoki Setsuichi, 100, 214
Araki Eikichi, 215
Araki Sadao, 77
Arita-Craigie settlement, 164
Arita Hachirō, 45, 148, 150, 164, 174, 176; on German occupation of Czechoslovakia, 160; on Nine-Power Treaty, 149; Pan-Asianist address by, 176–177
Arsène-Henry, Charles, 176, 184
Article X, 16, 38–39
Asano Ryōzō, 82
Asian Monroe Doctrine, 85–86, 115, 160
Asia-Pacific War, casualties, 1; Pacific theater and, 1, 210, 212. *See also* Sino-Japanese War
Atlantic Charter, 177, 203, 211
Australia, 19, 31
Austria, 148, 151
Axis Pact. *See* Tripartite Pact

balance of power system, 3, 14, 17, 19–20
Baldwin, Stanley, 51
Ballantine, Joseph W., 129
Barzun, Jacques, 145
Baty, Thomas, 78
The Beatles, 216
Beijing, 18, 19, 31, 38, 42, 107, 113; Sino-Japanese War and, 131, 133, 144, 147
Belgium, 20, 50, 139, 176
Bell, Edward Price, 92
Berlin, 1936 Olympics, 118
Bisson, T. A., 81
Borah, William E., 24, 40, 51
Boxer Rebellion, 25, 131
Bretton Woods conference (1944), 211, 212
Briand, Aristide, 24, 32, 33. *See also* Kellogg-Briand pact
British Council, 212, 226n35
Brussels conference (1937), 139
Buck, Pearl, 135
Bulkley, Sarah, 102–103
Burma, 211

Burma Road, 176
Byas, Hugh, 17, 62, 100, 129, 131, 143, 150, 172, 185, 190, 191; on February 26 incident, 116; Grew's relationship with, 108; Hiranuma labeled a fascist by, 155; on Japan in North China, 108, 114; on Konoe's appointment, 129; on Wang government, 174

Carnegie Endowment for International Peace, 32
Carnegie Foundation, 82
Chamberlain, Neville, 148, 160
Changchun, 52, 107
Chiang Kai-shek, 113, 134, 141, 153, 158, 172, 174, 204, 206; on cover of *Time*, 135; evacuation to Chongqing, 149; evacuation to Wuhan, 139; Jiangxi speech by, 132, 133; Konoe government frustration with, 143; Northern Expedition and, 42
Chicago, 75, 88, 136, 138–139
China, 22, 31, 126, 149, 150, 162, 174, 184; as alleged violator of Japanese rights, 43, 45, 52, 60; American bias toward, 29, 73, 90, 135, 144, 145, 166; disunity of, 31, 59; Japan trade with, 157; leased territories and, 11, 18, 25–27, 41; nationalism of, 19, 41–42, 131; Paris Peace Conference and, 18–19; as potential tinderbox, 22, 25; territorial integrity of, 18, 25, 28, 43, 48, 85, 149, 158, 171, 188; Twenty-One Demands imposed on, 18, 27. *See also* Sino-Japanese War; Kuomintang
China War. *See* Sino-Japanese War
Chongqing, 139, 149, 153, 164
Churchill, Winston, 176, 203
Clemenceau, Georges, 15, 17
collective security. *See* liberal internationalism
Communist Party, China (CCP), 31, 43, 107, 133
Conant, James B., 119
Congress of Vienna, 3, 13, 14
Coolidge, Calvin, 33
Cortissoz, Royal, 120, 121
Council on Foreign Relations, 55, 89, 215
Craigie, Robert, 144, 164

cultural diplomacy. *See* soft power; Kokusai Bunka Shinkōkai
cultural internationalism, 82
Czechoslovakia, 148, 151, 160

Dalian, 41, 77
Dan Inō, 83, 100, 119, 163, 214
Dan Takuma, 45, 53
Debuchi Katsuji, 11–12, 36, 37, 56, 65, 74
Dennett, Tyler, 207
destroyers-for-bases deal, 187
DeWolf Perry, James, 81
DiMaggio, Joe, 104
Dodd, William, 113–114
Dōmei News Agency, 110–111, 215
Draft Understanding, 7, 194–197, 201, 205
dualistic impressions of Japan, 7, 44, 53, 69, 73, 75, 96, 110, 150, 213; Byas and, 108, 116, 129; Grew and, 68, 77, 80, 85, 95, 108, 116, 132, 171, 214; skepticism about, 114, 133, 159, 171–172, 197
Dumbarton Oaks Conference (1944), 211–212
Dutch East Indies, 89, 175–176, 178, 190, 196, 204, 206

East Hebei Autonomous Council, 113, 131
Edgell, George, 122
Egypt, 127, 161
Emmerson, John K., 172
Ethiopia, 108, 113, 151

February 26 incident, 115–116
Finland, 171
Five-Power Treaty (1922), 23–25
Fleisher, Wilfred, 86, 134
Forbes, W. Cameron, 39, 48
Formosa. *See* Taiwan
Four Freedoms (1941), 154, 189–190
Four-Power Treaty (1922), 23, 25
Four Principles, 195, 196, 197, 203–204, 206
Fourteen Points (1918), 15, 15–16, 22, 28, 162
France, 18, 24–25, 40, 117, 148, 166, 167; Germany conquest of, 176, 178–179; Paris Peace Conference and, 15; Vichy government, 184, 201

French Indochina, 176, 184, 196, 201–202, 203–204, 205–207
Fundamentals of Our National Polity, 127

Garden Club of America, 100, 100–103, 102
Garner, John N., 89, 112
Gentlemen's Agreement of 1907, 30
George, David Lloyd, 14, 15, 23
Germany, 40, 153, 157, 201, 207; Anti-Comintern Pact and, 123, 126, 166; cultural agreement with Japan, 151; Manchukuo recognized by, 144; Munich conference and, 148; neighboring countries invaded by, 160, 166, 175–176, 178–179, 198, 199; non-aggression pact with Soviets, 166; Paris Peace Conference and, 15, 17; Shandong and, 18; Sino-Japanese War and, 132, 142; Tripartite Pact and, 184–185, 186–187, 197; Versailles Treaty violated by, 108, 117
Gō Seinosuke, 45
Goebbels, Joseph, 126, 185
Good Neighbor policy, 86
Great Britain, 29, 42, 43, 109, 210; Brussels conference and, 139; imperialism and, 18, 45, 89, 156, 203; lend-lease and, 189, 191; Manchurian crisis and, 40, 48, 50, 51, 52; Munich conference and, 148, 160; naval limitation and, 22–25, 34–35, 93; as obstruction to Japan's regionalism, 200, 205, 207, 209, 212; tensions with Japan, 150, 164, 176; Twenty-One Demands and, 18
Great Depression, 39, 42–43, 55, 73
Great Kantō earthquake, 29, 30
Greater Asia Association, 79, 141
Greater East Asia Co-Prosperity Sphere, 185, 189, 190, 199, 202, 210; Arita preliminary declaration of, 176; Hirohito surrender address and, 212–213; Matsuoka declaration of, 183–184; Matsuoka foreshadowing of, 60; 1941 Imperial Conference and, 200; Tōjō government and, 205–206, 211; Tokyo War Tribunal and, 214

Grew, Joseph C., 6, 68–69, 70, 181, 188; in conflict with Hornbeck, 137, 171–172; dualistic view of Japan by, 68, 77, 80, 85, 95, 108, 116, 132, 171, 186, 214; "Horse's Mouth" speech and, 168–169; on importance of Byas relationship, 108; on Japanese belligerency, 126, 134, 135, 145, 148, 169, 189, 190; on Japanese Special Exhibition of Art, 122; on KBS, 88, 103; as upset by Quarantine speech, 137
Griswold, A. Whitney, 166
Guam, 14, 25, 210
Guangzhou, 77, 145, 146, 147, 149
Gunther, John, 157
Guomindang. *See* Kuomintang

Hamaguchi Osachi, 35, 36, 42, 52, 93
Hamilton, Maxwell M., 77–79, 158–159, 170
Hamlet, 169, 206
Hanihara Masanao, 30
Harbin, 77, 133
Harding, Warren G., 21–23
Harvard University tercentenary, 119
have-not grievances. *See* realpolitik
Hawai'i, 14, 31, 175, 178, 207
Hay, John, 25–27, 28. *See also* Open Door policy
Hayashi Senjurō, 127, 128
Hearst, William Randolph, 136, 162, 166
Hebei-Chahar Political Council, 107–108, 131, 132
Hiranuma Kiichirō, 154–155, 164, 165, 166
Hirohito, Emperor Shōwa: cause of war with US explained by, 209, 212–213; Draft Understanding and Axis Pact linkage made by, 196; imperial conferences and, 142–143, 185, 200, 204, 205, 207; improved US-Japan relations desired by, 74, 112, 129; Japanese art loaned by, 119; Manchurian crisis and, 52, 66; Manchurian Incident and, 11, 41, 45, 48; Sino-Japanese War and, 132, 133, 134–135
Hiroshima, 1, 212

Hirota Kōki, 45, 67, 76, 91–92, 140, 143, 144, 241n15; China policy and, 80, 85, 114, 144; FDR criticized by, 114; Five-Ministers Conference (1936) and, 118; as perceived moderate, 75–76, 80, 85, 95, 116; soft power and, 79, 80–84, 87–88, 89, 93, 100, 103, 110, 112; Three Principles of, 112–113, 114

Hitler, Adolf, 108, 117, 160, 166, 206; mocking reply to FDR by, 160–161; Munich conference and, 148; popularity in Japan, 115, 148, 151, 181, 184–185, 192–193, 196–197, 199

Holmes, Edward J., 119, 122

Hong Kong, 148, 210

Hoover, Herbert, 35, 39, 58, 86, 93; Manchurian crisis and, 39, 40, 47, 50, 55

Horinouchi Kensuke, 75, 164, 165, 174

Hornbeck, Stanley H., 48, 71, 72, 81, 107, 108, 117, 146, 170; Grew's views in conflict with, 95, 137, 171–172; Konoe meeting with FDR opposed by, 203; recommends material pressure on Japan, 158, 182; on sanctity of postwar treaties, 65, 113; suspicion of goodwill trips and, 77, 82; visited by Kabayama, 111

House, Edward M., 89, 109–110, 137

Howard, Roy W., 74

Hughes, Charles Evans, 22–24, 26, 28, 30

Hull, Cordell, 68, 69, 86, 89, 115, 137, 145, 168, 170, 187, 190, 199; commencement addresses on treaty system by, 108–109; exchanges goodwill messages with Hirota, 80–81; Four Principles of, 195, 196, 197, 203–204, 206; on Japanese expansionism, 117, 139, 164–165, 174, 201; Konoe meeting with FDR opposed by, 203; Matsuoka described by, 73, 182, 197; naval talks with Japan and, 93; Nomura's talks with, 194–197, 201–202; on orderly processes, 113, 132, 157, 195; *Panay* attackers described by, 140; protest lodged with Konoe government by, 148–149; rejection of Plans A and B by, 205–207; Saitō's private talks with, 87–88;

Stimson's letter to, 135

Ickes, Harold L., 140, 183

ideology, 2, 7–8, 20, 35, 154, 159–160, 166, 185, 189, 197; definition of, 3. *See also* liberal internationalism; Pan-Asianism; world order

Immigration Act of 1924. *See* United States

Imperial Rule Assistance Association, 187–188

imperialism, late nineteenth century, 14, 89; in China, 18, 27, 50, 164; civilizing mission and, 5, 46, 56

India, 4, 211

Indochina. *See* French Indochina

Indonesia. *See* Dutch East Indies

Inoue Junnosuke, 53

Institute of Pacific Relations, 31, 34, 45, 58

Inukai Tsuyoshi, 40–41, 48, 49, 50, 53

Ishii Kikujirō, 45, 52, 83, 137, 157; on Asian Monroe Doctrine, 85; FDR visited by, 74; *Foreign Affairs* essay by, 47; on "Geneva atmosphere", 20–21; on Japanese backlash to naval conference, 34; on Japan's affinity with Italy and Germany, 185; Kellogg pact critiqued by, 33; negotiations with Lansing, 27–28

Ishiwara Kanji, 43

isolationism. *See* United States

Itagaki Seishirō, 43

Italy, 15, 19, 24, 40, 113, 132, 151; Japan cultural agreement with, 151; Konoe grateful for support of, 147; Manchukuo recognized by, 144. *See also* Mussolini, Benito

Japan: "ABCD encirclement" and, 187, 202; American cultural influence on, 106, 129; colonies of, 11, 14, 19, 54, 157; Control faction, army, 115, 116; entry in World War I, 13; fascism and, 155, 187–188; General Staff, army, 43, 44, 71, 132, 142, 199; General Staff, navy, 24, 34, 71, 142, 199; imperial conferences, 142–143, 185, 200, 204, 205, 207; Imperial Way faction, army, 96, 115; Major League all-stars tour of,

Index 263

97–99; Meiji Constitution, 71; Ministry of Foreign Affairs (MOFA), 21, 37–38, 66, 70, 82–83, 83, 146, 215; neutrality pact with Soviets, 192, 193–194, 199; 1940 Olympics and, 118, 129, 150; trade with US, 29, 66, 105, 126, 129, 156, 158, 165, 174; Tripartite Pact and, 184–186, 192, 194, 195–196, 197, 199, 200, 206; ultranationalists and, 36, 46, 53, 106, 115. *See also* Kokusai Bunka Shinkōkai (KBS); Pan-Asianism
Japan Pacific Association, 138
Japan Society of New York, 74, 81, 90, 100, 114, 120
Jewell, Edward, 120
Jiang Jieshi. *See* Chiang Kai-shek
Jinzhou. *See* Manchurian crisis
Johnson, Nelson T., 164

Kabayama Aisuke, 83, 108, 112, 119, 151, 214–215; establishment of Japan Culture Center and, 146; on impact of KBS garden tour, 101–102, 103; on importance of cultural diplomacy, 119, 170; *NIPPON* essay by, 92–93; US toured by, 111
Kaneko Kentarō, 81
Katō Shizue, 122
Katō Tomosaburō, 24–25, 26, 29
Kawai Tatsuo, 149
Kawakami, K. K., 46, 46–47, 89, 165, 185
KBS. *See* Kokusai Bunka Shinkōkai
Kearny, 205
Keller, Helen, 128
Kellogg, Frank B., 32
Kellogg-Briand pact (1928), 4, 32–34, 34–35, 61, 86, 165; Hull's Four Principles and, 195; Japan postwar constitution and, 213; Manchurian crisis and, 38, 38–39, 40, 48, 51, 55, 56; neutrality acts conflict with, 109
Kennan, George F., 19
Khalkin Gol, battles of, 163, 199
Kido Kōichi, 196
Kimmel, Husband E., 191–192
Kishi Nobusuke, 214
Kissinger, Henry, 17
Kita Ikki, 46
Knox, Frank, 92, 178, 187

Kokusai Bunka Shinkōkai (KBS), 6, 67, 99–100, 114, 119, 128, 151; Anesaki book tour and, 90; Asia-Pacific War and, 137, 210; establishment of, 83–84, 88, 90; funding for, 92; Garden Club tour and, 100–103; Japan Culture Center and, 146, 175; Konoe US visit and, 88–90; New York office, 90; New York World's Fair and, 162–163; *NIPPON* and, 92–93, 146–147, 186; Nō robes exhibition and, 100; postwar role and, 214, 214–215; propaganda report on, 170, 186; Special Loan Exhibition of Japanese Art and, 119–122; traveling library and, 147. *See also* soft power
Konoe Fumimaro, 45, 96, 130, 147, 148, 179, 199, 241n15; essay in *Liberty* by, 110; Hornbeck depicted by, 111; interest in Draft Understanding, 195–196, 196, 201; KBS involvement and, 83, 84, 88–90, 92; letters sent to FDR by, 138, 140; Manchurian Incident and, 131–132, 133, 134–135; on neutrality pact with Soviets, 194; New Order in East Asia declared by, 148–150; popularity of, 129, 190; resignation of cabinets of, 154, 200, 204–205; statements about Kuomintang made by, 143, 144, 150; summit with FDR desired by, 203–204; Tripartite Pact and, 185–186; worldview of, 89–90, 129–131, 139, 182, 188, 200
Konoe Hidemaro, 128, 129, 138
Koo, Wellington V. K., 18, 22
Korea, 1, 79, 111, 186, 214; Japanese colony of, 14, 54, 157; Japanese troops mobilized from, 11, 132, 153; March First Movement, 19
Kuomintang, 107, 145; American economic aid received by, 158, 174, 188; Chinese Communist Party and, 43, 107, 133; consolidation of power, 31, 41–42, 43; eviction from North China, 107, 112–113, 131, 132; Manchurian crisis policy of, 38, 40; propaganda and, 59, 90, 138, 145; Sino-Japanese War and, 132, 134, 139, 142, 143, 150, 164, 174. *See also* Chiang Kai-shek
Kurosawa, Akira, 216

Kurusu Saburō, 206, 207
Kwantung Army, 36, 41, 41–42, 47, 48, 54, 131; Manchurian Incident manufactured by, 11, 37, 39, 43–44, 44; Soviet battles in Mongolia with, 163–164
Kwantung Leased Territory, 11, 12
Kyoto, 34–35, 100, 205, 210, 212

La Guardia, Fiorella, 162
Lamont, Thomas W., 50, 89
Lansing-Ishii negotiations, 27–28, 58, 74
Leaf, Earl, 170, 186
League of Nations, 16; American absence in, 19, 20, 38, 40, 50–51, 62; Covenant of, 17, 19, 37, 55; enforcement powers of, 16; Manchurian policy and, 38, 40, 53, 59, 61; scope of activities, 21, 24, 31, 82. *See also* Lytton Commission; Lytton Report
League of Nations Association, 50
leased territories. *See* China
Ledoux, Louie, 100, 120, 121
lend-lease legislation, 191, 192
Lenin, Vladimir, 15
liberal internationalism, ideology of, 3, 5–6, 12, 15, 17, 203; collective security and, 16, 19, 29, 40, 54, 62, 216; limitations of, 38, 55, 61–62, 87, 90, 114, 216; world opinion and, 16, 33, 39, 48, 54, 55, 60. *See also* orderly processes; world order
Lin Yutang, 122
Lindbergh, Charles, 167, 191
Lindley, Ernest, 137
Lloyd, Harold, 129
Locarno treaties, 21, 117
Lodge, Henry Cabot, 30
Lodge, Henry Cabot, Jr., 33, 168
London naval conference (1930), 34–35
London naval talks (1935), 93
Los Angeles, 1932 Olympics, 56
Lost in Translation, 105
Lowell, A. Lawrence, 50
Luce, Henry, 128, 135, 191, 212
Ludlow Amendment, 140
Lytton Commission, 40, 52, 53, 54
Lytton Report, 57–58, 59, 61

MacDonald, Ramsay, 34, 35
Mack, Connie, 98
MacMurray, John V. A., 63, 107
Madame Kai-shek. *See* Song Meiling
MAGIC, 194, 201, 206, 207
Mahan, Alfred T., 68
Major League all-stars tour. *See* Japan
Makino Nobuaki, 115, 129
Manchurian crisis: hostilities in Jinzhou and, 11–12, 38, 41; hostilities in Shanghai and, 49–50, 52; Japan explanation for, 38, 44–47, 48, 51–52, 52, 54, 56, 59–61; as turning point in world affairs, 3, 12, 38, 159, 209. *See also* League of Nations; Lytton Commission; Lytton Report; Manchurian Incident
Manchurian Incident (1931), 11–12, 37, 43–44
Mao Zedong, 43
Marco Polo Bridge Incident (1937), 131–132, 133. *See also* Sino-Japanese War
Marquand, John P. *See Mr. Moto*
Matsudaira Tsuneo, 53
Matsui Iwane, 141
Matsukata Otohiko, 82
Matsumoto Shigeharu, 215
Matsuoka Yōsuke, 44, 59, 66, 241n15; background of, 58, 182; Draft Understanding and, 196, 197; Greater East Asia Co-Prosperity Sphere declared by, 183–184; Hitler and Nazi Germany admired by, 184, 185, 192–193, 197, 199; Hull's depiction of, 73, 182, 197; on ideological conflict, 182, 186, 189, 190, 196; Japan's cause in Manchuria defended by, 59–61; ouster of, 200; US toured by, 73–74; on world opinion, 59–60
McCormick, Robert, 136
Metropolitan Museum of Art, New York, 75, 100, 101
Minowa Saburo, 151
Minseitō party, 40, 42
modernity, 13, 14, 31
Molotov, Vyacheslav, 192, 193
Molotov-Ribbentrop pact. *See* Nazi-Soviet pact

Mongolia, 89, 163
Monroe Doctrine, 85–86, 115, 169, 174. *See also* Roosevelt Corollary
Morgenthau, Henry Jr., 148, 151, 158, 165, 167, 183
Mori Kaku, 44
Mr. and Mrs. America, 103
Mr. Moto, 117
Mukden. *See* Shenyang
Mukden Incident. *See* Manchurian Incident
Munich conference (1938), 148, 160
Museum of Fine Art, Boston, 75, 119–122, 121, 215
Mussolini, Benito, 108, 115, 148, 192; FDR letter to Hitler and, 160–161; Matsuoka's tribute to, 196
Myanmar. *See* Burma

Nagai Matsuzō, 210
Nagai Ryūtarō, 44, 138, 203
Nanjing, 42, 141, 147; bombing of, 136, 140; collaborative government in, 144, 174, 211, 213; massacre, 141
Nationalist Party. *See* Kuomintang
Natori Yōnosuke, 92
Nazi-Soviet pact (1939), 166
Netherlands, 175–176, 202, 206, 207
Netherlands East Indies. *See* Dutch East Indies
Neutrality acts, 109, 126, 137, 145, 159–160; arms embargo repeal and, 167–168
New Order in East Asia (1938), 148–151, 153, 155, 156, 164, 169, 171, 174
New Zealand, 31
NHK, 111, 151, 175
Nine-Power Treaty (1922), 28–29, 31, 43, 79, 86, 87, 139, 220n37; Manchurian crisis and, 39, 40, 47–48, 51, 55, 57, 61, 77, 90; North China and, 113; Sino-Japanese War and, 136, 144, 148–149, 158, 164, 168, 169, 195; Wang government and, 174–175, 188
NIPPON, 92–93, 111, 146–147, 163, 186
Nishida Kitaro, 46
Nitobe Inazō, 30, 45, 56–57, 66–67
Nō robes, exhibition, 100
Nomonhan. *See* Khalkin Gol

Nomura Kichisaburō, 169, 194, 199, 203; Hull's talks with, 194–197, 201–202; joint diplomacy with Kurusu, 206–207
Northern Expedition, 42
Nye, Gerald P., 112

O'Doul, Lefty, 104
Oikawa Koshirō, 200
Okada Keisuke, 91, 93, 115; soft power and, 92, 100, 103, 110, 112
Okakura Tenshin (Kakuzō), 5
Ōkawa Shūmei, 46
Open Door policy, 25–28, 48, 52, 148–149, 175
orderly processes, 3, 5, 20, 21, 25, 93, 211; Dennett on Japan and, 206–207; FDR on, 113, 209; Grew on, 169; Hull on, 88, 113, 132, 157, 195; League of Nations and, 40; Nine-Power Treaty and, 28, 139; Stimson on, 35, 51. *See also* liberal internationalism
Orlando, Vittorio, 15
Ōshima Hiroshi, 148, 198–199
Ott, Eugen, 184
Ozu Yasujirō, 216

Pan-Asianism, ideology of, 4–5, 5–6, 46, 127, 156; Japan as "stabilizing" influence and, 5, 57, 61, 85, 95, 118, 155, 169, 188–189; Japan's "civilizing mission" and, 46, 51–52, 56, 60, 61, 73, 81, 111; Sino-Japanese War and, 138, 140, 149, 150, 174, 176; soft power and, 6, 84, 90, 92, 99, 114, 119–120, 146–147, 151, 163, 210
Panay, 139–140, 141
Paris Peace Conference (1919), 15–20
Peabody, Endicott, 137
Pearl Harbor, 1, 178, 190, 207, 209
Peffer, Nathaniel, 113, 114, 123, 144, 156, 158, 166
Philippines, 14, 25, 31, 89, 112, 210, 211
Phillips, William, 82
Picasso, Pablo, 147
Pittman, Key, 115
Plans A and B, Japanese proposals of 1941, 205–207
Poland, 160, 166, 171, 172
Pollard, Robert T., 156

Price Committee. *See* American Committee for Non-Participation in Japanese Aggression
Pu Yi, Henry, 52, 80
public opinion polls, 145, 166, 168, 172, 190, 204
Puerto Rico, 14

Qing dynasty, 18, 25, 41, 52
Qiqihar, 39
quarantine speech (1937), 136–137, 140

Racial Equality clause (1919), 18–19, 44
realpolitik, 123, 156–157, 168; Japan's have-not grievances and, 2, 46, 110, 130, 157–158
Reinsch, Paul S., 22, 71
Reischauer, Robert K., 106, 134
Rhineland, 17, 117, 151
Ribbentrop, Joachim von, 144, 160, 199; Matsuoka's Berlin talks with, 192–193; Tripartite Pact and, 185
Richardson, James, 178
The Rising Tide of Color (1920), 56
Rockefeller, John D., III, 215
Rockefeller Center, 81, 146, 170, 186
Rockefeller Foundation, 82
Roosevelt, Franklin D., 67–68, 69, 119, 128, 166; economic pressure on Japan and, 136, 140, 144–145, 158, 165, 183, 202; isolationism and, 109, 137, 140–141, 159–160, 167–168, 177; Japanese goodwill visitors received by, 73, 74, 81–82, 89; on Kellogg-Briand pact, 136; Konoe letters received by, 138, 140; letters to Hitler and Mussolini sent by, 160–161; liberal principles and, 113, 136, 154, 159, 177, 189–190, 198, 203, 209; naval expansion and, 93, 178; on neutrality laws, 109, 126, 168; quarantine speech, 136–137; Stimson nonrecognition policy and, 67, 81, 107
Roosevelt, Theodore, 28, 68, 86. *See also* Roosevelt Corollary
Roosevelt Corollary (1904), 86
Root, Elihu, 28, 30, 62
Rōyama Masamichi, 89, 112, 131, 144
Russia, 18; Russo-Japanese War and, 13, 45, 46, 81, 193

Ruth, Babe, 97–98, 98, 104, 106

Saionji Kinmochi, 71, 90, 115, 116, 129–130
Saitō Hiroshi, 76–77, 78, 81, 89, 116–117; Hitler and Mussolini lauded by, 114–115; Japan policy explained by, 85, 117, 138; Japanese Special Exhibition of art and, 120; on naval talks, 93, 95; private talks with Hull initiated by, 87–88
Saitō Makoto, 53–54, 57, 67, 115
Sakatani Yoshirō, 14
San Diego, naval port of, 178
San Pedro, naval port of, 178
Sansom, George, 197
Satō Naotake, 127–128
Seiyūkai party, 40, 42, 53
Shandong province, 18–19, 29, 42
Shanghai. *See* Manchurian crisis; Sino-Japanese War
Shenyang, 11–12, 38–39, 41, 44, 71, 77
Shidehara Kijūrō, 26; Manchurian Incident and, 11–12, 44, 45; "Shidehara diplomacy" and, 21, 29, 40, 127
Shigemitsu Mamoru, 45, 83, 96, 100, 214; Japanese regionalism and, 51–52, 79, 164
Shiratori Toshio, 44, 49, 75, 77
Shotwell, James T., 32, 35
Shōwa Research Association, 89, 131, 149
Siam. *See* Thailand
Simon, John, 51
Singapore, 185, 190, 193, 197, 199, 210
Sino-Japanese War, 142, 144, 147, 149, 156, 172, 174; air raids on Chinese cities and, 135, 136, 145, 164; Marco Polo Bridge Incident and, 131–132, 133; Nanjing massacre and, 141; Shanghai and, 134–135, 139, 149
Smoot-Hawley tariff, 42
Smuts, Jan, 211
Society for International Cultural Relations. *See* Kokusai Bunka Shinkōkai
soft power, 6, 215; Japanese cultural diplomacy and, 2, 6–7, 67, 71, 83, 90, 95–96; Japanese information networks and, 110–111; Japanese public

diplomacy and, 73, 74, 81–82, 89, 111, 137–138; limits of Japan's, 93, 126, 147, 162–163, 175. *See also* Kokusai Bunka Shinkōkai
Song Meiling, 135
Song Zheyuan, 131
South Manchurian Railway Company, 27, 54, 58, 182; Japan's investment in, 45, 157; Manchurian Incident and, 11, 37, 39; propaganda and, 75, 111
Soviet Union, 20, 39, 206, 216; battles against Kwantung Army, 163–164; Germany invasion of, 198–199; neutrality pact with Japan, 192, 193–194, 199; pact with Germany, 166, 171; war on Japan declared by, 212
Spain, 118, 144
Special Loan Exhibition of Japanese Art (1936), 119–122, 121
Stahmer, Heinrich, 185
Stalin, Joseph, 123, 166, 171, 198; Matsuoka's negotiations with, 192–194
Stark, Harold, 191
Stimson, Henry L., 49, 50, 50–51, 53, 62, 135, 146, 178; on Asian Monroe Doctrine, 86; Kyoto spared by, 212, 241n9; Manchurian Incident and, 11–12, 37, 39–40; nonrecognition policy of, 41, 47–49, 67, 196; open letter to Borah, 51; sanctions on Japan urged by, 174, 183; speech to Council on Foreign Relations, 55–56. *See also* London naval conference
Stimson Doctrine, 48
Stravinsky, Igor, 13
Stresemann, Gustav, 33
Sudetenland, 148
Suetsugu Nobumasa, 142
Suzuki Kantarō, 115

Taft, Henry W., 81
Taft, Robert A., 168
Taishō, Emperor, 21
Taiwan, 14, 157
Takahashi Korekiyo, 115
Takamatsu Nobuhito, Prince, 83, 100, 119, 133, 214
Tanaka Giichi, 42
Thailand, 206, 211

Timperley, H. J., 141
Tōgō Shigenori, 205–206
Tōjō Hideki, 131, 183, 200–201, 205; negotiations with US and, 205–206; Pan-Asianism and, 210, 211
Tokugawa Iesato, 24, 52; cultural and public diplomacy of, 81, 83, 99, 102, 112, 128
Tokyo Giants, 104–105
Tokyo War Crimes Tribunal, 214
Tolischus, Otto, 197
Tripartite Pact (1940), 184–187, 194; US-Japan relations and, 194, 195–196, 197, 199, 200, 205–206
Trotsky, Leon, 15
Twenty-One Demands, 18, 27, 45, 84

Uchida Kōsai, 17, 54–55, 57, 67, 74–75, 75, 135
United Nations, 211, 214, 216
United States: attitudes toward Japan, negative, 30, 75, 135, 137, 140, 141, 145, 147, 150, 172, 187; attitudes toward Japan, positive, 29, 36, 56, 97–99, 102, 104, 112, 122, 128; entry in World War I, 13; halfway internationalism and, 3–4, 45, 50–51, 62, 65–66; Immigration Act of 1924, 29–31; imperialism and, 14, 25, 27; Japan occupied by, 213–215; League of Nations membership rejected by, 19; trade with Japan, 29, 66, 105, 129, 158, 165, 183, 202
US-Japan Commercial Treaty of 1911, 165, 174, 183

Vandenberg, Arthur H., 160, 168
Versailles Treaty. *See* Paris Peace Conference
Vichy government. *See* France
Villard, Oswald Garrison, 137–138
Vladivostok, 199

Wakatsuki Reijirō, 35, 40, 44; Japan's cause in Manchuria defended by, 47
Wallace, Henry, 162
Wang Jingwei, 174, 188, 195, 199, 213
Wang Zhengting, 18, 43; Japan's Pan-Asianism denounced by, 87

Warner, Langdon, 119, 121
Washington Conference (1921-22), 21–28, 30, 34, 51, 90
Welles, Sumner, 171, 183, 201, 206
Williams, Frederick V., 141
Wilson, Woodrow, 19–20, 22, 32–33, 161, 212; declaration of war requested by, 13; liberal internationalism and, 16–17, 62, 113–114, 203, 211; as proponent of new world order, 3, 14–15, 15; on Shandong, 17, 18–19; Twenty-One Demands and, 27. *See also* Fourteen Points
Wilsonianism. *See* liberal internationalism
world fairs, 75, 161–162
world opinion. *See* liberal internationalism
world order, competing ideas of, 3, 5–6, 37, 47, 79, 115, 159, 197, 207; FDR and, 177, 189–190, 198, 203, 209; Hull and, 108–109; Japanese officials and, 80, 149, 182, 184, 185, 190, 203, 209, 210; Stimson and, 53

World War I: as catalyst for new diplomacy, 12, 14, 23, 24, 32–33, 37, 54, 55, 86; ferocity of, 13, 14, 50
Wuhan, 139, 147, 149

Xie Jieshi, 57

Yamamoto Isoroku, 93
Yamato class battleship, 118
Yasukuni Shrine, 214
Yen, W. W., 59, 60, 65
Yonai Mitsumasa, 155–156, 172–174, 176, 178
Yoshida Shigeru, 117, 214
Yoshida Zengo, 183, 185
Yoshino Sakuzō, 17
Yoshino Shinji, 163
Yoshizawa Kenkichi, 38, 39, 45, 48, 119
Young, James R., 163

Zhang, Xueliang, 42
Zhang Zuolin, 42
Zhou Enlai, 133

About the Author

John Gripentrog is professor of history at Mars Hill University, a liberal arts institution near Asheville, North Carolina. He earned his Ph.D. from the University of Wisconsin–Madison and specializes in US foreign relations. His teaching and scholarly interests range widely, from the political, social, and cultural aspects of the American experience to the history of U.S.-Japan relations. Dr. Gripentrog is the recipient of the Robert S. Gibbs Outstanding Teaching Award at Mars Hill University as well as the Letters and Science Teaching Award at UW–Madison.